Stirring the Waters
The Influence of
Marie Clay

Edited by
Janet S. Gaffney
Billie J. Askew

HEINEMANN
Portsmouth, NH

Heinemann
A division of Reed Elsevier Inc.
361 Hanover Street
Portsmouth, NH 03801–3912
www.heinemann.com

Offices and agents throughout the world

The author and publisher wish to thank those who have generously given permission to reprint borrowed material:

Figure 4 from *Word Matters: Teaching Phonics and Spelling in the Reading/Writing Classroom* by Gay Su Pinnell and Irene C. Fountas. © 1998 by Gay Su Pinnell and Irene C. Fountas. Published by Heinemann, a division of Reed Elsevier, Inc., Portsmouth, NH. Reprinted with persmission of the publisher.

"Revealing and Telling: The Socialization of Attention in Learning to Read and Write" by Courtney Cazden originally appeared in *Educational Psychology* 1992 (12: 3 and 4). Published by Carfax Publishing Limited, Cambridge, MA. Reprinted by permission of the publisher.

"The Political and the Professional in Education: An Unnecessary Conflict" by Peter Mortimore and Jo Mortimore originally appeared in *The Journal of Education for Teaching* 1998 (24: 3). Published by Carfax Publishing Limited, Oxfordshire, UK. Reprinted by permission of the editors.

Library of Congress Cataloging-in-Publication Data
Stirring the waters : the influence of Marie Clay / edited by Janet S. Gaffney,
    Billie J. Askew.
        p.   cm.
    Includes bibliographical references.
    ISBN 0-325-00207-X
    1. Children—Language. 2. Language arts (Early childhood). 3. Reading (Early childhood). 4. Clay, Marie M.   I. Gaffney, Janet S.   II. Askew, Billie J.
LB1139.5.L35S85   1999
372.6—dc21   99-34929
                                        CIP

Editor: William Varner
Production: Elizabeth Valway
Cover design: Jenny Jensen Greenleaf, Greenleaf Illustration and Design
Manufacturing: Louise Richardson

Printed in the United States of America on acid-free paper
03 02 01 00 99 RRD 1 2 3 4 5

For Marie Clay
who, by her influence, has enhanced
the lives and literacy of children.

Contents

Foreword:
Theoretical Foundations
for Literacy Acquisition

RICHARD C. ANDERSON

Stirring the Waters celebrates Marie Clay as a major theorist of child literacy acquisition. Among her important theoretical innovations are the ideas of alternative routes to literacy acquisition and the child as a self-extending system. Not coincidentally, Clay is the originator of the Reading Recovery program. Previous discussions in the United States of Clay's contributions to literacy education have focused on Reading Recovery and have been preoccupied with whether the program works, or whether it works well enough considering its costs (Hiebert 1994; Pinnell et al. 1996; Shanahan and Barr 1995). How well does it work? How much does it cost? These are important questions, of course, and quintessentially American ones, but considering them has turned our attention away from deeper questions about the premises upon which the program is founded and the wider implications of these premises for literacy acquisition.

One foundational premise embodied in Reading Recovery is that there is not a single, fixed developmental path along which every child must travel. In his thoughtful chapter in this book, Stuart McNaughton develops the corollary that a "broad channel" curriculum caters to children on different developmental paths, whereas a "narrow channel" curriculum does not. Thus, Reading Recovery, in which an individual program is constructed from a rich variety of books, may provide stepping-stones for children with different understandings and lacunae. In contrast, an unvarying stream of "decodable texts" (Beck 1998) may be suitable only for children who meet restricted prerequisites.

It is not a coincidence that the hypothesis of alternative routes to literacy acquisition was promulgated by a New Zealand psychologist and educator. Every country has a "grammar of schooling" (Tyack and Tobin 1994) influenced by long-standing national education policies. The New Zealand policy of staggered school entry upsets a determinate view of developmental progression, as well as any strong sense of curriculum scope and sequence, and thus may enable less curriculum-bound program inventions such as Reading Recovery and Shared-Book Reading.

Even in America, where the conventional grammar of schooling might predispose one to be attracted to the idea of a fixed developmental progression (if we only knew what it was), there are clues that practicing teachers would accept, or already tacitly accept, the idea of alternative routes to the same eventual competencies. Prominent in the practical wisdom of teachers is that every child is different. Any theory that addresses the individuality of children, even theories such as that of learning styles, that lack a strong scientific basis, finds a ready audience among American schoolteachers.

The Reading Recovery teacher assuredly must be a reflective practitioner (Richardson 1998) and an empowered professional decision maker (Routman 1988), because each child's program is custom tailored through moment-by-moment and day-by-day decisions based on close observation of the child. The Reading Recovery teacher is invited to make many decisions, but at the same time to take other lesson features as givens. That there will be boundaries on decision making is inevitable; you cannot question everything at the same time. Decisions are impossible unless some conditions are accepted as given, at least provisionally. You cannot really hold all options open; trying to do so will hobble decision making. As Wittgenstein observed, for a door to swing, the hinges and frame must be fixed.

Three activity structures or *instructional frames*, within the typical Reading Recovery lesson are the repeated reading of familiar books, a writing activity, and the introduction and reading of a new book (Green, Weade, and Graham 1988). These three activities are a major reason for the effectiveness of Reading Recovery, although I know of only piecemeal empirical evidence in support of this judgment. Further, I am sure, although I have not conducted a poll, that experienced Reading Recovery personnel, as well as many authorities who have no association with Reading Recovery, would agree that when these three activities are skillfully executed, they are productive most of the time for most low-performing children—more productive than most other lesson activities. The three activities emphasize different facets of literacy so that, like a tripod, they form a stable platform for literacy acquisition. Thus, a Reading Recovery teacher is not invited to substitute a who, what, when, and where recitation for rereading a familiar book; drawing a picture for composing and writing a sentence; or reading a lovely poem aloud to a child for introducing a new book.

For the most part, Reading Recovery teachers take the instructional frames that constitute a lesson as given, and are able to concentrate on good within-frame decision making. Decisions are guided by a principled instructional strategy. The cornerstone of the strategy is that every child, especially the child whose initial progress is the slowest, must become a self-extending reader and writer. The teacher tries never to do for children what they can do for themselves. Books are selected that will place children at the frontiers of their competence. Prompts and questions are chosen to encourage children to solve reading and writing problems as independently as their current level of competence allows.

This book pays tribute to Marie Clay, one of the most remarkable educators and scholars of the twentieth century. It has been my honor to contribute this foreword and to comment briefly on two of Clay's ideas as they are realized in the Reading

Recovery program: alternative routes to literacy acquisition and the child as a self-extending system.

Richard C. Anderson
Center for the Study of Reading
University of Illinois at Urbana–Champaign

References

BECK, I. 1998. "Understanding Beginning Reading: A Journey Through Teaching and Research." In *Literacy for All*, edited by J. Osborn and F. Lehr, 11–31. New York: Guilford Press.

GREEN, J. L., WEADE, R., AND GRAHAM, K. 1988. "Lesson Construction and Student Participation: A Sociolinguistic Perspective on Lesson Construction and Reading." In *Multiple Perspective Analyses of Classroom Discourse*, edited by J. L. Green and J. O. Harker, 11–47. Norwood, N.J.: Ablex.

HIEBERT, E. 1994. "Reading Recovery in the United States: What Difference Does It Make to an Age Cohort?" *Educational Researcher* 23 (9): 15–25.

PINNELL, G. S. et al. 1996. "Response to Hiebert: What Difference Does Reading Recovery Make?" *Educational Researcher* 25 (7): 23–25.

RICHARDSON, V. 1998. "Professional Development in the Instruction of Reading." In *Literacy for All*, edited by J. Osborn and F. Lehr, 303–318. New York: Guilford Press.

ROUTMAN, R. 1988. *Transitions: From Literature to Literacy*. Portsmouth, N.H.: Heinemann.

SHANAHAN, T., AND BARR, R. 1995. "Reading Recovery: An Independent Evaluation of the Effects of an Early Instructional Intervention Program." *Reading Research Quarterly* 30: 958–996.

TYACK, D., AND TOBIN, W. 1994. "The 'Grammar' of Schooling: Why Has It Been So Hard to Change?" *American Educational Research Journal* 31: 453–479.

Marie M. Clay

Writing a tribute to Marie Clay is simultaneously an easy and an awesome task for exactly the same reason: She has accomplished so much. As reflected by the contributing authors in this volume, her influence transcends a single field of study and spans geographic borders.

Born in 1926 in Wellington, the capital city on the southern tip of the North Island, Clay is uniquely New Zealand—frugal and resourceful. Although education is a top priority in New Zealand, funding for schools and research leaves no room for excess and spurs ingenuity and cooperation. Historically, the national curriculum was developed and revised by educators, with the products of collegial work attributed to the New Zealand Department of Education rather than to individuals. From the beginning of their programs at a teachers college, preservice teachers work in schools, and they apprentice with master teachers as they enter the profession. These cultural features are footholds in Marie's work, as reflected in her concern for the "economic use of a child's learning time," and the central role that collegial interactions play in professional development.

Clay completed her teacher training at the Wellington College of Education and was awarded a primary teacher's certificate in 1945. At the same time, she was pursuing a bachelor of arts degree at the Wellington campus of the University of New Zealand. After graduating in 1946 with a senior scholarship in education that would support advanced study, she completed her master's thesis, "Teaching of Reading to Special Class Children," and was awarded a master of arts degree with honors in 1948. At the same time, she was employed as an assistant psychologist for the Department of Education. In 1950, Clay was awarded a Fulbright Scholarship and a Smith-Mundt grant to study developmental psychology and clinical child development at the University of Minnesota's Institute of Child Welfare.

On her return to New Zealand, Clay moved to the small town of Wanganui and continued to teach in the primary grades. Because of her interest in and expertise with children with special needs, the district placed many high-need students in her class.

The authors acknowledge the significant contribution of Ann Ballantyne and her colleagues, Christine Boocock, Blair Koefoed, and Barbara Watson, who constitute the National Reading Recovery Trainers Team in New Zealand, for their assistance with background information.

In 1955, Clay moved to Auckland and worked in the Department of Education's newly established Psychological Services.

In 1960, Clay was offered a temporary position at the University of Auckland to assist with a new diploma of educational psychology, a postgraduate training program for educational psychologists. Two years later, this became a permanent appointment. Clay continued to be involved with training school psychologists in consultation, testing, and measurement for the next twenty-five years.

Around the time that Clay was studying in Minnesota, Samuel Kirk and Barbara Bateman were developing the Illinois Test of Psycholinguistic Abilities (ITPA) at the University of Illinois. This test was designed to identify and explain underlying cognitive and language disorders and to guide remediation for children whose poor academic achievement was not attributable to intellectual, social, or emotional deficits. In the early 1960s when Clay was considering the focus of her dissertation research, she found herself in disagreement with the assumptions underlying the ITPA and other special-education assessments. Clay's developing criticism of the theoretical perspectives and the nature of instruction in the field of learning disabilities was a catalyst for much of her subsequent work. Her classic article, "Learning to Be Learning Disabled," represents the culmination of her thinking on issues of identification, assessment, and teaching students with learning disabilities (Clay 1987). Her positions challenging current practices in teaching, teacher education, and research are as relevant today as they were more than a decade ago.[1]

In 1963, Clay began to investigate her research question "Can we see the process of reading going astray close to the onset of instruction?" In her dissertation, "Emergent Reading Behaviour," she describes the week-by-week progress of one hundred children during their first year of school (Clay 1966). An important outcome of her dissertation and subsequent research was the development of reliable observation tools for the assessment and fine-grained analysis of consequential changes over time in children's early literacy learning. These assessments constitute *An Observation Survey of Early Literacy Achievement* (Clay 1993a), which has also been reconstructed and validated in the Spanish and Maori languages. Clay's observational methodology and clinical orientation have kept her close to the source of literacy learning—children and teachers. This proximity may partially account for her perspectives on literacy learning, which differ, sometimes dramatically, from those of other researchers. A compilation of her early research was published in *Reading: The Patterning of Complex Behaviour* (Clay 1979), which formed the basis of Clay's theoretical description of young children's developing control over literacy learning, as presented in *Becoming Literate: The Construction of Inner Control* (Clay 1991).

A permanent and, by 1973, senior member of the University faculty, Clay maintained a high level of contact with children, parents, and educators. Among her many commitments, she was an early member of the Reading Association in New Zealand, president of the Auckland Reading Association in 1971–1972, and coordinator of the New Zealand Reading Association Councils from 1971–1974. Clay was the first non-American to be elected president of the International Reading Association (IRA). During her term (1992–1993), Clay revitalized international participation in the work of the Association. As the 1995 recipient of the prestigious William S. Gray Citation of Merit, her contribution to invigorating the international emphasis of the IRA was acknowledged. "World-class scholar, researcher, and visionary educator, Marie Clay has inspired scholars, regenerated teachers, and touched the lives of children in all parts of the globe. An unwavering advocate for world literacy, she will always symbolize the *I* in IRA" (*Reading Today* 1995, 34).

Reading Recovery is one of Clay's important contributions to education. Like the pattern of her work, the program emanated from close involvement with and keen insight into those closest to the source. The research project was born from the concerns of classroom teachers who, despite well-designed classroom programs and good teaching, were not able to change the paths of progress for particular children. The driving question, stated with simple elegance, was "What is possible when we change the design and delivery of traditional education for the children that teachers find hard to teach?" (Clay 1993b, 97).

In 1976, Clay began to work—first with one research assistant, Sara (Sue) Robinson, then with a group of experienced primary educators including Barbara Watson—to develop an intervention that would bring the lowest children up to the average band of progress in their classrooms. These pioneers did not know, then, the possibilities that might be created for children, for teachers, and for schools with a different set of circumstances and assumptions.

Reading Recovery was developed and trialed in the short span of three years. Barbara Watson was appointed to the leadership team to contribute to this rapidly expanding effort. Field trials conducted in 1978 were replicated the following year in forty-eight Auckland schools. Reading Recovery became a national education program in New Zealand in 1983. Remarkably, Reading Recovery is now operating in most English-speaking countries (Australia, Canada, New Zealand, the United Kingdom, and the United States) and other jurisdictions (Anguilla, Bermuda, and Jersey), and has been redeveloped for use in the Spanish language. A redevelopment in the French language is underway.

Clay's role in developing and guiding the implementation of Reading Recovery is such a demanding and illustrious one that there is a danger that it will mask her accomplishments in other areas, including oral language (Clay, et al. 1983), writing (Clay 1975), and teaching-learning interactions that accommodate individuals with diverse starting points and rates of learning in typical primary classes (Clay 1998). Although literacy learning has been an early and abiding focus of her work, Clay's academic and intellectual curiosity has taken her along multiple paths of inquiry.

In 1980, Clay had her first opportunity for academic leave. In her report on this six-month sabbatical, she describes, among other things, an international conference on the study of counseling, a developmental psychology conference on the theme of language and cognition, and a scholarly search of the scarce and elusive literature on quadruplets and higher multiple births. The latter project culminated in a book with a catalog of reported cases (Clay 1989). In the spring of 1997, Marie spent an afternoon in Galveston, Texas in the home of Helen Kirk, who had been tracing the lives of twins and other children of multiple births for decades. The two women shared their fascination in nonstop conversation while Marie learned about the later lives of the siblings about whom she had written. On a seemingly different avenue, her interest in adolescent psychology is manifested in the book *Round About Twelve* (Clay and Oates 1983), which documents the interests, activities, perceptions, and behaviors of New Zealand youth on the threshold of adolescent changes. Clay's lens, once again, is sensitively focused on individuals on the verge of change.

When Marie Clay became a professor of education in 1975, she was the first woman professor at the University of Auckland. Clay has been the recipient of many prestigious honors. In 1978, she was awarded the International Citation of Merit at the IRA World Congress on Reading. The following year, she received the David H. Russell Award from the National Council of Teachers of English for distinguished research in the teaching of English. The citation for this award concluded with the words, "Hers has been a quiet voice of reason in a field frequently jarred by the conflicting cries of the marketplace. We do honor to the depth and scope of her scholarship and to the impact which it has made on the education of young children." In 1982, Clay was inducted into the Reading Hall of Fame. She was the recipient of the Mackie Medal in Education from the Australian and New Zealand Association for the Advancement of Science (1983) and the McKenzie Award from the New Zealand Association for Research in Education (1993). In 1993, she was also corecipient, with Gay Su Pinnell, of the Dana Award for Pioneering Achievements in Education.

Marie Clay's research and achievements in the fields of developmental psychology, school psychology, and education have been recognized by her peers: She was elected an honorary fellow of the New Zealand Educational Institute, a fellow of the New Zealand Psychological Society, and, in 1995, a fellow of the Royal Society of New Zealand. The latter was, in part, recognition of her extended efforts to have social science research recognized as worthy of state funding alongside other sciences. Clay served as chair of the Social Science Subcommittee of the New Zealand government's National Research Advisory Committee.

A major contribution of Marie Clay's has been to change the conversation about what is possible for individual learners when the teaching permits different routes to be taken to desired outcomes. This conversation is now embedded in diverse international educational systems. Our thinking has been stretched in ways that make some former assumptions about the lowest-achieving children intolerable. We now live inside of a new agreement about what is possible . . . an agreement, a paradigm that did not previously exist and that will shape future actions and conversations.

Janet S. Gaffney and Billie J. Askew

Note

1. See Vellutino, F. R., Scanlon, D. M., Sipay, E. R., Small, S. G., Pratt, A., Chen, R., and Denckla, M. B. 1996. "Cognitive Profiles of Difficult-to-Remediate and Readily Remediated Poor Readers: Early Intervention as a Vehicle for Distinguishing Between Cognitive and Experimental Deficits as Basic Causes of Specific Reading Disability." *Educational Psychology* 88: 601–638.

References

CLAY, M. M. 1966. "Emergent Reading Behaviour." Ph.D. diss., University of Auckland, Auckland.

———. 1975. *What Did I Write?* Portsmouth, N.H.: Heinemann.

———. 1979. *Reading: The Patterning of Complex Behaviour.* 2d ed. Auckland: Heinemann.

———. 1987. "Learning to Be Learning Disabled." *New Zealand Journal of Educational Studies* 22: 155–173.

———. 1989. *Quadruplets and Other Higher Multiple Births.* Philadelphia: J. B. Lippincott.

———. 1991. *Becoming Literate: The Construction of Inner Control.* Portsmouth, N.H.: Heinemann.

———. 1993a. *An Observation Survey of Early Literacy Achievement.* Portsmouth, N.H.: Heinemann.

———. 1993b. *Reading Recovery: A Guidebook for Teachers in Training.* Portsmouth, N.H.: Heinemann.

———. 1998. *By Different Paths to Common Outcomes.* York, Maine: Stenhouse.

CLAY, M. M., GILL, M., GLYNN, T., MCNAUGHTON, T., AND SALMON, K. 1983. *Record of Oral Language and Biks and Gutches.* Auckland: Heinemann.

CLAY, M. M., AND OATES, R. E. 1983. *Round About Twelve: Studies of New Zealand Form 2 Children in 1978.* Auckland: Department of Education.

Reading Today. 1995. "IRA Salutes Award Winners." *Reading Today.* June/July: 34.

Acknowledgments

We are grateful to Merle Levy whose editing expertise made our writing clearer. Teri Frerichs calmly and competently massaged the disks and pages into a single manuscript. William Varner, Acquisitions Editor at Heinemann, listened, nudged, and cheered at just the right times.

Introduction

This book is a tribute to the work of Marie Clay. Her research has influenced international communities of scholars in early literacy; early childhood, bilingual, and special education; developmental, cognitive, and school psychology; assessment; teacher education; professional development; systemic implementation; and research design. Clay's view of accommodating diversity by responding to individual children has permeated all aspects of her work. The constant in her perspective has been viewing the complexities of learning through an unfettered lens—the eyes of children.

This edited volume represents the depth and breadth of Clay's contribution to these wide-ranging disciplines. The authors are distinguished scholars from Australia, Canada, New Zealand, the United Kingdom, and the United States whose ideas have been stirred in some way by Clay. Like a pebble in a pond, the ripples of her influence move out in ever-widening circles—without the boundaries of disciplines or countries.

The contributors are connected by their association with and esteem for an outstanding scholar. The authors' acknowledgment of Clay's influence is the quality and depth of their own creative and scholarly work. Although the authors represent diverse perspectives, all share the bond of having been inspired in some way by Clay's work.

Each of the scholars invited to participate has a unique and personal story of connection with Clay. We were truly honored to listen to the cherished stories each contributor shared, and were awed by their overwhelming respect for her. We asked the authors to view the invitation as an opportunity to express creative new ideas—as a celebration of something that they were eager to share. Happily, every author we invited accepted our challenge.

This collection recognizes Marie Clay by the most significant means acknowledged by our profession—our work in honor of her work. The conversations that she has started are tributaries entering, meandering through, and absorbed by our personal programs of research. Our collective response makes a significant and enduring contribution to researchers and educators. Teachers, school psychologists, administrators, and researchers in multiple disciplines will be intrigued as they gain insight into the scope of Clay's interests and the interests of eminent scholars whose views have been stirred (or shaken) by hers.

Due to the international nature of the book, we chose to retain the spelling system selected by each author. Spelling is consistent within but not necessarily across chapters.

One

Developmental Diversity
and Beginning Literacy Instruction at School

STUART MCNAUGHTON

Marie Clay's (1988a) recent book introduces the questions that are the focus of this chapter. The title, *By Different Paths to Common Outcomes*, argues for diversity in early literacy development. What do we mean when we claim that children's emergent literacy can take different forms, that diversity is a feature of children's early learning? In this chapter I explore this challenge, initially by outlining the ways in which we can describe diversity in children's development. This discussion provides a background for examining two dimensions of effective instructional conditions for diverse literacy development. One is the need for a multifaceted curriculum that provides activities that can accommodate diversity, and a second concerns the ideas that teachers might have about the extent and nature of diversity; that is, their awareness of diversity. My claim is that teachers need to have well-developed ideas about diversity if school practices are to mediate more effectively between children's expertise and optimal development at school.

Concepts of Developmental Diversity

A number of phenomena have been used to index the presence of diversity. They include specific forms of knowledge before and upon entry to school which function as precursors for conventional school-based literacy (Sulzby and Teale 1991). The phenomena can also be culturally based differences in family literacy practices and their relationships with school literacy practices. Whichever phenomena provide the focus, our analyses are constrained by the theoretical position we adopt on a number of issues. An initial issue concerns the structure of development in terms of relationships between early diversity and learning to read and write at school. One can adopt a view of literacy development as unitary in nature, with skills and knowledge following a universal sequence. In this view, development is predictable and fixed because of the nature of literacy. Diversity can be ordered along this sequence (Goodman 1990).

A different view starts from the position that development in general may not be linear because of the presence of diversity in literacy experiences and knowledge.

However, conventional school literacy and the instructional conditions for it are relatively fixed, and some forms and combinations predispose children to learn easily at school. This view also means that diversity can be ordered along a predicted sequence for school literacy (Sulzby and Teale 1991).

There is a third view, that there are multiple potential pathways to conventional literacy. This has been Clay's (1975, 7) position, expressed in the early comment "I doubt whether there is a fixed sequence of learning through which all children must pass, the insights [and] the learning of conventions may be approached from a variety of directions." Clay (1966) first made this argument on the evidence of variation in children's knowledge upon entering school. She extended the claim through descriptions of concurrent strategies in emergent writing (Clay 1975), and more recently in a commentary on multiple forms of awareness children can develop from early acts of reading and writing (Clay 1998b).

The first two views lead to a similar instructional challenge: to build on the different levels of appropriate (precursor) development when beginning formal instruction in first-year classrooms. A central concern becomes to identify early literacy measures that indicate (that is, that correlate with or predict) progress in forms of reading and writing that are conventionally employed by schools. A body of research that is based on these two views provides evidence of demonstrable and robust relationships among such areas of literacy as alphabet knowledge, book knowledge, school-like talk, awareness of sounds in words, and early progress at school (Snow, Burns, and Griffen 1998). These are relationships of *actuality*, in which conventional literacy and instruction are assumed to be relatively fixed. But what if we radically changed some of the features of early reading and writing instruction? Imagine that the target conventionality was to be Qur'anic reading instruction. Then the correlates might look very different. Expertise in chanting and recitation might be indicative (Wagner and Spratt 1987). Or imagine that we had the most expert sorts of teachers, and they could pick wonderful varieties of knowledge that children brought with them to school, bypassing the ubiquitous "Matthew Effects." Under both scenarios the correlations might reduce, if not disappear.

This is, I think, the argument behind the third position. This "different routes to similar outcomes" position makes a distinction between *actuality* and *potentiality*. The diversity before school entrance may be acted on by both learner and teacher, creating multiple possible developmental pathways over the transition to school.

Clay's (1991, 3) own argument for this view is partly based on obvious evidence: "I think the underlying structure of literacy behaviours might be achieved in different ways. Successful readers and writers do emerge from many different types of programmes." This evidence, about different instructional conditions and their developmental characteristics, can be augmented by other sources. For example, development before school is characterised by multiple and concurrent forms of knowledge and strategies (Elster 1994; Phillips, Norris, and Mason 1996), and there is evidence that different components of reading and writing at school can have different sets of developmental precursors (Snow et al. 1991). The idea of potentiality introduces a second issue, an issue of developmental processes. How are we to account for diversity conceived as "different routes to similar outcomes"? For Clay (1991), the explanation is located in children's strategic invention and construction, as channelled by specific forms of teaching. It blends cognitive developmental and constructivist theorising with a focus on the dynamic properties of instructional conditions. Similarly, contemporary sociocultural or coconstructivist theorising describes children's development in terms of expertise in activities that contribute to family and community literacy practices. Socialisation processes, which include specific forms of guidance in activities, provide social platforms for children's constructions. Multiple forms of literacy are possible given the practices of different communities, which reflect and construct different social and cultural identities (Cole 1996; McNaughton 1995).

This view argues that different forms of literacy knowledge and expertise can develop before school, and can (or potentially could) provide multiple routes to learning at school. Instructional conditions mediate actual or potential relationships. The instructional challenge is to develop effective forms of mediation—"a starting programme should be so designed that it provides for engagement of different children in different ways on different levels from the beginning" (Clay 1991, 203). Before discussing this challenge it is important to review the nature of the development descriptions of diversity.

Plotting Developmental Diversity

Conventional Knowledge

Research descriptions of developmental diversity have used a number of measures, most often those of typical actual precursors to conventional literacy. A small set of measures of children's knowledge has been most consistently used. In New Zealand these measures have included letter identification, concepts about print, and writing vocabulary. (*Concepts about print* is a measure developed by Clay to describe children's understandings of the conventions of books, such as how a book is held and directionality of print). More recently, measures of phonemic awareness and various language measures relating to facility with stories have been added.

	n	Concepts	Letters	Writing
Clay (1966)	100	5.1	3.9	–
Clay (1985)	72	7.2	15.5	2.1
Nalder (1985)	16	6.8	13.6	2.1
McNaughton and Ka'ai (1990)	17	8.1	15.2	1.3
McNaughton (1997)	15	9.5	18.8	2.6

FIGURE 1–1 *Conventional literacy knowledge on entry to school: Means at five years in New Zealand Studies*

Several studies of children beginning formal instruction in New Zealand schools have common measures, as shown in Figure 1–1 on page 5 (adapted from McNaughton 1995). Children arrived at school with a range of conventional knowledge. In the later studies, five-year-olds knew an average of eight concepts (including how to hold a book, where the messages are in a book, directionality, and one-to-one correspondence); were able to identify fourteen or fifteen letters; and could write about two words, typically their name and one other word. The children's knowledge basis varied (in one study, between knowing five concepts and knowing eleven concepts; knowing no letters and knowing all fifty-four test letters; and writing no words and writing five words). To this interchild diversity can be added diversity in the profiles of this knowledge. In general, a relatively high correlation between knowledge scores is found (McNaughton 1997; Snow et al. 1991). Nevertheless, individual children can have both highs and lows. In the studies summarised in Figure 1–1, examples show a child identifying all letters, knowing nine concepts, but writing only one word; and a child knowing ten concepts, writing five words but identifying only eleven letters.

Yet another indication of diversity is the suggestion of an increase in preschool knowledge across decades. If Clay's (1966) original study is used as a benchmark, it appears that children are now arriving at school in New Zealand knowing more concepts and more letters. A recent trial of a school-entry assessment procedure provides even higher scores for fifty-five new entrants in eleven schools. They knew twelve concepts, twenty-one letters, and could write six words. A subsample of fifteen children who were less than four weeks into their school, shown in Figure 1–1 (McNaughton 1997), knew ten concepts, identified nineteen letters, and wrote three words.

These three sorts of diversity underline the historical, cultural, social, and ontogenetic properties of all developmental phenomena, including those associated with literacy development (Cole 1996). But this is a limited picture of the possible forms of expertise that children might bring with them to school. Only "products" of activities are examined, and in the relatively unusual and unfamiliar contexts of formal testing. Expertise situated in activities is not examined. For example, the variety of activities within which alphabet knowledge might be situated is not sampled; similarly, the variety of activities within which writing a name might be located is not sampled. When familiar contexts that are sensible to children are employed, children often display more knowledge (Wood 1997).

Family Literacy Activities

In addition to the theoretical approaches to diversity noted earlier, there are other possible descriptions of development. These use the notion of activity as a basis for analysis. In general, an activity in which children are learning provides ways of participating and forms of guidance. Participants hold goals, and develop expertise situated in the activity (McNaughton 1995). Again, New Zealand studies provide illustrative data. There are intensive descriptive studies of family members reading books to preschool children at home. They show that these events are widespread in New Zealand, although there are differences across families in the frequency of such reading and in the kinds of book used.

Of interest here, however, are descriptions of styles of reading, three of which constitute three distinct activities. The styles can be identified from the distinctive ways of participating, forms of guidance, and goals present during family book reading. A typical style described by researchers, and often associated with white middle-class families, involves the initiation of discussions focused on text meanings and familiar topics, a collaborative form of guidance that establishes and develops skills related to the focus. In this style, called *collaborative participation*, child and reader are often focused on the narrative and the life-to-text relationships. The interactions are like conversations, and the scaffolding that is provided by the reader guides the child into negotiating text meanings. A second style, *performance*, develops children's ability to recite portions of the text, maintaining the authority of the text through accurate objectification. The third style, the *display* style, is concerned with conveying items of knowledge such as colours, letters, or labels. Skills in identifying, as well as specific knowledge, are achieved through questioning routines that are initially controlled by the reader.

The three styles are not necessarily used exclusively; even with the same book, families can switch among styles to meet different purposes. They can adjust and modify their reading with children, switching between distinctive ways of participating, their forms of guidance, and their goals, thus demonstrating a kind of "textual dexterity" (McNaughton 1995).

Several studies have described how these styles are used by different families, including indigenous Maori families, Pakeha families (of European descent), and first- and second-generation Pacific Islands families living in New Zealand. The studies show that when storybooks are the vehicle and the children are three- and four-year-olds, Pakeha families tend to use the collaborative style almost exclusively. Other families, particularly Pacific Islands families, often use the performance and labeling style.

Qualifications need to be placed on these sorts of summaries. The variation in the use of different styles can be greater within a cultural group than among groups. But the studies indicate a tendency for Pakeha families to be more exclusive in their use of the collaborative style and for Maori families and Pacific Islands families to be more dexterous in using different styles.

Over time and with familiar books, these styles provide the activity base for particular sorts of expertise. The collaborative participation style, for example, is associated with comprehension strategies similar to those valued at school. The performance style is associated with (among other things) recitation memory; and the display style, particularly with young children, with learning about referents and referencing (McNaughton 1995).

Similar evidence for varied expertise situated within particular activities can be found in intensive studies of writing before school. We have explored children and their families' writing activities in a series of studies (McNaughton 1995). Several conclusions can be drawn. The first is that children experience, either directly or indirectly, many writing activities at home and in their community settings before they go to school. Second, these activities cover a range of forms and purposes. The range in one study was considerable. Examples of writing were collected from eighteen Maori, Pakeha, and Samoan families and their children over the six months before the children entered school. The children's personal or joint productions (in which the child did not necessarily complete the written product) were categorised by activity type into six kinds of texts (naming texts, narrative/descriptive texts, expository texts, labeling texts, message texts, and mixed texts) and into two categories that were demonstrations of conventions (writing strings of letters or numerals).

As with families in other countries, activities in which writing a name is a product were common. But, as other research has shown, a wide variety of writing activities occurred in these families (Heath 1983). More than eight hundred products were collected, and all but two families produced products from five or more activity categories. The range of categories tended to increase over time. There is a parallel to reading activities, in that families vary in terms of how frequently activities take place and how wide-ranging the activities are. Some families may be relatively narrowly focused; in others, children may be developing writing within several different activities. As children approach entry to school, patterns may vary further.

Effective Instruction

What do these descriptions mean for effective teaching? There is widespread agreement about the general properties of effective teaching (Darling-Hammond 1998). Expert teachers have knowledge about children that enables them to meet the needs of diverse students and create instructional events that connect with students' experiences. An effective teacher is able to solve the central problem of teaching identified by Bruner (1996, 45): "It is the issue of how human beings achieve a meeting of minds, experienced by teachers usually as 'how do I reach the children?' and by children as 'What's she trying to get at?'" The two sets of descriptions of children's diversity, one identifying specific knowledge and the other forms of embedded expertise, provide different sorts of information to a teacher. The descriptions of diversity provided by the second set add considerable complexity to Bruner's mediation problem.

In the second part of this chapter, I want to discuss some aspects of teaching that enable solutions to this problem in the face of diversity. The discussion focuses on the space afforded by curricula and how a curriculum enables or impedes the recognition of diversity. I also examine teachers' ideas about diversity in children's expertise and teaching strategies that might be used to recognise and capitalise on that diversity.

Wide Curricula

Curricula can be seen as vehicles for specifying and promoting valued forms of expertise. Although we seldom refer to explicit curricula for child rearing, families hold views about expected and valued forms of learning and development. For example, Valsiner (1987) uses the concept of a *zone of promoted actions* to describe how parents construct channels that increase the probability of some actions and decrease the probability of others. In a similar way, curricula can be conceived of as zones for promoting certain actions. The selection and specification of particular teaching and learning activities are based on views about expected and valued forms expertise. The activities increase the probability of some sorts of teaching and learning and decrease the probability of other sorts. For example, if the curriculum adopts high interest texts and emphasizes reading for meaning in the first year of instruction, the probability of certain forms of teaching and learning is heightened. It is likely that classroom talk relating to text topics and children's understanding; patterns of self-corrections; and meaning-related miscues will be higher in such a curriculum than in one that emphasizes activities of accurate discrimination of letter-sound relationships (McNaughton 1987).

Using this image, curricula can be considered further as providing wide or narrow channels for particular sorts of activities and expertise. A wide curriculum would provide a range of multifaceted activities that enabled teaching and learning to take place on a number of dimensions and in a number of different activity contexts. For example, explicit teaching of phonics can take place within text-based teaching (such as during guided oral reading and guided text writing), or it can take place outside of texts (such as in instructional episodes with letters and in worksheets), or it can take place in a combination of the two. But given that teacher-reader interactions and a teacher's incidental learning can be focused on several dimensions during text reading and writing (for example, strategies of decoding and strategies of comprehending), a curriculum that provides text-based activities would potentially be wider than one that did not. A clear claim follows: The wider the channel, the more diversity in skills and knowledge it is possible to accommodate.

Teachers' ideas and instructional strategies operate within the channel afforded by this curriculum. A specific tool of the curriculum for early instruction is the beginning reading text. Texts can also be seen as providing wide or narrow spaces for instruction. "Meaningful" texts are written typically in the form of simple narrations or expositions, and use language and illustrations in an optimal balance of complexity and familiarity for children along dimensions of structures, themes, vocabulary, and meanings. The narrative and expository features provide opportunities for multiple purposes and messages, both in the written text and in the illustrations that can accompany even the earliest texts. The space afforded by this sort of text and its illustrations creates a broad frame of reference for the discourse children and teachers engage in. With these texts conversational opportunities are plentiful. The potential for joint and personal understandings is wide, providing increased possibilities for children's topics and purposes to be aired, and enabling teachers to be informed and dexterous. The possibilities for shared meanings and for gaining the connections with which Bruner (1996) was concerned are greater. Teacher and student can both put more into and take more out of the act of reading.

Unplanned, or, more accurately, embedded learning can be substantial under appropriate conditions. For example, children can acquire incidental vocabulary when reading storybooks (Elley 1989), and can acquire substantial knowledge and awareness of phoneme-grapheme relationships even when the curriculum does not provide much explicit and text-independent teaching of this knowledge (McIntyre and Freppon 1994; Tunmer 1997).

There is clearly a need not to rely on one sort of text, but to have a variety of texts to provide space for diversity, including texts that are deliberately restrictive (Snow, Burns, and Griffen 1998). These may include *decodable* texts. A text that has strongly controlled phonic features almost inevitably is designed to restrict structures, themes, vocabulary, and meanings in the text and the representations in the illustrations. If these were the primary texts in keeping with a narrow curriculum, the possibilities for incidental and unplanned teaching and learning would be reduced. Even so, one has to consider carefully the functional properties of curricula and texts to determine if they do indeed afford the space and the conditions required for effective mediation. An example of inadvertent narrowing occurs in the internationalisation of even the most well-written narrative and expository texts. The "blanding" of illustrations can reduce messages about identity and the degree to which illustrations are familiar to different sets of local children (McLachlan 1996).

Ideas and Strategies

Teachers' abilities to respond to diversity within this wide curriculum depend on the properties of their expertise. One part of expertise is teachers' ideas about diversity. A second part is the strategies teachers use to capitalise on diversity. These are not simple things to change; the evidence is that the latter is in many respects dependent on the former, and our professional ideas are particularly difficult to change.

An intensive analysis of response to diversity comes from Megan Goodridge's (1995) study of writing lessons. The analysis comes in the form of an educational intervention. Before school, families prepared portfolios of children's writing products and descriptions of activities, which they shared with the teacher. It was assumed that demonstrating the range of writing activities that specific children had experience with (and had developed performances within) would lead to systematic use of this diversity within writing lessons. Although all the teachers appreciated this knowledge, it had little impact on how some of them interacted with the children as new entrants. In one instance, the child coming to school had often drawn types of cars and, with help, written labels for them. Although the teacher saw examples of this, the focus in the classroom on writing a "story" led her to dissuade the child from this form of writing. The strong focus on narrative seemed to restrict accommodation of the emergent expertise. Even when, as in this case, a child's initial writing is more expository in form, it can still be incorporated into guided writing and used as a base to develop narrative.

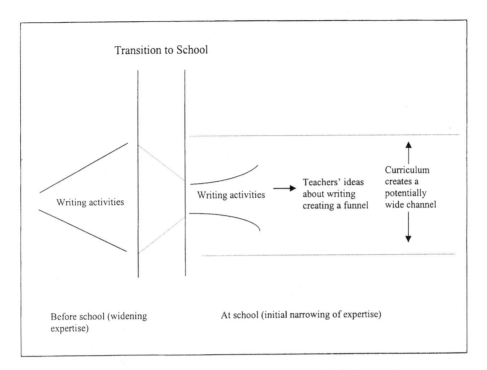

FIGURE 1–2 *Channels for expertise in writing over the transition to school: The case of a narrow funneling of emergent expertise*

This general outcome is illustrated in Figure 1–2, a graphic representation, in the form of a funnel hypothesis, of this situation. The hypothesis is that teachers' beliefs about what counts as reading or writing, or what counts as appropriate forms of expertise, create boundary conditions for "seeing" and responding to diverse forms. The widening activity base and the increasing diversity of emergent expertise is shown on the left, the transition to school in the center. On the right I have represented the potential in a curriculum for types (or genres) of writing to be developed further, and a focus that may often operate in beginning instruction.

The English curriculum in New Zealand (Ministry of Education 1995) provides space for identifying and responding to a variety of forms of language and literacy, but the activities selected, arranged, and deployed can, for beginning students, direct what was a diversifying emergent expertise through a narrowing of the curriculum as delivered. Modeling, conferencing, and other activities associated with the question "What is your story?" present a message that narrative in general—and personal recounting in particular—precedes, or at least is the building block to, other ways of writing. Thus, in the case of writing, teachers' beliefs about the priority of narrative and the form that instruction takes might limit their response to diversity.

In general this may be a perfectly defensible and workable teaching decision. It may be that children's immediate intention to recount, to be the narrator, is the most effective vehicle to promote the learning of mechanics and to provide a bridge to other forms of writing. Having immediate meaning and personalised sense driving the acquisition is, arguably, a very powerful basis for instruction. Also, the potential for establishing shared understandings and utilising personal and culturally framed topics is present in written narratives. The emphasis on narrative provides a "wide" instructional activity within which personal expertise is more likely to be seen. But this may not, for a particular student, be the only, or the best, tributary into the wide channel. The need is for adaptability and diversity. The curriculum and associated tools create the space for this diversity, but our ideas and interactional practices may get in the way.

Diversity Awareness

A major developmental step in expertise takes place as children become aware of parts of their actions (Clay 1998a). The general notion of awareness is useful in studies of teachers' expertise, too (Sternberg 1998). Within the ideas or "folk theories" (Olson and Bruner 1996) a teacher brings to instructional encounters are a set of ideas about the nature of literacy and the potential for diversity. This can be called *diversity awareness* (in literacy). Diversity awareness refers to the degree to which a teacher is aware of how much he or she knows about individual children's expertise in literacy, including family and community-based forms and functions. In writing it may be quite restricted. Year-one teachers' expectations about expertise on entry to school is limited mostly to items of conventional knowledge, and even here the evidence suggests mismatches between expectations and systematic assessment (Glasswell, McNaughton, and Parr 1993).

Having well-articulated knowledge about one's students is clearly a feature of effective teaching (Darling-Hammond 1998), but it is particularly important in the context of diversity. New Zealand educators' beliefs in their instructional practices were shaken by the results of the 1992 International Educational Achievement (IEA) comparisons of literacy achievement (Elley 1992). While supporting claims that the teaching of reading was relatively robust in terms of international levels of achievement, they demonstrated a disturbing gap between students whose first language was English and those whose first language was not English. Close examination of the IEA data shows that teachers who are successful in reducing this "language gap" assess their students' progress frequently, indicating that they personalise instruction (Wilkinson 1998).

How do teachers develop this awareness? One source is professional ideas constructed in preservice and inservice education. This is where our models of development become so important, both for our understanding of what develops (structures) and for our understanding of process. The three positions sketched in the introduction are likely to be associated with different sorts of awareness, because diversity is signified differently in each position.

A second source is the presence of reflective problem solving, the ability to teach oneself. This does not happen by chance. It happens when teachers are prepared to see and solve Bruner's (1996) "presenting problem," to find best-fit solutions without being restricted by received wisdom or structured lesson plans.

The collective reflection of early problem solving in New Zealand's history of reading instruction for Maori children provides an interesting case in point. The history of teaching in what were called the "native schools" shows that some teachers debated the best strategies for teaching children to read in English through Maori. Their strategies included developing purpose-built and experientially based texts, in some cases in Maori. This happened when the prevailing official position was to reject the first language and to use imported phonics-based readers. The historical data contain a suggestion that teaching in mainstream classrooms, which came to have the hallmarks of natural language texts and being child centered, may have been strongly influenced by the results of the reflective problem solving of teachers teaching in native schools (Simon 1998).

Instructional Strategies

Having ideas that enable a modicum of diversity awareness is a necessary condition for developing instructional strategies that respond effectively to diversity. But the relationship between ideas and actions, particularly for a professional expert, is not simple. The strategies teachers need fall into two main areas, identifying and connecting. The argument to this point suggests that identifying involves assessing more than conventional knowledge. Conventional measures need to be augmented with ways of identifying the activities with which children are familiar, providing understandings of their situated expertise. The portfolios described earlier are one such means. But the more general strategy is tapping into families' and early childhood educators' knowledge, and seeking examples. This strategy may mean that teachers have a range of early literacy tasks that they use to assess children's situated expertise; for example, singing the alphabet, memorising and reciting texts, and writing lists and letters. Some general strategies apply, such as using knowledge of common literacy events within a community. Here is where time spent with children and with their communities can be very important (Darling-Hammond 1998). However, other ideas may constrain the degree to which identification strategies can be deployed. Because year-one teachers tend to be more open to parent contact, parents and teachers engage in more contact at this level than at other levels (Booth and Dunn 1996; Parr et al. 1993). Yet despite this contact, teachers and researchers focus on guiding parents' involvement in school activities, but in return parents are viewed as having little guidance to offer teachers in matters of pedagogy and curriculum (Booth and Dunn 1996).

Connecting with children's expertise is part of the notion of building or bridging. How does a teacher do this? Having identified possible forms of expertise, including activity structures, the teacher's role is to create joint activity. The concept of activity includes having shared goals, shared understandings about means for achieving those goals, and shared ideas about participation.

Developing effective instructional activities is dependent on learner and teacher having the same understandings of what Gwenneth Phillips (1998) calls "the context of the task." Only when the teacher can see the task from the learner's perspective and when the learner understands what the teacher means can a generative connection occur. Connecting then involves the teacher's sharing the child's familiar activity and from there guiding the expertise towards those forms that are also needed in the curriculum. This may mean shifting to explicit description and explanation of purposes and processes. For example, if recitation of memorised text is a familiar activity for a child, this activity can be incorporated more deliberately (it may already be incorporated indirectly) in beginning reading instruction. From memorised texts, goals of decoding and comprehension can be developed. Or, if labeling drawings of cars is a familiar activity, using it as a basis for developing narrative about those cars can be a means of connecting.

Conclusions

Researchers have an important role in the development, maintenance, and questioning of pedagogical theories. The grand assumptions we make and the working principles we draw on influence (or should influence) and are informed by educational practices. Marie Clay has consistently argued against simple models of development that are unidimensional and linear, models that are problematic theoretically and that do not make much sense in the context of the activities and the diversity that researchers in emergent literacy have been plotting. The position elaborated here argues for an increase in our awareness, an increase in the degree to which we might see and respond to diversity in literacy.

References

BOOTH, A., AND DUNN, J. F., EDS. 1996. *Family-School Links: How Do They Affect Educational Outcomes?* Hillsdale, N.J.: Lawrence Erlbaum.

BRUNER, J. 1996. *Culture and Education*: Cambridge: Harvard University Press.

CLAY, M. M. 1966. "Emergent Reading Behaviour." Ph.D. diss., University of Auckland, Auckland.

———. 1975. *What Did I Write?* Auckland: Heinemann.

———. 1985. "Engaging with the School System." *New Zealand Journal of Educational Studies* 20: 20–38.

———. 1991. *Becoming Literate: The Construction of Inner Control.* Auckland: Heinemann.

———. 1998a. *By Different Paths to Common Outcomes.* York, Maine: Stenhouse.

———. 1998b. "From Acts to Awareness in Early Literacy." *Children's Issues: Journal of the Children's Issues Centre* 2 (1): 12–20.

COLE, M. 1996. *Cultural Psychology: A Once and Future Discipline*. Cambridge: Harvard University Press.

DARLING-HAMMOND, L. 1998. "Teachers and Teaching: Testing Policy Hypotheses from a National Commission Report." *Educational Researcher* 27 (1): 5–15.

ELLEY, W. 1989. "Vocabulary Acquisition from Listening to Stories." *Reading Research Quarterly* 24 (2): 176–186.

———. 1992. *How in the World Do Students Read?* New York: International Association for the Evaluation of Educational Achievement.

ELSTER, C. 1994. "Patterns Within Preschoolers' Emergent Readings." *Reading Research Quarterly* 29 (4): 403–417.

GLASSWELL, K., MCNAUGHTON, S., AND PARR, J. 1993. "Teachers' Expectations of Children's Knowledge About Writing on Entry to J1." Paper presented at the annual conference of the New Zealand Association for Research in Education, Hamilton, New Zealand, 2–5 December 1993.

GOODMAN, Y. 1990. *How Children Construct Literacy*. Newark, N.J.: International Reading Association.

GOODRIDGE, M. 1995. "Activity Systems for Writing: A Co-Constructivist Analysis of Children's Emergent Writing Development at Home and in the Transition to School." Ph.D. diss., University of Auckland, Auckland.

HEATH, S. B. 1983. *Ways with Words: Language, Life, and Work in Communities and Classrooms*. Cambridge: Cambridge University Press.

MCINTYRE, E. AND FREPPON, P. A. 1994. "A Comparison of Children's Development of Alphabetic Knowledge in a Skills-Based and a Whole Language Classroom." *Research in the Teaching of English* 28 (4): 381–417.

MCNAUGHTON, S. 1987. *Being Skilled: The Socialisations of Learning to Read*. London: Methuen.

———. 1995. *Patterns of Emergent Literacy: Processes of Development and Transition*. Auckland: Oxford University Press.

———. 1996. "The Power of Visual Language: Maori in Illustrations in Beginning Readers." Master's thesis, University of Auckland, Auckland.

———. 1997. "Story Retelling: A Collaborative Activity for Describing and Assessing Children's Language at School Entry." Report to the New Zealand Ministry of Education, April.

MCNAUGHTON, S., AND KA'AI. 1990. "Two Studies of Transitions: Socialisations of Literacy and Te Hiringa Take Take." Report to the New Zealand Ministry of Education. Education Department, University of Auckland.

MINISTRY OF EDUCATION. 1995. *English in the New Zealand Curriculum*. Wellington: Learning Media.

NALDER, S. 1985. "Emergent Reading." Unpublished report. Auckland Reading Advisory Service.

OLSON, D. R., AND BRUNER, J. S. 1996. "Folk Psychology and Folk Pedagogy." In *The Handbook of Education and Human Development: New Models of Learning, Teaching, and Schooling*, edited by D. R. Olson and N. Torrance. Cambridge: Blackwell.

PARR, J., McNAUGHTON. S., TIMPERLEY, H., AND ROBINSON, V. 1993. "Bridging the Gap: Practices of Collaboration Between Home and Junior School." *Australian Journal of Early Childhood* 18 (3): 35–42.

PHILLIPS, G. 1998. "An Analysis of the Co-Construction of Context in Beginning Reading Instruction." Ph.D. diss., University of Auckland, Auckland.

PHILLIPS, L. M., NORRIS, S. P., AND MASON, J. M. 1996. "Longitudinal Effects of Early Literacy Concepts on Reading Achievement: A Kindergarten Intervention and Five-Year Follow-up." *Journal of Literacy Research* 28: 173–195.

SIMON, J., ED. 1998. *Nga Kura Maori: The Native School System 1867–1969*. Auckland: Auckland University Press.

SNOW, C. E., BARNES, W. S., CHANDLER, J., GOODMAN, I. F., AND HEMPHILL, L. 1991. *Unfulfilled Expectations: Home and School Influences on Literacy*. Cambridge: Harvard University Press.

SNOW, C. E., BURNS, S., AND GRIFFEN, P., EDS. 1998. *Preventing Reading Difficulties in Young Children*. Washington, D.C.: National Academy Press.

STERNBERG, R. J. 1998. "Abilities Are Forms of Developing Expertise." *Educational Researcher* 27 (3): 11–20.

SULZBY, E., AND TEALE, W. 1991. "Emergent Literacy." In Vol. 2 of *Handbook of Reading Research*, edited by P. D. Pearson, R. Barr, M. L. Kamil, and P. Mosenthal. New York: Longman.

TUNMER, W. 1997. "Language-Related and Cognitive Motivational Factors in Beginning Literacy Instruction: An Overview." Paper presented at the conference Reading on Track: Research Results for Teaching Reading, Massey University, 17–18 July 1997.

VALSINER, J. 1987. *Culture and the Development of Children's Action*. Chichester England: Wiley.

WAGNER, D. A., AND SPRATT, J. E. 1987. "Cognitive Consequences of Contrasting Pedagogies: The Effects of Quranic Pre-Schooling in Morocco." *Child Development* 58: 1207–1219.

WERTSCH, J. V. 1991. *Voices of the Mind: A Sociocultural Approach to Mediated Actions*. Cambridge: Harvard University Press.

WILKINSON, I. A. G. 1998. "Dealing with Diversity: Achievement Gaps in Reading Literacy Among New Zealand Students." *Reading Research Quarterly* 33 (2): 144–167.

WOOD, D. 1997. *How Children Think and Learn*. 2nd ed. London: Blackwell.

Two

There Are x Kinds of Learners in a Single Class: Diversity Without Individual Differences

DAVID R. OLSON

I once asked Marie Clay, whose work I greatly admire, to contribute to a volume on education and human development I was organizing. I asked her to write about the problem of human diversity, as I was particularly impressed by the sensitivity of her program, Reading Recovery, in meeting the particular and special needs of each beginning reader. At the same time, I recognized that her approach to diversity was completely different from the one common in the psychological literature, where the same topic is treated under the category of *individual differences*. The difference, in a word, was that Marie Clay treated all learners as unique, in that each requires a specialized program, and yet as basically similar, in the sense that all learners must master the same knowledge. It is this enigma, commonality and difference, I examine in this chapter.

The problem of human diversity is commonly considered to be identical to the problem of individual differences. People, after all, do differ. With the exception of identical twins, no two persons in the total human population of some four billion are the same in appearance. To a man-eating lion or to a microbe, this diversity goes unnoticed. But human beings are expert at detecting difference, to the extent that we do not confuse any two individuals. We are just as diverse psychologically as we are physically, and we are just as attuned to these differences as we are to physical differences. How we react to this diversity makes all the difference.

Categorizing or classifying individuals on the basis of traits is one traditional way. In the Homeric legends, the actions of Achilles are explained by his courage and pride, that of Odysseus by his foresight and wiliness. We, too, may think that there are basically two kinds of people: those who are pleasant, informed, and cooperative—people who are more or less like Marie Clay, me, and you, dear reader—and those others who are argumentative, opinionated, inflexible, and selfish. Categorizing people is one of life's small, usually harmless, pleasures, but for psychologists and educators, classifications are a way of life—by age, by grade, by success in schooling; more recently by traits such as giftedness, hyperactivity, intellectual ability, visual thinking, and the myriad traits discovered by personality theorists.

17

In psychology, individual difference is a particular theoretical stance or orientation to the problem of human diversity. It classifies persons on the basis of values on particular dimensions or traits, such as intelligence or style. Personality theory ascribes traits and dispositions to persons as a means of explaining behavior—and, in particular, differences in behavior—and ultimately, in assigning persons to roles. The tradition goes back to Galton's early studies of human variability and to Binet's pioneering work on mental abilities. To this day, Binet and his successors account for some 25 percent of the variance on a variety of school-like tasks on the basis of performance on IQ tests. The usual explanation is that the IQ test captures some underlying trait, ability, or capacity that is then seen as accounting for, and thereby explaining, performance on other tasks. Other traits, such as open-mindedness, persistence, or impulsivity, are then added to the lists of traits in the hope of explaining more of the variance.

There are a number of problems with this tradition, some of which are well known. Best known is the potential confusion between correlation and cause. The well-known correlation between IQ and reading ability, for example, is often seen as a causal relationship; the capacity indicated by IQ tests being exploited in learning to read. However, the relationship could indicate common beliefs and strategies called upon in both IQ tests and reading tests. Metalinguistic knowledge is one such candidate, in that a large part of IQ is linguistic competence; possessing an adequate stock of metalinguistic concepts, such as word, letter, sound, meaning, and intention, may mediate that relation.

Second, equally well known is the temptation to indulge in the spurious transformation of a trait into an entity. Thus the IQ, which began as a description, came to be thought of as an attribute, a real entity. Alfred North Whitehead spoke of the fallacy of "misplaced concreteness," the attempt to treat adjectival properties as actual entities. For example, *truth* is a relation between a statement and a state of affairs, but thinkers through the centuries have been tempted to think of truth as something that exists independently of all statements: the true facts, the Truth. Similarly, *intelligence* is sometimes mistakenly taken as a entity or a thing, a possession. Intelligence is better thought of as an abstract description of the relation between strategies and tasks. It is not a possession, a mechanism, or a capacity. Speaking more generally, relations are not things, and intelligence is a relation. Thinking of intelligence as an explanatory entity is a form of circular reasoning similar to that of Moliere's M. Jourdain, who advanced the celebrated claim that sleeping potions achieved their effect through their "dormative powers."

Third, there is the well-known problem of labeling. Once a child is persuaded that he or she is dull or gifted, the appellation may become a self-fulfilling prophesy. Clay noted this in the labeling of children as dyslexic: If a child is labelled as dyslexic, the condition becomes the explanation of educational failure, in contrast to the more accessible alternatives such as tutoring and practice. Hacking (1996) examined the effects of the eighteenth-century invention of the statistical notion of normal on psychological theory. Rather than seeing persons as possessing a common human nature, deviations from the statistical mean came to be seen as abnormal, offering individuals a host of alternative explanations for failure in addition to the traditional ones of opportunity and effort.

But there are other less well-known problems with defining human diversity in terms of individual differences: This approach misrepresents the goals of psychological explanation, it deflects attention from the more basic determinants of action, and it leads to counterproductive programs of education and remediation. All of these may be traced to a common base—a failure to come to grips with the problem of intentionality, with what persons think, want, and try to do and the role of intentionality in accounting for human diversity.

This alternative also goes back to antiquity. Auerbach ([1946] 1991) contrasted the Homeric style of depicting human action in terms of traits (wily Odysseus) with the Old Testament style of accounting in terms of the beliefs, hopes, and, roughly, intentions of the actors. Auerbach wrote:

> Abraham's actions are explained not only by what is happening to him at the moment, nor yet only by his character [unlike Achilles and Odysseus], but by his previous history; he remembers, he is constantly conscious of, what God has promised him and what God has already accomplished for him—his soul is torn between desperate rebellion and hopeful expectation. (12)

Let us consider briefly how a theory of intentionality allows us to see the problem of diversity in a new light.

Psychological Explanations: Doings *versus* Happenings

One branch of psychology, experimental psychology, has looked for the universal in persons; for example, just as each human has a nose, two legs, and a spleen, even given inexhaustible diversity, so too all humans have visual systems, memory systems, and a capacity for learning. The other branch, differential psychology, has attempted to capture the ways in which people differ with respect to those fixed features—for example, some learn more quickly, remember better, or detect patterns more successfully than others.

What modern cognitive psychology has contributed to this picture is that these general putative differences in memory, perception, and learning are not themselves general explanatory properties or traits, but rather reflections of the current state of the knowledge structures of the individual involved. Patterns are quickly recognized if one is familiar with the alternatives. Chess masters see patterns on a chess board in terms of attacking and defending, moves that are invisible to a novice. A mathematician sees a string of numbers as a list of primes; an amateur sees it only as an arbitrary list. Failure to see a pattern or a relationship cannot be explained or treated in terms of a trait or an ability, but rather in terms of what the perceiver knows, believes, wants, and tries. This, of course, complicates the psychologists' task in that what a person knows or believes is infinitely more diverse that any list of hypothetical traits would ever suggest. A difference between children, for example, could result from something as simple as one child taking the numeral 0 to be the letter O. This is a knowledge difference, not a trait difference; an Abraham, not an Odysseus.

This shift in explanation corresponds to a pervasive shift in psychological theory, from a causal theory to what may be loosely called an *interpretive* or *intentionalist* theory. Understanding, sense making, was central to John Dewey's effort to provide a new psychology for the educational process. He contrasted *doings*, the actions of persons, with *happenings*, events that resulted from outside causes. Traditional psychology, Dewey argued, explained a person's behavior according to what happened to them; behavior should, rather, be explained in terms of what people, including learners, were doing or trying to do. What people are doing, are trying to do, or think they are doing makes up much of the modern cognitive sciences, with their emphasis on representation and consciousness. To this day, psychological explanation veers between these two poles—causal events and structures—that push behavior, rather than relying on intentional states, including beliefs and plans, that allow people to do things. Trait theory is part of that earlier causal psychology.

As in any other science, psychology attempts to advance a minimum number of principles to explain the broadest possible range of phenomena. For example, gravity explains not only terrestrial events, but also celestial ones. Traits are advanced on the same basis: One trait, such as intelligence, can explain performance on a variety of tasks. A trait or disposition functions as a causal and explanatory principle. Although the empirical basis of trait theory is correctional, traits are often seen as causal states or mechanisms that are recruited in a variety of contexts. If successful, that theory would achieve the scientific goal of reducing behavioral complexity to a manageable set of factors. However, the idea that behavior could be explained according to a few causal factors has fallen under serious criticism in the cognitive sciences. This first became clear in the linguistic sciences: No set of causal factors is capable of generating the infinite set of sentences that a speaker routinely generates. The search is now for the set of generative principles that actors employ in producing sentences, thoughts, and actions, rather than for the causes of the behavior. Thus psychological explanation has increasingly relied on what is sometimes called *intentional causation* in opposition to mechanical causation. In a sense, intentional causes are not causes at all, but rather the reasons for action, including the beliefs, desires, hopes, and intentions of agents in particular environments. From this view, behavior is less mechanically caused than it is intentionally, consciously, and deliberately chosen.

Traits are poor cousins in such explanations, in that they are assumed to operate causally and outside of the scope the beliefs and other conscious intentional states of actors. Intentional causality operates on the basis of beliefs, feelings, and goals that are accessible to consciousness, hence to revision, on the basis of new evidence, as well as to planning and accountability. Actors are responsible for what they do as long as that action is under their control. Intentionalistic psychology puts much of that behavior under the agent's control; hence, it subjects that behavior to responsibility and accountability and ultimately, to pedagogy.

This is not to deny outright the possible causal effects of nonintentional dispositions acting outside and overriding a person's expressed beliefs and goals. Infants are notorious for their "irrationality," which is to say, they act automatically and reflexively. Attachment, for example, would seem to be a fundamental disposition, as are some other encapsulated cognitive functions. Such dispositions may turn into intentional states such as beliefs, desires, and intentions, as learners acquire a language for reflecting on those dispositions. Furthermore, such dispositions may be better thought of as rules called into play in certain contexts than as simple causal mechanisms. Attachment may thus be thought of as a complex set of perception-emotion-action rules rather than as a simple causal mechanism. Stanovich (1999) has suggested a useful middle ground between caused and chosen behavior by distinguishing between algorithmic and deliberative processes in thinking and by showing that in many contexts, automatic, algorithmic rules, as well as more deliberative ones, are at play.

Psychological explanation, then, depends on finding out the beliefs, rules, theories, and other representations and misrepresentations held by persons that lead to particular forms of action. Differences are the product of these different representations, rather than a particular set of traits.

The Insider's View of Action

We attribute traits to others that they would rarely if ever ascribe to themselves. This is known as the *attribution fallacy*. Ascribing traits such as craziness or intelligence is an outsider's game. Sometimes the ascription is socially necessary, as when we ascribe madness to someone who sincerely believes he is Jesus Christ (see, for example, *The Three Christs of Ypsilanti*, Rokeach 1964). The point is that such ascription is entirely from a third-person stance, not from the perspective of the actor. Actors explain their own actions according to beliefs and desires rather than traits. When asked why we missed the bus, we are more likely to explain that we thought the bus left an hour later or from a different corner than to mention a trait such as tardiness. Others may be tempted to see such behavior as the product of a such a disposition. Similarly, an outsider may explain that a student solved a problem because she is "clever"; the student herself would more correctly and informatively say she solved it because she recognized that the problem had the same form as the one in the textbook. The actor sees his or her own actions in a different way than the theorist sees them.

Piaget is well known for his discoveries about how children view their own actions—ways of viewing that frequently lead to actions that adults had previously seen as products of ignorance or habit. In studies of conservation with young children, Piaget found that it was not simply that young children did not know about quantity; it was that they conflated quantity with extent, and consequently could be led into error by distracting arrays. Piaget's approach to children's cognition may usefully be contrasted with that of Binet, the inventor of the IQ test. Binet's goal was to classify individuals in terms of ability; Piaget's was to find out what subjects were doing—and thought they were doing—when they approached the very tasks that Binet has used to classify persons.

As a consequence of its third-person or objectivist stance, the trait theory of individual difference is more useful for thinking about others than about oneself. Indeed, if children adopt the objectivist stance in explaining their own behavior, they may render that behavior autonomous and out of the reach of their own responsible intentional actions. If a person is late because of a trait, the trait is responsible for the failure; conversely, if a person is late because of beliefs and intentions, he or she is responsible for amending those beliefs and intentions and for his or her ultimate success or failure.

Trait theory inherited its objectivist stance from behaviorism. Early in the twentieth century, scientific scruples led psychologists to downplay anything resembling "spiritual" or "mental" powers, including beliefs and intentions, and to search for mechanical causes of behavior. Behaviorism was the product of those scruples; action was seen to be caused, in the same way that the path of a particle was caused, even if the causes were complex. The "cognitive revolution" was in part responsible for bringing intentionality and intentional causation back into respectability, because computational devices could be designed to manifest, through naturalistic causal mechanisms, actions that, had they occurred in a person, would have been seen as intentional.

Persons as Learners

A collection of traits never gives a genuine picture of a person; a person is not an integrated set of such traits. A person is a self with a set of beliefs and expectations, coupled with a set of sensitivities that is employed in setting and monitoring the outcomes of actions based on those beliefs and expectations. Put simply, people know and believe, want, and try, and they integrate all of these actions in their attempts to act successfully and in their attempts to understand what is going on around them. Pedagogy, as we shall see, must accommodate those perceptions and orientations and must achieve some mutuality of goals and procedures between teacher and student. Those beliefs and goals are far more specific than any general trait can detect.

This confusion between person as self and person as a collection of traits is at its tragicomic worst in popular television shows in which people, in a rather desperate search for romance and matrimony, attempt to describe their idealized mate. For example, he or she should be kind, intelligent, ambitious, and sincere, and should possess a sense of humor and a good physique. The attempt is, in my view, seriously misguided. One does not fall in love with, or live satisfactorily with, a collection of traits. One is attracted to, and must come to know, a person. Indeed, the path to marital grief is to interpret every unexpected action of a spouse as an indication of some underlying, perhaps familial, disposition. Successful counseling, like successful teaching, is a matter of leading people to see or interpret actions in a corresponding way. One must come to love a person not by ascribing traits to him or her, but by understanding. Traits (except perhaps the trait of solvency) are only adjectivally relevant; that is, they may usefully modify our description of a person, but they do not capture a person, a self.

Human resource specialists are faced with the difficult, if not impossible, task of assigning persons to positions by means of personal traits, even if the relationships are extremely tenuous. Consequently, assessments are sometimes supplemented by more direct evidence of performance in similar roles on previous occasions. The best evidence that someone can skin a cat is that he or she has previously succeeded in doing just that.

Classification of students is little different. Classifying children as slow or gifted is based on unwarranted assumptions about underlying traits. More appropriate would be to classify children on the basis of what they do or have done rather than on the basis of an assumed trait. Thus, children could qualify for advanced math if they succeed in basic math. In this way, advantage is earned, not bequeathed. Trait descriptions are also ascriptions. Students may come to internalize the ascriptions, thereby becoming only what they are said to be—the problem of labeling. If learners are told that they are unable or unworthy, they may come to believe it, with the consequence that they fail to exert the effort needed. Students make mistakes not because of a disposition, but because of a misunderstanding. They are responsible for correcting such misunderstandings, and teachers are responsible for detecting, diagnosing, and assisting in the correction of those misunderstandings.

Pedagogy: From Learning to Understanding

It is in pedagogy that trait theory has elicited the most questionable results. If action is the product of traits and dispositions such as intelligence, critical thinking ability, open-mindedness, or tolerance, it is tempting to design programs to increase those traits or abilities. Critical-thinking programs are a case in point. Cognitive virtues such as critical thinking and open-mindedness, in my view, are better approached in less general terms. One can be taught to consider more options and apply useful strategies in the particular domains represented by the major scientific and humanistic disciplines.

One approach that has attracted much attention is the attempt to connect aptitudes or cognitive traits with treatments, under the assumption that some personal traits may help to specify the appropriate pedagogy (Cronbach and Snow 1997). That idea, however inspired, has yielded disappointingly little. The problem is that it takes the notion of traits too seriously, while ignoring the problems of intentionality. The effects of instruction are not to be seen as the simple outcomes of applying certain procedures to learners with certain characteristics. Learners are people with intentional states, including beliefs, goals, and feelings. Once recognized, the whole pedagogical enterprise changes its focus from producing effects to helping learners achieve their goals. This shift in orientation is often described as "learner-centered," which indeed it is. That label, however, is of limited value, as attention to the traits of learners may also be justified as being learner centered. What is required is that learners be treated as intentional beings who are responsible for their own beliefs, goals, and actions, as well as their understandings and misunderstandings.

Understanding is the critical concept here. The role of the teacher is not simply to produce some effects in a learner, but to produce understanding. This can only be done by connecting to the beliefs, desires, and goals of the learner. Failure should not be seen as a natural consequence of diversity. Modern pedagogy is built on a universalist assumption—that everyone can learn—and on the belief that learning is the product of understanding, not merely of compliance. Consequently, teaching is, so far as is possible, attuned to the beliefs and understanding of the learner.

Trait characterizations of individual differences fail to give access to the genuine problems of dealing with diversity. This is shown perhaps most clearly in the work of Marie Clay. Poor readers are helped because each is treated as an individual, possessing the cognitive resources needed for learning, but all erring in their own ways. Their errors are not just behavioral, but are the product of misunderstandings. Accommodating diversity is the invention of techniques for addressing these misunderstandings. In fact, in a task like reading, there are only a limited number of ways in which learners can go wrong, and those working with readers must be expert in detecting these ways. It is important, however, that these ways of going wrong not be captured in terms as general as traits. Problems are more specifically cognitive and affective—for example, failure to understand that expressions are composed of distinctive words that are represented in the writing system, that words can be decomposed into a small set of recognizable sounds represented by letters of the alphabet, or that the ideas expressed must make sense to the reader.

How, then, are we to treat the problem of diversity? Just as Clay does. Instruction is premised not on assumptions of deep differences in cognitive or other general abilities, but on many shallow differences in understanding. The question is not "What ability does this student lack?" but rather "What is the learner doing, trying to do, understanding, misunderstanding?" The solution is achieved not by the teacher's delivering truths but rather by the teacher's achieving an intersubjective mutuality with the learner. Teacher and student must come to share an understanding, a common way of looking at language, reading, and the world.

This goal is somewhat utopian in many, perhaps most, school contexts. Fortunately, such intersubjectivity between teacher and student is not essential for all learning. It is adequate for the learner to come up with his or her own understandings, interpretations, and misinterpretations, as long as these understandings do not lead the learner too far astray. Further, some mutuality can be achievable through group work, group projects and discussion, classroom reports and written reports, tests, and other assignments. But when the problems are more serious, there is little alternative to the sort of intensive, one-on-one interventions implemented in programs such as Reading Recovery or by sympathetic and knowledgeable reading instructors.

Conclusion

Paradoxically, perhaps, I am suggesting that the problem of human diversity is not well served by theories of individual differences. People, including children, differ. It is our attempts to make sense of this diversity that have gone awry. Human beings are more complex than our theories have generally allowed. Psychology seemed like a promising discipline as long as it could, like the Almighty on the Day of Judgment, separate the sheep from the goats. Alas, psychology has not succeeded in providing anything approaching that ability to classify. There are simply too many ways in which people differ for any such approach to succeed. People do differ, and teaching must accommodate differences. But diversity is not the same as "individual differences." Although individual differences, characterized as enduring, causal, objectivized properties of individuals, are perhaps of some use in conducting impersonal, institutional functions, such as assigning an individual to a role in a bank or a mental institution, they fail to connect with the actor's own self or point of view. When diversity is seen as a product of intentionality, that is, of the beliefs, values, goals, and consciousness of individuals, diversity can be accommodated through mutual enterprises and mutual understandings. This is at the heart of Clay's successful pedagogy.

References

AUERBACH, E. [1946] 1991. *Mimesis: The Representation of Reality in Western Literature.* Princeton: Princeton University Press.

CRONBACH, L., AND SNOW, R. 1997. *Aptitudes and Instructional Methods: A Handbook of Research on Interactions.* New York: Irvington.

HACKING, I. 1996. "Normal People." In *Modes of Thought,* edited by D. Olson and N. Torrance. Cambridge: Cambridge University Press.

ROKEACH, M. 1964. *The Three Christs of Ypsilanti: A Psychological Study.* New York: Knopf.

STANOVICH, K. 1999. *Who Is Rational? Studies of Individual Differences in Reasoning.* Mahwah, N.J.: Erlbaum.

Three

Unpacking Literate Achievement

PETER JOHNSTON

It is popular to argue that schools should be held accountable for student achievement, particularly literate achievement. It is also popular among researchers to study factors that affect student achievement. But what does it mean to "achieve" in literacy? Or what might it mean? It is easy for those outside the classroom to reduce achievement to scores on a standardized test, but there is evidence that this practice trivializes the learning that takes place (Murphy 1998). It is like assessing health by examining the speed with which a person runs a mile, ignoring the complex personal, social, emotional, and political learnings that are part of more or less healthy living. A teenager with a sub-six-minute mile can become a twenty-year-old couch tuber with an attitude, or die an anorexic. The same is certainly true for something as pervasive and consequential as literacy achievement. In this chapter, then, I will explore what it means, and might mean, to achieve in literacy. Although there is considerable concern over the misrepresentation of literate achievement by standardized tests (Johnston 1992; Murphy 1998), there has been substantially less demonstration of what is being left out, that is, exactly what of significance is achieved beyond the standardized test. This becomes particularly important when pressures are applied to teachers through tests, because under such circumstances the unmeasured aspects of achievement become excluded from instruction (Johnston 1998; Smith 1991).

My interest in these matters has been piqued by my involvement in a study of exemplary teachers. Our experience is that two exemplary teachers can be very different in the ways they go about teaching. There are similarities, certainly, as many studies attest (Haberman 1995; Pressley, Rankin, and Yokio 1996; Thomas and Barksdale-Ladd 1995), but there are very real differences that doubtless have consequences for

This report is based on research undertaken at the Center on English Learning and Achievement (CELA) at the University at Albany. The research was supported in part under the Research and Development Centers Program (award no. R305A60005) as administered by the Office of Educational Research and Improvement (OERI), U.S. Department of Education. However, the contents do not necessarily represent the positions or policies of the Department of Education, OERI, or the Institute on Student Achievement.

This chapter has been improved by feedback from Arthur Applebee, Janet Gaffney, and Virginia Goatley. It has also been shaped by discussions among the researchers at CELA.

students' literate learning. For example, I have often noticed in classrooms and tutoring programs such as Reading Recovery that teachers must tread a careful line between the pace of instruction for immediate efficiency, and the wait-time necessary to develop reflection and self-correction. It might not be the case that there are always trade-offs, but we must know the potential trade-offs in order to make reasoned judgments.

Consider this example. Terri Thorkildsen (in press) asked children in a direct instruction–oriented school and an inquiry-oriented school about their theories on the fairness of testing practices. The premises of these two approaches to education more-or-less line up with monological and dialogical patterns of talk. The children in the direct instruction school felt that tests were a good and fair way to find out about students' understanding and, indeed, to motivate children to learn—they could see little other reason to learn. They didn't like the idea of time spent on discussion, because then, for example, "you might give someone else the answer." By contrast, the children in the inquiry-oriented school felt that tests would not be a good idea, not least because they would take time away from discussion, which they valued as a good source of learning. Which set of understandings would we prefer if these two groups scored equally on standardized tests? What if they did not score equally? How important is children's understanding of what it means to learn and the significance of other people in the process?

Candidates for Literate Achievement

When my youngest daughter was in kindergarten, she was occupied one night writing a letter to a boy. It read (with spelling conventionalized), "Dear Gavin. I hope your birthday was fun. Do you know that my birthday is coming up? Love Sam." What struck me was that although she had limited control of the conventions of spelling, she had considerable control of some of the other relevant social conventions, such as her attention to the social niceties of her audience's interests before introducing her own (perhaps especially with a boy). But more important, because the letter spread to both sides of the page, she had written along the side "Turn over," commenting as she did so that he might not know it was continued on the other side. I consider her ability to imagine someone else's experience and use that to regulate her literate practices in this way an important achievement. I say this not merely because it happened when she was writing, but because it is a central aspect of literate competence—whether or not it is being exercised in the immediate context of print. It is this competence that enables her to construct believable characters, write plausible dialogue, anticipate necessary arguments for persuasion, etc. Although it is clearly a literate competence, and she is demonstrating it in kindergarten, according to some views of development, this ability to take a distant other's point of view would be a "developmentally inappropriate" addition to a kindergarten curriculum. I have certainly not seen a "social imagination" on any curriculum documents, although increasingly it seems to me not only appropriate but a central component of development (Dyson 1993; Johnston 1993).

28

Over the years I have also been surprised by the complexity of logic and syntax used by children, sometimes on paper, to persuade—usually, in the case of my own children, to address the unsatisfactory nature of our house rules (see also Newkirk 1989). Similarly, I have been struck by the complexity of philosophical thought children can demonstrate, although developmental theories suggest those thoughts should not be happening (see, for example, Matthews 1984). These, too, do not appear in curriculum or standards documents. If we have no place for such matters in our theories of development, our notions of literacy, or our curricula or standards for achievement, then teachers and parents will also be less likely to engage children in ways that will foster such development. These achievements would then be excluded from the curriculum simply because we lack the necessary theories, research strategies, or imagination—deficiencies that we will likely pass on to our children.

When considering literate achievement, I do not wish to exclude children's command of print conventions—spelling, word recognition, etc. Rather, I want to argue that these capture only a limited portion of literate competence. In this paper, without denying the significance of the achievements we attempt to measure with tests, I describe some of the dimensions of literate achievement that are left out, and make an argument for including them in what counts. Some of what I describe will possibly draw the reaction, "That's not literacy." Indeed, when we divide up the curriculum into pieces—science, social studies, reading, writing, math, etc.—some of what I describe will be in gray areas and some will simply not appear. These are exactly the aspects of learning that get squeezed out of the classroom in the press to name and secure "outcomes," particularly high-profile ones (Johnston 1998). Because literacy is pervasive across the curriculum, it is particularly vulnerable to these exclusions: What part of science is literate? Is the logic of scientific argument only a literate matter when it is written down? Is talk about historical records part of literacy?

Some resistance to what I will call *literate achievement* will arise from the belief that, if it is to count as literate, it must immediately involve the act of reading or writing. Such an argument holds that talking about a book one has read might count as literate, but talking with someone about a book they have read, or about a book one heard read on a tape, would not count as literate. I will argue instead, along with Applebee (1996), Heath (1990), Gee (1996), Wells and Chang-Wells (1992), and others, that in a literate society the distinction between oral and written discourse is not particularly helpful. In a literate society children must learn ways of representing and interacting. These ways are reciprocally influenced by print.

The notion of what it means to be literate in English has changed substantially over the past few decades, and remains a matter of contention. In the United States, the "basic" view of literacy is still popular. Proponents argue for a definition tied solely to making sounds out of print (Sweet 1997). Whatever else is acquired in the process of becoming literate is not viewed as being about literacy. Contrasting views explore more subtle and elaborate understandings. For example, literate thinking has come to mean "all those uses of language in which its symbolic potential is deliberately exploited as . . . an intentionally controlled tool for thinking and feeling" (Wells and

Chang-Wells 1992, 77). In this framework literate achievement constitutes a matter of intellectual development rather than merely expansion of communicative or translation skills. The distinction is not trivial. If literacy is viewed this way, it becomes a tool for building conscious control over learning and for developing independence. It makes possible a critical and reflective stance toward knowledge, knowledge development, and the language used to represent knowledge.

Whether or not this is accomplished is a matter of the instructional interactions in the classroom. Following Vygotsky (1978) and others (Gee 1996; Langer 1995; Rogoff and Toma 1997), I assume that the literate interactions in which children participate are not simply a vehicle for learning, but also a major part of what they learn. Consequently, these must count as literate achievements with implications both for individual students and for the literate communities of which they are a part. On a simple level, then, when a teacher engages students' talk in particular ways, using particular terms, she is specifying the nature of the talk that should take place in the particular discipline—the register, the genre, the word choices. For example, beginning in early adolescence there is a shift in language acquisition toward an expanded Greco-Latin vocabulary—the vocabulary that marks "academic" literacy. Part of literate achievement, then, is revealed in the facility with which children use academic vocabulary and discourse forms, whether or not in the immediate context of print.

The way in which the teacher engages students in talk also specifies transparent, yet powerful, literate dimensions. For example, in learning science in school, children learn what counts as science, who does it, who asks the questions, what counts as an acceptable question, the acceptable sources of evidence, and what it means to know and not know. These understandings are brought to bear on children's sense-making engagements with print, just as they are with children's spoken engagements. Children learn these subtleties in the tacit (and related) ways they learn about femininity and masculinity (Gilbert 1989; Malinowitz 1995), as unstated presuppositions. Because they are unstated, they are transparent and hard to contest (Todorov 1996), yet they provide the infrastructure of literate development. To learn that one has nothing of significance to say is certainly an understanding that will be part of literate interactions, even though it might have been acquired in oral engagements. What do we make of a fourth-grade student who, when asked if there are different kinds of readers in his class, says, "There's ones like the people who's not good and the people who are good"? When asked if he likes to contribute to discussions of books, he says, "Not really. 'Cause I think what Mrs. Wilson does is right. She sort of starts off easy and then she gets real hard with the questions." Asked whether he ever disagrees with the other students in discussions he observes, "No. 'Cause they usually be right." The child's literacy instruction appears to have produced achievements that should give us pause. First, he is not becoming prepared to participate productively in a democratic society—a society based on the premise of collaborative development of visions to guide social action. Second, rather than learning a self-extending system of knowledge development in which he uses literate conversations to extend his own thinking, he appears to have learned a self-limiting system. He has certainly achieved an understanding of himself as a literate knower that will not serve him well in the long run. There are two interrelated aspects of this that I would like to explore, the epistemological and the social.

Epistemology

Epistemology is from the Greek words *episteme* (knowledge) and *logos* (discourse). Simply stated, a person's epistemology is his or her theory of knowledge and knowing, which on the face of it sounds esoteric and innocuous. But Parker Palmer (1993) puts his pen nicely on the epistemological problem. He observes:

> At its deepest reaches, education gave me an identity as a knower. It answered the question "Who am I?" [but, it also answered the question] "what is the world?" . . . and the same knowledge that gave me a picture of myself and the world also defined the relation of the two. . . . What is the nature of the knower? What is the nature of the known? And what is the nature of the relations between the two? (20)

These are all questions of identity and relationship, but they are also achievements that are fundamental to literacy.

Though there are several ways of classifying epistemological stances, a common distinction is between constructed and received knowing (Belenky et al. 1986). I will caricature this dichotomy somewhat to sharpen the distinctions in the interests of space, and because it relates readily to Nystrand and his colleagues' distinction between monologic and dialogic instruction (Nystrand et al. 1997). Received knowers feel that knowledge is "out there" and that someone in authority will be able to give them the knowledge they need to receive. Knowledge comes in facts, and clear transmission of these facts is the central part of learning. Received knowers are uncomfortable with ambiguity, expecting things to be right or wrong, and they do not see discussion as a useful means of learning. Their own experiences and feelings are not part of real knowledge and are kept separate from their literate learning. They are not in a position to make knowledge. The ubiquitous IRE (initiate-respond-evaluate) classroom interaction format is very conducive to a theory of received knowing, and is very comfortable for a received knower.

Constructed knowers value conversations as a means of learning, particularly conversations in which people share not-quite-fully formed ideas in the process of collaboratively constructing meaning. They expect and value multiple perspectives. They are comfortable with ambiguity and feel a moral responsibility for the knowledge they construct, thus they are obliged to adopt a critical stance toward information sources. These characteristics mean that they keep issues open longer and are likely to be less judgmental. They view their own and others' experiences as important sources of information, among others.

As a simple example to ponder, Ellen Adams (1995) documents an exchange that took place while she read aloud to her second graders from *Pompei, Buried Alive*. She makes a connection with an earlier book, noting that Pompei is in Greece. One of her more capable readers interjects, "Uh . . . I don't mean to tell you how to teach or anything but I remember my father saying that Vesuvius was in Italy." Adams immediately concedes her error and tacitly apologizes, saying that she should have known that Vesuvius was in Italy. The student responds, "Well, you can't know everything."

But one of the less able readers in the class asks, puzzled, "Aren't teachers supposed to know everything?"

"No," she says, "but I try learning something new each day."

To this a third student adds, "Wow, you must know a lot Mrs. Adams. I mean you're old." (Summarized from Adams 1995, 137–138.)

This last observation aside, the two other students (more able and less able readers) appear to have very different understandings about knowledge and its sources and about themselves as knowers.

Knowing always entails a relationship between the knower and the known. In most classrooms this relationship is distancing, controlling, and dualistic. Reality is presented as separate from us, to be known through the teacher or textbook. In science instruction, the "objects" of our attention are routinely presented as separate from us, the scientist's role being to maintain the distance (and height) necessary for an "objective" view. Children are "gently disciplined" (Foucault 1977) to split their inner feelings and intuitions from their outer world—feeling from "reality"—and knowing from morality and ethics. The tool used to pry them apart is language. The careful separation of knowledge and experience is particularly marked for those in special education or in lower reading groups, and for those from lower-class backgrounds (Anyon 1981; Bryson 1993; Page 1991). These students often carefully maintain a separation between texts or school knowledge and life experience, ultimately in spite of teachers' efforts to heal the split (Jones 1991). As Palmer (1993, 21) points out, over time "our epistemology is quietly transformed into our ethic, [forming] the values by which we live our lives."

In other words, there are more or less desirable theories about knowledge that are quietly achieved through literacy instruction in relation to literature, science, social studies, and any other domain. The classrooms we have been studying recently have been selected in part because they integrate various parts of the curriculum, so consider for a moment science as a venue for developing children's epistemology. The word *science* is from the Latin word for knowledge, or *to know.* Until relatively recently, school science was presented as the acquisition of facts that had been verified by scientific procedures and authorized by scientists—a received knowing stance consistent, too, with reading and literature instruction (Cazden 1988; Dillon 1988; Nystrand et al. 1997). A clear depiction of this is provided by Driver and her colleagues (Driver et al. 1996, 125) in the following exchange between students and an interviewer. The students have read about the controversy surrounding continental drift theory, and the significance of a theoretical mechanism for resolving the controversy. In the interview, however, on no occasion do they refer to the mechanism. Notice what they do refer to:

I: So do you think the theory that the continents were once stuck together is sensible?
S: Yes.

S: Yes.

I: Why?

S: Because we know. Because we have that Wegener bloke . . .

S: So many textbooks have said that this is right.

Current views on science curriculum suggest encouraging a different stance. For example, the National Research Council (1996, 105) National Science Education Standards stress the need for "an appreciation of 'how we know' what we know in science." In other words, the idea is to help children develop a productive epistemology into which literacy can be infused. And, as I have already noted, epistemologies entail relationships with other knowers as well as with knowledge and the process of knowing. These relationships are also fused to the epistemology.

Consider the current nature of these relationships. The monologue of the average eighth-grade English classroom in the United States is enlivened by fifty seconds of dialogue a day, a figure that drops to fifteen seconds in ninth grade (Nystrand et al. 1997). This unidirectional relationship has often been documented in elementary school too, in the ubiquitous IRE interaction pattern (Dillon 1988). This pattern, in which the teacher *initiates*, usually with a question, a child *responds*, and the teacher *evaluates* the response, results in students often looking at the teacher even when their peers are speaking (Cazden 1988). Not only is the general pattern of interaction singularly monologic, but it is singularly solitary. In science classes, for example, U.S. students are rarely encouraged by their teacher to interact with the ideas of other students. Tsuchida and Lewis (cited in Rogoff and Toma 1997) found that teachers encouraged children to elaborate on each other's ideas in only 7 percent of lessons, to express agreement in only 3 percent of lessons, and to express disagreement in only 3 percent of lessons. By contrast, in Japanese classrooms the figures were 40 percent (elaborate), 20 percent (agree), and 40 percent (disagree). Even when U.S. students worked in groups, which they do less frequently, they tended to work as individuals—without sharing ideas—rather than working as a group. In a similar contrast, Toma (cited in Rogoff and Toma 1997, 484) found that in discussions the proportion of student utterances addressing other students' comments was 81 percent in her Japanese sample and less than 12 percent in her U.S. sample. These literate relationships are an integral part of the literacy that students learn and take into their adult lives in a democracy, and of whatever occupations (senators, members of congress, teachers, researchers) they choose.

An Example for Speculation

For this past year, my colleagues and I have been studying classrooms that were selected in part because they were led by exemplary teachers, and in part because the teachers integrated their instruction in various ways across language arts and some of the disciplines. Although "integration" was variously defined, with disciplines still often marked off by language and scheduling, literate language and practices were inseparably distributed throughout. The following example is one that primarily involves a topic that might be classified as science. Although I could have drawn more from literature discussions, I have chosen science to emphasize the broader issues of literate thinking. I will draw your attention to the epistemological, scientific, and social aspects that students are learning.

What struck me first about this fourth-grade classroom was that the students sustained conversations relating to books, science, spelling, or math (these were not always easily distinguishable) for up to an hour and a quarter at a time, sometimes picking them up again over a period of days, and with relatively limited contributions by the teacher. An example of this was when some ducklings were hatched in the classroom incubator. The children, having documented the changes in the eggs on charts and graphs, were constantly interested in the hatchlings, of which there were three by the time this particular discussion occurred. Joan, the teacher, opens the discussion with "I'm going to be writing questions as I hear people talking and I expect you will too. I haven't worked with ducks before so I'll have a lot of questions." The students have observed the younger duckling being pecked by the other ducklings and, unprompted, they begin to generate theories to explain it. Shirley fairly quickly introduces the idea of a pecking order. Chase suggests they peck each other because it's "like teething rings for babies." Alex's explanation is that it's like older siblings. Jack returns to Chase's idea that babies put everything in their mouths and mothers complain, "You don't know where that's been."

Shirley elaborates her pecking-order theory, noting that "The weaker and sicker ducks get pecked on." Jack disagrees. He thinks the other ducks know the duckling is younger, just like they were, implying that the older ducks would take that into account and give the younger one a break. Gordon agrees.

Laura adds, "I disagree with Shirley because [evidence] and I agree with Jack and Gordon because [observation], and . . . [observation] . . . So . . . [hypothesis] . . . because . . . [observation] . . . But . . . [observation]."

Joan suggests that "What scientists do when they have questions is to experiment."

The discussion is picked up again with the birth of a fourth duckling, and the students decide to experiment to see what will happen. Joan asks that everyone "be writing what they think will happen." She then invites them to share what they have written, beginning with a weaker student, Lane. The students then call on each other to comment and add their own proposals. Joan takes a brief poll and finds the students are divided.

Joan summarizes a comment by Clem both for confirmation and to make sure it is heard by all. She adds, "I hear you, and others, talking about time." She connects this to the science teacher's discussion of "variables," then connects it to the suggestion yesterday that it might be territorial behavior. She then brings up Art's question about what would happen if the tank were larger, a question that suggests an active attempt to explore covariance in the ecological system, with the goal of choosing between theories.

Aja suggests another possibility, that it is like a gang, and "if you're strong enough you can be part of the gang and they make fun of the geeky girls."

Joan puts the ducklings in the tank and the children giggle with excitement, commenting, "They're scared."

Joan asks, "Is that an observation?", prompting them to distinguish data from theory. She adds, "Jessie's writing down what she thinks, so she won't forget it." This writing promotes reflection. There is lots of conversation and commentary.

The ducklings continue to occasionally peck one another. Clem proposes a new hypothesis—that it is like monkeys' grooming behavior, suggesting that maybe it's not aggressive. The conversation continues and includes:

"All the ducklings did it at the beginning" (a new observation on covariation).

"Maybe it's not that bad—you just don't know," Jake says, following up on Clem's suggestion and keeping the taken-for-granted aggressive motive open for examination.

"Maybe they like to peck, and they are bored with pecking the food," following up on the "teething ring" proposal.

The next day, the following exchange occurs:

JOAN: So my question to people at the farm would be what would happen to this duck in the wild?

JACK: Well the mother's there so really . . . and they're all brothers and sisters, so I doubt they'd do what they're doing now when they're out in the open so they have more room to run around and more things to explore and peck at.

LAUREL: //Oh, oh. . . .

JOAN: I notice, Laurel, that when he was talking it sort of jogged your mind— what were you thinking?

LAUREL: Maybe they're territorial. Like, that brown one's sitting there right now. He was sitting there and that one started pecking him, so, like, maybe they're territorial.

SASHA: What do you mean?

LAUREL: Like they don't want to share their property. Sort of like a farmer . . . Oh, like, what's that show? [*describes a movie*]

AJA: That Darn Cat. . . .

Aja adds another theory before Joan helps them schedule observations for the rest of the day. Some of the children go on the Internet to seek answers to their questions.

Throughout, most of the children write down their observations and hypotheses, as Joan points out, so they don't forget. She also points out that, as scientists, the difficult part is not getting so engrossed that you forget to keep notes. She adds, "It's so easy to talk about it and not write it down, and yet a scientist would be writing it all down because he'd want to have evidence and come back and think about it."

Along the way, the students have given directions to Joan as to which ducks to put together in which circumstances, controlling selected variables to test for covariation.

The pecking issues reemerge when a group of children undertakes another study. For homework they have designed an experiment to study the ducklings' preference for water, a question generated from their observations. They prepare the experiment during lunchtime, borrowing a sand tray from a kindergarten teacher. The large tub space used in the experiment incidentally provides the opportunity to add weight to the territorial hypothesis about the pecking, which the students quickly notice and record as the pecking has stopped.

What Achievements Are These?

Several literate achievements are apparent to me in these interactions. First, a particular epistemological frame has been established, one that appears to be developmentally ahead of its time. Second, the understandings that might be called "scientific literacy" (though this distinction might not be necessary) are also developmentally advanced. Third, the social side of the literate practices of these children is distinctive and has significance for their participation in democratic living. These three matters are quite intertwined with one another.

Epistemology

What is the theory of knowledge implicit in these conversations? The overall set of interactions implies that knowing (in this case in the discipline of science) involves collaborative construction of meaning, with each student being an active agent in the process of construction. With her opening statement, Joan disabuses the students of the idea that she is the source of knowledge in this domain. By not answering their questions and by inviting their contributions, she asserts the relevance of their experience and observation, and their responsibility to seek answers. She presses this responsibility by assuming that, naturally, people will be interested in these answers and in forming a committee of "only those who are serious" to find answers at home and on the Internet. In another discussion Joan has had the students start by listing their questions, or "wonderings," followed by their "surprises." The students have many of both. They are aware that their questions are important and should be taken seriously—they are written down and posted publicly with names attached, followed through on, and engaged by other students.

These students were also comfortable with ambiguity and complexity, with keeping questions open: "Maybe it's not that bad—you just don't know." There was an unusual amount of "tentative talk," in which students put out half-formed ideas and possibilities without apparent fear that they would look foolish. They clearly value discussion and take each other's comments and observations seriously. They engage the ideas, supporting, challenging, and building them over an extended period of time. These characteristics are all features of constructive knowers, not of received knowers (Belenky et al. 1986), in spite of the fact that most research on these epistemological stances places this development in late adolescence or some time in adulthood (if it occurs at all).

In answer to the question "who am I as a knower?" we have evidence from which to surmise the children's choice of identity. Consider the fact that these children have become able to formulate and pursue a research problem—a competence that Kuhn and her colleagues (Kuhn et al. 1995) have shown to be slow to develop in many adults. The students thought through the study for homework, committing their ideas to paper, and prepared it in their lunch hour, suggesting personal commitment to knowledge production and a sense of agency in the matter. The relevant conversation was pursued for three days on and off by the children, accompanied by persistent observation, record keeping, and generation of numerous hypotheses. The nature of these students' participation fits what Wells and Chang-Wells (1992, 99) assert is an important literate function of schooling, bringing "the individual's knowledge, and also the processes by which it is acquired, under conscious monitoring, so that she or he may take active and intentional control over her or his own learning and be able to make connections between knowledge acquired in school and that which is acquired in practical life situations outside the classroom." In this framework, the identity children are building as knowers is evident. They have confidence in the significance of their experience and their questions—enough confidence to respectfully disagree with each other and with the teacher—and are compelled to seek evidence for their theories.

In their adopted epistemological position, the answer to the question, "What is the relationship between the knower and the known?" is captured by Belenky and her colleagues in their description of constructed knowers as "the opening of the mind and the heart to embrace the world" (Belenky et al. 1986, 141). Their talk and their handling of the ducklings suggests that these students feel connected to the "objects" of their study. Their theorizing about the ducks' behavior was grounded in human analogies, and I suspect that, together with the extended contact time with the ducklings, these analogies contributed to raising the children's awareness of the ethical nature of science.

Indeed, two other conversations explicitly addressed this matter. One was an extensive discussion of whether to dissect the overdue eggs, and which one to dissect, given the small, but perhaps estimable, possibility that the inhabitants were still alive. Joan worked both sides of this balance between the objective stance and the personal stance. In one day she noted, "If I were its mother, I would want to get it out of there (where it was being pecked)," and urged children not to get so caught up in the ducklings that they forgot to write their observations and hypotheses. The other discussion was about the significance of naming the ducklings, particularly in the face of their leaving the classroom at the end of the week. There was the issue of who has the right to name and the question of whether it made sense to name under the circumstances. As Gordon pointed out, "What if we called Joan 'Teacher' and she called us 'Hey you'? It just wouldn't be the same."

Even from a very narrow view of literacy, this epistemological achievement should be regarded as significant. For example, Kardash and Scholes (1996) found that undergraduate students' epistemologies influenced their reading of articles that contained mixed evidence. Students whose epistemologies were more constructivist (as these children were demonstrating) were more likely to write conclusions that reflected the inconclusive nature of the article. However, there is reason to believe that the significance goes well beyond that. Indeed, to the extent that this epistemology becomes part of all literate engagements, including the sense of agency and moral commitment in the construction of knowledge, this is no trivial achievement.

Scientific Literacy

To approach the knowledge-construction issue from another perspective, consider these students' understandings of "science." According to Kuhn and her colleagues (Kuhn et al. 1995) there are three interrelated areas of understanding to be developed in science education. First, there is the habit of mind of scientific thinking, with its underlying metacognitive and metastrategic aspects. Second, there is the understanding of the concrete practice of doing science—how people put together and negotiate scientific understandings, including how personal and social issues play a role, for example, in deciding what counts as evidence. Third, there is the understanding of the larger social and cultural context in which science is done, and the ways in which science impacts society. In these terms, these students reveal a remarkable grasp of the necessities of scientists. To begin with, they collaboratively and extensively explored the "pecking" problem space, generating and selecting theories to test, and selecting the means and evidence for the testing. They have, I believe, a sense that this is how knowledge is pursued, and that the collaborative part of it is fundamental. The theories and "facts" of science have to be engaged in public debate (Kuhn et al. 1995). Normal scientific inquiry involves theorizing and testing, usually, multiple theories. Groups of scientists engage in a process of debate as they articulate theory and evidence, much as lawyers act as advocates. This social process becomes internalized so that scientists are constantly aware of audience concerns and logic.

Second, these students are aware that data and theory are separate and that their theories need justification through data. They also have an idea of what sort of evidence would distinguish among their theories—a concept not normally developed in this age group and not often developed in adults. Certainly, graduate students (and often their mentors) still wrestle with these matters. Furthermore, these students are becoming competent at seeking disconfirming evidence. As babies we are very good at theorizing about the world and confirming our theories. We are not particularly good at attending to disconfirming evidence. As a counter to this, Joan asks the children to notice questions and surprises. Surprises, in particular, are places where current taken-for-granted theories are questioned. She highlights the significance of this by commenting, "Based on what I'm learning here [in the text and the discussion], what I always believed to be true is not true." At the same time, she demonstrates keeping questions open, and potentially revising her knowledge, but she is also keeping track of the sources of her knowledge. By tuning the students' attention to the feeling of surprise, Joan builds an executive self-correction system, a propensity to use violations of expectation to modify personal theories.

It is also intriguing that most of the hypotheses were generated by the children "stepping into the ducklings," just as they did when trying to understand a piece of literature—a connection explicitly made on one occasion by Aja, and later by Joan. The strategy turned up a lot in their literature studies, but in both domains it represents a particularly valuable strategic use of language. As Matthews (1984, 67) points out, "an imaginative use of examples is one of the most important techniques for making progress in an abstract discussion" (whether or not it is written down), as might occur in philosophy, ethics, the practice of law, science, and most other disciplines. Some might protest that personification of animals is not really appropriate in science, where objectivity is important. Yet such analogical reasoning has a prominent place in the thinking of expert scientists (Clement 1991). It expands the problem space and is a powerful way of modifying or developing entirely new problem representations. Indeed, Tweney (1991) argues that without it, Faraday would have remained a bottle-washer in Sir Humphry Davey's laboratory.

I am compelled to believe that these students are being well prepared to be scientists, but equally well prepared to be citizens—to participate actively in the collaborative decision making of a democracy. Although they sometimes looked to the teacher as recorder (or perhaps the chart as record), they usually looked at relevant peers during the discussion. Joan often added comments like "I love the way you're really listening to one another," and on the rare occasions they did not, Joan pointed out that they needed to do so. In the process of this conversation, the students supported and disagreed with each other respectfully—a feature that is, regrettably, soemtimes missing from current scientific debates.

Driver and her colleagues (Driver et al. 1996) argue that children need this understanding of the nature of science—knowledge about the production of knowledge—for several reasons. Aside from blunt economic survival of both individual and society, they point to the need to appreciate it to preserve and advance the culture. More interesting, however, is the argument that understanding the nature of science has been found to improve conceptual learning of scientific topics. Further, they argue that in order to participate actively in the democratic decision-making process, citizens must understand the nature of science and of knowledge, particularly the socio-scientific issues. Even reading the newspaper is complicated without this knowledge. Finally, they argue that there are commonalities between everyday scientific thinking and moral/ethical judgment in science and the scientific community.

In other words, we cannot simply argue that a scientific habit of mind is an optional extra. It does not seem possible to read or write science without it. But, more importantly, it is part of the very fabric of activity in a literate democracy. For example, every citizen is required to perform jury service, and judicial reasoning "is an informal, individualized process of approximating truth and reasonableness" (Lawrence 1991, 61)—commonly in a print context. As with science, it requires us to disentangle our emotional and logical sensibilities, without denying either. The idea is to develop the competence to productively engage feeling with reason to solve problems in emotionally charged social circumstances. To make this a "literate" achievement in the narrower sense of literacy, this competence is developed also through discussions around literature, where students learn to recognize their own and others' feelings and motives, and the evidence, or sources of authority, necessary to distinguish one from the other. This is a necessary part of learning to untangle (not separate) them.

Social Literacy

In the conversation I reported, spread over several days, children have attended to each others' ideas and used them for intellectual leverage. These students are developing strategies for managing social resources, and this ability does not "just happen." For example, in our study we found students classified as very capable who found collaborative literate activities difficult (though one reported that her goal was to change this). Some did not yet value the experiences of others as sources of learning. In this classroom, though, children are learning a way of thinking about and engaging others in mutual (not identical) understanding—developing intersubjectivity. In particular, they are learning to value each other as resources to scaffold their own thinking. Their experience in these engagements is one of expanded intellect, again with attendant emotional ties. Joan often spent time helping children transform their concerns into "big questions," which are ones that a range of people can become involved in contributing to. These questions are a means for recruiting the social resources to expand the intellectual capacity brought to bear on a problem.

Our field notes and interviews revealed important behaviors based on children's knowledge of one another, such as knowing the reading and writing interests and foibles of others in the class. Through their discussion of books, students were developing a deeper understanding of each other. This is the basis of the social commitment necessary to fuel a democracy, and of the social imagination necessary for everything from persuasive writing to convincing character creation. In our interviews, we asked students about books they had read and who else would be interested in those books and why. In some classrooms, children figured into their recommendations a knowledge of both other children's predilections, and their ability. At the same time as being clearly aware of one another's relative competence, they did not see its significance as an issue of power, but as one of managing relevant contributions. Furthermore, in classes like Joan's, where children were often involved in forming and managing committees to accomplish particular literate projects such as accounting, book discussion groups, and research, they were often able to talk about the nature of the group process and where it was breaking down. This form of analysis is necessary for collaborative group efforts to be effective, and is highly valued in all spheres of life outside of school (Johnson and Johnson 1989).

Another way of viewing this social side of literacy is as distributed intelligence and the scaffolding of thought. In the many discussions I witnessed, the ability to participate in lots of tentative talk (something many adults do with difficulty) seemed important not only for its epistemological significance, but also because it is necessary for the collaborative problem solving found in business enterprises and in participatory democracy. The openness of discussion maximizes the possibilities of distributed cognition—the system of collective thought in which the whole is more than the sum of the parts (Salomon 1993). This distributed thinking is not simply the context for literate thinking, but a kind of literate thinking in itself (Resnick 1991). In addition, it provides the scaffold for the development of important aspects of individual literate cognition. In most schools, children have all executive learning decisions made for them—what to read, when to read, what problems to engage in and in which order, what to write, and so forth. At some point, the assignments stop and we are somehow surprised at how students fail to transfer their learning to "real life" (Perkins 1993). In theory, if not in practice, this executive decision making is at some point passed on to the child through "scaffolding." But even then, the learner is not normally given control of building the scaffold—choosing what to scaffold, when, how, and for what purpose. People do ultimately have to choose their physical and social environments, and the choice will have an impact on their psychological development. In the conversation I described above, children are deciding what to study and how to study it, carrying out the actions, and making the decisions in a socially responsible community. This is the collective executive function upon which children can scaffold their intellectual development. To the extent that they gain control of the organization of such learning environments, they have control of the scaffolding of their own literate development.

Common Threads

In my analysis of this particular classroom, I have stressed the social side of literacy particularly because the social is largely missing from images of literacy, certainly in the United States. Not only do classrooms reflect the isolated individual, but also posters intended to encourage reading consistently portray individuals. This individualistic view is enforced by assessment systems that isolate individuals and draw attention only to the achievement of isolated individuals, regardless of what might be accomplished in a social setting. In this context, collaborative sense-making—the coconstruction of meaning—generally draws little interest. Researchers (and teachers) approach literate achievement as if it were something contained in the isolated mind of the individual. But it is becoming increasingly clear that thinking, and hence literate learning, is often best viewed as socially mediated activity that lies as much in the relationships among minds as in any one mind (Rogoff and Toma 1997; Salomon 1993). In other words, part of becoming literate is learning how to use other's literate thinking as a tool to extend both individual and collective literate thought. Shared literate thought, then, is not simply a process or a scaffolding strategy, but an achievement.

There are several ways to consider the significance of this. First, outside of school, collaborative problem solving through literate engagements is common. Second, children who are able to engage others' ideas in joint meaning-construction are more likely to gain skill and understanding than children whose interactions are not so focused (Light and Glachan 1994). Third, because individual thinking takes place in the context of social engagement, the individual plays a role in constructing the environment in which his or her thinking develops. The role can be active or passive. Fourth, a democratic society is in some ways predicated on the maximization of distributed intelligence. In other words, we might argue, as do those with an interest in "metacognition," that the collective reflection engendered in these interactions must become internalized. But if we fail to consider the competence of being able to arrange social resources in this manner with the expectation of expanded collective and individual consciousness, we will be missing the heart of a democratic community and of a democratic individual. We can talk about the characteristics of social commitment and independence of judgment that are necessary for democracy to flourish, but if we develop distributed cognition simply as an optional extra, not as something that's integral to children's habits of mind, we will have failed to advance democracy. In other words, there is clearly an argument to be made for counting as a literate achievement an inclination on toward intersubjectivity that helps children learn to develop the collective mind (Crook 1994). In large part, this inclination lies in the kind of epistemology children acquire.

There should be no doubt that such a set will serve children well in literate concerns outside of school, whether civic or economic; however, the civic is critical and often neglected. According to Benjamin Barber (1984), strong democracy "can be defined as politics in the participatory mode where conflict is resolved in the absence of an independent ground through a participatory process of ongoing, proximate self-legislation." Citizenship, according to Barber, "is a dynamic relationship among strangers who are transformed into neighbors, whose commonality derives from expanding consciousness rather than geographical proximity." Futhermore, it seems to me that a just, caring democracy cannot exist without social commitment, collaborative action, and independent judgment. Educating a committed citizenry who will productively engage one another in dialogue, and who feel sufficiently connected to balance the tensions between individual and community (Barber 1984), means acquiring *literate practices in which they can confront one another respectfully, organize and value collaborative literate experiences, and value their own and others' learning.* We might think of this as maximizing the potential of distributed intelligence. We should certainly ask whether our literate practices in schools embody these requirements. Doing so might have us think differently about social development—about "maturity"—another kind of "achievement." As Pradl (1996, 18) points out, we might value "mature dependency." Infants, because they are unable to survive without their mothers, determine the immature end of the dependency continuum. At its opposite is not the independence of the rugged individual, but rather the kind of relationship that is possible between friends, lovers, learners, workers, and a wife and husband. Each involves a kind of reciprocal dependency that in fact defines maturity (a social concept) as opposed to self-sufficiency (an individual concept).

In thinking about the range of possible literate achievements, I was motivated in part by the possibility that there are subtle trade-offs that are made by good teachers who teach in different ways. Perhaps we can have our cake and eat it sometimes, but we must investigate the potential trade-offs, which means expanding our thinking about what counts as literate achievement. To some extent, our limited views of the possibilities of literate thinking for children are a result of the notions of development and the notions of literacy we have lived with for so long. But unless we arrogantly view our culture as having reached the epitome of civilization, our goal thus being one of mere maintenance, we must approach research on children's literacy development in ways that explore literate development with an eye toward the productive evolution of our society. This means opening ourselves to the possibility of developing in children literacies that many adults have barely glimpsed, but that we see occurring in some children in some situations in some classrooms. It means considering exceptional examples of children's literate competence to be concrete examples of more general possibility, rather than of exceptionality.

References

ADAMS, E. L. 1995. "A Descriptive Study of Second Graders' Conversations About Books." Ph.D. diss., State University of New York at Albany.

ANYON, J. 1981. "Social Class and School Knowledge." *Curriculum Inquiry* 11: 3–41.

APPLEBEE, A. N. 1996. *Curriculum as Conversation: Transforming Traditions of Teaching and Learning.* Chicago: University of Chicago Press.

BARBER, B. 1984. *Strong Democracy: Participatory Politics for a New Age.* Berkeley: University of California Press.

BELENKY, M. F., CLINCHY, B. M., GOLDBERGER, N. R., AND TARULE, J. M. 1986. *Women's Ways of Knowing: The Development of Self, Voice, and Mind.* New York: Basic Books.

BRYSON, M. 1993. "School-Based Epistemologies?: Exploring Conceptions of How, What, and Why Students Know." *Learning Disabilities Quarterly* 16 (4): 299–316.

CAZDEN, C. 1988. *Classroom Discourse: The Language of Teaching and Learning.* Portsmouth, N.H.: Heinemann.

CLEMENT, J. 1991. "Nonformal Reasoning in Experts and in Science Students: The Use of Analogies, Extreme Cases, and Physical Intuition." In *Informal Reasoning and Education*, edited by J. F. Voss, D. N. Perkins, and J. W. Segal, 345–362. Hillsdale, N.J.: Lawrence Erlbaum.

COUNCIL, N. R. 1996. *National Science Education Standards.* Washington, D.C.: National Academy Press.

CROOK, C. 1994. *Computers and the Collaborative Experience of Learning.* London: Routledge.

DILLON, J. T. 1988. "The Remedial Status of Student Questioning." *Curriculum Studies* 20: 197–210.

DRIVER, R., LEACH, J., MILLAR, R., AND SCOTT, P. 1996. *Young People's Images of Science.* Buckingham, U.K.: Open University Press.

DYSON, A. H. 1993. *Social Worlds of Children Learning to Write in an Urban Primary School.* New York: Teachers College Press.

FOUCAULT, M. 1977. *Discipline and Punish.* New York: Pantheon.

GEE, J. P. 1996. *Social Linguistics and Literacies: Ideology in Discourses.* 2d ed. London: Falmer Press.

GILBERT, P. 1989. "Personally (and Passively) Yours: Girls, Literacy and Education." *Oxford Review of Education* 15 (3): 257–265.

HABERMAN, M. 1995. *Star Teachers of Children in Poverty.* West Lafayette, Ind.: Kappa Delta Pi.

HEATH, S. B. 1990. "The Sense of Being Literate: Historical and Cross-Cultural Features." In *Handbook of Reading Research,* edited by R. Barr, M. Kamil, P. Mosenthal, and P. D. Pearson. White Plains, N.Y.: Longman.

JOHNSON, D. W., AND JOHNSON, R. T. 1989. *Cooperation and Competition: Theory and Research.* Edina, Minn.: Interaction.

JOHNSTON, P. H. 1992. *Constructive Evaluation of Literate Activity.* White Plains, N.Y.: Longman.

———. 1993. "Assessment and Literate 'Development'." *The Reading Teacher* 46 (5): 428–429.

———. 1998. "The Consequences of the Use of Standarized Tests." In *Fragile Evidence: A Critique of Reading Assessment,* edited by S. Murphy, 89–101. Mahwah, N.J.: Lawrence Erlbaum.

JONES, A. 1991. *"At School I've Got a Chance." Culture/Privilege: Pacific Islands and Pakeha Girls at School.* Palmerston North, New Zealand: Dunmore Press.

KARDASH, C. M., AND SCHOLES, R. J. 1996. "Effects of Preexisting Beliefs, Epistemological Beliefs, and Need for Cognition on Interpretation of Controversial Issues." *Journal of Educational Psychology* 88 (2): 260–271.

KUHN, D., GARCIA-MILA, M., ZOHAR, A., AND ANDERSON, C. 1995. *Strategies of Knowledge Acquisition.* (Vol. 60, #4). Chicago: Society for Research in Child Development.

LANGER, J. A. 1995. *Envisioning Literature: Literary Understanding and Literature Instruction.* New York: Teachers College Press.

LAWRENCE, J. A. 1991. "Informal Reasoning in the Judicial System." In *Informal Reasoning and Education,* edited by J. F. Voss, D. N. Perkins, and J. W. Segal, 59–81. Hillsdale, N.J.: Lawrence Erlbaum.

LIGHT, P., AND GLACHAN, M. 1994. "Facilitation of Individual Problem Solving Through Peer Interaction." *Educational Psychology* 5: 217–225.

MALINOWITZ, H. 1995. *Textual Orientations: Lesbian and Gay Students and the Making of Discourse Communities.* Portsmouth, N.H.: Boynton/Cook, Heinemann.

MATTHEWS, G. 1984. *Dialogues with Children.* Cambridge, MA: Harvard University Press.

MURPHY, S., ED.. 1998. *Fragile Evidence: A Critique of Reading Assessment.* Mahwah, N.J.: Lawrence Erlbaum.

NATIONAL RESEARCH COUNCIL. 1996. *National Science Education Standards.* Washington, D.C.: National Academy Press.

NEWKIRK, T. 1989. *More Than Stories: The Range of Children's Writing.* Portsmouth, N.H.: Heinemann.

NEWKIRK, T., AND MCLURE, P. 1992. *Listening In: Children Talk About Books (and Other Things)*. Portsmouth, N.H: Heinemann.

NYSTRAND, M., GAMORAN, A., KACHUR, R., AND PRENDERGAST, C. 1997. *Opening Dialogue: Understanding the Dynamics of Language and Learning in the English Classroom*. New York: Teachers College Press.

PAGE, R. N. 1991. *Lower Track Classrooms: A Curricular and Cultural Perspective*. New York: Teachers College Press.

PALMER, P. J. 1993. *To Know As We Are Known: Education As a Spiritual Journey*. San Francisco: HarperCollins.

PERKINS, D. N. 1993. "Person-Plus: A Distributed View of Thinking and Learning." In *Distributed Cognitions: Psychological and Educational Considerations*, edited by G. Salomon, 88–110. New York: Cambridge University Press.

PRADL, G. M. 1996. "Reading and Democracy: The Enduring Influence of Louise Rosenblatt." *The New Advocate* 9 (1): 9–22.

PRESSLEY, M., RANKIN, J., AND YOKIO, L. 1996. "A Survey of Instructional Practice of Primary Teachers Nominated as Effective in Promoting Literacy." *The Elementary School Journal* 96: 363–384.

RESNICK, L. B. 1991. "Shared Cognition: Thinking as Social Practice." In *Socially Shared Cognitions*, edited by L. Resnick, J. Levine, and S. Behrend, 1–19. Hillsdale, N.J.: Erlbaum.

ROGOFF, B., AND TOMA, C. 1997. "Shared Thinking: Community and Institutional Variations." *Discourse Processes* 23: 471–497.

SALOMON, G. 1993. "No Distribution Without Individuals' Cognition: A Dynamic Interactional View." In *Distributed Cognitions: Psychological and Educational Considerations*, edited by G. Salomon, 111–138. New York: Cambridge University Press.

SMITH, M. L. 1991. "Put to the Test: The Effects of External Testing on Teachers." *Educational Researcher* 20 (5): 8–11.

SWEET, R. W. 1997. "Don't Read, Don't Tell: Clinton's Phony War on Illiteracy." *Policy Review* May/June: 38–42.

THOMAS, K. F., AND BARKSDALE-LADD, M. A. 1995. "Effective Literacy Classrooms: Teachers and Students Exploring Literacy Together." In *Inquiries into Literacy Theory and Practice. Forty-Sixth Yearbook of the National Reading Conference*, edited by C. K. Kinzer, K. A. Hinchman, and D. J. Leu, 37–53. Chicago: National Reading Conference.

THORKILDSEN, T. A. in press. "The Way Tests Teach: Children's Theories of How Much Testing is Fair in School." In *Education, Culture, and Values, Vol. III, Classroom Issues: Practice, Pedagogy, and Curriculum*, edited by M. Leicester, C. Modgil, and S. Modgil. London: Falmer Press.

TODOROV, T. 1996. "Living Alone Together." *New Literary History* 27 (1): 1–14.

TWENEY, R. D. 1991. "Informal Reasoning in Science." In *Informal Reasoning and Education*, edited by J. F. Voss, D. N. Perkins, and J. W. Segal, 3–16. Hillsdale, N.J.: Lawrence Erlbaum.

VYGOTSKY, L. S. 1978. *Mind in Society: The Development of Higher Psychological Processes.* Cambridge, Mass.: Harvard University Press.

WELLS, G., AND CHANG-WELLS, G. L. 1992. *Constructing Knowledge Together: Classrooms as Centers of Inquiry and Literacy.* Portsmouth, N.H.: Heinemann.

Four

Creating Independent Learners

BARBARA WATSON

"You learn by trying to think in your head" was five-year-old Anna's response to the question, "How do you learn?" She seemed to be suggesting that learning came from what *you* thought about in *your* head. Concern among many teachers, researchers, and theorists about didactic instruction (telling) leads to suggestions that the attention given to "over teaching" may limit the opportunities for children to engage in this kind of self-generated, self-monitored, and self-constructed learning that Anna seemed to know about. However, if the focus is solely on the child and the role of teaching is underemphasized, opportunities for independent learning may be equally limited.

What Is Independent Learning?

There has been a degree of vagueness about the notion of independent learning. The term *independent* occurs frequently in educational writing, but the word and its derivations appear to be used in a variety of ways. Independence has been described by some researchers as simply working without adult supervision, and by others as acting independently of adults or not depending on instruction. For Ferreiro and Teberosky (1982), independent learners "can comprehend the production mechanism of knowledge and consequently be creators of knowledge" (18).

The study of independent learning leads to an understanding of the way young learners move to building cognitive competencies and constructing some "inner generating system" that allows them to further their learning by their own efforts (Clay 1991b, 42). These mental activities generated by children are unseen processes. Hence, the nature of independent learning, like the concept of higher-order thinking discussed by Resnick (1987), is difficult to explain precisely. However, it may be possible to observe children engaging in certain kinds of behaviours that indicate that independent learning is taking place. The idea of inferring inner processing from behaviour may be illustrated by two examples. Resnick (1987) suggested that higher-order thinking can be recognized when it occurs. For example, from various practical problem-solving tasks in mathematics, it can be inferred that children who are regulating their own understanding of procedures, checking for consistency, and attempting to relate

47

what is known to new material are "constructing meaning"; that is, they are engaging in interpretive work rather than in mechanical manipulations. In Reading Recovery (Clay 1993), an early intervention program for young readers and writers, inferences are made about the use of nonobservable strategies from careful observation of the child's responses in reading. Described by Clay, and inferred from text-reading behaviour such as, for example, noticing and correcting errors, is a range of "in-the-head" strategies developed by readers who are involved in searching, monitoring, and self-correcting, which form "a self-extending system of strategies" (1991a, 3). For independent learning, it could be inferred from observed behaviour that children may, by their own activity, be generating and directing some of the processes involved in learning. Evidence of such active processing can, therefore, be gathered by identifying specific behaviours that can indicate that there is an opportunity for children to learn more for themselves.

For these reasons, it seemed appropriate to explore ways in which school beginners may operate when they are learning how to learn for themselves by adopting a view of children as constructive learners who may initiate and extend their own learning. Within such a constructive framework, independent learning was defined as:

> Knowing how to initiate and direct the processes of learning by working on grouping things together and categorizing them, by linking new information to what is already known, and by resolving inconsistencies while constantly altering and reorganizing ideas as experiences increase. (Watson 1993, 3)

There are many different ways in which children may indicate they are initiating and controlling their learning. Evidence of active processing may be gathered by identifying specific behaviours that indicate that there is an opportunity for children to learn more for themselves. In the following example (Watson 1993, 1), five-year-old Nicky was engaging in independent behaviour.

> Nicky was sewing a gingerbread man shape drawn with marker pen on hessian material. She was going to stitch around it with wool.
> Nicky reached for a ball of yellow wool and threaded her needle with the loose end. She then cut a long piece of wool off the ball, pulled it until the two ends were together and tied a knot. She began sewing by pushing the needle in the material and pulling the attached wool through. Then Nicky noticed that the knot was on the wrong side of the hessian (i.e., on the front). She looked at the other side, then turned back to where the knot was and looked carefully at it. Picking up the scissors, she cut the knot off and pulled the wool out. Nicky tied another knot and started sewing again, carefully pushing the needle up from underneath this time. After pulling the wool through, she checked to see that the knot was on the correct side then, satisfied it was, she carried on sewing. (5.3 years)

Nicky, working alone, spontaneously resolved a problem. Initially she made a mistake that she noticed and then, by her own resources, she sorted out the problem and solved it successfully. Her behaviour shows that she thought it through by herself, indicating a degree of cognitive engagement. Nicky was therefore working on her own learning.

In another example, Anna's behaviour indicates how she is attempting to make links for herself by relating information and discovering similarities. The teacher is helping her to understand the difference between what she had noticed from her knowledge of a previously known word and the new word.

Anna was composing and writing a story to go with a picture she had drawn about being scared. Anna had written the word *we* herself. The teacher was helping with the next word, *were*, which she had written for Anna to copy into her story.

> ANNA: [*to the teacher*] Maybe you wrote "we" there [*pointing to the letters "we" in "were"*].
> TEACHER: No, no! That belongs there. I didn't write "we." "Were," the beginning looks like "w" doesn't it? It's longer. It's got bits added. That makes it say "were."
> ANNA: Ohhh! Oh, I thought . . . .
> TEACHER: If we only wrote that much [*covered final "re"*] what would it say?
> ANNA: "We."
> TEACHER: Yes [*uncovered rest of the word*]. But it's a long word.
> ANNA: "We" and "were." That's . . . that's got "we" . . . you see . . . in it [*pointing to "were"*]
> TEACHER: It has. Yes. It certainly doesn't say "we" any more, does it? It says "were."
> ANNA: Mmmm.
> (5.3 years)

Why Foster Independent Learning?

The argument is not that all children's learning should be independent, but that if increasing proportions of children's early learning were undertaken from this perspective, there would be benefits. Children might be able to increase their learning power if they were oriented toward making some decisions about their learning, and if a proportion of learning opportunities arose from situations in which they were able to generate and direct their activities. By way of contrast, situations in which children rely solely on didactically delivered instruction from the teacher would appear to create dependence and limit opportunities for learning. Glynn (1983) claimed that independent learning in classrooms can occur only when there are sufficient opportunities to engage in academic behaviours outside the direct control of teachers.

Improved education is an important issue. Schools have been given the task of enhancing academic learning. For the educational enterprise to be successful, schools have a responsibility to provide learning of the highest quality across the whole curriculum. The challenge of improving the effectiveness of early education and promoting valuable learning experiences in schools calls for continued attention to children's active role in learning, so that each child gets the best start possible. Bloom (1964) suggested that early success leads to continuing success and that early failures are multiplied, stating, "early achievement in school has a powerful effect on later achievement" (41). If children are independent learners who know how to learn, and the environment is suitably supportive, they have more opportunities to engage in powerful learning experiences. Such active, individual effort may lead them to be able to further their learning. It allows for going beyond teaching (McNaughton 1985).

The active involvement of most children in some of their own learning is alleged to be a feature of learning in early childhood (DeLoache and Brown 1987). By making available at school some learning opportunities that capitalize on children's prior learning experiences and that begin with children's competencies, teachers enable children to continue with some of their own learning. According to Clark (1991), such a provision is similar to and consistent with the way in which children learn in their preschool years. Such continuity of learning experiences could facilitate the transition to formal schooling and the continued development of independent learning.

All children in a class should be helped by facilitation of independent learning. For example, self-sufficient children should be able to explore some activities for themselves. The teacher is thus free to foster similar learning with children who need extra attention because they have had less opportunity or incentive for such learning prior to school. If, as Clay (1985) suggests, the differences between children are likely to be greater at this time than at any other, focusing on each individual child in ways that encourage independent learning should provide a setting for maximum learning in classes. Being able to manage school programs to reach individual children and then to deal with them in ways that foster independence should allow the teacher to meet more effectively the wide range of development levels that exist in first classes. Clay (1991a) argued that working more intensively in the ways described above with the low-progress children, and those needing guidance in particular areas, provides individual assistance and support that is both effective and efficient.

Change in learning over time should be facilitated. If teachers were responding effectively to each child by adapting and adjusting their teaching to the child's particular responses, thus leading to higher levels of operating (Vygotsky 1978), it is possible that the child could be developing generic knowledge about how to learn. It has been shown that, as the child works on different kinds of information, generic competencies or facilitating interrelationships that power subsequent learning are constructed (Bruner 1973; Clay 1991a; Glynn 1983).

How Can Independent Learning Be Facilitated?

Integral to the provision of independent learning opportunities from the earliest days at school is the view that learning is something the child does, while the teacher arranges for that child to continue to learn how to learn. A significant link to the ways in which children can extend their learning is found as teachers observe and interact with learners engaged in tasks and activities. According to Wood (1998), allowing freedom for children to explore and learn on their own, and avoiding limiting their scope for engaging in such learning, can maximize effective cognitive development. But this is not always sufficient. Evidence about children's early learning suggests that attention must be given to the contribution of the school environment, in particular to the place of quality teaching in interactions for enhancing children's opportunities to gain more independent control (Clay 1998).

Changing interactions between teacher and child enable children to assume increasing responsibility for their learning (Yopp and Singer 1994), but this requires teachers to develop a responsiveness to the child's initiatives when creating learning contexts (Clay 1991a, 1998). Teachers must be sensitive and perceptive observers of what children can do, and must be able to respond to their need for assistance or for greater autonomy (Rogoff 1990). Effective interactions provide a learning situation that is both challenging and supportive, and that adjusts to the child's developing understanding. This association—between the active child as an independent learner and the active teacher facilitating such learning (Cazden 1991)—became the focus of the research. The challenge was to find out what occurs.

Capturing Independent Learning

To explore this challenge, it seemed appropriate to observe closely and record children's early encounters with school learning. One objective was to attempt to identify and characterize some of the essential qualities involved in independent learning. The other was to identify the kinds of opportunities teachers created that are necessary for promoting and supporting such learning.

Two Auckland teachers' beginner (new entrant) classrooms were used for study. The eight children selected for observation, four in each classroom, were the two boys and two girls in each class who had most recently started school. A period of two weeks at the beginning of their schooling and another two-week period three months later, four weeks in all, were the observation times. The school year (New Zealand) began in February. The observations were undertaken in September and December. Observations were made throughout the whole school day, which was from 9 a.m. until 3 p.m.

Two kinds of recording were used to obtain as much behavioural data as possible about what the teacher and the identified children were doing in each classroom. First, all teacher-child and peer interactions involving a target child were recorded verbatim by a two-way audio recording using radio microphones, supplemented with written notes. One radio microphone, worn by the teacher, captured all interactions with the target child in any setting by a remote control device, which meant that unrelated teacher talk was avoided. A separate radio microphone, attached to a small storybook that was moved by the observer as necessary, recorded all the target children's conversations. Continuous ten-minute observation samples of each child were made, with the child being observed rotated randomly in sequence throughout the day. Second, detailed written field notes were made of all the nonverbal engagement of the children during each ten-minute observation sequence.

From everything that occurred in the classrooms, three kinds of situations (called *episodes*) were identified: episodes of *activity* (a child working without talking to others), episodes of *teacher-child interaction* (one-on-one dialogue alone or within a group), and *peer interaction* (a child talking to other children). Whole class teaching was excluded.

Beginning Classrooms

There are some typical features of new entrant classrooms in New Zealand schools (Department of Education 1985; Ministry of Education 1996). From their first encounter with school, five-year-olds are involved in academic matters. Teachers provide children with extensive opportunities for talking and listening; for reading, writing, and numeracy learning; for developing science, nature study, social studies, and health concepts; and for engaging in art and craft, music and movement, and drama and physical education. These opportunities are provided in a context of integrated activities that span a broad national curriculum. Children are exposed to a literacy-based program that immerses them in oral language and book language, and in which early writing tasks form an integral part. The environment is rich in print. A wide range of mathematical apparatus and environmental materials aims to foster the development of early numeracy concepts and skills. Experiences through environmental studies and expressive activities using different art forms, craft construction, acting, and musical activities are also available. Together with literacy activities, these experiences are often incorporated into topic, interest, or thematic studies, creating opportunities for integrating activities. The expressive work and creative exploration in which the children engage is displayed on walls in classrooms, foyers, and corridors.

Children in New Zealand begin school on their fifth birthday (Birch and Birch 1970), so they enter school at any point in the school year, except that following school holidays, a small cluster of children may start together. The first or beginning class is usually referred to as the "new entrant" class. Children stay in this class for varying lengths of time, for the organizational pattern of the junior school (K–2) over the first three years is flexible and relatively unstructured. While the school day is from 9 a.m. to 3 p.m., children just starting school sometimes go home an hour earlier than the others for the first few weeks as they adjust to the new environment.

The term *formal instruction* applies to children being helped to acquire and to improve literacy, numeracy, and other school-related learning. It does not imply a formal approach to instruction nor to the learning context. The classroom setting is best characterized as informal and flexible. Children move around the room or even outside it when they are involved in tasks in small groups or alone. Working in this way, they frequently talk with those working near them, so there is a constant hum of chatter. The teacher works with the whole class only occasionally; more often, she will work with small groups in various parts of the room. She may move among the children as they engage in tasks, setting up individual teaching interchanges. In these classrooms the intention is to have children working within a social context of interaction and involvement.

The analysis of the nature and incidence of independent learning in new entrant children's behaviour, together with the teaching interactions that support or promote opportunities for independent learning, forms the focus of the next sections of this chapter. The final section discusses the nature of the association between the active child as an independent learner in school and the role of the assisting adult.

Observing Behaviour in the Classrooms

Across all curriculum areas, instances of independent learning were observed and identified as *child-directed acts*: instances of behaviour containing identifying features indicating that the child, in some way, may be generating and directing by his or her own activity the processes involved in learning. These child-directed acts were assigned to one of six categories:

1. Showing relationships
2. Checking
3. Trying and testing

4. Attending to errors
5. Working at difficulties
6. Rehearsing and repeating

Each category contained many different behaviours. Some examples of child-directed acts from across the curriculum, coded into categories, are described below.

Showing relationships consisted of making links or connections between objects or ideas, discovering similarities and regularities, detecting patterns, or relating and grouping information from different sources. An example of how children clearly indicated the way in which they were relating objects comes from Nicky, who makes the connection between the uses of pig's hair that had been discussed earlier and a product, a paste brush in this instance. The comment followed a farm visit.

> NICKY: [*to Sue, a child nearby*] Do you know what? That bit's from a pig! [*pointing to the bristles on the paste brush*]
> SUE: What?
> NICKY: That bit is from a pig. Miss Cox told us this morning.

Renee drew on what she knew, linking this knowledge to what she noticed in the print in the following discussion.

> TEACHER: Can you look at that big, long word "butterfly" and look at "bedtime." Can you see anything that is the same about *butterfly* and *bedtime*?
> RENEE: They're both long.

TEACHER: Yes. Anything else the same?
RENEE: They both start with "b."
TEACHER: They do! Just like "baby."
RENEE: And "boy."
TEACHER: You're right!

Checking was being aware of one's own processing, performance, or both, including planning, rehearsing, and mediating through nonverbal or self-verbalizations; monitoring, comparing, confirming, and evaluating. Among the examples of children checking on their own performance was how they commented on their success. Renee was doing an alphabet task, matching alphabet cards by making a pile for each letter.

RENEE: [*added letters n and b correctly to existing piles and then did the same with the letter q; turned to Marilyn the child beside her*] I'm getting some right! [*proudly*]

Sometimes the children monitored their performance in more than one way. Toby both commented on his own achievement and identified what he thought he did not know when it was in a different place in the story. He also asked for help. After he finished reading his new storybook once for himself, Toby went to the teacher who was sitting near his reading group listening to the children reading.

TOBY: I can read it!
TEACHER: Hmmm [*smiling*].
TOBY: [*began reading accurately*] Who's going to lick the bowl [*added in an extra word "No," then read*] I am [*continued to read accurately*].
No, I am! I am! I am! I am! I am! Stop! said Dad.
[*Paused and asked the teacher*] What's that word? [*pointing to "I am"*]
TEACHER: I am [*pointing to each word as she said it slowly*].
TOBY: [*read*] I am.

Trying and testing was searching for alternatives; exploring and checking options; and predicting or testing something out and confirming, revising, or rejecting it. Sometimes children were observed to work persistently on trying to solve a problem. Phillip was accepting and rejecting hypotheses as he worked on a jigsaw.

Phillip tipped out the jigsaw puzzle of a rocket. He started to put the pieces in, beginning with the smallest ones from the nose of the rocket and continuing in order of size. He found the base of the rocket and put that in. He tried each of the four pieces that were left in the next space, turning the last piece four different ways to see if it would fit. He continued trying each of the pieces until he was called to join a group by the teacher.

Composing one's own message was an example of trying and testing. Lyle was writing a story about Santa Claus after the teacher had read a book about Christmas to the class.

LYLE: [*wrote carefully*] The s . . . [*called to the teacher*] Miss Cox! Miss Cox! Look
  what I did [*showed his writing*].
TEACHER: What did you write?
LYLE: [*read*] The ah . . . The ah . . .
TEACHER: [*read what he'd written*] The "s" . . . What do you want to write?
LYLE: Santa . . . [*writing episode continues*].

Adam confirmed the result of testing his hypothesis by commenting on the outcome. He had chosen to go outside with other children to the water tray on the veran-
dah of the classroom. He was working with a variety of plastic containers in the water.
  Adam picked up a funnel and poured water into it, watching it go right through.
Then he put his index finger on the end and held it there tightly. Brian poured water
into the funnel for him. Adam kept his finger on the bottom. When the funnel was full
he took his finger off. (Said aloud to himself) "There it goes! There it goes! There goes
the water!" (as the water flowed out).
  Attending to errors was correcting or attempting to correct an error made (i.e., one
that arises from the child's own performance), discovering inconsistencies and
attempting to resolve or resolving the dissonance of conflict by seeking solutions. Of
the many examples that might be given to illustrate how the children noticed errors
and tried to do something about them, often successfully, the following instances indicate the variation this category covered. Adam had just dictated a story for his picture
to the teacher, who had written the story in Adam's book for him, leaving space under
each line of text. She asked him to write his story in the space and left him.
  Adam began to write his story underneath the teacher's scribing. He wrote two
words, but had started writing the second line of the story instead of the first. He
looked at what he had done and realized it was wrong. Looking around, he called to
the teacher across the room.

ADAM: Mrs. Sengler, I've doned a mistake! Mrs. Sengler, I've doned a mistake.
TEACHER: [*came over and worked with him*]
[*And a little later when he made the letter g the wrong way*]
ADAM: [*Aloud to himself, expressively*] Doned a mistake again.

The children read new reading books for themselves after the teacher had introduced the story to them. This is Toby's first attempt at *The Bear Family*.

TOBY: [*began reading aloud*] Here is Father Bear.
TEXT: Here is Father Bear.
TOBY: Mother [*stopped*] Here (spontaneous self-correction) is Mother Bear.
TEXT: Here is Mother Bear.

Working at difficulties was actively meeting difficulties (i.e., obstacles) and working
on finding solutions by making discriminatory judgements. Some of the situations
where children tried to work at difficulties are illustrated in the following examples.

55

Toby was making a face puppet out of a round piece of cardboard. He was trying to make a small hole in the top to put a piece of string through. He folded the top edge over and tried to cut a hole with the scissors.

TOBY: I couldn't [*to Matu nearby*]. I'll have another try.
MATU: Try with mine [*handed over his scissors*].
TOBY: If I cut this way I'll do it . . . [*tried again and cut a bit more out, making a bigger hole—smiled broadly*]. Done the hole! [*to Matu*] I need string now.

Sometimes the obstacle is not easily overcome. Anna had decided to make a doll's house in the making area. She had chosen a cardboard box for the house and had used pieces of cardboard to make some walls. She searched through all the boxes available and then went over to the teacher, who was working with children on the carpet area. Anna waited nearby until the teacher was free.

ANNA: I can't find something to be a fridge (refrigerator).
TEACHER: You can't find . . . ?
ANNA: Something to be a fridge
TEACHER: Something to be a fridge! Mmmmm! [*in a warm, understanding voice*]
ANNA: Something that would be right for a fridge. But I can't find anything!
TEACHER: How about hunting for a little, tiny box?
ANNA: I know. That's what . . . that's what I were . . . I was looking for a little box [*shows shape with hands*].
TEACHER: There's bound to be some in those big boxes in there.
ANNA: I've had a look there. Right down to the bottom of one.
TEACHER: Lamond brought some matchboxes today. Would they be any use?
ANNA: [*raised eyebrows, shrugged*] Mmmmm!
TEACHER: Lamond is busy with Mrs. Lern at the moment. He put them in the making room. They might be in among the big boxes.
ANNA: Mmmmm! [*thoughtfully*] Well, I'll just have to cut it (i.e., cut down a big box to make the fridge) [*goes off*].

Rehearsing and repeating was engaging in the early stages of reading, writing, and manipulating, or improving one's own performance by purposefully repeating or practising a task. The first examples cover the area of engaging in early (preparatory) learning.

Rachael chose to go to the writing area, taking a piece of work she had done earlier in the day.

Rachael picked up a black felt pen, and on the paper she had worked on previously began to write letters and letterlike forms beside those already there.

In the class library area, Adam had picked up a book called *The Three Little Pigs*. After a while he opened it and began to read.

> Adam: [*read aloud, inventing the text*] He went to look for a house. [*turned page*] Please give me some bricks. Please. Yes, you can make bricks for a house [*turned page*]. Give me some sticks. Give some sticks. Yes. Give me some sticks and you can make a house [*turned page*] and [*continued until the end of the story*].

A final example shows how children often purposefully repeated or practised a task. Phillip, working on a mathematics task, had been asked to make a pattern of a person with geometric shapes on top of the one made on a card.

> Phillip reached out for the circle and triangle he needed for the head and body, the two squares for the legs, and two for the arms and placed them on the shape to complete the figure. He looked at what he had done, then tipped the shapes off and started to do the task again, completing it quickly.

These examples are mainly of short interactions or activity situations illustrating one child-directed act. A considerable number of longer episodes that contained many child-directed acts were recorded.

What Was Occurring?

It was the cognitive engagement of children in child-directed acts signifying independent learning that was of paramount interest, and a considerable amount of data was available for analysis. Of the 1,526 episodes recorded, 51 percent contained 1,335 child-directed acts, which signaled that children may be generating and directing their learning in some way. Only these episodes were used for further analysis and interpretation.

A striking feature of these data was the range and the number of child-directed acts emerging in the different categories, even at the time children were new to school (Figure 4–1). There was considerable variation in the percentage of occurrence across different categories (3 percent to 44 percent), although the percentages within each category at each observation time were similar.

Observation time			Category			
	Showing relationships	*Checking*	*Trying & testing*	*Attending to errors*	*Working at difficulties*	*Rehearsing & repeating*
1	4.34	23.33	8.31	2.77	7.39	13.86
2	43.35	18.29	10.86	5.54	3.77	18.18

FIGURE 4–1   *Incidence of child-directed acts in each of six categories at each observation time (%)*

The children were consistent in their levels of engagement in each of the four categories with the most independent learning. The ranking was the same at both observation times. By far the most commonly occurring child-directed acts at both Times 1 and 2 were those included in *showing relationships*. This facet of learning, discovering, and making connections by attempting to relate information to things that the children already knew (e.g., Nicky pointing out that the brushes' bristles were pig's hair) appeared to be integral to many of ways of learning that the new entrant children were being encouraged to explore. Activities were designed with opportunities for the children to create or construct the task, so their responses were individual. They were not merely playing, nor were they reproducing the teacher's product. They were participating in thinking activities, which could account for the substantial level of engagement in this category.

As they worked on varied tasks with different materials, and talked about them with others, the children were also observed to be monitoring their own performance by *checking* on themselves in different ways (e.g., Renee proudly exclaiming, "I'm getting some right!"). An average of 20 percent of child-directed acts were observed to fall in this category across both observation times. Being able to check on oneself requires the freedom to do so. The finding indicated that in these two classroom settings, children felt confident enough to monitor and evaluate their own performance and products.

Approximately 16 percent of the child-directed acts were in the *rehearsing and repeating* category. A relatively wide range of behaviour was captured in this category, including instances of engagement in very early literacy and numeracy activities (e.g., Adam inventing the text for *The Three Little Pigs*) as well as instances when a child returned to previously novel tasks (e.g., when Phillip quickly remade his successfully completed geometric puzzle). What seems necessary for self-initiated rehearsal and practice is an acceptance by teachers of its importance, together with opportunities and encouragement for it to take place. Children must have sufficient choice in decision making as well as time to carry out these activities. The level of behaviour occurring in this category suggests that these requirements were being met.

Child-directed acts occurred most frequently in the three categories described above, and a distinction can be made between these and the remaining three categories (*trying and testing, attending to errors*, and *working at difficulties*). The first three involve less complex processing than the latter three. As expected, there were fewer child-directed acts associated with the more complex processing categories, but considering the type of behaviours involved (problem solving on novel text, noticing and solving errors for oneself, overcoming obstacles), it is still interesting to note their appearance. Over a relatively short time these new entrants were building what appeared to be developing control over these processing behaviours.

The average proportion of child-directed acts over the two observation times in the *trying and testing* category—involving children searching, predicting, and checking options—was approximately 10 percent. Included in this category were testing hypotheses and the solving that learners needed to engage in as they approached tasks in certain areas (e.g., Adam testing his hypothesis about how to stop water going through a funnel with his finger). What seems to be important to enable children to develop strategies for such problem solving is that they have suitable opportunities, that meaningful learning tasks are available and, particularly, that these tasks are at an appropriate level to enable each child to build on existing competencies and to use developing strategies effectively. From the early emergence of children's active exploration as indicated by this category, these conditions can be assumed to have been met to some degree.

In the categories concerning *attending to errors* and *working at difficulties*, there was an average of approximately 4 percent and 6 percent of child-directed acts, respectively. Attending to errors involved awareness of the existence of an error by the children (e.g., Adam exclaiming "I've doned a mistake!" when he started on the incorrect line). It also involved evidence of searching in an attempt to achieve a correct fit by their own initiative (e.g., spontaneous self-correction by Toby when reading *The Bear Family*). Children have to feel able to take risks and have the incentive to seek a solution in order to notice and then try to correct their own errors. Evidence of this behaviour suggests that this was happening.

There was also evidence that in these learning contexts children were able to meet and work on obstacles (e.g., Toby tussling with making a hole to hang his cardboard puppet). Child-directed acts in the *working at difficulties* category (which applied to all curriculum areas except literacy activities) emerged in different situations. These data suggest that children were being presented with difficulties to solve and were given encouragement to solve them.

In summary, the categories reflect a conceptual analysis of the notion of independent learning so as to identify aspects of behaviour that indicate children were initiating and directing some of the processes involved in learning for themselves. They signified independent learning. The findings suggest that the children were actively engaged in pursuing their own learning in ways that matched both the definitions and categories that were derived from them. As they worked on tasks within different curriculum areas, these five-year-olds were making many links to things they knew and demonstrating that they were, over time, building a greater understanding of relationships. They were monitoring their own behaviour in different ways and practising the new behaviours they were learning to control, thus developing more fluent responding. Sometimes they were testing out and revising options, and developing alternative approaches to problem solving. Less often, they were noticing their errors and attempting to deal with them, initiating some active problem solving when they began to tussle with some of the particular difficulties encountered. These constructive behaviours were observed in the children's actions (activity) and in their talk with others (interactions).

Capturing Teacher Behaviour

The ways in which the two teachers helped children to learn more for themselves in teacher-child interactions in relatively complex classroom settings were of particular importance. The aim was to identify facilitative teacher moves—the teaching related to creating opportunities that could assist the child to learn more about how to learn in interactions throughout the school day. In such teaching moves, the teachers were judged to be facilitating independent learning, fostering behaviour that could assist children to take their own learning further.

All the situations in which the teacher was interacting with one of the children being observed (teacher-child interactions) were reanalysed to examine the teacher's behaviour. In the systematic analysis of these one-to-one interactions, the teaching moves that created opportunities likely to promote and support independent learning were identified and described. This form of teacher behaviour was called *facilitative teacher moves*. To identify facilitative teacher moves, the six categories of child behaviour were applied to teacher behaviour. All of the teacher moves in teacher-child interactions that were related to creating opportunities that could assist the child to engage in independent learning were coded into the appropriate category. Each interaction consisted of turns of talk taken by the teacher and the child. Within these, each facilitative teacher move was categorized to match the child behaviour categories. Wood and Wood (1983) spoke of such coding schemes in cases like this as taking the *mirror image* of categories of child behaviour.

The teacher behaviour considered to provide opportunities to promote and support independent learning was encompassed in a variety of ways in each category. For example, the teacher might be extending the children's responses when teaching them something new about how things are linked (*showing relationships*); inviting anticipation of the text when reading a new book (*trying and testing*); or requesting a reason from the children when helping them to solve an error (*attending to errors*). All remaining teacher behaviour was classified as *other*, allowing for a distinction to be made between those teaching moves that were relevant to facilitating independent learning and those that were not.

There was a wide variety of data in the teacher-child interactions. Not only did interactions occur in different settings, but the length of the interactions varied considerably. They included extended brief interchanges and conversations that could continue throughout much of the ten-minute behaviour sample. The teacher-child interactions occurred in both one-to-one and within-group settings. These two situations were identified for analysis. The distinction was considered relevant because analysing teacher behaviours that occurred in the two settings may show variation in the teaching moves related to enhancing independent learning. For example, Cazden (1988) suggested that teachers may make more cognitive demands in small-group than one-to-one settings. Others have emphasized the importance and value of one-to-one interactions in early schooling (Clay 1985; Wood 1998).

How Did the Teachers Teach?

There were 5,582 teacher moves and considerable variability in the length of moves. This teacher behaviour was analyzed in detail, independently of child behaviour. The

Observation time	Teacher behaviour	
	Facilitative	*Other*
1	61.87	38.13
2	63.03	36.9

FIGURE 4–2 *Incidence of facilitative and other teacher behaviour in two classrooms at each observation time (%)*

data are presented as a percentage of the total instances of teacher behaviour observed.

The incidence of *facilitative teacher behaviour* was considerably higher than that of *other* behaviour at both observation times, as indicated in Figure 4–2. Both teachers were creating many opportunities (up to 63 percent) within teacher-child interactions to assist the children to become more independent as learners. Much of their teaching was focused on fostering and supporting independent learning.

Both teachers were found to be skilled at promoting learning opportunities for these school beginners by attending closely to each child's needs and fostering change in appropriate directions within activities suitable for each individual's development. Many of their teaching moves seemed to be directed specifically towards assisting children to become "learners in control" (Glynn 1992, 1). The teachers were each cueing, prompting, linking, shaping, supporting, and praising children's efforts in many different ways. They were also eliciting responses from children by inviting their views or interpretations, and requesting reasons for actions undertaken, as well as modeling and explaining new or difficult aspects for the children.

Some of these teaching moves are illustrated in the following interaction, which occurred when Lyle was writing a story to go with the spider web he'd drawn on an overhead transparency.

LYLE: [*had written "The spider od"*]—[*was composing*] and, and, and. . . .
TEACHER: You read what you've written.
LYLE: The [*paused*]
TEACHER: Good. [*encouragingly*]
LYLE: What does that say? [*no response from teacher*] spider [*read slowly*]
TEACHER: You're right! You're right!
LYLE: [*reread*] The spider . . . I think I'll have to write "and" now.
TEACHER: What was your story? Tell me the whole story from the beginning. The spider . . . [*prompting*]
LYLE: The spider is, is . . . in, in.
TEACHER: Do you want that to say "is"? [*pointing to "od" that he'd written*]
LYLE: [*nodded—teacher rubbed "od" out for him*] Do . . . did I say "and" too?
TEACHER: Well, you tell me your story. The spider . . .

LYLE: Is [*wrote "is"*] is in [*wrote "n" for "in." Looked at it. Shook his head*]

TEACHER: Try it out there. [*on scrap paper*] You're nearly right.

LYLE: [*wrote "up"*]—[*teacher rubbed out "n"*]. [*wrote "up" in story*] a [*wrote "a"*] Done it! Done it!

TEACHER: What did you write?

LYLE: "A," "a." I did "a."

TEACHER: Read it now.

LYLE: [*read*] The spider is up in . . . on

TEACHER: On. What will it start with?

LYLE: "O" [*letter name*]

TEACHER: Right. Is that what you want to write? Are you sure that's . . .

LYLE: On [*teacher rubbed out "a"*]—[*wrote "on"*]

TEACHER: Good, you did know how to write "on." Read it. [*pointed while child read*]

LYLE: The spider is up on [*generated*] the web. [*wrote "te" —looked at it*] Oh! [*squeezed in an "h" between the letters for <u>the</u>—read aloud for himself*] The spider is up on the . . . web.

TEACHER: Web, web [*saying slowly*] web, what will it start with?

LYLE: /D/, /d/

TEACHER: It starts with? You say it. [*child nearby said /w/*]

LYLE: /W/

TEACHER: What does the "w" look like? Do one there. [*pointed to scrap paper*]

LYLE: [*wrote "w" correctly*]

TEACHER: Good boy, and the rest of it is like that. [*wrote rest of word "eb" on paper for him to copy*]

LYLE: I know how to do a "e." [*as he copied "eb"—read*] The spider is up on the web.

TEACHER: That's right. Good. Go and put it on the screen [*of the overhead projector*] and read it to us all.

Note: "a" indicates letter name; /a/ indicates letter sound

Lyle was helped to use his existing knowledge, and from this starting point was encouraged to try to reach out to learn more about what was new for him in writing. The teacher modeled what she felt he was not yet ready to attempt. She adjusted her support according to her knowledge of what the child could control and her understanding of what he was trying to learn. Such teaching, which has been described as *assisted performance* by some educators, is here seen as a form of facilitative behaviour.

This example and others indicate that the ways the teachers shared in joint interactions with children were compatible with Smith's (1993) account of the kinds of teaching interactions that would occur in "the Vygotskian classroom" (57). She described how both teacher and child became actively engaged in shared tasks for extended periods, particularly during early learning stages. Children were thus able to advance in their zone of proximal development (Vygotsky 1978).

Both teachers in this study appeared to expect, and encourage, children to use and build on what they knew and could do. They often praised the children's efforts, sometimes coaxed them to try to do new things, and supported their attempts, however uncertain. When appropriate, the teachers showed or told the children what to do. This could be interpreted as fostering access to what Bruner (1990) called "new kinds of knowledge" and understanding by asking questions and presenting challenges aimed at helping children to think, to test out options, and to relate what they already knew to new experiences. In such ways one could say the teachers were fostering constructive processes; that is, helping the children to negotiate and construct meaning through purposeful activity as they interacted with them. Teachers participated in this way in shared contexts with children when, for example, discussing mathematics or science concepts, reading books, writing stories, or working on a construction problem.

Figure 4–2 also shows a striking consistency in the extent of facilitative behaviour at both observation times. The policy of continuous school entry for five-year-olds into New Zealand schools may provide a partial explanation for this uniformity, for while this study observed school beginners near the start of their schooling and twelve weeks later, these particular children entered an ongoing classroom context that had been established for some eight months. In order to cope with this kind of situation, the teachers had developed particular ways of working with children in an environment with interest areas, materials, equipment, and classroom routines in place. Within each class there were some children who had been at school from the beginning of the year until the time the observation began. It could be expected, therefore, that the kind and style of teaching patterns established would not be altered to any great extent for new children, but that the teachers would respond to the child's initiatives, assisting each child as appropriate. The teachers could be said to be working from each child's agenda. The following episode illustrates how the teachers worked from individual children's competencies, responding to personal starting points. In a mathematics activity, the teacher was helping a small group of children make relative judgements by grouping coloured sticks. She initiated an individual interchange with Toby, starting from the one coloured stick he had in front of him. Her teaching moves built on his responses, furthering his understanding of specific number concepts by helping him use concrete materials to confirm his hypothesis.

TEACHER: Toby, what can you tell me about one?
TOBY: Well . . . One is less number than two.
TEACHER: Less, is it? Good!
TOBY: And nought's lesser.
TEACHER: Yes!
TOBY: Umm . . . One number is less than two and there's ummm. . . .
TEACHER: What about three?
TOBY: It's ummm . . .
TEACHER: Is it more than or less than one?
TOBY: It's more.

TEACHER: Is it? How do you know three is more than one?

TOBY: Ummm . . . it's ummmm . . . got three . . . and umm one's only one stick.

TEACHER: All right. Leave your one stick there. Now get three and put three there. [*pointed*] We'll see if it's more.

TOBY: [*puts three sticks down*]

TEACHER: Now, is three more than one?

TOBY: Yup. [*nodded*]

TEACHER: How can you tell?

TOBY: Cause that is only one [*pointed to one stick*] and that's one, two, three. [*pointed to each stick in the other set*]

TEACHER: Well done!

Such individual meeting and extending of children's learning levels did not only take place when the teacher was working with a single child. Often, particularly when children were composing and writing their own stories, the teacher would provide individual help for a few children at the same time while sitting with them at a group table.

Clay's (1985) description of teachers of new entrants providing "a rich set of opportunities" (23) could well be applied to the teaching-learning experiences available to the children in this study. Individual intellectual effort was being enhanced in interactions with teachers who were sensitively observing and responding to what children were actually doing, thus ensuring they were continuing on independent learning routes. The more teaching follows a child's agenda, the more it will be appropriate for each child's learning and, therefore, likely to assist such learning.

Where Did Facilitative Teacher Behaviour Occur?

The facilitative teacher behaviour shown in Figure 4–3 provided insights into the attention teachers gave to each specific form of behaviour that in the research was considered to foster independent learning.

Observation time	Category					
	Showing relationships	*Checking*	*Trying & testing*	*Attending to errors*	*Working at difficulties*	*Rehearsing & repeating*
1	31.95	24.92	18.85	2.56	2.51	18.21
2	32.11	26.52	12.62	5.11	6.23	17.41

FIGURE 4–3 *Facilitative teacher behaviour in each of six categories at each observation time (%)*

Four categories accounted for the majority of facilitative teacher behaviour at each observation time. There was a relatively high percentage of facilitative behaviour in both the *showing relationships* and *checking* categories. Teachers were consistent over both observations, with from 25 percent to 32 percent of moves in teacher-child interactions related to these two categories.

In *showing relationships* children were being assisted to identify and relate information to help them understand how different things are connected. The following example, from a story-sharing time, indicates the links being encouraged between letters and something very familiar—the children's names.

> LOUISE: He's got a "T" on it. [*his tee-shirt*]
> TEACHER: He's got a "T." "T"' for . . . ? "T" for Toots. That's his name. If you wore your letter of your name you'd have a . . . ?
> LYLE: "T!"
> TEACHER: "L." "L' for Lyle.
> LYLE: [*smiled*]
> TEACHER: And you'd have an "M." "M" for Michael. [*to Michael*] Nicky would have a . . . ?
> NICKY: "N."
> TEACHER: "N" for Nicky. [*continued for all the children in the group*]

The teachers also helped children to monitor their actions (*checking*) in many different ways across curriculum areas. In a group session in mathematics, the children were asked to get two things that matched. Renee chose a numeral card for eight and a picture card with eight flowers.

> TEACHER: Why did you choose those two?
> RENEE: They both are eight.
> TEACHER: Would you like to check for us in a loud voice so we can hear?
> RENEE: [*paused*]
> TEACHER: How can you check?
> RENEE: By counting.
> TEACHER: [*smiled*] Okay. You point and count for us.
> RENEE: [*pointed to and counted each flower on the card*]
> TEACHER: Were there eight?
> RENEE: Yes. [*smiling*]

The consistent attention that teachers gave to encouraging children to attend to very early literacy and numeracy activities and to revisit and reexplore familiar tasks at both observation times was apparent in the *rehearsing and repeating* category of facilitative teacher moves. That teachers were fostering these opportunities indicated that they understood the value of practice to achieve fluent responses and of informal opportunities to explore printed material and reinforce number skills in children's development. In the following example the teacher was encouraging children to return to books she had introduced and read with them.

> TEACHER: Now in the box today are some books that we've already read before, and I would like you to choose one that you would like to read all by yourself . . . and then you can try and read it here and then take it home to read to someone there. If you get stuck I'll give you a helping hand. [*she held up each book, giving its title, as she spread them all out on the carpet*]

In the *trying and testing* category teachers in this study were providing opportunities for children to use and enhance their problem-solving strategies, to search, to predict, and to explore and check options, early in their schooling. This suggested that with the kinds of learning experiences the teachers were providing, there was an expectation that children would be, in a sense, negotiating meaning and understanding. An example from the teaching of reading to new entrants illustrates aspects of the complexity involved in teaching for active processing. The children had been exposed to meaningful books from the start and were encouraged to expect reading to make sense. These teachers shared books with the children. They read to the children and introduced new storybooks by talking about the story and reading it to and with the children. Children were thus prepared to read the story for themselves. (In the example // indicates deleted text.)

> TEACHER: [*holding up the small book so all the children in the group of six could see the pictures and the text*] This book's called *Sleeping Out*. What does "sleeping out" mean?
>
> TOBY: Camping.
>
> TEACHER: Mmm. Camping means sleeping outside. How many of you have slept outside? // Who has never slept outside? // What's it like in a tent, Lucas?
>
> LUCAS: Well, you can hear all sorts of different noises and scratching. //
>
> TEACHER: Let's look at what happens to these people when they go sleeping out. Whereabouts are they camping? // What could it be? // Who do you think? // I wonder what other sounds they heard?

These excerpts illustrate how the teacher explored the main ideas of the story, built on children's prior knowledge, and encouraged the children to anticipate both the events in the story and the text. She was fostering comprehension, helping children learn how to use the pictures and the text to think about the rest of the story. As usual, the children were able to respond in individual ways. Such situations, according to Smith (1993), demonstrate the teacher's ability to work in the zone of proximal development with a group. A somewhat lower occurrence of teacher behaviour in the *trying and testing* category at Time 2 may be explained by a shift in emphasis from an initial teacher effort to help children search out and check options, to one of encouraging them to process more of the information for themselves.

The low overall percentages in the *attending to errors* and *working at difficulties* categories is probably a reflection of the relative complexity of these behaviours. By Time 2, the incidence in these categories was still low. But there were clear indications that, as the children adjusted to the new environment of formal schoolwork, the teachers were able to move them gradually towards developing competencies in these relatively complex behaviours.

The examples below illustrate this. The children were being helped to learn more about how to notice and attempt to correct their errors, as in this seriation task in mathematics.

> TEACHER: I want you to have a think about the sizes of those ones. [*pointing*] See if you can fix that little part. It's tricky!

The teachers were supporting the children to overcome obstacles.

> TEACHER: Yes, you need a piece of wool about that length. Can you thread the needle?
> RACHAEL: [*shook head*]
> TEACHER: You have a try.
> RACHAEL: [*took wool and needle*]
> TEACHER: Squeeze it. Squeeze it with your fingers. Squeeze it tight like this. [*showed Rachael how to do it on another piece of wool*]
> RACHAEL: [*tried*]
> TEACHER: Tight. Roll it like that. Make it so that you can't really see it, Rachael. Squeeze it in there like that. [*showed her*]
> RACHAEL: [*did so*]
> TEACHER: That's right. That's right. And push the needle down over the top.
> RACHAEL: Like that?
> TEACHER: [*nodded*]
> RACHAEL: [*kept trying to thread the needle*] I can't put it in. I can't really do it.
> TEACHER: [*watching, came closer*] I'll squeeze it with my fingers and you can push the needle over the top.
> RACHAEL: [*did so*]
> TEACHER: You push that needle down. Good girl! That's it! Right! There you are! You've done it. Pull it through.
> RACHAEL: [*pulled the wool right through*]
> TEACHER: Oh! Let's do it again.
> RACHAEL: [*went to use the pointed end of the needle. Noticed that it was wrong. Turned it around to the other end so that she had the eye by the wool the teacher was holding. Threaded it successfully*]

It appeared that the teachers were in various ways and contexts maximizing children's access to learning within school, acknowledging the behaviours that had emerged in preschool contexts and building on this learning. By fostering continuity of development, the teachers were allowing the continuation of child initiatives, contrary to a trend in some educators' concerns that the styles of home and school learning can remain isolated from one another (e.g., Glynn 1992). At the same time, these two teachers were consistently focusing on helping children to construct understanding of meaning and develop new skills.

An Interactive View of Teaching and Learning: Independent Learning in the School Setting

The children in this study were approaching much of their learning independently, engaging in interesting, authentic tasks without requiring the teacher to be working with them all of the time. Through active involvement, they expanded their own repertoires of learning. In their attempts to understand and negotiate meanings in individual ways, they were drawing on what they knew and controlled, working on different kinds of information, thinking through what they were doing for themselves, and reaching and often checking their own solutions.

The children were not dependent on an adult for most of their actions. They did not require the teacher to constantly tell them what to do or how to carry out each task. They proceeded using their own initiative, requesting help only when the complexity of the task was beyond their capabilities. There was no pattern established of waiting for help, or of believing they could not carry out the tasks. An expectation that children could operate independently prevailed. By continuous encouragement to build on their own strengths and with support for their efforts, a momentum was established and maintained. One could almost say that the teachers required and expected children to engage in independent learning.

There were many instances of activities and interactions initiated by the children, as well as situations initiated by the teachers, that provided opportunities for independent learning. Significantly, a considerable proportion of the children's tasks were open-ended. The children constructed their own responses (generating their own stories to write) and created their own products (painting individual pictures) without constraints imposed by the teacher or the task. They were not given preset activities where the answers to problems were previously determined. Thus, the learning opportunities to which they had access can be clearly distinguished from mere busywork (such as colouring in geometric shapes on a worksheet). Pupils can work on tasks industriously and even productively, but such activity may not necessarily be "engaging children's minds" (Katz and Chard 1989). Access to learning experiences from across a wide-ranging curriculum, pitched at a level that was neither too limiting nor too daunting, enabled the children in the study to succeed in what they were doing and to build a foundation that could support their ongoing success as learners (cf. Clay 1991b).

A Different Way of Teaching

From this research there emerges a way of teaching that has features that distinguish it from instruction as it is commonly defined. It is not instruction in either sense referred to by Katz and Chard (1989). They distinguish *direct (didactic) instruction*, which applies to a whole class or to ability groups, from *systematic instruction*, defined as "an approach to teaching individual children a progression of interrelated subskills" (10). Both of these kinds of instruction are likely to arise from and follow the teacher's predetermined agenda.

The teaching observed in this study is best described as representing an interactive approach to teaching and learning. The view of the child as a constructive learner is integrated with the role of the assisting adult, in this instance a classroom teacher. In the tradition of Vygotsky and Bruner, the children moved from being supported to participate just beyond their present competence, to internalize activities shared with the teacher, and, as a result, to advance their capabilities for managing problem solving independently.

The main thrust is helping children progress in each curriculum area predominantly, but not solely, by their own actions. Parallels can be drawn with what has been observed in Reading Recovery (Clay 1993) for children experiencing difficulty in early literacy learning. In that programme, while children are active in constructing their action systems, the teacher plays a very active role in assisting learning. An important difference is that in the present study the interdependence of child and teacher activity was achieved in different settings within classes of children.

The Role of Active Teachers

The identification and description of "quality" one-to-one interactions with an "adult expert" are particular features of this study. Independent learning was supported and enhanced by particular teacher activity. This is a significant issue if Vygotsky (1978) is correct, and it is child activity of this kind, supported by a teacher acting in particular ways, that provides a basis for developing independent learning. Creating contexts for learning in which children are operating for some of the time as independent learners who are gradually assuming increasing control over their learning means "more not less competence on the part of teachers" (Glynn 1984, 17). How this competence is manifested is central to understanding the teacher's role in promoting independent learning. It is important, if any clear distinctions are to be made between instruction as commonly defined and assisting children to engage in independent learning, that three general points be raised about aspects of the facilitation processes.

1. Responsiveness to Children

Clear images of how teachers perceived children as learners are illustrated. Each child was interpreted as following a personal agenda determined in part by background factors exclusive to that child, and the teachers took their cues for attempts at facilitative behaviour from that. The teachers were involved in helping to meld curriculum goals through children's agendas by the contexts they created. They showed an adaptability to new children with different backgrounds, and deftness in their responses to individual learners. There was encouragement for children to use their initiative, combined with the sure knowledge that the teacher would be available to support that initiative and unlikely to compromise it by taking over. The teachers showed a respect for the child's ability to achieve personal goals. Both teachers had developed a way of reacting to the child's responses to learning with openness. Working from the child's actions and responding to very different starting points, the teachers acknowledged and sought to make use of what each individual child knew and did. The teachers were closely observing how children were responding by listening carefully to what they were saying, and by watching how the children went about different curriculum tasks, trying to gain insights into the children's thinking and levels of understanding. The shared activity observed was reflective of a significantly different kind of relationship between teacher and child, with regard to knowledge and understanding, than has been portrayed in many classrooms. It was the kind of responsiveness that allowed all the children to develop as independent learners, adding support to the position held by Clay (1991a), McNaughton (1991), and Wood (1998) that teaching contingent on children's responses and reflecting shared understandings helps children build a processing system that enables them to direct their own processes of learning. This result appears to have been achieved by facilitative teaching.

2. Effective Teaching in Classrooms

Ongoing monitoring of children's progress provided a foundation for the teachers' decisions to help each child move in appropriate directions. The teachers had to make judgements about what they would do with a child's initiated activity, using their skills in organizing the enthusiasm that each child brought or developed. They were making split-second decisions, choosing the facilitative style suited to individual children yet still consistent with the curriculum requirements of the whole class of new entrants. Although the two teachers were interpreted as having a similar general idea of how to work with new entrant children from a variety of backgrounds, they were observed at times to foster the learning and understanding of children in different ways. For example, one teacher used a style of questioning that coaxed the children to think as much as possible for themselves by turning things back to the children for further reflection, by getting them to elaborate and extend their responses, and by asking for reasons, while acknowledging her emphasis to them ("You're doing good thinking"). A variation in style of questioning and comment developed by the other teacher focused at times on helping the children understand concepts and ideas by eliciting responses with leading questions. Prompting the children to make links with everyday experiences was combined with explaining and summarizing how things worked, and with possible reasons for what was happening ("They're sad because their baby bird died"). One of the implications for inservice work is that there are unlikely to be any particular forms, or set sequences, or patterns of words, or questions, that will be effective in fostering independent learning. Based on the evidence of this study, an important prerequisite is effective management skills.

3. Managing the Classroom Environment

A sharpened awareness of the importance of organization and management skills emerged. The teachers had created and sustained an environment to enhance the opportunities children had for independent learning. These opportunities occurred through a style of teaching incorporating facilitative moves in one-to-one teaching interactions and small-group teaching, and in the way the settings were arranged and operated to allow opportunities for the children to work on their own for a considerable proportion of the time. Several levels of management were involved. Although there was variation between the two classrooms, both were prepared and operated in a way that acknowledged the presence of a wide range of learners with different needs. Children had access to a diversity of tasks and materials that spanned all curriculum areas and provided a wide range of experiences. They were specifically encouraged to engage in activities that enabled them to build on their present competencies, such as reading increasingly difficult short books matched to their current level of ability, and, from the first week of school, creating their own stories in writing. The many tasks and activities available provided opportunities for developing children's knowledge and understanding.

These teachers had a responsibility for children's learning in each curriculum area, and goals that had to be achieved. This was not perceived as a rigid, predetermined set of skills that had to be mastered. The teachers were not constrained by a curriculum dominated by workbooks or "ditto" sheets. Nor did publishers dictate the teaching programme by the materials they offered. Rather, the two teachers fostered the development of skills and strategies through access to a diversity of activities that allowed for open-ended responses by each child. They did this within a responsive context in which they arranged for frequent access to individual children within a range of situations: one-to-one settings, informal groupings, and small-group teaching. The flexibility inherent in these settings appeared to maximize children's opportunities to learn.

A Way Forward

This study offers a beginning. The details of the teacher-child interactions create a vivid impression of what the children and teachers were doing. These teachers did not follow a specific set of rules or procedures. Nor did they carry out their teaching in the same way, although the outcomes were similar. Thus, the study does not provide other teachers with a structure to follow, but with examples they can test against their own experience and setting, and whose relevance they can reflect upon as they set up environments for young children in school.

There is a Maori saying in New Zealand:

Nau te rourou Naku te rourou Ka ngawari aki ngamahi.
(With your expertise and mine the task will be easier).

These words capture the essence of what occurred in these two classrooms. Learning came from the collaborative efforts of teacher and child—for the independent learning observed to occur so early in schooling was the outcome of the activity of the child and of deliberately planned teaching that allowed for responding to and enhancing each child's growing control.

Acknowledgment

This report originates from the author's Ph.D. research. The advice, guidance, and support of Dame Professor Marie Clay, Associate Professor Viviene Robinson, and Dr. Judy Parr as supervisors of this research are gratefully acknowledged, as is the assistance of Professor Tony McNaughton. Special thanks belongs to the two teachers and the children who contributed so generously to the study.

References

BIRCH, J. W., AND BIRCH, J. R. 1970. *Preschool Education and School Admission Practices in New Zealand*. Pittsburg: University of Pittsburg, University Center for International Studies.

BLOOM, B. S. 1964. *Stability and Change in Human Characteristics*. New York: John Wiley and Sons.

BRUNER, J. S. 1973. "Organization of Early Skilled Action." *Child Development* 44:1–11.

———. 1990. *Acts of Meaning*. Cambridge: Harvard University Press.

CAZDEN, C. B. 1988. *Interactions Between Maori Children and Pakeha Teachers*. Auckland: Auckland Reading Association, Council of New Zealand Reading Association Inc.

———. 1991. "Contemporary Issues and Future Directions: Active Learners and Active Teachers." In *Handbook of Research on Teaching the English Language Arts*, edited by J. Flood, J. M. Jensen, D. Lapp, and J. S. Squire, 418–422. New York: Macmillan.

CLARK, M. M. 1991. "Ten C's for Early Education." Paper presented at "The First Years of School," Fourth Australia and New Zealand Conference, Auckland, New Zealand.

CLAY, M. M. 1985. "Engaging with the School System: A Study of Interactions in New Entrant Classrooms." *New Zealand Journal of Educational Studies* 20 (1): 20–38.

———. 1991a. *Becoming Literate: The Construction of Inner Control*. Auckland: Heinemann.

————. 1991b. "Child Development." In *Handbook of Research on Teaching the English Language Arts*, edited by J. Flood, J. M. Jensen, D. Lapp, and J. S. Squire, 40–45. New York: McMillan.

————. 1993. *Reading Recovery: A Guide Book for Teachers in Training*. Auckland: Heinemann.

————. 1998. *By Different Paths to Common Outcomes*. York, Maine: Stenhouse.

DeLoache, J.S., and Brown, A. L. 1987. "The Early Emergence of Planning Skills in Children." In *Making Sense*, edited by J. Bruner and H. Haste, 108–130. London: Methuen.

Department of Education. 1985. *Reading in the Junior Classes*. Wellington, New Zealand: Learning Media.

Ferreiro, E., and Teberosky, A. 1982. *Literacy Before Schooling*. Exeter, N.H.: Heinemann.

Glynn, T. 1983. "Building an Effective Teaching Environment." In *Psychological Aspects of Learning and Teaching*, edited by K. Wheldall, and R. Riding, 40–62. London: Croom Helm.

————. 1984. "Contexts for Independent Learning." Inaugural address. September. University of Otago, New Zealand.

————. 1992. *Learners in Control: Responding to Children's Writing*. Unpublished Manuscript. University of Otago, New Zealand.

Katz, L. G., and Chard, S. C. 1989. *Engaging Children's Minds: The Project Approach*. Norwood, N.J.: Ablex.

McNaughton, S. 1985. "Beyond Teaching: The Development of Independence in Learning to Read." Keynote address presented to the Eleventh Annual Conference of the Australian Reading Association, July, Brisbane, Australia.

————. 1987. *Being Skilled: The Socializations of Learning to Read*. London: Methuen.

————. 1991. "Do Children Construct Their Literacy Development?" Paper presented to the 16th National Conference of the Australian Reading Association, May, Adelaide, Australia.

Ministry of Education. 1996. *The Learner as a Reader*. Wellington, New Zealand: Learning Media Ltd.

Resnick, L. B. 1987. *Education and Learning to Think*. Washington, D.C.: National Academy Press.

Rogoff, B. 1990. *Apprenticeship in Thinking: Cognitive Development in Social Context*. New York: Oxford University Press.

Smith, A. B. 1993. "Early Childhood Educare: Seeking a Theoretical Framework in Vygotsky's Work." *International Journal of Early Years Education* 1 (1): 47–61.

Vygotsky, L. S. 1978. *Mind in Society*. Cambridge, Mass.: Harvard University Press.

Watson, B. 1993. "Facilitating Independent Learning Early in the First Year of School." Unpublished Ph.D. thesis, University of Auckland, New Zealand.

WOOD, D. 1998. *How Children Think and Learn: The Social Contexts of Cognitive Development.* 2d ed. Cambridge, Mass.: Basil Blackwell.

WOOD, H., AND WOOD, D. 1983. "Questioning the Pre-School Child." *Educational Review* 35 (2): 149–162.

YOPP, H. K., AND SINGER, H. 1994. "Toward an Interactive Reading Instructional Model: Explanation of Activation of Linguistic Awareness and Metalinguistic Ability in Learning to Read." In *Theoretical Models and Processes of Reading*, 3d ed., edited by R. Ruddell, M. Ruddell, and H. Singer, 381–390. Delaware, Md.: International Reading Association.

Five

Reading Recovery:
Waves of Influence on Literacy Education

BILLIE J. ASKEW AND JANET S. GAFFNEY

In the new physics of quantum mechanics, the conception of the world is based on the interconnections of subatomic particles (bundles of energy), which appear as waves of probabilities (Zukav 1979). Consistent with a systems approach to schools, an occurrence at any part of the system influences the entire network of relationships (Gaffney and Paynter 1994; Garmston and Wellman 1995). Any act, including observing, influences future probabilities (Garmston and Wellman 1995). Reading Recovery, a school-based early intervention program, has influenced the network of relationships within educational systems at school, district, and national levels. Each time one teacher succeeds with one child, the wave of future probabilities for a literate society increases.

Reading Recovery has influenced early literacy education in an unprecedented way. Although it is a challenging task, our goal is to identify a few areas that have had significant and lasting effects on literacy education. These areas are worthy of examination for at least two reasons: Our analysis may contribute to a deeper understanding of the complex and comprehensive nature of Reading Recovery as a systemic intervention, and educators may use the insights from Reading Recovery to design and implement effective interventions in other areas of literacy learning.

Three waves of influence are addressed in this chapter:

- Teaching and learning within a theory of reading and writing continuous text
- Development of professional expertise
- A system for implementing, sustaining, and expanding an intervention in schools and systems

Helping children learn to read and write by reading books and writing stories is based on a quite different theory than is teaching children by other schemes. We examine some fundamental assumptions of Clay's theory of reading and writing continuous text. When literacy learning is based on continuous text rather than systematic and sequential learning of prescribed sets of items, different teaching-learning interactions are required. These complex interactions mirror the acts of real reading and writing. We discuss the complex relationships that undergird teacher-child interactions by exploring ideas such as the effects of observing on teaching, the unique nature of individual paths of progress, the role of teachers' cognitions about children's learning, and the significance of acceleration in the learning process.

In a problem-solving model that is based on teaching children, professional development focuses on the expansion of teaching capacity through the development of expertise. Expertise is defined as the ability to solve problems in novel ways, rather than through skilled use of routine practices or procedures. Professional development is child driven in its implementation and evaluation. Critical factors for a solid framework of professional development are the melding of theory and practice; robust initial training followed by continuing support, collegiality, and guidance; and accountability for children's progress.

Clay (1997) presents a conceptual framework for guiding discussion of implementation issues by using three concentric circles. The inner circle represents the children's learning; the second circle represents training teachers to solve problems; and the outer circle represents implementing the program within an education system. The outer circle focuses on how decisions made by education systems support or threaten the quality of Reading Recovery within that system. We examine structures that support effective implementations that have been replicated in a variety of settings. We also share a proposal for considering Reading Recovery as a model for redesigning education.

Teaching and Learning Within a Theory of Reading and Writing Continuous Text

> Being able to observe and interact with a child in order to discover what she knows, understands, and can do, takes time, considerable knowledge and skill. (Wood 1988, 224)

Any theory about how children learn implies a corresponding theory of instruction (Wood 1988, 75). In the Russian language, the inextricable link between teaching and learning is made by combining the two ideas in the single word *obuchenie* (Wertsch and Rogoff 1984). To understand changes in children's reading and writing as they are just getting underway with print, one must examine both teaching and learning (Clay 1991a). The complexity of this interactive process intensifies with the realization that evaluating only the *responses* of the learner and the teacher reveals just a portion of the picture. Looking only at what the child *does*, without considering the child's *cognitions*, is insufficient; the understandings of both child and teacher must also be considered.

Teachers strive to understand the unique ways in which each child makes sense of the world, including the world of print. The teacher uses a child's responses to infer what sense the child is making of reading and writing—that is, to understand the child's theory. Teachers develop their own theories about how children learn to read and write and they use these general theories to explain the responses of individual children. The juxtaposition of the teacher's personal theory of acquisition with her interpretation of an individual child's responses drives the teaching. "Both the teacher and the child exhibit behaviours and both operate on cognitions" (Clay 1991a, 233).

"A model of reading acquisition which defines reading as working on continuous texts with the story as the focal point of attention describes word-solving in somewhat different ways from a theory that regards reading new words in isolation as the significant activity" (Clay 1991a, 340). Therefore, learning how to read and write using meaningful, connected text leads to actions and understandings on the part of children that differ from those that result if the starting point is isolated letters or words. Because teachers have the opportunity to observe quite different responses when continuous text, rather than words and letters, is used, the children's responses influence and are influenced by the teachers' interpretations and shape their teaching moves.

Consider a response to a question that is often asked about Reading Recovery: "How can the lowest-achieving children start reading books and writing stories on the first day?" Implicit in this question is the conviction that knowledge of items such as letters and words precedes text reading and that these items are the most beneficial starting point for all children. In isolation, however, these items offer little information for the construction of a response, especially by children with limited knowledge reserves.

Now consider the kinds of information that are available for word solving when words are embedded in text. A child may rely on oral language, the gist of the story, and knowledge of the world as well as knowledge of print (letters, word parts, and words). With continuous text, children can use any of these avenues to solve a problem. Because there are multiple routes to the same solution, children construct responses using their own available resources, whether they are meager or substantial. Children's varied responses during story reading yield rich and textured descriptions for teachers' development of personal theories and observations of the idiosyncratic responses of individual children.

Children's construction of both errors and correct responses gives the teacher insight into the kinds of information that a child is noticing. The use of stories enables children access to the text through any level of language that is accessible to them, including story, page, sentence, phrase, words, word parts, and letters. In fact, access to multiple levels permits children to confirm or disconfirm their own responses through triangulation of data.

Consider a clothing metaphor (J. M. Methven, personal communication, 1997). A specific piece of clothing, for example a suit, has characteristics such as color, fabric, style, and size. Any of these characteristics, alone or in combination, may persuade or dissuade the shopper from purchasing the suit. Analogously, when a child considers or produces a response, the "fit" of features from any level of language may lead the child to accept or reject his own candidate response. As with shopping, the child is sometimes led to accept incorrect responses that do not fit *all* criteria, lending credence to the statement that some errors are better than others.

As a child reads and writes continuous text, the teacher notices the aspects of oral and written language that the child is using and neglecting. Thus, the teacher's next move incorporates observation-based information about *this* child's immediate response to *this* text. Naturally, the response patterns of individual children vary across texts and differ from those of other children. Likewise, effective teaching varies in ways that correspond to a child's response, rather than to a prescriptive formula or curriculum sequence.

Attending to the "responding history" of a child requires a quarter-turn in thinking for many educators: "There is change over time, not only in what is known, but also in how reading is carried out" (Clay 1993b, 7–8). Observations over time are required if one is to detect patterns in the ways in which a child approaches reading and writing tasks, rather than merely to inventory a child's item knowledge at a single point in time. This type of observation-interpretation reflects the sophisticated nature of the teaching craft.

The theory that drives good early literacy teaching, however, has two parts. The first part is the teacher's knowledge and use of each child's responding history; the teacher's knowledge of the ever-increasing corpus of information available to the child; and the child's ever-developing repertoire of ways to use this information. Looking only at what the child does, however, is insufficient. The second requisite is that teachers note whether the movement is in appropriate directions (Clay 1993b, 3). The focus is on learning trajectories, rather than on predictable stepwise gains (Lave 1996).

Through systematic observation of heterogeneous learners over time, teachers gain a sense of typical trajectories of literacy learning in order to weigh the progress of individual children. The child's performance must be examined in light of how good readers learn to read and how good writers learn to write (Clay 1993a). Efficient teaching enables each child to take his or her own path to this destination, rather than restricting all children to a single route, which would not be viable for some children. Teachers "can allow children to take different learning paths to the same outcomes because they are clearly aware of the learning that is occurring" (Clay 1993a, 4). In other words, the destination is known, but there are many ways to get there.

An Interesting Change Occurs in Teachers Who Observe Closely

Teachers who observe closely begin to question educational assumptions (Clay 1998). Close observation of children as they learn how to read and write is both challenging and intriguing. When teachers observe what children are doing with the intent to understand what children are noticing, they improve the quality of their teaching interactions. Johnston cautions us that "standing where the learner stands in order to see his world is not easy, and it is something that you must want to do" (Johnston 1992, 552).

When teachers interact with children with the assumption that their responses are nonrandom, they are searching for legitimate rationales for children's behaviors. By trying out different hypotheses in subsequent teaching interactions, teachers come to expand and deepen their own thinking about how children learn to read and write. Thus, conscious reflection on the observation is essential for improving the quality of teaching interactions. Fullan and Hargreaves (1991) differentiate between weak and strong forms of reflection. Strong reflection is carried out with the clear purpose of critically examining the aspects of teaching that help or hinder students' learning. Teachers "who intentionally and systematically observe student ability assume that such inquiry can and will lead to changes in their teaching, in their students, and in themselves" (Wansart 1995, 169).

The teacher's interpretation and the nature of the tasks in which children are engaged will affect the conclusions that are drawn from observations. What teachers attend to while observing is influenced by their interpretive frame and, in a reciprocal manner, the results of the observation may shape their next view of the world. In an interview, Michael Armstrong suggests that the distinction between observation and theory is diminished when the description of the observations is close and sufficiently rich. "I have become convinced that the thing that holds up progress in developing any sort of satisfying theory of childhood or of intellectual growth is the inability, our inability, to understand the idea of description at a sufficiently profound level. So that in a way there is, should be, an art of description which is of such a kind that it does actually embrace or contain within itself all the theory that we actually require" (Engel 1984, 355).

The nature of the tasks in which children are engaged matters. Based on deep descriptions of children's learning, Armstrong contends that "the thought of children is not to be seen either as some kind of trial run for adult thought or as simply acquiring techniques later to be used or as something impossibly naive and different" (Engel 1984, 354). He posits that children are engaging in the same kind of thought as adults, but have limited technical means to solve the same kinds of substantive problems. The use of continuous text is necessary to support young children's evolving expertise in writing and reading so that they gain experience in solving problems that typify advanced learners. When teachers observe children writing and reading continuous text, rather than selected aspects of literacy, they will notice that children take varied routes to common outcomes.

Children Can Be Supported to Learn How to Go About Their Own Literacy Learning

Hampton (personal communication, 1997) used the concept of *range of motion* to describe the access of persons with physical disabilities to activities in their environment. His premise is that a person's range of motion is expanded or restricted by alterable environmental factors, not by the inalterable physical condition. He illustrates the concept with examples of factors that support or restrict the access of persons with disabilities to social and recreational activities in housing, transportation, restaurants, and other facilities (e.g., fitness centers, dance clubs, bars). Hampton described a young man with quadriplegia who had access to the workplace in a large city, but who, once he returned to his apartment, was virtually stuck and unable to access the community and businesses that he could see from his window. Thus, the degree to which a handicap is disabling depends upon the range of motion permitted in the context.

A child's range of motion in literacy is also dependent upon accessibility within the learning environment. When teachers develop "tasks with scope" (Clay 1996, 216), children can approach learning by making connections with what they already know and can do—resulting in multiple entry points to new learning (Clay 1998). Thus, tasks with scope have an elasticity that permits different children to attend to different information and enables individual students to expand their learning on diverse knowledge continuums simultaneously. Alternatively, "tasks directed to the learning of items of knowledge, skills or concepts in a prescribed order do not allow for different routes to different outcomes" (Clay 1996, 216).

Text-based instruction in reading and writing expands children's range of motion by allowing them to link what they know with any aspect of the new learning and to move out from their starting point in any direction. Multiple entry points and multiple routes to the end goal of literacy learning prevent children from getting stuck in inaccessible learning contexts. Teaching in reading and writing that is based on text may be motivating, stimulating, and meaningful, but the primary advantage is that "*any competence the child has is allowed to contribute to the output*" (Clay 1998, 190). A text becomes an invitation to children to build onto whatever knowledge they have about how books work, how language sounds, how words work, and common letter sequences in reading and writing. In this way, children initiate processing, and their actions are windows for teachers to better learn how to encourage this building up and out of new learning in any direction.

> In human literacy learning and teaching there are many differing ladders, many ways to climb, many kinds of powers in climbing, and an amazing capacity in human learners of all ages to climb on more than one ladder at once. How to organize school genuinely for diversity in literacy, treating its multidimensionality as a resource rather than a liability and providing various ways to climb high, is a challenge we continue to face as educators and citizens. (Erickson 1991, x)

How do teachers help children become active participants in their own learning? Fortunately, "we do not have to solve the problems of teaching on our own: We have the constructive learner as our strongest ally" (Clay 1996, 215). Some children, however, suspend their constructive prowess when confronted with print. The teacher's role is to do whatever it takes to ensure that the reading and writing tasks encourage the active involvement of young children. Children with lean prior knowledge and limited response repertoires offer the greatest challenge. In these cases, skillful teaching is required to determine competencies, ensure that the reading and writing tasks are accessible, and call upon children to rely on their own resources. Because the teacher is clear about a child's competencies, he or she is free to do things for the child that are not within reach, to help the child to do things that are almost within reach, and to expect the child to act on things that are within reach.

When teaching consistently calls for the child to act on increasingly challenging tasks with "just right" scaffolds for support, the balance of teacher and child activity shifts to the child. With such opportunities, children not only develop constructive responses, they become "bold enough to use them" (Clay 1998, 190). The goal is for children to take over the learning task and work independently while discovering new things for themselves, both when working with a teacher and when working alone (Askew and Fountas 1998).

"Teachers Think About Their Teaching" (Clay 1991b, 55)

According to teacher-education research, experience is necessary but not sufficient for the development of expertise (Bereiter and Scardamalia 1993). A common character-istic of experts across domains is their skill in recognizing and interpreting patterns (Johnston 1997), particularly high-significance patterns (Bereiter and Scardamalia 1993). The patterns of child responses that teachers consider important are contin-gent upon their personal theories.

So, how do we check our own theories? If we observe closely, the behaviors of the children will signal when our theories and, therefore, our teaching have gone wrong. Because hard-to-teach students may have some unusual patterns of responding (and some of these may be due to how they have been taught), teachers need to develop expertise in using and interpreting observations in order to evaluate their own teach-ing. Teachers may challenge the assumptions that underlie their teaching by evaluat-ing a child's progress along multiple trajectories of learning how to read and write. Some productive questions to use in assessing teaching are

- What does this child control?
- What connections is this child making?
- Is the child going beyond the information given into new territories (Bruner 1964; Clay 1998, 54)?
- Is there evidence of shifts in the child's competencies and the teacher's responses?

Reading Recovery teachers become vigilant about their assumptions. Teachers make assumptions about instructional sequences, essential learning, gradients of tasks, rate of learning, and the kind and amount of teaching that is needed. They also make assumptions about the potential, competencies, confusions, understandings, and progress of the individual children they are teaching. The close evaluation of one's own teaching and focused discussions with colleagues about jointly observed teaching sessions generate opportunities for uncovering incorrect assumptions (Clay 1991b, 68–69; Gaffney and Anderson 1991, 195).

Fine-grained observations promote the sophisticated analysis and discussion of teaching-learning interactions. Reading Recovery teachers use jointly observed lessons to leverage professional discussions in which they try out their explanations for the actions of the teacher and child whom they are observing. Multiple perspectives are reflected in the articulation of varied hypotheses that lead to thoughtful discussions about literacy teaching and learning. Central to the resolution of discrepancies among teachers is the undeniable evidence of the learner and teacher before them. Over time, teachers fine-tune their observations and interpretations, contributing to their development as high-craft teachers. Reading Recovery teachers confirm Benton's (cited in Taylor 1990, 19) statement that "observing kids is about us changing our thinking" and our teaching. The alternative is also true: Sometimes when we change our teaching, we revise our thinking.

The complexity of teaching is acknowledged when the craft is approached in a problem-solving manner. Quality teaching-learning interactions are particularly critical for young children who are experiencing difficulty in getting underway in reading and writing. "My position on good teaching is that it arises out of the understanding teachers have of their craft and never out of prescriptive programs" (Clay 1998, 130). Instruction that is based on *a priori* sequence restricts the learning of both children and teachers. "The difference between experts and experienced nonexperts is not that one does things well and the other does things badly. Rather the expert addresses problems whereas the nonexpert carries out practiced routines" (Bereiter and Scardamalia 1993, 11).

In Reading Recovery, high-craft teachers are responsive to children in ways that are theoretically consistent with learning to read and write continuous text (Clay 1998). "In the end, I suspect that excellent teachers will do what they have always done: grow. And the growing will be as it has ever been: the result of their tuning in to their students, responding to them, and learning from and with them even as they 'teach' them" (Lindfors 1987, 386).

Acceleration Is a Surprising and Even Contradictory Phenomenon

Most children develop self-extending systems that expand their learning and capacity to learn in ways that are seemingly effortless; others do not. The intention of Reading Recovery teaching is to help children who are not making adequate progress in their class programs to achieve accelerated rates of progress. To change the learning velocity of the children on the tail end of the achievement distribution is unprecedented and flies in the face of logic. Attention to rate of learning is a significant aspect of Reading Recovery and one of the outcomes that challenges the status quo in literacy educa-tion. Reading Recovery teaching acknowledges the "economical use of a child's learn-ing time" (Clay 1993b, 61).

How can educators expect to change the slope of the trajectories of literacy learn-ing for children whose progress is offtrack? Astute observation of the idiosyncratic response patterns of individual children and the skilled use of robust teaching proce-dures is required to reverse the extant trend. However, "teaching is neither necessary nor sufficient to produce learning"(Lave 1996, 157). A teacher cannot produce or induce acceleration; acceleration is what the child does (Clay 1993b).

Teaching with text provides a wide range of opportunities for learning and fosters accelerated rates of learning. We don't have enough time to *teach* the child everything he'll need to know how to do, so we help the child to develop a way to learn on his own in an active, constructive manner by being a coworker. With the teacher as guide, the child negotiates the layers of language in texts, using familiar landmarks and noticing novel features. Texts that offer sufficient familiarity with a smattering of new ways to crisscross the many levels of language nudge, stretch, and propel a child's learning into new territories. Children's fascination with stories and information is in the forefront of their attention, while in the background their knowledge accumulates and their competencies in navigating longer and more challenging texts increase. The child's expertise in negotiating a variety of texts with different kinds of inherent support expands in range and increases in efficiency—signaling the development of a self-extending system (Clay 1993b).

The elemental principle of acceleration, then, is that a significant change in learning is a change in the *rate* of learning. Each new connection that a child generates among his or her networks of knowledge increases the probabilities of further connections—leading not only to a change in learning, but also to a change in learning capacity and, thus, rate. A problem-solving approach leverages learning in complex domains. "Finding a solution to even a small problem confirms that what you did to get to the solution is a useful way to go about this process" (Clay 1995) and leverages future learning. Because text offers at least ten levels of language, children may enter and move among the levels quickly or slowly as the task requires and solve problems using any resources available to them. Quality teaching-learning interactions with text yield possibilities for bursts of insight and small leaps in understanding, rather than progression on a ladder of trivial gains.

Development of Professional Expertise

> Students' right to learn is directly tied to their teachers' opportunities to learn what they need to know to teach well. (Darling-Hammond 1996, 6)

The Reading Recovery staff-development model ties teacher learning to student learning in extraordinary ways. The unique three-tiered training model provides yet another wave of influence from Clay's work in Reading Recovery.

Reading Recovery teachers must learn to be responsive to the learner and to make effective decisions on the run, based on evidence of the child's responses. Each lesson is designed for a particular child at a particular point in that child's program. No package of teaching materials can substitute for the teacher's ability to design a program that is determined by the child's performance and that calls for highly skilled, moment-to-moment decisions during each lesson (Clay 1992, 1993b). This special kind of teaching calls for a unique training scheme.

Clay (1993b) refers to professional development in Reading Recovery as a hierarchy of expertise. Three levels of professional staffing provide a stable training structure: university trainers who train and support teacher leaders; system-level teacher leaders (or tutors in some countries) who train and support teachers; and school-based teachers who work with the hardest-to-teach children. At each level of training, the roles of the professionals, as well as their use of theory, are different (Clay 1992). The expertise of the teacher is highlighted here.

The Training of Teachers Promotes Unique Interactions Between Practice and Theory

> The training has forever changed the way I view literacy learning. I now realize how complex the process is!
> *Reading Recovery Teacher in Training*

Reading Recovery training values the experiences that teachers bring to the situation. Teachers work from their existing theories and practices while gradually acquiring new theories about how they and their students perform and how they should perform. By the end of their year-long inservice course, teachers are able to "question, challenge, discuss, work out courses of action, and explain their decisions in ways they could all understand because these new theories were shared and explicit" (Clay 1982, 194). How does this happen?

The critical parts of the year-long initial training of teachers are the weekly (or fortnightly, outside the United States) demonstration lessons using a one-way glass screen, and the discussion sessions that follow. During the live lessons taught by members of the class, teachers are able to observe and talk about what they think the child is doing and why the teacher may have responded as she did. A trained teacher leader guides the talk during the lesson and the subsequent discussion, using the observed behavior of the child and teacher to help the group learn to describe, analyze, make inferences, and challenge themselves and their colleagues. Teachers begin to develop their own theories in this way, theories that are grounded in the specifics of teaching and that foster problem solving (Pinnell 1991).

"Teachers . . . start with diverse assumptions about learning to read and write and these differences are a strength within their collegial network" (Clay 1997, 663). The challenges in teacher training also relate to uncovering hidden assumptions that are antagonistic to the progress of the hardest-to-teach children. During demonstration lessons, teachers articulate their ideas and open up their assumptions about literacy learning and teaching interactions for public consideration by the other trainees. They also learn to check on their own assumptions about teaching and to change their assumptions based on clearly observed data (Clay 1991b).

Therefore, while the emphasis during sessions using the one-way glass is sometimes on putting what is seen into words, equally important is articulating how what is seen conflicts with what was assumed. "Bringing the implicit, whether observed or assumed, into a verbal form which allows discussion and revision is an essential part of training" (Clay 1997, 663). The Reading Recovery training model at all levels, then, is based on the assumption that language is a key factor in building theories. It is through language that we represent our experiences to others and refine and extend it for ourselves. "Through language interactions with other people, we expand our experiences, try out our ideas, and formulate or reformulate understandings of a particular phenomenon" (Pinnell 1991, 182).

Clay (1982) refers to *observation* as the key word in the development and implementation of this inservice program. The unique feature is the potential for multilevel observation and learning that is embedded in the situation. Child-driven data gathered from observations provide a common or shared experience that becomes the content for teacher discussion. In addition to their explicit articulation about observed teacher-child interactions, teachers are introduced to teaching procedures and concepts using a guidebook as a reference source. The Reading Recovery guidebook for teachers in training (Clay 1993b) is used as a basis for the discussion of individual children and teacher decisions, as well as for clarification of concepts and teaching procedures, building bridges between practice and theory.

Both practice and theory building are driven by behavioral data in Reading Recovery. Daily records of child behaviors and teacher decisions provide a check on practice and a vehicle for building theories about teaching and learning. As teachers acquire case-by-case knowledge that builds their capacity for making decisions and solving problems, they develop expertise by examining their own practices. All theory building, then, is checked against practice—child by child. As in all instances of building relationships between theory and practice, teachers must be flexible and tentative, observing constantly and altering their assumptions based on a child's behaviors (Clay 1997).

After an independent evaluation of Reading Recovery in New Zealand, two senior members of Her Majesty's Inspectorate offered this observation about the training of Reading Recovery teachers:

> What was particularly gratifying was to observe moments when the teachers made connections between theory and experience, bringing the latter to bear in reflecting on their own practice. In effect, they were achieving two purposes at once: constructing a framework of conceptual understanding with which to underpin and develop their own work in the programme and refining their own practice. (Office of Her Majesty's Chief Inspector of Schools 1994, 155)

Teacher Change Is Supported Through Networks of Guidance and Collegiality

> It's an exciting journey—not only watching my students develop but experiencing my own growth as well as that of my peers.
> *Reading Recovery Teacher in Training*

Although much is written about the ways in which teachers support children and their learning, much less is written about the support that an adult needs in order to support a child's learning. In their discussion of two tiers of scaffolding, Gaffney and Anderson (1991) propose that the first tier (teacher-child interaction) forms the essential content of the second tier (teacher training). The Reading Recovery teacher development model includes extensive and multipurpose networks to support teachers' initial and ongoing training and learning.

The key person in the initial and ongoing training of Reading Recovery teachers is the teacher leader, whose role is complex and requires a wide range of skills in a variety of areas. The teacher leader must have a thorough and academic understanding of the theoretical concepts on which the program is based; awareness of the organizational, professional, and child-development issues associated with the program; and extensive experience in the workings of an elementary school (Clay 1982). According to Clay (1992), teacher leaders exemplify Goodlad's (1977) "redirecting system." They teach children, train teachers, educate local educators, negotiate the program's local implementation, and advocate maintaining the integrity of the program in the interest of effective results. Therefore, they must be insistent, persistent, and uncompromising in order to prevent a return to old practices.

In the initial training of teachers, the network begins with a trained teacher leader and a group of teachers in training. The teacher leader guides the teachers in challenging talk about lessons and the discussions that follow lessons. Teachers are challenged to form hypotheses about the child's performance, to present evidence to support or disconfirm the hypotheses, to provide rationales for their decisions, and to suggest alternative instructional procedural decisions (Gaffney and Anderson 1991). While the Reading Recovery teacher course creates many challenges, the teacher leader creates an atmosphere of collaboration within the group. The network of learners in the group continues to provide support for each other throughout the year and in subsequent years.

During the initial training and in the following years, teacher leaders make on-site visits as schedules allow. These visits help with communication about the school's program, support for the teaching of children, and assistance with particularly challenging children. Colleague visits are encouraged, broadening the network of support among peers.

After the initial year of training, teachers continue to participate in ongoing professional development sessions, called "continuing contact." They continue to teach for their colleagues and to discuss their programs. These sessions provide collaborative opportunities for teachers to maintain responsiveness to individual children, to question the effectiveness of their practices, to get help from their peers with hard-to-teach children, and to consider how new knowledge in the field relates to their practice (Clay 1992).

Reading Recovery does not exist as an isolated venture in a district, state, or region. Each Reading Recovery site is connected to a larger whole. University trainers help to maintain connections across sites locally, nationally, and internationally. These trainers offer ongoing professional development for the network of teacher leaders.

Trainers, teacher leaders, and teachers collaborate across the network. Teachers build networks with other Reading Recovery teachers, Reading Recovery site coordinators, local administrators, and their colleagues in classrooms. They build school teams that form a network for solving program problems locally. teacher leaders who are supported by university trainers in turn support the teachers in their efforts. Ongoing professional development at every level of the training scheme preserves the network—both the expertise needed for working with hard-to-teach children and the ability to respond to unique needs and challenges in schools.

Reading Recovery Provides a Demonstration of an Effective Teacher-Development Model

Reading Recovery has opened some doors in my mind that can never be shut!
Reading Recovery Teacher in Training

Reading Recovery serves as an exemplar for effective teacher development. "Effective professional development involves teachers both as learners and as teachers and allows them to struggle with the uncertainties that accompany each role" (Darling-Hammond and McLaughlin 1995, 598). Reading Recovery teacher training embodies each of the characteristics of a good professional development model proposed by Darling-Hammond and McLaughlin (1995):

- teachers engaged in concrete tasks of teaching, assessment, observation, and reflection that illuminate learning
- grounded in participants' inquiry, reflection, and experimentation
- collaborative, involving a sharing of knowledge
- connected to and derived from teachers' work with children
- sustained, ongoing, intensive, and supported by coaching, modeling, and collaborative problem solving on specific problems of practice
- connected to other aspects of school change

Their model calls for teachers to confront research and theory directly, regularly engage in evaluating their practice, and use their colleagues for mutual assistance. Reading Recovery has institutionalized these characteristics of professional development at all levels of expertise.

Pinnell's (1997a) characteristics of the Reading Recovery teacher-development model closely match those offered by Darling-Hammond and McLaughlin (1995) and others. She suggests that Reading Recovery provides

- a structure that builds strong content knowledge
- observation of phenomena that are important to participants and that they encounter in their daily work

- guidance from an expert
- daily work of an investigative nature
- use of careful records to guide those investigations
- case examples for the group to consider together
- a group of professional colleagues who work together across time
- recognition of the central role of language in learning

Returning to Clay's original research question about what is possible for children, we can also ask what is possible for teachers when this comprehensive network is used to train and support the teachers of the hardest-to-teach children. P. David Pearson suggests that the Reading Recovery training model provides evidence of yet another wave of Reading Recovery's influence:

> Reading Recovery has managed to operationalize that vague notion that teachers ought to reflect on their own practice. That behind the glass play by play analysis and the collegial debriefing with the teacher after her teaching session represent some of the best teacher education I have witnessed in my 28-year history in the field. (Clay 1997, 663)

Implementing, Sustaining, and Expanding an Intervention in Schools and Systems

> In too many cases, where ideas deserved consideration, the processes through which they were implemented were self-defeating . . . the process of implementation requires an understanding of the settings in which these ideas have to take root. That understanding is frequently faulty and incomplete. (Sarason 1991, 99)

Literacy interventions such as Reading Recovery cannot be considered isolated phenomena in schools. Complex interventions need problem-solving processes that call for a clear understanding of the conceptual congruity of all aspects of the theory, intervention, and training underlying the innovation (Gaffney and Paynter 1994). Therefore, a third wave of Reading Recovery's influence on literacy education is the carefully planned system for implementing the program in an existing education system.

Systemic Implementation of Reading Recovery Has Not Been Left to Chance

> Institutional changes that are both sweeping and practical don't endure and succeed by chance. (Wilson and Daviss 1994, 26)

A structured process guides the implementation of Reading Recovery within an education system. Reading Recovery has been called a systemic intervention, which Clay (1987, 1990, 1992) views as the processes involved in opening the system to accommodate and support the innovation. It involves solving the problem of placement of the intervention into an existing education system. Reading Recovery implementers understand that the failure to build an innovation into the normal structures and practices of the organization leads to the disappearance of many reforms (Fullan and Miles 1992).

Because of the complexity of systemic relationships, a successful innovation will be cohesive both internally and with the host system and its stakeholders (Clay 1992). Both internal and external structures guiding successful implementation merit consideration. Reading Recovery's internal and external structures offer a model for implementation of other innovations:

Structures for Supporting Internal Cohesion
- An established and documented intervention (Bernard van Leer Foundation 1991).
- Standards and guidelines for protecting teaching and training that are revised when contexts and understandings change.
- An intensive long-term professional development model that continues after the initial year, with a built-in renewal system to support teaching effectiveness.
- Networks within and across the three tiers of Reading Recovery professionals (university-based trainers, system-based teacher leaders, and school-based teachers), with university training centers providing leadership.
- An established system of providing evaluative evidence of the program's outcomes and benefits.
- A dynamic system for incorporating changing theories (Pinnell 1997b).

Structures for Supporting External Cohesion
- Organized training schemes that deliberately attend to issues of implementation.
- Long-range planning with the expectation that the intervention will be structured to work over time (Fullan and Miles 1992).
- A system for problem solving through established networks.
- A system for dissemination and expansion at all levels.
- Structures for preserving program quality while placing the innovation into the context of an existing system.
- Processes for building shared understandings among the stakeholders.
- Interpretation of the needs and successes of individual implementations relative to the age of the implementation.

Even with structures in place to protect the internal and external cohesion of an innovation, the downsizing of an innovation to fit a local school climate can result in uncertainties and institutional insecurities (Huberman and Miles 1982). While Reading Recovery involves a means of solving the problem of placing the innovation into an existing system, some cautions are noted:

> The art in the change process is that changes should not distort or diminish its payoff and any changes should be explicitly referred to theories of what is occurring.

Compromise, or unthinking adaptations, can readily change the impact of the innovation and reduce its capacity to deliver effective results. During periods of expansion every effort should be made to ensure that the parts of the programme retain their cohesion and link with other parts of the programme. (Clay 1987)

Reading Recovery Has Been Successfully Replicated in a Variety of Settings

Educational practices are not generally considered exportable because educational systems are organized and managed differently and operate with different political agendas (Clay 1997). Yet Reading Recovery has been successfully transplanted into a wide variety of educational systems. Successful program longevity has been enjoyed in New Zealand, Australia, the United States, the United Kingdom, Canada, Jersey, Bermuda, and Anguilla. The United States has also implemented Reading Recovery in a number of Department of Defense schools around the world. Reading Recovery, then, operates in many diverse settings in several countries that differ in their structural, historical, cultural, and educational ways. Sustained replications across such diverse systems attest to the strength of the structures in place for program implementation.

"The differences in educational cultures and practices call for problem-solving the theory of the early intervention into the beliefs, practices and academic literature of a new education system" (Clay 1992, 31). While staying true to the theory and design of the program, Clay offers examples of Reading Recovery adaptations experienced across several countries to accommodate such diversity. Acceptable adaptations have included word tests designed to reflect the frequency with which words are used in local reading books; schemes for making the transition for the child from Reading Recovery to local classroom programs easier; responses to practical issues, such as the availability of appropriate storybooks for children; and adjustment of time of entry into the program to the local education environment.

Data from several countries also offer evidence that Reading Recovery is successful in a variety of socioeconomic, sociocultural, and sociolinguistic settings. Studies from New Zealand (Clay 1993b), England (Hobsbaum 1995), and the United States (Compton et al. 1995; Frasier et al. 1996) have documented surprisingly successful results with children whose first language was not English. Early results in Reading Recovery in Spanish, or *Descubriendo la Lectura*, indicate patterns of success similar to those in studies of Reading Recovery in English (Escamilla 1994; Escamilla et al. 1998). Canadians are currently exploring the redevelopment of Reading Recovery in French.

Reading Recovery has also been successful in a wide range of school settings, including urban, rural, suburban, and small-town settings. According to Pinnell, Lyons, and Jones (1996), "areas of high need usually require more problem solving, greater effort, and more time, but success has been demonstrated" (24). They cite data from an economically disadvantaged system representing a highly diverse population in New York City as an example of progress in a large urban setting (Jaggar and Smith-Burke 1995).

The measure of successful replication is tied to student outcomes. Reading Recovery is unique in its collection of outcome data on every child. Various reporting systems have been used in countries implementing Reading Recovery, with full accountability calling for describing the outcomes for all children served by the program. There are two optimal outcomes for children served by Reading Recovery, and both are positive: Children may be successfully discontinued from the program or recommended for additional assessment with consideration for longer-term assistance. Both outcomes benefit the individual child and the system.

Reading Recovery uses replication studies to document program outcomes for all children served, adhering to duplication of methods, instruments, and time lines across numerous sites. "Replication is important in all sciences because it is through replication that scientists verify research results" (Frymier et al. 1989, 228).

Reading Recovery has used two types of replication methodology to determine program effectiveness: systematic replication and simultaneous replication (Lyons 1998). In reporting on thirteen years of data in the United States, Lyons found consistent outcomes for children served in English and in Spanish. A large majority of the children with opportunities for full programs were successful in reaching literacy performance within an average range of their classrooms. Similar findings are reported in New Zealand (Clay 1993b; Kerslake 1998) and England (Hobsbaum 1995). Confidence in Reading Recovery is therefore increased through repeated results with different students across different settings.

There is also evidence across several countries that the effects of Reading Recovery are long lasting (Askew et al. 1998; Clay 1993b; Hobsbaum 1995; Rowe 1995; Shanahan and Barr 1995). Several of these studies further indicate that school experiences following Reading Recovery tend to distribute former Reading Recovery children across a range more similar to that of the general school population (Rowe 1995).

Sustained Effort Is Required for Success

Beyond attention to the initial implementation, tremendous effort is required to sustain any successful program. Reading Recovery implementers recognize a number of factors that are critical for sustaining strong innovations.

Shared ownership of the program is essential (Fullan 1985) for sustaining a successful implementation. The first principle for guiding both long-term and short-term reforms of instructional support programs is that "all staff are responsible for the education of all students" (Allington and Walmsley 1995, 26.)

Implementers across Reading Recovery sites are creating district-level teams and school-based teams as structures for building shared understandings and for solving program problems (Sievering and Sorsen 1994). Over a period of years, team members learn from their Reading Recovery teacher leaders, site coordinators, and teachers how an effective Reading Recovery program can be implemented to serve the children in the school and the system. Administrators at all levels are essential to the communication among stakeholders.

These Reading Recovery teams must learn to run their own programs by addressing issues such as (a) identifying the stakeholders and their roles; (b) creating the interface between Reading Recovery and comprehensive literacy initiatives for the school or system; (c) determining Reading Recovery staffing needs; (d) developing a plan for moving toward full implementation; (e) creating funding options to ensure adequate staffing; (f) setting priorities for ensuring daily lessons during the year and extending services as feasible; (g) documenting program effectiveness; and (h) making the program effects visible to others in the school, the community, and the district.

Sustaining high-quality teaching and training is also essential for program success. The selection of highly successful Reading Recovery teachers and teacher leaders underlies the potential for success. Skillful teachers are needed for children who require special help. In addition to needing experience with children whose progress is normal, Reading Recovery teachers must be flexible in doing different things with different children. High-quality ongoing training must complement the quality of these teachers' initial training. Continuing sessions for trained Reading Recovery teachers represent the assistance required for the refinement of teaching expertise and for responding to changes in schools.

To sustain a successful Reading Recovery program, schools and systems work tenaciously toward full coverage or full implementation. A school or a system has reached full implementation when there is sufficient trained-teacher time available to serve all of the children defined as needing the service in the school, the district, or the state. Only at the stage of full coverage will there be a dramatic decrease in the number of children with reading and writing difficulties in subsequent grades. An established plan for reaching full implementation makes it easier to allocate the necessary resources to meet the program goals.

Clay (1994) defines partial implementation as a time to be lived through and a period that reveals all the implementation difficulties. It is a time for persistence and a focus on the success of individual students. As schools and districts move toward full coverage, many problems disappear. Flexible staffing plans are important in working toward full implementation. Schools with a cadre of trained Reading Recovery teachers have the capacity for serving all needy children within a workable and flexible framework.

To sustain any successful program, schools and systems must document their programs. Visible outcomes influence program continuation and improvement. While student outcomes for Reading Recovery children are reported annually at the district or site level and at the national level, it is also important for schools to the document outcomes of their local programs. Many Reading Recovery school teams are now preparing brief reports that provide feedback on accomplishments and offer data to inform planning.

Finally, successfully sustained interventions have plans for monitoring children after the intervention has ended. Clay (1993b) suggests that schools adopt a watchdog role for former Reading Recovery children and monitor their progress sensitively, providing further help if needed. She cautions that "although Reading Recovery children may perform well in their classes they remain at-risk children for two or more years after completion of their program" (96). Many school teams appoint an advocate for all children served by Reading Recovery, to monitor their subsequent progress and to champion their literacy goals.

Adopting a prevention program such as Reading Recovery is an investment for school systems. That investment is protected only to the extent to which the system adheres to high-quality implementation standards. For example, a lack of commitment to daily instruction for the hardest-to-teach children will probably affect the investment adversely. Outcomes are based on the decisions made by the investors.

Reading Recovery Is One Model for Redesigning Education

Nobel Prize-winning physicist and educational reformer Kenneth Wilson and educational journalist Bennett Daviss (1994) argue that education has no redesign process that enables it to build on its past experience of change. They define a *redesign process* as the integration of research, dissemination, and refinement by which innovations are originated, improved, and made affordable. The redesign process in industry measures improvement against four criteria: "capitalizing on success, improving quality, expanding usefulness, and keeping the selling price of each unit as affordable as possible for as many consumers as possible" (30).

According to Wilson and Daviss, Reading Recovery gives U.S. education a more complete framework than any other single program on which to model a redesign process. They cite Reading Recovery as one of the most successful education reforms in U.S. schools and suggest that it is thoroughly grounded in the process of redesign:

> The program does incorporate several key features of a successful redesign process. It has shaped its methods according to the results of its own and others' research. It has tested and honed its techniques through years of trials and refinements, analogous to industry's processes of product prototyping and test marketing. It equips its specialists with a common body of proven knowledge and skills that allow instructors to tailor each lesson to each child's needs—rather than expecting every child to adapt an identical course of lessons that moves at an inflexible pace. Equally important, the program maintains rigorous systems of self-evaluation or quality control, and offers ongoing training and support to the teachers and schools—"dealers," in effect—that adopt it. (Wilson and Daviss 1994, 50–51)

Wilson and Daviss contend that "Reading Recovery offers education in the United States its first real demonstration of the power of a process combining research, development (including ongoing teacher education), marketing, and technical support in an orchestrated system of change" (76). They suggest that Reading Recovery encourages the process of educational design in three ways:

1. It demonstrates that a well-designed education program can be replicated across a wide array of cultures and locations while yielding consistently superior results.
2. It indicates that an investment of money and effort in educational design can yield dramatic rewards.
3. It demonstrates that when educators find a program that meets these two criteria and can earn a good return, schools are willing to make it a top budget priority.

The Challenge to Implementers

Unlike many other innovations, Reading Recovery has planned for implementation, dissemination, expansion, and continuation. However, there is no room for being content with the current status of implementation. The multiple contexts in which an intervention resides are ever-changing.

> The environment within which the innovation is generated is itself changing. Its success will be affected by the economy, political stability, social expectations, labour market, education's relations to other societal sectors, unions, and the state of technological change and educational development. Financing, decision-making, support structures, size of the system, and the relation of the individual school to the system at large, and the goals of the innovation, are important factors also. Any educational change will be embedded in a network of these factors and any one of the factors may undergo a shift which in turn facilitates or hinders the process of mounting the innovation. (Clay 1992, 41)

Reading Recovery implementation is subject to a network of change forces and thus requires an understanding of these forces. Training of teacher leaders includes attention to change processes. Acknowledging that Reading Recovery is challenging enables implementers to understand and accept the change forces (Fullan 1993) that will inevitably come:

- being able simultaneously to push for change while allowing self-learning to unfold
- being prepared for a journey of uncertainty
- seeing problems as sources of creative resolution
- having a vision without being blinded by it
- having internal cohesion but with an external orientation
- valuing personal change as a route to system change

Therefore, while the model for implementation of this program has created waves of influence, Reading Recovery professionals continue to explore and refine the process of redesign. When Clay first asked what is possible for the children, could we have imagined the impact of what is possible for teachers, for schools, and for systems? The explorations continue across all levels of education systems around the world and create exciting conversations among educators about what is possible.

References

ALLINGTON, R. L., AND WALMSLEY, S. A. 1995. *No Quick Fix: Rethinking Literacy Programs in America's Elementary Schools*. Newark, Del.: International Reading Association.

ASKEW, B. J., AND FOUNTAS, I. C. 1998. "Building an Early Reading Process: Active from the Start!" *The Reading Teacher* 52: 126–134.

ASKEW, B. J., FOUNTAS, I. C., LYONS, C. A., PINNELL, G. S., AND SCHMITT, M. 1998. *Reading Recovery Review: Understandings, Outcomes, and Implications*. Columbus, Ohio: Reading Recovery Council of North America.

BERNARD VAN LEER FOUNDATION. 1991. "Dissemination." *Bernard van Leer Foundation Newsletter* 62 April: 1–11.

BEREITER, C., AND SCARDAMALIA, M. 1993. *Surpassing Ourselves: An Inquiry into the Nature and Implications of Expertise*. Peru, Ill.: Open Court.

BRUNER, J. S. 1964. "Going Beyond the Information Given." In *Contemporary Approaches to Cognition*, J. S. Bruner, E. Brunswik, L. Festinger, F. Heider, K. F. Muenzinger, C. E. Osgood, and D. Rapaport, contributors. Cambridge: Harvard University Press.

CLAY, M.M. 1982. *Observing Young Readers*. Portsmouth, N.H.: Heinemann.

———. 1987. "Implementing Reading Recovery: Systemic Adaptations to an Educational Innovation." *New Zealand Journal of Educational Studies* 22: 35–58.

———. 1990. "The Reading Recovery Programme, 1984–88: Coverage, Outcomes and Education Board District Figures." *New Zealand Journal of Educational Studies* 25: 61–70.

———. 1991a. *Becoming Literate: The Construction of Inner Control*. Portsmouth, N.H.: Heinemann.

———. 1991b. "Reading Recovery Surprises." In *Bridges to Literacy: Learning from Reading Recovery*, edited by D. E. Ford, C. A. Lyons, and G. S. Pinnell, 55–74. Portsmouth, N.H.: Heinemann.

———. 1992. "Reading Recovery: The Wider Implications of an Educational Innovation." In *Prevention of Reading Failure*, edited by A. Watson and S. Badenhop, 22–47. New York: Ashton Scholastic. Reprinted in *Literacy, Teaching and Learning: An International Journal of Early Literacy* 1994, 1: 121–141.

———. 1993a. *An Observation Survey of Early Literacy Achievement*. Portsmouth, N.H.: Heinemann.

———. 1993b. *Reading Recovery: A Guidebook for Teachers-in-Training*. Portsmouth, N.H.: Heinemann.

————. 1994. Report on Meeting on Reading Recovery Implementation, Raleigh, North Carolina. December 5–6, 1994.

————. July, 1995. Can we observe change over time in development? Presentation at the Second International Reading Recovery Institute. Palm Springs, Calif.

————. 1996. "Accommodating Diversity in Early Literacy Learning." In *The Handbook of Education and Human Development: New Models of Learning, Teaching, and Schooling*, edited by D. R. Olson and N. Torrance, 202–224. Cambridge, Mass.: Blackwell.

————. 1997. "International Perspectives on Reading Recovery." In *Handbook of Research on Teaching Literacy through the Communicative and Visual Arts*, edited by J. Flood, S. B. Heath, and D. Lapp, 655–667. New York: Macmillan Library Reference USA.

————. 1998. *By Different Paths to Common Outcomes*. York, Maine: Stenhouse.

COMPTON, C., ASKEW, B. J., FRASIER, D. F., AND RODRIGUEZ, Y. 1995. *Reading Recovery Report: 1998–1995*. Denton, Tex.: Texas Woman's University.

DARLING-HAMMOND, L. 1996. "The Right to Learn and the Advancement of Teaching: Research, Policy, and Practice for Democratic Education." *Educational Researcher* 25: 5–17.

DARLING-HAMMOND, L., AND MCLAUGHLIN, M. W. 1995. "Policies That Support Professional Development in an Era of Reform." *Phi Delta Kappan* 76: 597–604.

ENGEL, B. S. 1984." Interview with Michael Armstrong." *The Elementary School Journal* 84: 350–356.

ERICKSON, F. 1991. Foreword to *Literacy for a Diverse Society: Perspectives, Practices, and Social Policies*, edited by E. H. Hiebert, vii–x. New York: Teachers College Press.

ESCAMILLA, K. 1994. "Descubriendo La Lectura: An Early Literacy Intervention Literacy Program in Spanish." *Literacy, Teaching and Learning: An International Journal of Early Literacy* 1: 57–70.

ESCAMILLA, K., LOERA, M., RUIZ, O., AND RODRIGUEZ, Y. 1998. "Examination of Sustaining Effects in Descubriendo La Lectura Programs." *Literacy Teaching and Learning: An International Journal of Reading and Writing* 3 (2): 59–78.

FRASIER, D. F., ASKEW, B. J., RODRIGUEZ, Y., AND COMPTON, C. 1996. *Reading Recovery Report: 1998–1996* . Denton, Tex.: Texas Woman's University.

FRYMIER, J., BARBER, L., GANSNEDER, B., AND ROBERTSON, N. 1989. "Simultaneous Replication: A Technique for Large-Scale Research." *Phi Delta Kappan* 71: 228–231.

FULLAN, M. G. 1985. "Change Processes and Strategies at the Local Level." *The Elementary School Journal* 85: 391–421.

————. 1993. *Change Forces: Probing the Depths of Educational Reform*. Bristol, Pa.: The Falmer Press.

FULLAN, M., AND HARGREAVES, A. 1991. *What's Worth Fighting for in Your School?* New York: Teachers College Press.

FULLAN, M. G., AND MILES, M. B. 1992. "Getting Reform Right: What Works and What Doesn't." *Phi Delta Kappan* 7: 744–752.

GAFFNEY, J. S., AND ANDERSON, R. C. 1991. "Two-Tiered Scaffolding: Congruent Processes of Teaching and Learning." In *Literacy for a Diverse Society: Perspectives, Programs, and Policies*, edited by E. H. Hiebert, 184–198. New York: Teachers College Press.

GAFFNEY, J. S., AND PAYNTER, S. Y. 1994. "The Role of Early Literacy Interventions in the Transformation of Educational Systems." *Literacy, Teaching and Learning: An International Journal of Early Literacy* 1: 23–29.

GARMSTON, R., AND WELLMAN, B. 1995. "Adaptive Schools in a Quantum Universe." *Educational Leadership* 52: 6–12.

GOODLAD, J. I. 1977. *Networking and Educational Improvement: Reflections on a Strategy.* Washington, D.C.: National Institute of Education.

HOBSBAUM, A. 1995. "Reading Recovery in England." *Literacy, Teaching and Learning: An International Journal of Early Literacy* 1: 21–39.

HUBERMAN, A. M., AND MILES, M. B. 1982. *Innovations Up Close: A Field Study in Twelve School Settings.* Andover, Mass.: The Network, Inc.

JAGGAR, A. M., AND SMITH-BURKE, M. T. 1995. *Follow-up Study of RR Children in Community School District # 2, New York City.* New York: New York University Reading Recovery Project, School of Education.

JOHNSTON, P. H. 1992. *Constructive Evaluation of Literate Activity.* New York: Longman.

———. 1997. *Knowing Literacy: Constructive Literacy Assessment.* York, Maine: Stenhouse.

KERSLAKE, J. 1998. "Reading Recovery Data for 1996." *The Research Division Bulletin.* Wellington, New Zealand: Ministry of Education.

LAVE, J. 1996. "Teaching, as Learning, in Practice." *Mind, Culture, and Activity* 3: 149–164.

LINDFORS, J. W. 1987. *Children's Language and Learning.* 2d ed. Englewood Cliffs, N.J.: Prentice-Hall.

LYONS, C. A. 1998. "Reading Recovery in the United States: More Than a Decade of Data." *Literacy Teaching and Learning: An International Journal of Early Reading and Writing* 3 (1): 77–92.

OFFICE OF HER MAJESTY'S CHIEF INSPECTOR OF SCHOOLS. 1994. "Reading Recovery in New Zealand." *Literacy, Teaching and Learning: An International Journal of Early Literacy* 1: 143–162. Reprinted with permission from HMSO Publications, Norwich.

PINNELL, G. S. 1991. "Teachers and Children Learning." In *Bridges to Literacy: Learning from Reading Recovery*, edited by D. E. DeFord, C. A. Lyons, and G. S. Pinnell, 171–187. Portsmouth, N.H.: Heinemann.

———. 1997a. "An Inquiry-Based Model for Educating Teachers of Literacy." In *Research in Reading Recovery*, edited by S. L. Swartz and A. F. Klein, 6–17. Portsmouth N.H.: Heinemann.

————. 1997b. "Reading Recovery: A Review of Research." In *Handbook of Research on Teaching Literacy Through the Communicative and Visual Arts*, edited by J. Flood, S. B. Heath, and D. Lapp, 638–654. New York: Macmillan Library Reference USA.

PINNELL, G. S., LYONS, C., AND JONES, N. 1996. "Response to Hiebert: What Differences Does Reading Recovery Make?" *Educational Researcher* 25: 23–25.

ROWE, K. J. 1995. "Factors Affecting Students' Progress in Reading: Key Findings from a Longitudinal Study." *Literacy, Teaching and Learning: An International Journal of Early Literacy* 1: 57–110.

SARASON, S. B. 1991. *The Predictable Failure of Education Reform: Can We Change Course Before It's Too Late?* San Francisco: Jossey-Bass.

SHANAHAN, T., AND BARR, R. 1995. "Reading Recovery: An Independent Evaluation of the Effects of an Early Instructional Intervention for At-Risk Learners." *Reading Research Quarterly* 30: 958–996.

SIEVERING, B., AND SORSEN, C. 1994. "The Whole Is Greater Than the Sum of Its Parts." *Network News* Fall: 1–2; 7.

TAYLOR, D. 1990. "Teaching with Testing: Assessing the Complexity of Children's Literacy Learning." *English Education* 22: 4–74.

WANSART, W. L. 1995. "Teaching as a Way of Knowing: Observing and Responding to Students' Abilities." *Remedial and Special Education* 16: 166–177.

WERTSCH, J. V., AND ROGOFF, B. 1984. Editors' Notes in *Children's Learning in the "Zone of Proximal Development,"* edited by V. Rogoff and J. V. Wertsch, 1–6. San Francisco: Jossey-Bass.

WILSON, K. G., AND DAVISS, B. 1994. *Redesigning Education.* New York: Henry Holt.

WOOD, D. 1988. *How Children Think and Learn.* Cambridge, Mass.: Basil Blackwell.

ZUKAV, G. 1979. *The Dancing Wu Li Masters: An Overview of the New Physics.* New York: William Morrow.

Six

Language and Literacy as Epistemology

BRIDIE RABAN

During the last thirty years I have been a reading teacher, researcher, and literacy educator, with an especial interest in the early childhood years. Such specialisation has given me the opportunity to observe many changes and developments in the field of literacy learning and teaching. From an initial emphasis on teaching reading as a series of increasingly sophisticated subskills and abilities that progressed in a linear fashion towards proficiency, my understanding over this period of time has moved to a focus on early literacy, first from the perspective of the learner of literacy, second from that of a learner of language, and more recently as a complex and subtle social constructivism, with the learner making sense of the world at a range of different levels. Clay (1969) in New Zealand, Goodman (1967) in America, and Ferreiro and Teberosky (1982) in Argentina, along with other researchers across the world, demonstrated the internal logic, consistency, and complexity of the learner's activity. Early steps in the process of written-language learning, for instance, were shown to be unlike the activity of the proficient reader and writer, and this finding was to have a profound influence on both theory and practice. Literacy learning has come to be seen within a much larger framework of language learning generally (Snow 1991), and this is paralleled by a focus on making meanings through a range of resources available to the learner (Wells 1986).

These changes and developments in theory and practice have also significantly influenced teacher education; they have not been confined to the knowledge base of reading teachers, but have influenced the knowledge base of all teachers because they concern the related views of the learner, learning generally, and language learning in particular. Whether spoken or written, language has a special place in every education system because it is both the medium and the focus of instruction in teaching reading and writing, and consequently there is now an expected minimum knowledge base required of all teachers. To ensure student progress, therefore, teachers will need to know

- the range and complexity of language
- relationships between language and learning

99

- differences between spoken and written language
- contexts for language learning
- ways of responding to children's spoken and written language
- what makes language work

The Range and Complexity of Language

A traditional model of language (Figure 6–1) has drawn a distinction between spoken and written language on the one hand, and production and reception of language on the other.

What we do when we listen (or read), and what we do when we speak (or write) is to make meanings. Whereas spoken and written language activities are different in many ways, they are the same processes inasmuch as both are creating meanings as the language string progresses. Meanings are not in the words themselves; meanings are in the minds of those who are engaged in the thinking that is being expressed. The highly skilled activities of becoming a reader of your own writing and a listener of your own speech illustrate the necessity to distinguish between these activities. However, the relationship between them will not equate to any simple translation that production

Traditional Model of Language		
	SPOKEN	WRITTEN
PRODUCTION	Speaking	Writing
RECEPTION	Listening	Reading

FIGURE 6–1 *Traditional model of language*

through speaking leads, through development, to reception through reading (Raban 1984, 1988).

The Kingman Report (Department of Education and Science 1988), giving advice to the British government concerning the knowledge about language required by all teachers, used a different model of language and language development.

Language is defined here as inherently variable, with the standard variety being only one kind, and with different varieties of language revealed through specific uses in certain contexts. Language is seen here to relate to intellectual and social development as well as to personal and aesthetic need. Language is acknowledged to express identity, enable cooperation, and confer freedom on those who have access to and control over a wide repertoire of language strategies. Language use is considered active and dynamic, whether the user is speaking or listening. In addition, language is seen here as multifaceted, not only at the level of language structure, but also through use and in variety. Thus, language learning is considered recursive in the sense that through active use, language is extended, enriched, and restructured, not necessarily in any linear fashion. As children experience language through social and intellectual interactions, they become more able to marshal their linguistic resources towards increasing levels of sophistication.

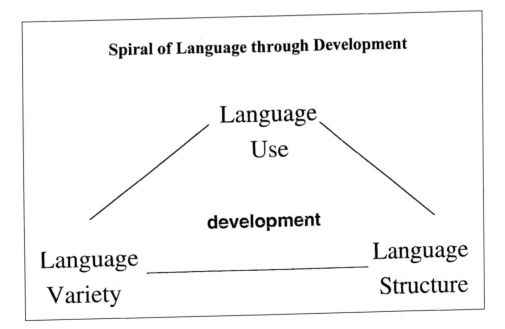

FIGURE 6–2 *Spiral of language through development*

Marie Clay's observations of young children has prompted this view many years before the Kingman Report:

> Observation of children suggests that they do not learn about language on any one level of organisation *before* they manipulate units at higher levels. (Many teaching schemes imply that this is so.) . . . As a child learns . . . there is a rich intermingling of language learning *across* levels which probably accounts in some way for the fast progress which the best children can make. A simplification achieved by dealing firstly with letters, then with words, and finally with word groups may be easy for teachers to understand but children learn on all levels at once. (Clay 1975, 19)

This perceptive interpretation of numerous observations highlights the fact that it isn't language that young children are learning primarily, although they are; they are learning foremost *through* language. With respect to the relationship between spoken and written language and thought, a more intricate model of language in use (Figure 6–3) can map the ground for language and learning within a school context.

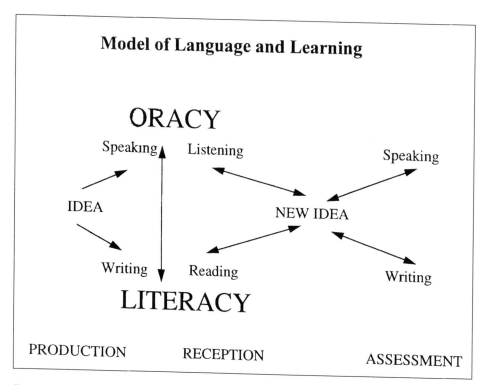

FIGURE 6–3 *Model of language and learning*

Figure 6–3 illustrates how our ideas, our thinking, can be coded in either spoken or written language. However, we need to remember that linguistically coded thought is not the only form of thinking. For example, we can also think visually, artistically, architecturally, and mathematically, as well as musically. Nevertheless, ideas can be expressed through both spoken and written language, and this is the preferred mode for most forms of education. While speaking and writing, we create meanings for ourselves; we recreate them afresh through listening and through reading. Although the activities of production and reception may be different, they share the same process of making meaning. These new ideas can thus be coded in both speaking and writing and are available for inspection by others. We can both demonstrate and rework our ideas for assessment, and this is an integral part of the educative process. The central thread of this model of language in use (Figure 6–3) is the salience of thinking and learning that is taking place through language.

Clearly, the range and complexity of language includes many facets. For instance, first, language cannot be considered apart from the people who use language. Second, all speakers and writers are teachers of language because they constantly demonstrate how language captures and conveys meanings. Third, although all languages are equally effective in achieving this purpose, it is worth remembering that some languages are more powerful than others and consequently render some people more persuasive than others, not necessarily because their arguments are more cogent or more complete. Beyond all these factors, language remains a related set of subsystems over which the young learner comes to gain control with increasing sophistication through using language for a variety of purposes and engaging with others who provide appropriate and supportive feedback. In this sense language is defined by audience, by context, and by purpose.

Peters (1985) illustrates clearly how writing that is rich in purpose lifts the child's writing ability way beyond what is typically produced through normal classroom demands. Peters gives many examples, and in one notable example of writing from the same six-year-old boy, she notes that his written work in class is repetitive and stilted:

I went to norfolk.
I went to the beach.
I went to (crossed out) to (crossed out) the slot machines.
I went fishing.
I went swimming.

The teacher responds to this piece of writing, written as a response to a request for writing about the summer holidays, with "well tried." This same child, at the same time at home, placed a letter to the teeth angels under his pillow. Because the child was asking for some money for a tooth that was now lost, extra care was taken, not only with the spelling, crossing out, and handwriting, but also with the syntax and clarity of the writing. This letter comes off the page with a verve and vitality missing from the classroom piece:

> Dear teeth Angels I lost my tooth under the seat of my car please can you find for me
> and give me the money

Peters provides us with many more examples of what she refers to as "urgent" writing, where it is important for writers to make themselves understood because real and, at times, vital information is being conveyed. Here we see the power of audience, context, and purpose in supporting and extending language learning for another student. For Stella, the sale of her family was a real concern. She left this notice on the board at school:

> <u>For</u>   <u>Sale</u>
> <u>Mum</u> and <u>dad</u> 2 ´p
> dad in bad condition
> mum in half good and bad
> condition brother and sister
> bad condition price 15p
> See me <u>Stella</u> class 4B
> in playground.
> (source unknown)

Clearly, Stella is in earnest, and she is keen not to be seen as being either greedy or unreasonable in her offer. If she asks for too much money, she might jeopardise the deal.

Relationships Between Language and Learning

Language and learning can be seen in relation along a continuum that extends from *transmission* to *interpretation*. This continuum represents how talk in classrooms is organised for different purposes. At the extreme of transmission alone, the one who "knows" does all the talking. If this person is the teacher, then there is little room for student talk, as what is inside the teacher's head is transmitted to the students through talk. At the other extreme, students are invited to join in the talk, which is designed by the teacher to encourage and engage the students in making their own meanings through interpretation and collaborative exchanges.

The transmission extreme of this continuum offers a particular view of learning. This is a view of sending or transmitting knowledge between speakers and listeners or readers and writers. This view is coupled with a sense that students will succeed or fail to receive the transmitted messages, which will then need to be repeated over and over again to achieve successful transmission. Within this context, successful transmission of information is assessed through students' talk and writing as far as these language modes literally reflect knowledge. From this point of view, learning is equivalent to an accumulation of information, similar to threading beads onto a string—it assumes that meaning is to be found in the words themselves, it focuses on outcomes, and it has a product orientation. An overemphasis on this model of learning can inadvertently render students as passive learners.

The view at the other extreme of this spectrum sees language as a means of interpretation. Students interpret what they hear and read by drawing on their previous experience, and by successive approximations they come to understand; they come to learn. In an important sense at this extreme of interpretation, knowledge is filtered by individual experiences. Educationally, from this point of view, talking and writing will be for learning and not for assessment. Students make knowledge their own; they make meanings for themselves rather than memorise what their teachers tell them. This interpretation focuses on a process orientation, and at this end of the continuum, students are perceived as active learners with responsibility for their own understanding. The extreme of this view will see few of us sharing conventional notions of the world, but this commonality becomes possible because the majority of our experiences are similar and we thereby bring similar knowledge bases to bear on fresh experiences. In this way, we all have the chance for agreed understandings.

Within this context of interpretative understandings, collaborative learning has a powerful role. Sharing and communicating with others enables the individual student to explore and create a depth of meaning not always available to the isolated thinker. It is at the overlay of cognitive, social, and communicative activity that students develop their own understandings; through communication and collaboration with others, they develop shared understandings.

When students are using talk in collaborative learning, as teachers we need to know: What are they doing? How are they learning? and What are they learning? When we observe what they are doing, we see students sharing, sorting, reviewing ideas, justifying points of view, reordering, questioning, speculating, arguing, supporting with evidence, summarising, hypothesising, building on previous ideas, getting information, seeking clarification, and exploring cause and effect. Through these processes they are not only refining their language, but also refining their thinking. They are reordering what they already know, applying what they know to a new context, and making connections between already known information and between the known and the new information. These students will be building bridges between where they have been with their thinking and where they are going.

In this intellectual adventure, students are learning to understand information in fresh and creative ways; they are learning to elicit appropriate information, to make their thinking explicit, to share their attitudes, and to use the language of leaning effectively. Therefore, in asking ourselves the question Why should students talk?, we see that talk can help them to connect new ideas to old ones. Indeed, in this sense, talking may help learning more than listening because language accesses past experience, which will provide a context for new learning. This is a powerful activity within the contexts of, in particular, guided reading and writing.

What we are discovering is that for students to succeed, the following criteria need to be met. First, students will need a clear understanding of the tasks teachers set and the motivation to perform them. Second, students need to know the criteria by which successful performance will be judged. Third, students will require opportunities to explore ideas, as well as to reach conclusions. Students will also require the support of someone more knowledgeable who extends and encourages them whilst still leaving them with the initiative and responsibility (Wells 1980).

Differences Between Spoken and Written Language

In contrast to spoken language, writing has the capacity to transcend time and space, and in this way overcomes the needs of immediacy. In this sense written language provides for readers who may not have the common shared purpose typically assumed of speakers and listeners. For instance, speakers and listeners experience a wealth of nonverbal information that acts as support for meaning. Similarly, speakers can modify what they say in ways that writers can't; speakers can do this by registering in the moment what listeners are reflecting back to them in terms of understandings. The writer, on the other hand, can assume nothing. The writer will need to be explicit concerning everything for the reader, because writers can never make assumptions about their readers, who are probably transposed from them in both time and space. Therefore, in an important sense, text is *hard* to read. The activity of reading is monotonous and uninterrupted. It defies the give-and-take of speakers and listeners that lends conversations the opportunity of interruptions, keeping the process more alive and interesting for immediate participants. Because of this, as writers, we can make no assumptions about our reader, and we have to put everything in the text. In an important sense, the final organisation of written material bears little, if any, relationship to the writer's thinking processes.

However, examples of young children's early attempts at written language show their reliance on their knowledge of spoken language. For instance, Stuart can show his reader that he knows how to say "EEEEE.T." by stressing the E and putting many horizontal lines there in the letter E itself. He also knows about capital letters and full stops for abbreviations, although this knowledge is less secure, as he places full stops both before and after the letters E.T.

Contexts for Language Learning

Children's homes and the schools they enter can offer very different contexts for language learning. Hannon (1995, 39) points out these distinctions in a number of ways. For instance, at home the child is in a close and continuous relationship with a few adults, problems encountered are authentic, and conversations can be extended and often happen spontaneously. In contrast, children may well experience a discontinuity in these experiences when they start attending school. In school, the adults are less familiar, problems are contrived, conversations are brief, and frequently spontaneity can be discouraged with such a large number of students in the same room. Because the context for language learning in school can be so very different from that at home, teachers need to plan for talk in school rather than just let it happen. Students will require the kinds of talk that support and assist new ideas and concepts, that demonstrate understanding, and that give them increasing responsibility over their own learning.

Working with groups of students in this way will require teachers to manipulate a wide repertoire of skills, including strategies that promote talk. These strategies will include brainstorming ideas; sharing, writing, and telling a story; giving instructions and directions; telling or asking someone else and reporting back; solving a problem together or investigating something; and drawing, painting, model-making, dramatisation, role-play, and interviewing someone. These interactive opportunities are typically rich with meaning for children within the context of their own homes. In particular, these kinds of talk are determined by their usefulness. Throughout children's experience of these opportunities, their language learning appears continual, effortless, and incidental to the main purpose of their activities. Language learning in these instances will be both collaborative and vicarious as children both experience and observe successful interactions, through language, that achieve their ambitions and their different purposes. A further characteristic of successful language learning under these circumstances will be the chance for children to reach towards a more sophisticated linguistic repertoire and to make approximations while doing so, but without the risk of a sense of failure.

At the start of school, these characteristics of successful language learning may need to be carried across into school to provide children with a sense of continuity. For instance, once students feel that their performance is falling short of expectations, apart from their desire to get things done, they may well stop exploring their world through language and, incidentally, cease to explore language itself, thereby limiting their access to this rich resource for their learning and their thinking. Some of the kinds of talk that will contribute to continued learning include reporting, informing, telling, explaining, questioning, exploring, suggesting, hypothesising, imagining, evaluating, speculating, responding to questions, narrating, arguing, persuading, summarising, collaborating, and expressing feelings. Indeed, the significance of talk in school will depend on the roles that communicators take (Howe 1989). For example, students need to have the opportunity to be "experts" while their teacher takes on the role of "skillful ignoramus." In this way a communication gap can be created between the speaker and the listener, as students use increasingly precise language to inform a naive listener. Students need to experience both of these roles so that they can feel the pressure that this places on their language. The need to explain ideas clearly and precisely, the need to answer increasingly focused questions, the need to make yourself understood and to understand will put language under a press that results in language growth, learning, and development. As Barnes (1976) has pointed out:

> It is when students are required to use language to grapple with new experience, or to order old experience in a new way, that they are most likely to find it necessary to use language differently. (76)

Ways of Responding to Students' Work

During the early stages of teaching literacy, the language experience approach has taken on a significant role in combining spoken and written language in a dynamic fashion. Language experience draws on individual children's spoken language resources and enables them to watch what they say being transformed into written language. There has long been tension between two points of view. One says that the scribe should write exactly what the child says, nonstandard forms and all. The other argues that the scribe should translate the child's spoken trace to the standard form of language. While for the teacher, the urge may be conventionally to standardise the child's speech in writing, we know that children will read back exactly what they have said, regardless of what the scribe writes. Because of this, and also because one of the purposes of the activity is to find an opening into literacy, it seems counterproductive to change what the child says in any way. However, giving children access to standard forms of their language still resides at the heart of language education.

Edwards (1985) identifies a way of achieving all these positive objectives. She uses as an example a script from Mrs R.'s class, which is composed of many students from non-English-speaking backgrounds. Mrs R. writes precisely what each child says. In one example, she writes

> I went to ballet. You can do
> gymnastics. They done gymnastics
> and I done ballet.

In response, Mrs. R. initially remarks on the content of what the child has said, then models appropriate grammatical form, thereby illustrating to the child the value placed on her efforts, while at the same time extending her linguistic repertoire. Mrs. R. responds by writing:

> What an energetic crowd!
> I did ballet when I was little too.

Teacher comments of this kind follow the pattern of responding first to the content of the child's message and only second responding to the surface features of the language, not by overt correction, but by using the more subtle and powerful resources of modeling and demonstration. By responding in writing to children's writing, we can leave a trace that indicates to others that we have a positive strategy for dealing with nonstandard forms of students' language.

Below are other examples of this response strategy.

> S: Me and Dad and Mum and Michael and Fluffy went for a walk. Fluffy got lost and he crawled into a snake's body. He tried to get out. Then he breaked the snake's body.
> T: I'm glad he got out!

He broke the snake wide open!

S: My Mummy flied to the beach.

T: Did she enjoy it?
   I flew to the beach for a holiday as well.

S: Isobel swam to the deep end. She almost drowned, she friend's mum throwed out a ring to save her.

T: She didn't drown?
   Her friend's mum threw out a ring just in time.

S: And then while they was in their beds asleep, well, Santa came down the chimney.

T: Did Santa leave some presents? I bet they were surprised in the morning.

Responding in this way shows the teacher in the role of active listener, responding to content first and then modeling and demonstrating standard form. In an important sense, by responding to the meaning of the written message first, an appropriate emphasis is placed on the ideas and thoughts rather than the language for its own sake. As Marie Clay (1991, 291) reminds us, "reading with understanding is more than reading the words."

What Makes Language Work?

As native speakers ourselves, we have intuitions that alert us when language goes wrong. This ability is at the basis of jokes and other forms of verbal humour, intended or not. Banner headlines in newspapers and advertisements are notorious opportunities for such linguistic slips. For instance, the *New Scientist* advertised recently for a "Sterile Production Manager" and the "for sale" column of the local newspaper listed "A pram for a baby with rubber tyres" along with "A house for a family of three with electric fittings." Native speakers will be aware of something odd about these snippets but may not be able to analyse why they are inappropriate. Effective language learning, however, takes place when this implicit awareness is consolidated by explicit language knowledge (Carter 1991). The jury is still out on whether this intuition involves the explicit teaching of grammar, for instance, or the explicit and systematic experience of language in use for a variety of purposes.

Teachers' beliefs and practices will be demonstrated through our uses of language within contexts of learning. For instance, they are shown through the patterns of relationships between teachers and students. What kinds of emphasis are placed first on the teacher as the sole source for knowledge? Second, as teacher control through selected student responses? Third, using the teacher as a resource with students communicating together? Or last, students engaging in self-communication by talking to themselves? Beliefs concerning the role of language in teaching and learning are demonstrated by what form the curriculum takes: a set of facts, a body of knowledge, or ways of inquiring. How schools and classrooms are organised for learning and teaching will also reveal beliefs and understandings concerning what happens in classrooms.

Are students grouped into classes by age or otherwise? Are small groups and learning centres familiar classroom management techniques? Who does most of the talking and for what purposes?

The work of Marie Clay (1991) has added considerable insight to the debate concerning learning language, learning about language, learning, and teaching. Although many may argue about appropriate theories of language for educational purposes, Clay has helped me to clarify that I am working with a theory of learning, and with a theory of teaching (Wells 1994). These theories of learning and of teaching are in their turn informed by theories of epistemology that embrace knowledge as being both given and public *and* created and personal. Between these extremes of rationalism and postmodern perspectives, students experience and come to understand their world through the meanings beyond the words of any language. Indeed, my own experience of the National Oracy Project in Britain strengthens this argument further, and rereading the collected papers (Norman 1994) reminds me that these views and ideas continue to fascinate both scholars and practitioners.

References

BARNES, D. 1976. *From Communication to Curriculum.* Harmondsworth, England: Penguin Books.

CARTER, R., ED. 1991. *Knowledge About Language.* London: Hodder and Stoughton.

CLAY, M. M. 1969. "Reading Errors and Self-Correction Behaviour." *British Journal of Educational Psychology* 39: 47–56.

———. 1975. *What Did I Write?* Auckland: Heinemann.

———. 1991. *Becoming Literate: The Construction of Inner Control.* Auckland: Heinemann.

DEPARTMENT OF EDUCATION AND SCIENCE. 1988. "The Kingman Report." Report of the committee of inquiry into the teaching of English language. London: Her Majesty's Stationery Office.

EDWARDS, V. K. 1985. "Beyond Babel." In *Practical Ways to Teach Writing,* edited by B. Raban. East Grinstead, England: Ward Lock.

FERREIRO, E., AND TEBEROSKY, A. 1982. *Literacy Before Schooling.* Portsmouth, N.H.: Heinemann.

GOODMAN, K. S. 1967. "Reading: A Psycholinguistic Guessing Game." *Journal of the Reading Specialist* 6: 126–135.

HANNON, P. 1995. *Literacy, Home and School: Research and Practice in Teaching Literacy with Parents.* London: The Falmer Press.

HOWE, A. 1989. *Expanding Horizons.* Sheffield, England: National Association for Teachers of English.

NORMAN, K. 1994. *Thinking Voices: The Work of the National Oracy Project.* London: Hodder and Stoughton.

PETERS, M. 1985. "Purposeful Writing." In *Practical Ways to Teach Writing*, edited by B. Raban. East Grinstead, England: Ward Lock.

RABAN, B. 1984. "Observing Children Learning to Read." Ph.D. diss., University of Reading, Faculty of Education.

———. 1988. "Language and Literacy Relationships: Some Reflections." *British Journal of Educational Research* 14 (3): 12–25.

SNOW, C. E. (1991). "The Theoretical Basis for Relationships Between Language and Literacy in Development." *Journal of Research in Childhood Education*, 6: 30–46.

WELLS, C. G. 1980. "Apprenticeship in Meaning." In *Children's Language* Vol. 2, edited by K. Nelson. New York: Gardiner Press.

———. 1986. *The Meaning Makers: Children Learning Language and Learning to Use Language*. Portsmouth N.H.: Heinemann.

———. 1994. "The Centrality of Talk in Education." In *Thinking Voices*, edited by K. Norman. London: Hodder and Stoughton.

Seven

The Gift of Story

CHARLOTTE S. HUCK

Narrative as a Way of Thinking

Each person's life is a story. We read stories about others to know who we are and how others feel and think, and to discover what we might become. We read stories to experience more lives than the one we are allotted. Stories are universal. Ursula Le Guin (1989) tells us that there have been societies that did not use the wheel, but there have been no societies that did not tell stories. Story telling or narrative is a way of thinking. We tell ourselves stories throughout our days. Barbara Hardy (1978) of the University of London suggests that all our constructs of reality are in fact stories that we tell ourselves about how the world works. She maintains that the narrative is the most common and effective form of ordering our world today:

> We dream in narrative, day-dream in narrative, remember, anticipate, hope, despair, believe, doubt, plan, revise, criticize, construct, gossip, learn, hate, love by narrative. In order to really live, we make up stories about ourselves and others, about the personal as well as the social past and future. (13)

If narrative is characteristic of adults' thinking, it is even more typical of children's. It has been estimated that some 80 percent of children's thinking can be described as narrative. Send a naughty child to his room, and he thinks of all the places that he'll run away to, just as in Sendak's (1963) *Where the Wild Things Are*. This is the appeal of this classic story: It taps into the wellsprings of all the stories that children have been telling themselves. Yet it provides a more satisfying conclusion than many of their imaginings, for it ends with Max's coming home to find his supper waiting for him as a symbol of his mother's love and reconciliation. Stories can resolve problems even for young children.

Adapted from a speech presented at the Reading Recovery Conference, Columbus, Ohio, January 30, 1994

Babies Need Books

We need to plant the love of reading early and deep. Marie Clay recognized this when she and Dorothy Butler wrote *Reading Begins at Home* in 1979. Butler (1998) has just revised this book. She tells us that when a parent cuddles a child and reads a story, such as *Time for Bed* (Fox 1993), the youngster associates reading and story with love and pleasure. Much talk usually accompanies a parent's sharing of this story as mother or father points to a baby colt or lamb in the pictures. Huttenlocher (1997) has found that the size of a toddler's vocabulary is strongly correlated with how much the mother talks to the child. The critical factor appears to be the number of times a child hears different words spoken to her. Reading stories aloud becomes the perfect means to share a large vocabulary of different words and to attach special meaning to them in relation to the child's life experiences.

Recent research on brain development confirms the importance of the practice of reading aloud to very young children. Some of the most interesting brain research has been done by Huttenlocher (1997), who found that the brain quadruples in size from birth to age three. The number of synapses, or connections, increases twenty-fold in the first months of life and peaks at eight months of age. Those synapses that are not stimulated tend to slough off, until they stabilize at around seven years of age. Hubel and Wiesel (1970) demonstrated this effect dramatically by sewing the eyelids of kittens together so they received no visual stimulation. When their eyes finally were opened, the physical structure of the eye was normal, but the cats were "blind," showing that if the brain cells are not stimulated at the right time, they will be lost.

Reading aloud to the young child is vital for the early stimulation of the brain, as are talking, singing, and hearing nursery rhymes. We have quantities of research that proves that reading aloud to young children has a positive effect on their ability to learn to read. In her classic study of early readers, Durkin (1966) found they all came from homes that valued books, and they had all been read to from an early age. Thorndike's (1973) study of reading in fifteen different countries found the same thing to be true around the world. An important longitudinal study by Wells (1986) proved that hearing stories in the preschool years can have lasting benefit. He followed children from the time they could speak through school-leaving age. Of all the activities he studied in this nine-year period, only one was significantly related to the acquisition of literacy—listening to stories. Anderson et al.'s report (1985) for the Commission on Reading again emphasized that the single most important activity for building the knowledge required for eventual success in reading is reading aloud to children.

MacLean, Bryant, and Bradley (1987) suggest that sharing nursery rhymes with preschool children makes a difference in their learning to read. These psychologists believe that rhymes develop children's sensitivities to the sounds of language just as the alliteration of "Little Boy Blue come *blow* your horn" emphasizes the beginning sound of B. Rather than teach phonemic awareness directly, we should share many rhymes and finger plays with children and let them absorb these sounds naturally.

114

The Power of Reading Aloud

What is so powerful about children hearing stories read aloud? First of all, hearing a good story read aloud provides fun and entertainment. I can think of one father who read *Froggy Gets Dressed* (London 1992) with such gusto and expression that his four-year-old son took it to bed with him and asked for his father to read it every night for weeks! He joined in on the "F-r-o-o-g-y" calls and in no time was "reading" the story to his best friend. Never underestimate the power of a well-loved story to take a child into reading.

In addition to providing pleasure and motivation to read, reading aloud provides many educational values. It develops book language, which is not the same as every-day conversation. One child, who was telling about something that had happened in her family, said that her father "exclaimed." We seldom use that word in talking, so she must have learned it from hearing it read aloud or reading it herself. Another six-year-old stumbled over the word *sturdy* when he was reading about the third little pig's brick house. "Oh," he said, "that's just another word for strong." A new word was learned in the context of a story.

Besides developing vocabulary, reading aloud helps the young child develop what Marie Clay (1982) calls "concepts of print":

Where to begin on a page.
Directionality: that we read from top to bottom and from left to right.
The function of some punctuation, such as a question mark.
The one-to-one correspondence of words.
The stability of print: it always tells the same story.

Without direct teaching, a child absorbs this knowledge by sitting next to a parent and observing his reading. I remember reading *The Blanket* (Burningham 1976) to an eighteen-month-old toddler. After we had read it three times, she wanted to hear it again. So I gave her the book upside down with the back cover facing up and said, "All right, only you tell me where to begin." She turned the book right side up, opened the pages, went past the title page, and pointed to the first word in the text! She knew all those concepts of print at eighteen months. And she certainly understood something about the ability of print to give her the same pleasure in a story that she asked to hear four times!

Creating Rich Literacy Environments

While we are laying a foundation for the child's beginning reading by reading to him, it is important that the child derive pleasure from such activities. I can think of one couple that is creating a rich literacy environment in their home. Their children are surrounded by books. There are books in every room of the house. The children each have bookcases in their bedrooms, filled with books they have received for Christmas and birthdays. Their parents read to them four and five times a day. They go to the library at least once a week for story time and to check out books. Before their vacation in northern Wisconsin, they checked out such books as *Up North at the Cabin* (Chall 1992), *Salt Hands* (Aragon 1989), and *All the Places to Love* (MacLachlan 1994). Books enrich every one of their experiences and are a part of all that this family does. These children see their parents reading and enjoying books much in the same way that Coles (1989), as described in his book *The Call of Stories*, observed his parents reading and enjoying books together. It is no wonder that both these children are beginning to read *before* they go to school with seemingly no instruction at all. Yet, of course, they have received quantities of instruction, by example. They are learning to read as naturally as they learned to talk and walk.

It would be wonderful if all children were as fortunate as are those of my friends, but of course they are not. Many middle- and upper-class children today come from literacy-deprived homes. They may have a computer and TV, but no books. They never see their parents read, because they do not read. Other children are living in real poverty without adequate shelter, food, or clothing. Their first encounter with books may be on their first day of school.

Schools need to create the same rich literacy environment that my friends have in their home. Every classroom should be flooded with books. There should be low bookshelves with books displayed at the child's eye level. Primary teachers should read aloud three to four times a day—not just on Friday afternoon. I can think of one teacher who regularly went to the public library to take out books for her class. She would return with bags full of books and enthusiastically talk about each title, sometimes giving one child a book she had carefully chosen just for him. She made the very selection of books exciting.

You should be able to walk into a classroom and recognize that this is a teacher who values books and wants her students to become book lovers. I remember visiting one first grade where there must have been twenty versions of Little Red Riding Hood on a table. The children had book-marked all the pictures of the wolves in the stories. Then they talked about which wolf was the scariest one, the funniest one, the largest one. The children had made a large story map of Little Red Riding Hood that showed her route through the woods from her house to her grandmother's house. Dictated captions labeled the two houses, the woods, the wolf, and the woodcutter.

In another activity, two children were arranging the books on one bookshelf into special categories. They determined what those categories should be, so they had fat books, Mother Goose books, books by Pat Hutchins, the "Three" books like *The Three Little Pigs*, and books with pretty pictures on their covers. As childish as these categories were, they included an author grouping because the children were studying the books by Pat Hutchins, and two genre groupings, Mother Goose and folktales (identified by the specific motif of "three"). Looking for pretty pictures on the covers provided an opportunity for much discussion and decision making. In brief, this was a classroom that reflected children's enjoyment of and involvement with books.

Books also were used to enrich all areas of the curriculum. Before taking a nature walk, the children heard the story of *What Joe Saw* (Hines 1996). Then each of them tried to be as thorough in their observations as Joe was. They drew careful pictures of what they wanted to report about their observations. Some of them brought back specimens, which they labeled and displayed. They used simple identification books to find the names of their samples. Books were used for both story and reference in this exciting classroom.

Not only should classrooms have well-stocked libraries; every school should have a library and a trained librarian. Two recent large-scale studies report that nearly all elementary teachers are now using trade books in their reading and language arts programs (Canney 1993; Strickland et al. 1994). Unfortunately, the number of school libraries has declined in the last ten years. For example, in California schools spent only seventy-six cents per pupil on trade books compared to the national average of slightly more than seven dollars per student (Gorman 1995). This is a disgrace. Books must be easily and readily accessible if we want our students to become readers.

While a computer in every classroom may be desirable, it will never take the place of many exciting trade books. A child can always put a paperback in her desk drawer or backpack; she can hardly do that with a computer. I firmly believe that children need books, many books, before bytes.

What to Read

Not only should children have access to a quantity of books, but they should be the very best books available for children. Teachers need to select quality literature to read aloud, stories that may be beyond the children's reading ability but not their interest level. I've collected a group of what I call love stories to read to young children. Today so many of our children are neglected and even abused. They need to hear stories of reaffirmation and love. My favorites include *Guess How Much I Love You* (McBratney 1995), *Koala Lou* (Fox 1988), and *Owl Babies* (Waddell 1992). For children who are eight or nine years old, I'll read *Amazing Grace* (Hoffman 1991), *Thank You Mr. Falker* (Polacco 1998), and *Eleanor* (Cooney 1998), all stories that help children identify with the problems of others, that develop compassion and understanding.

One of my favorite quotations is from Chukovsky (1963), a Russian poet and the author of that remarkable book, *From Two to Five*. He says: "The goal of every storyteller consists of fostering in the child, at whatever cost, compassion and humanness, this miraculous ability of man to be disturbed by another being's misfortune, to feel joy about another being's happiness, to experience another's fate as your own" (138).

Young children need to hear stories that will develop their imagination, help them to soar on the wings of another's imagination. Folk- and fairy tales have enriched children's imaginations for many years. Three hundred years after Charles Perrault wrote his first book of fairy tales, I adapted one of them, *Toads and Diamonds*

(1996), for children to read today, and they still delight in the story of the good sister's gift of jewels and flowers and the bad sister's gift of slithering snakes and hopping toads. I also retold my favorite fairy tale from when I was a child, *Princess Furball* (1989). This is a gutsy version of Cinderella, for Furball has no fairy godmother to send her to the ball in a coach; she has to devise her own way of gaining the attention of the king.

Children enjoy comparing the different versions of Cinderella and the good sister/bad sister theme in other books. As they compare the similarities and differences in these stories, they begin to do critical reading, as when they read how different cultures have interpreted similar stories.

Stories set in different time periods or geographical areas stretch children's imaginations to consider what living in that period or place must have been like. Barbara Cooney's remarkable story *Island Boy* (1988) details the life of a young boy growing up on an island off the coast of Maine. Except for the time when he was master of a ship, Matthais lived on the island until he was an old man, just as his father before him had done. In *Hattie and the Wild Waves*, Cooney (1990) describes the life of her mother growing up in an affluent Victorian family. These stories with their beautiful pictures give children a sense of the varied past of our forefathers as much as Laura Ingalls Wilder's *Little House* series give them a sense of the pioneers. Teachers and librarians need to introduce children to these stories to extend their horizons through time and space.

Rereading Stories

Rereading stories is essential to the development of early literacy. Think how many times a child hears bedtime stories. I was in a bookstore not too long ago and was asked to recommend a book for an eighteen-month-old child. I said, "Well you can't go wrong with *Goodnight Moon*" (Brown 1947). A father was standing nearby and overheard me. He spoke up and said: "Just be prepared to read it over and over again."

Very young children do develop favorite books that they request again and again. This is equally true as children begin to take on reading. I can think of one first-grade teacher who each Friday recorded which book each of her children had chosen to read during independent reading time. At first, she said she was concerned when children listed the same book week after week. Then she realized that these were the very children who were becoming readers. Rereading familiar books gave them a feeling of power and success over the process of reading.

Teachers need to reread favorite stories, too. If it is a good book, children will gain more and retain more with each rereading. One of the best primary teachers I know had this to say about reading to children:

> I read to my children a lot—a whole lot! I'll read anywhere from one to three stories at a time. Sometimes I'll reread a favorite story twice. And I read four to five times a day. I read to the whole group, to small groups of four or five children, and to individual children. While I'm reading to the group, I'll encourage them to join in on the

refrains. With individuals I may point to words, talk about what a word is. I put songs, poems, and refrains on chart paper so children will try to read them by themselves. And I'll read stories *over and over again*, just the way children hear bedtime stories. It's not unusual for me to read a book twenty times in one month! (Hepler 1982, 2–3).

How many of you would consider rereading the same story twenty times?

Every Reading Recovery lesson begins with rereading a familiar story. But of all the stories you read with children during their lessons, do you know which ones are their favorites? Perhaps on the last day of the week you could look at all the little books a child had read that week and let him select his favorite to reread. Even going back and rereading a book he read early on in his lessons gives a child a sense of power and accomplishment, because now it is so easy to read. Rereading stories can serve many purposes.

Time for Children to Read

All children must have time every day to read books of their own choosing. We know children and adults are reading less than they did in the past. In fact, George Steiner maintained in his R. R. Bowker Memorial Lecture (1985) that the great age of reading is behind us. Anderson et al. (1985) report that the amount of independent, silent reading children do in school is significantly related to gain in reading achievement. At the same time, they disclosed a study of fifth graders that showed that for the majority of the children, reading from books occupies less than 1 percent of their free time. More than half of these children reported reading less than four minutes a day! If the time children spend reading outside of school is shrinking, we must reorder our priorities and provide more time in school for free reading. Independent reading is a major source of reading fluency.

Even young children in kindergarten and early primary grades should be given time to read books they want to read. The most popular books are usually those with a predictable text that builds on what children already know, such as the days of the week or numbers, or predictable story structures, such as the use of three in folktales. These structures provide a kind of scaffold for children to help them to know what comes next. If, for example, the first Billy Goat Gruff goes trip trapping over the bridge, the child knows that he will be followed by the second Billy Goat Gruff and the third one. Many predictable books are built on the following structures:

- Knowledge of days of the week: Ward (1988) *Cookie's Week.*
- Number knowledge: Carle (1969) *The Very Hungry Caterpillar.*
- Repetition in cumulative stories: Hayes (1986) *This Is the Bear*; Taback (1997) *There Was an Old Lady Who Swallowed a Fly.*
- Use of three in folktales: Barton (1991) *The Three Bears*; Marshall (1989) *The Three Little Pigs*; Galdone (1973) *The Three Billy Goats Gruff.*
- Question and answer stories: Hill (1980) *Where's Spot?*; Martin (1983) *Brown Bear, Brown Bear, What Do You See?*; Williams (1989) *I Went Walking.*

Frequently, children will want to reread a story that a teacher has read aloud. Again, familiarity with the text makes it easier to read. I recall seeing two at-risk first graders working together to read *The Three Bears* after their teacher had read it to them. Looking at the pictures, they told the story to each other except when it came to the dialogue, when they read the text of "Who's been eating my porridge?" and "Who's been sitting in my chair?" They recognized the look of the printed conversation and read it dramatically, even taking the roles of the father bear and the baby bear. Reading to these children had helped them learn to read.

Today we have many "little books" with a single story. These are short, simple tales that children can read with 90 percent accuracy in order to give them a sense of accomplishment. Some of them tell good stories, such as *The Greedy Cat* (Cowley 1983) and *Mrs. Wishy-Washy* (Cowley 1980), but some of them sound like basal reader stories that have been cut apart and made into separate books. It is a disservice to children to keep them reading these books if they can read real books. Increasingly, trade books publishers are producing simple, easy-to-read stories by well-known authors and illustrators. These have the imaginative quality of authentic literature.

I'll never forget watching a boy in Reading Recovery read Wildsmith's (1982) *Cat on the Mat*. He became so excited while rereading it that he hissed like the cat as he was turning to that page. Simple as that story is, it has beautiful pictures, a nasty cat as the main character, a climax, and a predictable plot. I'm convinced that only real books make real readers, books with real stories where something happens. When children have heard many fine books, they become surprisingly sophisticated in their sense of story. They know about characters, actions, plot, and resolution. This sense of story provides a structure that helps children read for meaning. Non-stories or artificial stories written with decodable texts do not provide children with a predictable structure. They may help children pronounce words, but they use forced language and provide little enjoyment. Margaret Meek (1982) reminds us that it is the power of literature to make readers: "Literature, not reading lessons, teaches children to read in ways that no basal reader can, because literature is read, if at all, with passion, with desire."

Making Books Memorable

Besides reading to children and providing time for children to read books of their own choosing, it is important to let children talk about a book, link it to their experiences, somehow make it memorable. I visited one kindergarten that at story time divided the children into groups of five. (They had student teachers and parent assistance, so they could do this.) Each group heard several stories and then had time to talk about the stories. When they heard Henkes's (1993) *Owen*, a wonderful story about Owen and his attachment to his blanket, each child could describe their comfort objects and things that had happened to them. In this way, each child had an opportunity to tell her personal story in relation to the story she had heard.

Teachers have found numerous exciting ways to make books memorable for young children. Many a first-grade teacher has hidden a gingerbread man and then conducted a search throughout the school for the runaway boy. Frequently, the search ends up in the cafeteria, where all the children eat gingerbread men, or in the kitchen, where they bake the cookies themselves. These children can then retell the story during shared reading and illustrate their big book. They can write the recipe and describe how they baked the cookies. Others can write about the search for the runaway boy. Recording what they have just done is one way all children can participate in shared writing.

The teacher can copy the story and send it home in an envelope containing a cut-out gingerbread man, or a fox and an old lady and old man. Then children can reread the story to their parents and retell the story with the cutouts. The next day, they can write their own version of the story in a gingerbread-shaped storybook. Every story can be revisited many times and made memorable with appropriate activities.

One group of first graders chose different folktales to share with the group. Parents were alerted, and children practiced their reading of the story at home. Then each child sat in a specially decorated chair and read their story to the group. They also brought an appropriate treat to go with the story, such as the basket of cookies Red Riding Hood was carrying to her grandmother. When the child finished reading the story, the cookies were passed out, and the reader donated her red cloak to the fairy tale museum. The cloak was labeled and displayed on a fairy tale bulletin-board museum along with a mitten from *The Mitten* (Brett 1989), an artificial snake for *Toads and Diamonds* (Huck 1996), and a thimble for *The Sleeping Beauty* (Hutton 1979).

A group of kindergarten children made a large mural depicting Mother Goose characters. They labeled the characters, then wrote their thoughts in cartoon blurbs above them. Peter Pumpkin says, "I'm glad I put her in a pumpkin shell," while his wife mutters, "I'm going to get out of here soon." The children had read aloud and looked at the illustrations of many versions of Mother Goose tales before they decided which characters to paint.

In addition to Mother Goose or folktale studies, young children enjoy learning about the books by particular author-illustrators, such as Pat Hutchins, Barbara Cooney, or Donald Crews. You will want to read *The Girl with the Brown Crayon* (Paley 1997), by the only kindergarten teacher to have received a MacArthur Fellowship. In this book she describes the many stories that her kindergarten children told and dramatized as the result of a study of the books by Leo Leonni.

Such studies help children see the connections among stories, to begin to build a frame of reference for literature. Just as you don't want to read isolated words, neither do you want to read isolated books. By grouping books by theme, genre, or author, you help children link stories to their experience or to other stories. One of my favorite expressions is "linking is thinking."

Drama is certainly another way to make books memorable. One first-grade group dramatized Tolstoy's (1968) well-loved *The Great Big Enormous Turnip* by letting one child be the father who plants the turnip and then calls his wife to help him pull it up.

She in turn calls the granddaughter, who calls the dog, who calls the cat, who calls the mouse. When they all pull, the turnip comes out. The children made a facsimile of a turnip and put it in a paper bag to be pulled out at the right moment. A simple cumulative story turned out to be a wonderful one to involve many children in its dramatization. The next day another group of children played the story. The dialogue became richer with each reenactment. Most important, the children loved the story. They made life-sized figures of the characters for an outstanding mural, and they wrote about both the dramatizations and how they made their mural.

Teachers need to find creative ways for children to respond to books, as well as ways to make books memorable. In a study of literature-based curricula in six high-poverty schools, Allington (1996) found few art or drama activities linked to the reading that children were doing. These are such simple and obvious follow-up activities to enrich the reading of well-loved stories.

Another disappointment in the Allington study was the weak link that his team observed between reading and writing activities. In my work with teachers, books always served as springboards for children's own writing. After hearing *Goodnight Moon* (Brown 1947), kindergarten children made a class story including their own special "Good Nights" (Huck et al. 1997). Using the language pattern in *Brown Bear, Brown Bear, What Do You See?* (Martin 1983), one group of first graders composed a Halloween book:

> Monster, monster, what do you see?
> I see a white ghost looking at me.
> Ghost, ghost, what do you see?
> I see a black cat looking at me.

Another group synthesized their knowledge of folktales by making their chart read: "Papa Bear, Papa Bear what do you see?" followed by Mamma Bear, Baby Bear, Goldilocks, The Little Red Hen, and the Three Little Pigs.

Children can be encouraged to write to authors, provided they have something that they want to respond to or a sincere question. Just writing to an author for the sake of writing a letter should not be encouraged. I always answer children's letters that are really sincere and original. My favorite comments about *Princess Furball* (Huck 1989) came from second graders' letters with their own spellings:

> Your book reminded me of the golden sun . . . I like the coat of one thousand anamils. I want you to come to this school. I wanted to complement you on your book. . . .
> *Lindsay*

> The best part I liked was when she was all curled up in the tree. How long did it take you to make the book? How did you get the ideas to make the story? The reason that I liked when princess furball was curled up in the tree was because I like bears and she looked like a bear to me. So thats why I liked it.
> *Dinah*

I like you book Princes Furball. My best part was wanh she woke the gowns to the ball. Why was the cook so menh? It wod be nice if you came to our school and talk about your book. Do you like my writing? You are a good writer I tinkeh you are a fabeus writer. You no jusst wate to write . . .

Elizabeth Jane

Two nine-year-olds worked together on a project about stories. They each wrote their explanation of what they thought stories were and then together they composed a story. Let me share one child's definition of a story:

A story is a mind-full of a life of someone or something wich has been writen down on paper. A story is a bit of wrighting that tells of a time that someone or something has had. It mite be just in the mind or it can be real.

That is what a story is.

What greater legacy could a teacher have than to teach children how to read and to love reading at the same time. It lies within the power of each teacher to give children the gift of story—a "mind-full of life."

References

ANDERSON, R. C., HIEBERT, E. H., SCOTT, J. A., AND WILKINSON, I. A. G. 1985. *Becoming a Nation of Readers: The Report of the Commission on Reading*. Washington, D.C.: U.S. Department of Education, National Institute of Education.

ALLINGTON, R. 1996. "Literature-Based Curricula in High-Poverty Schools." In *The First R: Every Child's Right to Read*, edited by M. Graves, P. Van Broek, and B. Taylord. New York: Teachers College Press.

BUTLER, D. 1998. *Reading Begins at Home: Sharing the Joy of Books with Children from Birth to Six*. Rev. ed. Portsmouth, N.H.: Heinemann.

BUTLER, D., AND CLAY, M. 1979. *Reading Begins at Home*. Auckland: Heinemann.

CANNEY, G. 1993. "Teachers' Preferences for Reading Materials." *Reading Improvement* 30: 238–245.

CHUKOVSKY, K. 1963. *From Two to Five*. Translated by M. Morton. Berkeley: University of California Press.

CLAY, M. 1982. *The Early Detection of Reading Difficulties*. Auckland: Heinemann.

COLES, R. 1989. *The Call of Stories*: Boston: Houghton Mifflin.

DURKIN, D. 1966. *Children Who Read Early*. New York: Teachers College Press.

GORMAN, M. 1995. "The Domino Effect, or Why Literacy Depends on All Libraries." *School Library Journal* (April): 27–29.

HARDY, B. 1978. "Narrative as a Primary Act of the Mind." In *The Cool Web: The Pattern of Children's Reading*, edited by M. Meek, A. Warlow, and G. Barton. New York: Atheneum.

HEPLER, S. 1982. *The Best of the Web*. Columbus, Ohio: Center for Reading, Language Arts and Children's Literature, College of Education, The Ohio State University.

HUBEL, D. H., AND WIESEL, T. N. 1970. "The Period of Susceptibility to the Physiological Effects of Unilateral Eye Closure in Kittens." *Journal of Physiology* 206: 419–436.

HUCK, C. ET AL. 1997. *Children's Literature in the Elementary School*. 6th ed. New York: McGraw-Hill.

HUTTENLOCHER, J. 1994. "Synaptogenesis in Human Cerebral Cortex." In *Human Behavior and the Developing Brain*, edited by G. Dawson and K. Fisher. New York: Guilford Press.

———. 1997 Quoted in "How to Build a Baby's Brain," by G. Begley. *Newsweek* special edition (Spring/Summer): 31.

LE GUIN, U. 1989. *The Language of the Night: Essays on Fantasy and Science Fiction*. New York: The Women's Press.

MACLEAN, M., BRYANT, P., AND BRADLEY, L. 1987. "Rhymes, Nursery Rhymes, and Reading in Early Childhood." *Merrill-Palmer Quarterly* 33: 255–282.

MEEK, M. 1982. "What Counts as Evidence in Theories of Children's Literature?" *Theory into Practice* 21:290. Columbus: Ohio State University, College of Education.

PALEY, V. 1997. *The Girl with the Brown Crayon*. Cambridge: Harvard University Press.

STEINER, G. 1985. "R. R. Bowker Memorial Lecture." *Publisher's Weekly*, May 24.

STRICKLAND, D., WALMSLEY, S., BRONKS, G., AND WEISS, K. 1994. *School Book Clubs and Literacy Development: A Descriptive Study*. Rep. No. 2.22. Albany: State University of New York, National Research Center on Literature Teaching and Learning.

THORNDIKE, R. L. 1973. "Reading Comprehension." *Education in 15 Countries: An Empirical Study*, Vol. 3. International studies in education. New York: Holstead Wiley.

WELLS, G. 1986. *The Meaning Makers*. Portsmouth, N.H.: Heinemann.

Children's Books

ARAGON, J. C. 1989. *Salt Hands*. Illustrated by T. Rand. New York: Dutton.

BARTON, B. 1991. *The Three Bears*. New York: HarperCollins.

BRETT, J. 1989. *The Mitten*. New York: Putnam's.

BROWN, M. W. 1947. *Goodnight Moon*. Illustrated by C. Hurd. New York: HarperCollins.

BURNINGHAM, J. 1976. *The Blanket*. New York: Crowell.

CARLE, E. 1969. *The Very Hungry Caterpillar*. New York: World.

CHALL, M. W. 1992. *Up North at the Cabin*. Illustrated by S. Johnson. New York: Lothrop.

COONEY, B. 1988. *Island Boy*. New York: Viking.

———. 1990. *Hattie and the Wild Waves*. New York: Viking.

——— . 1998. *Eleanor*. New York: Viking.

COWLEY, J. 1980. *Mrs. Wishy-Washy.* Illustrated by E. Fuller. Auckland, N.Z.: Shortland.

———. 1983. *The Greedy Cat.* Illustrated by R. Belton. Wellington, N.Z.: Department of Education.

FOX, M. 1988. *Koala Lou.* Illustrated by P. Lofts. San Diego, Calif.: Harcourt, Brace, Jovanovich.

———. 1993. *Time for Bed.* Illustrated by J. Dyer. San Diego, Calif.: Harcourt Brace.

GALDONE, P. 1973. *The Three Billy Goats Gruff.* New York: Seabury Press.

HAYES, S. 1986. *This Is the Bear.* Illustrated by H. Craig. New York: Lippincott.

HENKES, K. 1993. *Owen.* New York: Greenwillow.

HILL, E. 1980. *Where's Spot?* New York: Putnam's.

HINES, A. 1996. *What Joe Saw.* New York: Greenwillow.

HOFFMAN, M. 1991. *Amazing Grace.* Illustrated by C. Binch. New York: Dial.

HUCK, C. 1989. *Princess Furball.* Illustrated by A. Lobel. New York: Greenwillow.

———. 1996. *Toads and Diamonds.* Illustrated by A. Lobel. New York: Greenwillow.

HUTTON, W. 1979. *The Sleeping Beauty.* New York: Atheneum.

LONDON, J. 1992. *Froggy Gets Dressed.* Illustrated by F. Remkiewicz. New York: Viking.

McBRATNEY, S. 1995. *Guess How Much I Love You.* Illustrated by A. Jeram. Cambridge, Mass.: Candlewick Press.

MACLACHLAN, P. 1994. *All the Places to Love.* Illustrated by M. Wimmer. New York: HarperCollins.

MARSHALL, J. 1989. *The Three Little Pigs.* New York: Dial.

MARTIN, B. 1983. *Brown Bear, Brown Bear, What Do You See?* Illustrated by E. Carle. New York: Holt, Rinehart & Winston.

POLACCO, P. 1998. *Thank You Mr. Falker.* New York: Philomal.

SENDAK, M. 1963. *Where the Wild Things Are.* New York: HarperCollins.

TABACK, S. 1997. *There Was an Old Lady Who Swallowed a Fly.* New York: Viking.

TOLSTOY, A. 1968. *The Great Big Enormous Turnip.* Illustrated by H. Oxenbury. London: Heinemann.

WADDELL, M. 1992. *Owl Babies.* Illustrated by P. Benson. Cambridge, Mass.: Candlewick Press.

WARD, C. 1988. *Cookie's Week.* Illustrated by T. de Paola. New York: Putnam's.

WILDER, L. 1953. *Little House in the Big Woods.* Illustrated by G. Williams. New York: HarperCollins.

WILDSMITH, B. 1982. *Cat on the Mat.* Oxford: Oxford University Press.

WILLIAMS, S. 1989. *I Went Walking.* Illustrated by J. Vivas. San Diego, Calif.: Harcourt, Brace, Jovanovich.

Eight

Writing (Dallas) Cowboys: A Dialogic Perspective on the "What Did I Write?" Question

ANNE HAAS DYSON

Wenona and Marcel are discussing their busy lives as hockey players, football team participants, and students. After singing a round of "We Are the Champions," they reminisce and commiserate over their grueling sports schedule.

MARCEL: 'Member they [another hockey team] lost to us last year? We went to the world champions.

WENONA: We *was* the world champions. . . . We gotta play at night time, you know.

MARCEL: And my football game is at night. . . . We gotta play at Arizona, Texas, San Fran//cisco//—

WENONA: //cisco// um Stockton. That's a long way. . . . Now, how we kids gonna do our homework?

Marcel and Wenona were six-year-olds, and their intense discussion took place during the daily writing time in their first-grade class. They were small children, just figuring out this new school task, but they transformed their relationship to each other and to school itself through an imagined context built through talk. In their evoked world, they were competent, powerful people, beset with responsibilities. A favorite movie (*D2: Mighty Ducks*) provided a coach and a group song; and televised football provided them with a team—the Dallas Cowboys—and at least the idea of an itinerary.

Like Marcel and Wenona, children are "scavengers of form and theme" (Goldman, 1988, 143). They build peer cultures—local, emergent, and negotiated—by

The research reported herein was supported through the generosity of the Spencer Foundation, although the findings and opinions expressed are not necessarily shared by that organization. Much-appreciated support was also forthcoming from the Committee on Research of the University of California, Berkeley. This chapter, written in appreciation of Marie Clay, is a variant of the full research report, titled "Coach Bombay's Kids Learn to Write: Children's Appropriation of Media Material for School Literacy"; that report appears in *Research in the Teaching of English*, 1999, 33 (4). I thank my hardworking project research assistant, Soyoung Lee.

appropriating material from available cultural repositories, including the popular media (Dyson 1993, 1997; Sutton-Smith et al. 1995). These verbal play spaces and the use of media texts as play material have become more important in childhood today than they were in earlier times. Physical play space and time have decreased (e.g., because of less free time during recess, more structured after-school programs, unsafe city streets). At the same time, the commercial media have increased children's independent access to story, song, and other forms of cultural expression. Indeed, most children enter school with common textual material from the radio, videos, and television, rather than from adult storytellers or readers.

And yet, in the decades of professional and public preoccupation with matters of letters and sounds, literacy research and pedagogy in the United States have seemed oblivious to this experiential quality of contemporary childhood. Although there is voiced concern about the quality and quantity of available media, there is little attention given to the role of that media in the interplay of children's social and school lives. Children have available, and must learn to differentiate among, an enormous range of texts from diverse institutions, among them family, church, school, and the popular media themselves. Surely all these texts and the complex social lives they index must figure in particular ways into children's literacy learning and thus into their experience of early school curricula.

As a student myself of children's social lives and literacy learning, my imagination was captured by the imagination of Marcel and his friends. I wondered what kinds of shared media experiences undergirded their imagined landscape. How, if at all, did their comfortable maneuvering on that media-saturated landscape assist them in venturing onto the print-saturated ground of school, and especially in their initial forays into school composing? This chapter is drawn from an ethnographic study in Marcel's classroom in which I addressed these questions. It focuses in particular on the children's use of sports media, which are themselves linked to children's movies—for example, *D2: Mighty Ducks* (Arnet, Kerner, and Liberman 1994) and *Space Jam* (Falk et al., 1996)—and, through those movies, popular songs, like "We Are the Champions" (Mercury 1995). Before exploring these questions in this chapter, I explain briefly the perspectives on language learning and child literacy that guided this project.

Children as Voice Borrowers and Text Scavengers

Children learn language through participating in the social practices or activities of their everyday lives. These activities "come packed with [ideologies] about what is natural, mature, morally right, or aesthetically pleasing" (Miller and Goodnow 1995, 6). Thus, children's subjectivities (their senses of themselves and their own possibilities for action) develop along with their symbolic resources and cognitive capacities (Bruner 1990). In the view of the language philosopher Bakhtin (1981), in learning speech, children are entering into social dialogues; they are engaging with particular others in socially valued ways and, at the same time, they are entering ideological ones; that is, they are learning the words available to them, given their role, their status, their place.

Children's senses of possible selves and possible dialogues are quite audible in their story telling and play. They literally appropriate appealing or powerful voices, especially those that are aesthetically marked and affectively charged (e.g., Garvey 1990; Miller et al. 1993; Miller and Mehler 1994). Interwoven in their storytelling and play are complex discourses of "time, space, geography, religion, gender roles, biology, and the natural world" (Nelson 1996, 218). In school, children learn symbolic tools like writing and disciplinary taxonomies and genres that help them gain distance from, differentiate, and recontextualize these discourses in the "scientific" ones of school (Vygotsky 1962).

Learning written language, however, differs in a fundamental way from learning speech, in that it is a more deliberate, less spontaneous process. In learning to speak, children appropriate words that name an experience physically shared with others. These "used" words (Bakhtin 1986) become saturated with meaning and thus became a basis for "inner speech"—the ability to think with words (Vygotsky 1987). In learning to write, children move in quite the opposite direction; they engage with that just-emerging inner speech, reflecting on and choosing words that must themselves be represented on paper.

As Marie Clay noted, children may begin by attending to the outer form of the written system, attempting letter and letterlike marks, and then, with brash confidence or simple trust, asking an adult, "What did I write?" Children seek guidance wherever they can, finding and remembering bits of words from bulletin boards, blackboards, and books; when their alphabetic sense allows, they listen for letter names and sounds in their own pronunciations of words. Not surprisingly, given their grappling with making speech an object on paper, children may also attend to appealing voices and *liftable* texts—bits of texts that call attention to themselves through formal properties of speech or graphics (rhythm, rhyme, layout) and thus stand out from their verbal surroundings (Bauman and Briggs 1990). In Marcel's classroom, for example, along with family and friends' names, children wrote bits of songs, commercials, and superhero themes (e.g., "Go Go Power Rangers").

Given that it is social intention and participation that energize and organizes the complex writing act, children must figure out not only *how* to write but *what* and *why*, given their present lives as children. Control of the writing process begins when children deliberately plan a message and then search for, or invent, spellings. Their efforts, as Clay (1975) suggested, reveal their understandings and confusions about all levels of language at once (e.g., graphic forms, orthographic connections, sentence structures, and semantic sense). And yet messages do not come from thin air, nor do they emerge directly from expressive hearts. Their themes and forms—their very words—come from others; they are improvised revoicings. As individuals we have no choice but to use the public communication systems, and in our complex travels through society's social spheres, we accumulate the used words that are our ticket to societal participation (Bakhtin 1981).

Indeed, the very first composed texts of young schoolchildren may reveal, as surely as Marcel's and Wenona's play, children's powers as scavengers of form and theme, and the diversity of their textual and knowledge resources. Those resources are likely to have roots in social worlds other than that of the school itself, whose "selective traditions" and particular textual values must be learned (Dyson 1993; Williams 1965, 66). Moreover, children are apt to offer words to peers and teachers who do not share their own tastes, interests, and values—football, for instance. Children may be surprised by the unintended interpretations and unanticipated responses their words bring, which is why a deliberateness about crafting words may be linked to a deliberateness (i.e., a sophistication about) social worlds (Bakhtin 1981), and this link may be especially evident for children privileged to attend socioculturally diverse classrooms like Marcel's (Dyson 1997). For this reason, too, the question, "What did I write?" is not only the question of the naive young writer, but also of the most sophisticated one: The meanings of our texts are revealed only in the meeting of authors and others in particular moments.

In brief, media texts provide children with conceptual knowledge, communicative forms and features, and a pool of potential characters, plots, and themes. Thus, the freely written texts of even the very youngest schoolchildren are situated within a complex of overlapping social worlds, and inherent in this diversity—this Bakhtinian "hybridization"—are children's challenges as writers. Children grapple with the semiotic, graphic, and linguistic conventions of written language, yes. But they also grapple with the varied social dialogues or relationships they can enact through writing, and, moreover, with the ideological tensions undergirding those dialogues. After a review of methods, I illustrate this point with the "epic rivalries" of sports media as situated within the local loyalties and traditions of Marcel and his friends (Willis 1990, 112).

A Child Culture and Its Texts: Rita, Marcel, and the Brothers and the Sisters

Marcel's (K–5) school was officially described as having the "greatest crosstown span" in this East San Francisco Bay district (i.e., the greatest socioeconomic mix). Approximately half the school's children were African American, approximately one-third were European American, and the rest were of varied Latino and Asian ancestries. Manuel's first-grade teacher was Rita, who had begun teaching in the London primary schools of the 1960s. Rita's curriculum included both open-ended activities (e.g., writing workshop, where the children wrote and drew relatively freely, followed by class sharing) and more teacher-directed ones (e.g., assigned tasks in study units, in which children wrote and drew as part of social studies and science learning).

In any classroom there are both official and unofficial social spheres (D'Amato 1987; Goffman 1961). I stumbled into an unofficial sphere on an informal visit to Rita's room, when I overheard Marcel and a small group of peers, all African American, who designated themselves "the brothers and sisters": Marcel, Wenona, Denise, Vanessa, Noah, and Lakeisha. That designation was linked to the use of "brothers and sisters" to refer to solidarity in the African American tradition, but it was much more literal. Their elaborate narrative play was based on being "fake" siblings.

For example, in one kind of play, the children reported what happened or predicted what would happen "at home" when they had some dramatic encounter with each other and "their" mother. In another, the children went home with each other after school (although, as their parents confirmed, only Marcel and Wenona had *ever* even been inside the other's home). Marcel's closest "siblings" were Wenona and Noah, with whom he regularly engaged in team travel plans, as in the opening anecdote.

In the fall of 1996, I began to document (through observation and audiotaping) the children's participation in school activities, especially but not exclusively composing events, and to photocopy their written work, as well as that of all class members. During the 1996–1997 school year, I collected data over an eight-month period, approximately four to six hours per week.

My own relationship with the children evolved over time. As a middle-aged white woman, I made no effort to become one of the gang. I was "busy" writing in my notebook, because I was "interested in children," and I wouldn't "tell on them." Denise, however, made some familial sense of me. She deemed me a "fake mama." As far as I could tell, a fake mama could sit and listen and, when asked, her children could explain their ways to her. "Speak to me when you—ever you need to again," Wenona said after I'd asked about her coach and her teams.

Media leads from the children were all verified, and original sources documented, primarily through the efforts of the project research assistant, Soyoung Lee, who was herself helped by many kind souls at local video and music stores. Soyoung and I even watched videotaped football play-off games—something neither one of us had ever done before. I also met with parents to discuss my findings and their feelings about the media.

The (Unofficial) Social Usefulness of Media References

To construct an interpretation—a response to the "What's happening?" question about the children, literacy, and the media—I studied my field notes for all episodes of child references to media. By studying the content and interactional patterns of such episodes, I developed a description of the social functions the media served, including sports media. First, the media provided a source of *pleasure*, or just stimulation—a function most often served by songs, including sports-related ones. For example, as they worked on a class assignment, Wenona suggested to Marcel that they sing the *Space Jam* title song because "it's boring just sitting here." (*Space Jam* is a movie featuring basketball player Michael Jordan, "toon" Bugs Bunny, and selected colleagues of both.)

Second, media shows provided a potential source of *displayed knowledge*. Marcel, Samuel, and Zephenia often repeated teams and scores to each other, after an opening "Did you see the game?" Third, the media provided material serving *affiliation and differentiation* in varied, sometimes overlapping, social spheres; for sports media, this was especially, but not exclusively, the case for boys. For example, a preference for particular teams and players was openly acknowledged through T-shirts, declared favorite

colors (Marcel's was Dallas Cowboy blue), and reported personal and family preferences, as in the following vignette:

> *Wenona is completing a journal entry on her three nephews: T-bird, Damien, and Char-*
> *lie. She comments to her designated "fake" sister Lakeisha:*

WENONA: One of the boys like the 49ers. I don't know who this boy gonna like—
      he gonna like Dallas. . . . [The other nephew] like black too. I don't
      know why, unless the Raiders [whose team color is black]—
LAKEISHA: I don't [like the Raiders].
WENONA: I do. 'Cause my family like the Raiders, but we're still Dallas.

On another occasion, after Lakeisha had threatened to tell Rita about a rule violation
of Wenona's, the latter child shrugged, "Yeah. So you can be a 49er. Forty-niners tell,
not Dallas."

Fourth, the media provided contextual material for *unofficial play*. As already
noted, Marcel and Wenona played hockey for Coach Bombay and football for Dallas.
Finally, and most important for this analysis, cultural media could provide resources
for *participation in, negotiation with, and transformation of, official school contexts*. It is this
latter function that is highlighted in this chapter.

Media Material Appropriated for (Official) Use

As media references in field notes were studied, all children's writing workshop products were examined for the textual or content material appropriated from the media.
From sports media, the children appropriated a relatively wide range of material,
including the following:

1. Content
   a. Names (e.g., teams, players).
   b. Entire events (reported happenings), which could serve as topics of personal
      experience and evaluative texts (i.e., as something a child watched or liked or
      both) or even of written exchanges with peers or adults (i.e., as an experience
      about which a child could seek, through written inquiry, another's opinion or
      team preference).
   c. Concepts/knowledge, which could be
      i. recontextualized within writing practices modeled and practiced at school,
         including composing lists (e.g., of teams, players, home cities, and states),
         information reports (e.g., "I know that Michael Jordan is a superstar"), and
         fictional accounts (e.g., of having to travel to the play-offs on the weekend
         and having "made three thousand touchdowns").
      ii. recontextualized as reference points for scaffolding the use of cultural tools
         and knowledge emphasized in school (e.g., using teams' home sites as refer-
         ence points for figuring out maps).

2. Communicative forms
   a. Entire textual forms (e.g., announcements of upcoming games, reports of game results)
   b. Discourse features of those forms (e.g., location adjective [city or state name] before team name, as in "Dallas Cowboys" or "Minnesota Vikings"; time adverbs and adverbial phrases, as in "Tonight, Dallas will play at Miami"; dramatic, sometimes violent action verbs, as in "The 49ers got whipped on Sunday"; omission of verbs in announcing upcoming games and/or score reporting, as in "The Bulls 304 Warriors 463" [see Hoyle 1989]).
3. Graphic conventions
   a. Graphic arrangement (e.g., of game results on television).
   b. Symbols (e.g., of teams and commercial products).
4. Voiced utterances (i.e., particular lines spoken by narrators or characters, including "fans").
5. Ideologies (e.g., of race, gender, and power), which could not only be recontextualized in child talk, drawing, and writing (e.g., pictures of muscle-bound football players) but also become the focus of official and critical discussions among children and teacher (e.g., Rita discussed gender preferences for sports media with the class). In the unofficial world, dominant ideologies were countered by *movie* references (e.g., Wenona countered Marcel's denial of girls' right to play football with reference to *Mighty Ducks*, in which a fictional hockey team includes a girl).

As this broad range of appropriated material emerged, I asked as I analyzed my field note data, what kinds of tensions (i.e., semiotic, social, and ideological) arose when children recontextualized media material in official school texts? How could those tensions be resolved? It is this latter analysis, which builds on all the others, that I draw upon below, in an analytic narrative featuring Marcel, the Dallas Cowboys, and Marcel's official and unofficial worlds.

Marcel and the Written Word

First Contact Across Boundaries

In September of his first-grade year, Marcel was six years and eight months. He was named after a football player, said his mother, from the time when sports figures were "role models for our children." Marcel's interest in sports surfaced early on in his writing-workshop book. Along with names of family members and friends were the names of football teams and the numbers of favorite players (like No. 22, Dallas Cowboy Emmitt Smith, and No. 88, Cowboy Michael Irvin). A drawing of a football field (Figure 8–1) suggests some of the complex knowledge embedded in his sports entries, much of it potentially school valued (e.g., counting by tens, writing and reading two-digit numbers, graphic design and page arrangement, labeling, and symbol use).

FIGURE 8–1   *Marcel's detailed football field*

Within the month, Marcel, like his classmates, began to appropriate brief forms from the class-generated "things to write about" list (e.g., "I like _____," "I went_____"), inserting names or other chosen content into the blanks. By December, he began to write media-influenced textual forms: sports reports and announcements. These forms were salient to him and manageable (liftable) for a just-beginning writer. His initial efforts were syntactically awkward, but they did contain key information and structural features, as in the following example:

> The Dallas Cowboys and the 49ers and Texas g [against] The 49ers got Wt [whipped] on Sunday

Marcel's texts, however, were deceptively simple; they did not entail the straightforward reporting readers might imagine. That "Dallas Cowboys" text, for example, was mediating primarily Marcel's participation in unofficial play in the brothers' and sisters' world, not knowledge display, as illustrated below:

> *During writing time, Marcel and Noah discuss the 49ers' recent win over the Atlanta Falcons. Nonetheless, Marcel draws a Dallas Cowboy. Noah, in an apparent act of affiliation, decides to draw a football player too:*

NOAH: Oh! Are you making a football [player]? I'm gonna make a football [player].

> *Noah's player soon becomes "me. These are my muscles." He also adds an invented "baby brother" football player. As he draws, he narrates a version of the Monday night football event: "Forty-niners tackle the Atlanta Falcons."*
> *Marcel responds to Noah's play with "Jerry Rice. Jerry Rice," and draws that 49ers player. He soon returns, though, to the Cowboy figure and to Dallas ("Noah, look! This is Dallas."). Marcel pronounces the final score "20 to 23, Dallas." As he begins to write his report, Wenona comes over and shows Marcel her journal piece—a drawing of a cheerleader. Marcel explains:*

MARCEL: She cheerleads for Texas. (*I look puzzled.*) For me.
ANNE: Oh, she cheerleads for *you*. Where?
WENONA: In Texas.
MARCEL: Mm m.
WENONA: And sometimes we go to um Grove St. Park to practice. Sometimes.

Marcel used his knowledge of sports media to make contact with the official world and to produce what is, in fact, a valued form: an informational text. But, in truth, that text was mediating Marcel's participation in different social worlds, with different interests, practices, and values. His traversing of different social boundaries, not to mention states, was not yet producing audible tensions, but it would sound eventually.

Moreover, Marcel's appropriation of sports material suggested semiotic as well as social tensions. Marcel needed to translate the names of football teams from their audiovisual source to the printed page and, needing help, he sought out a states map, an available and officially valued cultural tool. This simple act stopped him in his tracks, so to speak. On the map's symbolic canvas, not all of the teams were readily visible:

Wenona and Marcel are sitting together during writing workshop. Marcel wants to write about football but needs some spelling help. He retrieves a classroom aid—a states map. At first Marcel looks for Kansas City (home of the Chiefs) on the map, but then he spots a familiar place.

MARCEL: And there's Texas right here! (*He is pointing to Texas.*) And Oakland, where's Oakland? Is this Oakland? (*turning to me*)

ANNE: That's Oregon. Oakland's gonna be in California. Here's the Bay. You see the Bay? Well, Oakland's right near the Bay, right?

MARCEL: Where's Minnesota [Vikings]?

ANNE: It's right here.

MARCEL: Good. Here's Texas.

WENONA: Texas! Where? (*She leans over the map, head-to-head with Marcel.*)

MARCEL: Go like this, going down, straight down (*running his finger down the map from Minnesota to Texas*). You got to cross the whole town. You gotta cross the whole town to get to Texas.

Marcel *has abandoned his writing now and is completely absorbed in the map. He shows Wenona another route, a longer one, through California.*

MARCEL: Go like this. Go down. Go down California, cut across here. And there's Texas. That'd be a long way from California.

WENONA: I want Oakland.

MARCEL: Oakland is easy to find. (*pointing to map*)

ANNE: That's Oregon.

MARCEL: OH MY GOD! . . . Here's Arizona [Cardinals]. . . . Is this Minnesota?

WENONA: Yeah! Like on Mighty Ducks. They say "Minnesota something." (*Notice how Wenona is locating Minnesota in a dimly recalled utterance from a movie, just as Marcel's notion of unfamiliar states is rooted in sports media utterances and, more specifically, team names.*)

MARCEL: From Minnesota—from Minnesota to Arizona takes a long time. . . .

Geographic information embedded in Marcel's sports talk was unsettled and reorganized as it was recontextualized within—and, in fact, became a reference point for participating in—the literacy practice of map reading. As his finger traversed the bor-

FIGURE 8–2 *Marcel's sports report*

ders of states, the distinction between city names and state names was becoming an issue ("OH MY GOD!").

Marcel's interest in maps continued. Within a few weeks of the above event, he wrote the sports report presented in Figure 8–2. That text has a clear semiotic link to its media resource: The teams ("Minnesota" and "Dallas") and their respective scores are laid out as they would be on a TV screen, rather than using prose style, as would be done in print media. Moreover, Marcel's talk during this event revealed his grappling with the place of those teams on the map, as well as in his official and unofficial social worlds. In the following vignette, all references to geographic concepts are underlined.

> *Marcel is sitting by Lakeisha and a parent volunteer, Cindy. Lakeisha is his fake sister and understands that he plays for a winning team—Dallas. Cindy is not a relative; she understands that Marcel is a little boy who seems to have the facts about Dallas's play-off fate wrong. I, as fake Mama and researcher, am not sure whether or not Marcel knows that, in the official world, Dallas lost, but, listening to his talk, I am quite sure he understands that he is negotiating different world views.*

MARCEL: (to Lakeisha) I know what I want to write about. "The Dallas Cowboys beat Carolina."

CINDY: They [Dallas] lost. Did you watch the game?
MARCEL: They're out! Out of the play-offs?
SALLY: They're like the 49ers now.

Marcel changes his writing plans. He begins, The Dallas, then stops, gets the states map, and begins to copy Minnesota, which Dallas had beat the previous week. (See Figure 8–2.)

MARCEL: (*to the table generally, as he looks at the map*) It's got all the states right here.
(*to himself as he writes Minnesota*) Minnesota, Minnesota, Minnesota, Minnesota . . . to the city of dreams. Minnesota, Minnesota, Minnesota, to the city of dreams. (Pause) Dallas, Texas. Dallas, Texas. Dallas, Texas. (*to the table*) This has all the states, right here. I have all the states, right over here. . . .
I'm writing "Dallas against Minnesota."

Marcel writes Minne for "Minnesota," positioning that truncated word under Dallas, column fashion, just as it would be on the television screen. He rereads "Dallas against Minnesota."
Marcel then recites "Dallas, Texas" several times before writing in Texas.

MARCEL: It [the score]—it was, 15—no 15 to 48.
LAKEISHA: Where's Berkeley [on that map]?
MARCEL: In California (pointing). (*Notice that Marcel now expects only the state name to be on the map, and he knows the state name is California.*)
Marcel rewrites Minne and Dallas in another column, placing the scores after them, again, like on a television screen. (See Figure 8–2.)
MARCEL: (*to Cindy*) This says, "Dallas against Minnesota. In Texas. 15 to 48." It has the cities of the teams.
(*to Lakeisha*) I be home tomorrow, only me and Wenona will be home late. 'Cause me and Wenona got practice. . . . I still got to go to football practice. . . . Wenona got cheerleading.

Marcel and Wenona will both be home with Mama and Lakeisha tomorrow, but they'll be late. The Cowboys may be out of the play-offs, but Marcel's "still got to go to football practice," and Wenona's "got cheerleading."

In sum, Marcel, like his peers, was sensitive to the importance of *written* material in school contexts. His simple, brief early texts belie the complexity of the composing time interplay of official and unofficial worlds and the potentially productive social and semiotic tensions thus generated.

Orderly Transformations Through New Social Dialogues

By January, Marcel, like his peers, was becoming a more comfortable writer, producing longer texts (averaging approximately twenty-four words per entry). That new length accompanied a new genre diversity, as Marcel continued to recontextualize media material in new communicative practices learned in school. Many of these genres were learned during the course of a space unit Rita introduced in early January. The unit's early lessons were accompanied by displayed lists of planets and charts of space facts; sometimes those facts were reviewed in a dialogue game in which pairs of children first asked other pairs "Did you know that . . . ?" and then reported during sharing time that "I learned that. . . ."

In his own writing, Marcel too made use of list making and fact reporting. After making a list of planet names for an assigned space-writing task (one in which Rita explicitly told him *not* to write about the Dallas Cowboys), Marcel began to fill his writing-workshop book with lists—about football, yes, but also about cities and states. First came a list of teams ("Green Bay, Dallas, Bears, 49ers"), and then a team list that included locales (e.g., "The Green Bay Packers and the Carolina Panthers, the Dallas Cowboys, the New York Giants, the New York Jets"), and, finally, a list of just states (see Figure 8–3):

The state of Texas
The state of Arizona
The state of New York
The state of Minnesota
The state of Kansas

Marcel's named states and their accompanying illustration of a helmeted man left little doubt about the origin of his efforts. His football team expertise thus continued to be reorganized and recontextualized in taxonomic form, not only through the mediational support of a symbolic tool (a map), but also through a new communicative practice (list making).

In addition to list making, Marcel began writing information texts that displayed his football expertise; these texts were more elaborate and more "officially" truthful than his reports of game results. His first such text (fifty words, which was twice his and the class's average) began modestly with his announced intention to write that "Desmond Howard made 3,079 touchdowns."

"Yeah, right," said Noah skeptically. Then, Jamal declared that Desmond Howard played for the 49ers.

"He didn't play for the 49ers," Marcel said firmly, "He played for the Green Bay Packers [but not, as it happens] for his whole life."

Marcel recorded this fact, wrote about a player who did switch teams, and, finally, reported the Super Bowl results:

Desmond Howard made 3,079 touchdowns.
He played for the Green Bay Packers.
Dion Sanders played for the 49ers and the Dallas Cowboys.
The Carolina Panthers played in the Super Bowl.
But they lost the Super Bowl against the Green Bay

Packers [actually, the Packers played the Patriots]. And the Green Bay Packers were the World Champions again. [spelling and punctuation corrected for ease of reading.]

"I did more. I did more writing," said Marcel to Noah when he was done. "Rita's gonna be so proud of me. . . . That was the tightest story I ever told."

FIGURE 8–3   *Marcel's list of states, all of which have football teams*

"How many football players do you know about?" asked Vanessa when he shared.

"I know about twenty-nine," replied Marcel, looking very pleased with himself.

Marcel's expertise in football, his interest in travel across states (especially Texas), and his experience with lists and reports, seemed to culminate late in the year when he became fascinated with a book about tornadoes read by Ms. Sheng, the school librarian. The book includes both a states map and an illustration of a television weather reporter pointing to a U.S. map (Bramley 1988). Marcel's assigned end-of-year thank-you letter to Ms. Sheng quite quickly became a report on tornadoes' travel across states, old familiar states:

> Dear Miss Sheng:
>
> I love the book of tornadoes. Because the tornado sucks up things that gets in its way. The tornadoes are very very dangerous because it can suck you up and throw you in the cloud. That's the tornado cloud's job. When the tornado is done, it goes back to the cloud and there [are] tornadoes in Florida. There may be some tornadoes in Arizona. But there no tornadoes in Berkeley, California because it is so hot in spring. The sun is so hot. On the news there was a twister in Texas yesterday in the morning. A tornado in the morning.
>
> from Marcel [spelling and punctuation corrected for ease of reading]

Marcel's mother told me that currently, in the second grade—a year after he wrote the above text and began his fascination with the weather—he still checks the sky each morning for funnel clouds in his assumed role as family weatherman, and he still considers "the tornado book" his favorite.

Thus, Marcel, like his peers, used school-valued practices to organize and display knowledge from unofficial sources. These practices included list making and reporting and involved using cultural tools like geographic taxonomies and representations that allow one to trace movement across space. One of my favorite such hybrids of official and unofficial material was produced by Noah; it is a report on *Space Jam* and Michael Jordan ("one of my favorite men"). It began, "I know that Michael Jordan is a superstar and he know that he goes on Space Jam . . . He gots the moves. . . ." However, the recontextualization of material across social and semiotic boundaries did not always go so smoothly.

Contested Transformations and Hidden Dialogues

Sometimes children's texts were unruly hybrids, less compatible with official textual structures and uncontained by official school practices. As the school year progressed, children became more sensitive to social boundaries—and to writing's potential to maintain or disrupt them. During the unit on space, not only did Rita caution Marcel against football as a topic for his science text, Noah and Wenona strongly objected to Marcel's suggestion that they name their invented planet "Pizza Planet," based on the movie *Toy Story* (Arnold, Guggenheim, and Lasseter 1995). They wanted a proper name, like Saturn (Noah's suggestion).

Moreover, children began to engage in surreptitious writing. They made private lists of "club" members, which they kept in their backpacks or stashed in their cubbies. Marcel's was named the "BC" club, after a popular radio station's BC [Breakfast Club]. These clubs were more exclusionary than those Rita advocated (i.e., "Everybody Clubs"). The children also made what might be called *double-coded symbols*, symbols interpreted differently for different social spheres. For example, one day Wenona wrote the digit *2* in her writing book, which was "how old her nephews were" on the official school stage, but how many times she, Marcel, and Noah would "beat up" Jamal on the unofficial one. (This was more a "snap" than an actual threat, since hitting was forbidden, but "remember, Mama said she don't care if we snap at somebody.")

The more writing became a functional tool in children's social lives and the more deliberate they became about minding social boundaries of appropriateness, the more potential the children, and their addressees, had to exercise power by heightening border tensions. Tensions could be heightened if authors abandoned double-coding and openly read an alternative meaning; tensions could also be heightened if authors made salient unofficial (and potentially unacceptable) sources, or if addressees resisted the recontextualization of material from particular sources.

One poignant example of child audience resistance to unofficial play material came near the end of the school year, when for the first time Marcel publicly declared his unofficial play-off responsibilities in a very official context: a text-sharing time. On this day, Marcel stood before his class and read two pieces. In one, he reported *watching* "the play-offs" on cable all weekend "till 6:30 in the morning" on Monday. In the second, he himself was *in* a nighttime play-off game and "made three thousand touchdowns."

Marcel's presentation of dubious facts about himself (not some distanced team) led to objections from unrelated peers, objections that emphasized Marcel's status as an adult-dependent child:

> JOHN: (*responding to Marcel's reading*) When you said you stayed up, did your mom know that you was um staying up till late?
> MARCEL: I I I was in the play-offs.
> JOHN: Yeah, did you mom know?
> MARCEL: No. . . .
> JOHN: Is that a made-up story?
> MARCEL: No.
> ZEPHENIA: Marcel, why were you out by yourself?
> MARCEL: I wasn't. My dad was the coach of my team.
> VANESSA: Oh. So you went with your dad. Your dad coached your team. . . . (*nodding at Marcel and then at her classmates in an affirming way*)

Marcel, under pressure, lowers his sights. He does not claim to play for Dallas, but rather for:

MARCEL: Peewees. (*Marcel is referring to the city teams for children.*)
ZEPHENIA: Peewees are 8 to 9.
MARCEL: I know, and they're 7 in second grade, and in first grade.

Rita, who pointed out that Marcel <u>was</u> on the team <u>in his writing</u>, thanks Marcel and moves on to the next child.

Marcel's genre or communicative practice in the above event is unruly and thus not easy to name or contain. On the surface, his piece about his own football playing was a *personal experience* text, a kind valued in school. But given its dubious truth value, John and Rita surmised that it must be a "story." However, the text was rooted in the brothers' and sisters' world, a serious world whose routines and games were seldom acknowledged as unreal; that world was about being powerful, responsible, and competent. The children's texts about their biological families and their school experiences were factual, or so my interviews with parents and Rita suggested. And texts about their "fake family" were true too, as long as one was inside that world. Still, given his audience, Marcel did attempt to negotiate a "true" context for his piece.

Marcel was not the only child to engage in this public negotiating. When a classmate asked Noah during sharing time about his drawing of the small football player, Noah named the figure "my baby brother." Rita articulated the official composing time boundary between what was true "in your story" and "in your family." For whatever reason—saving face in this public place or simply maintaining his overlapping location inside the unofficial world (where invented siblings were common)—Noah did not let go of that invented brother. When Rita inquired as to the baby's name, Noah (like Marcel) negotiated with the adult world: "My mother didn't got his name yet."

Marcel's play-off responsibilities and Noah's baby brother demonstrated something fundamental about childhood and writing. Labels and brief statements do not evolve smoothly into adultlike communicative practices, despite children's dependence on adult organization and guidance. Rather, they sometimes become uncontainable, brimming over with the social and ideological tensions of childhood itself. These tensions are not markers of unruly children, but of complex children, who are differentiating, organizing, and reorganizing both their semiotic and cultural resources and their ever-widening social and ideological worlds.

A Critical Imagination and Learning to Write

From something as simple as the small red score book in which I inscribed the narrative of a ball game, I saw the inception of what has become my life's work as a historian. (Goodwin 1997, 10)

Doris Kearns Goodwin traces the roots of her passion for history to the afternoons she spent as a six-year-old, huddled by the radio with pad and pencil, recording the names of baseball players and inning scores. She would use these jottings to jog her memory when she retold the game for her father. Just as Goodwin's involvement with sports media grew from and supported her relationship with her father, Marcel's was clearly rooted in his home, too, as his mother affirmed. But it was also functionally linked to his relationships with friends, peers, and adults in school.

Marcel's interest also supported more academic interests, including meteorology. Embedded within Marcel's engagement with sports media were mathematical and geographical, as well as textual, knowledge. His football teams, like the funnel clouds and hurricanes with which he became fascinated, traveled the states according to forecasted routes. That knowledge, recontextualized amid the complex social worlds and valued literacy practices of school, provided Marcel with entry points into new social dialogues or genres, as well as new ideologically charged dialogues. For example, the Dallas Cowboys were all men, cheered on by skimpily clad females, unlike Coach Bombay's fictional but coed hockey team, as Wenona in fact commented upon. (A child in the fifties, Goodwin seems to have taken the gender-divided world of famed players for granted.)

In the larger project from which I have drawn, children also freely appropriated material from popular music, animation, and film, and used that material to help build peer worlds that gave them a sense of belonging, competence, and fun. Embedded within that media use were varied kinds of physical, social, ideological, and, ultimately, textual knowledge. And yet in the literature on early school literacy, the appreciated sources of textual and conceptual knowledge and know-how are remarkably narrow, particularly given the tremendous changes that have taken place in theories about childhood, development, and literacy itself (e.g., New London Group 1996; Street 1995). Those valued sources are primarily experiences with books and with particular kinds of adult-child interactions about written texts (see, for example, Hemphill and Snow 1996), despite literacy's trend toward becoming a multimodal affair (epitomized by electronic texts). Further, discussions of literacy teaching seem permanently focused on a dichotomously posed, equally narrow issue of teaching phonics, of children, teachers, and their respective relationships only to and through the sounds of the letters—a breathtakingly anemic view of a complex symbol system open to different "points of entry and . . . path[s] of progress" (Clay 1975, 7).

Thus, no matter how important Goodwin views her social and literate relationship to baseball to be in her own intellectual history, it is likely that her early teachers were neither appreciative of nor disturbed by her interest, if they even knew about it. Surely, in the social categories by which our children are sorted, a contemporary child Doris would not be labeled "at risk," a fate more likely for children categorized like Marcel and his siblings (not white and middle-class). And this fate is not mitigated by the institutional imagination of schools, and the discursive imagination of early literacy research (Dyson 1995, in press), which turns a narrowly focused and concerned eye to children so categorized (Shepard 1991).

The "normative" child "ready for school," to whom all children are to conform by the year 2000, seldom has a presently complex world among other children, or guiding frameworks that originate outside the mediating influence of a parent or teacher's voice. Children's frames of reference and potential understandings, unarticulated but interwoven in their experiences, are filtered out, and thus so are understandings of symbolic media, discourse genres, communicative strategies; potential insights into societal categories like age, gender, and class; and social themes like collectivity and individuality, all of which is potentially constitutive of exactly what the school aims to teach.

Building on what children bring is an axiom in both developmental and multicultural education, but it is much harder to do than to say. Children's recontextualization of unofficial texts (their textual hybridization) can be difficult to hear, in part because teachers' ears are alerted to textual signposts that "sound" familiar, academic, and forward looking to *their* ears (Bakhtin 1986). Thus, it would be useful for teachers, as surely as for the children they teach, to remain alert to children's ever-evolving confrontation with the "What did I write?" question, with how their chosen words reverberate in particular situations. They might also work to differentiate social worlds and to appreciate the interplay of the resources those worlds offer; that is, to see communicative agency, textual knowledge, and embedded concepts in sources other than the usual ones.

For example, Marcel did not need football books—nor football fans as teachers— to learn to write. But he did need to use familiar textual practices and forms, and the embedded knowledge they contained, to make sense of new practices and knowledge. In the recontextualization process, Marcel, like children generally, would continue to benefit from classroom talking times when children are expected, allowed, and supported in presenting, elaborating on, and explaining their work. In such events, especially when they are interwoven with at least some open-ended activities, children's voices are more apt to reveal texts and practices needing to be named, and knowledge that can potentially be guided into new textual and social frames.

Creating such a "permeable" (Dyson 1993) curriculum surely entails grappling with complex ideological issues in children's terms. From preschool on, children are sensitive to the social meanings of appearance and possession differences that locally construct the meaning of race, gender, and social class (Ramsey 1998). On playgrounds, children have long confronted issues of physical domination and of sex, such as through boy/girl chase games and kissing games (Opie 1993). These aspects of social existence often underlie children's identification with, and attraction to, media figures (Dyson 1997). Thus, teachers willing to build on all of the children's resources must also help children develop a critical appreciation of how media texts both provide and shape their sense of pleasure and of a good life. (For an illustration of a teacher doing just this, see Dyson 1997; for discussions of media literacy and young children see Comber 1998; Kavanagh 1997; and Levin 1998.)

In the process of literacy teaching and learning, a teacher of young children needs a healthy dose of imagination, just as children do. A child must say some version of,

"Yes, I imagine I can do this." And a teacher must also view the present child as competent and, on that basis, imagine new possibilities. The new sociologists of childhood (e.g., James, Jenks, and Prout 1998) see this future-oriented view of childhood as problematic, because it blinds adults to children's current abilities and pleasures, to the importance of a present worth living. But I don't see time so easily separated. After all, Doris Goodwin's father never told her that he read the baseball game summaries in the newspaper; Marcel's mom never told him that there was little need to check the sky for funnel clouds; and Rita responded honestly, probed, sometimes contained, but never dismissed his symbols and agency—his Cowboys. All seemed to know that it is out of a respect for childhood, and a commitment to children's rights to a fulfilling and satisfying present, that the seeds of the future evolve.

References

ARNET, J., AND KERNER, J. (PRODUCERS), AND LIBERMAN, R. (DIRECTOR). 1994. *D2: Mighty Ducks* [film]. Burbank, Calif.: Walt Disney Pictures.

ARNOLD, B., AND GUGGENHEIM, R. (PRODUCERS), AND LASSETER, J. (DIRECTOR). 1995. *Toy Story* [film]. Burbank, Calif.: Walt Disney Pictures, in association with Pixar Corporation.

BAKHTIN, M. 1981. "Discourse in the Novel." In *The Dialogic Imagination: Four Essays by M. Bakhtin*, edited by C. Emerson and M. Holquist, 259–422. Austin: University of Texas Press.

———. 1986. *Speech Genres and Other Late Essays*. Austin: University of Texas Press.

BAUMAN, R., AND BRIGGS, C. C. 1990. "Poetics and Performance as Critical Perspectives on Language and Social Life." *Anthropological Review* 19: 59–88.

BRAMLEY, F. M. 1988. *Tornado Alert*. New York: HarperCollins.

BRUNER, J. 1990. *Acts of Meaning*. Cambridge: Harvard University Press.

CLAY, M. 1975. *What Did I Write?* Auckland: Heinemann.

COMBER, B. 1998. "Coming, Ready or Not: Changing What Counts as Early Literacy." Keynote address to the Seventh Annual Australia and New Zealand Conference on the First Years of School, Canberra, January 1998.

D'AMATO, J. D. 1987. "The Belly of the Beast: On Cultural Difference, Caste Like Status, and the Politics of School." *Anthropology and Education Quarterly* 18: 357–360.

DYSON, A. HAAS. 1993. *Social Worlds of Children Learning to Write in an Urban Primary School*. New York: Teachers College Press.

———. 1995. "Writing Children: Reinventing the Development of Childhood Literacy." *Written Communication* 12: 3–46.

———. 1997. *Writing Super Heroes: Contemporary Childhood, Popular Culture, and Classroom Literacy*. New York: Teachers College Press.

————. In press. "Transforming Transfer: Unruly Children, Contrary Texts, and the Persistence of the Pedagogical Order." To appear in *Review of Research in Education (RRE): Vol. 2*, edited by A. Iran-Nejad and P. D. Pearson. Washington, D.C.: American Educational Research Association.

FALK, D., REITMAN, I., AND ROSS, K. (PRODUCERS), AND CERVONE, T., PYTKA, J., AND SMITH, B. (DIRECTORS). 1996. *Space Jam* [film]. Burbank, Calif.: Warner Brothers.

GARVEY, C. 1990. *Play*. Enl. ed. Cambridge: Harvard University Press.

GOFFMAN, I. 1961. *Asylums*. Garden City, N.Y.: Anchor Books.

GOLDMAN, L. R. 1998. *Child's Play: Myth, Mimesis, and Make-Believe*. London: Routledge.

GOODWIN, D. K. 1997. *Wait Till Next Year: A Memoir*. New York: Simon & Schuster.

HEMPHILL, L., AND SNOW, C. 1996. "Language and Literacy Development: Discontinuities and Differences." In *The Handbook of Education and Human Development: New Models of Learning, Teaching, and Schooling*, edited by D. Olson and N. Torrance, 173–201. London: Blackwell.

HOYLE, S. 1989. "Forms and Footings in Boys' Sports Casting." *Text* 9: 153–173.

JAMES, A., JENKS, C., AND PROUT, A. 1998. *Theorizing Childhood*. New York: Teachers College Press.

KAVANAGH, K. 1997. *Texts on Television: School Literacies Through Viewing in the First Years of School*. Adelaide, South Australia: Department for Education and Children's Services.

LEVIN, D. E. 1998. *Remote Control Childhood?: Combating the Hazards of Media Culture*. Washington, D.C.: National Association for the Education of Young Children.

MERCURY, F. (WRITER). 1995. "We Are the Champions." In *D2: Mighty Ducks: The Soundtrack*. [CD]. Burbank, Calif.: Hollywood Records.

MILLER, P.J., AND GOODNOW, J. J. 1995. "Cultural Practices: Toward an Integration of Culture and Development." In *Cultural Practices as Contexts for Development*, edited by J. J. Goodnow, P. J. Miller, and F. Kessel, No. 67, *New Directions in Child Development* 5–16. San Francisco: Jossey Bass.

MILLER, P. J., HOOGSTRA, L., MINTZ, J., FUNG, H., AND WILLIAMS, K. 1993. "Troubles in the Garden and How They Get Resolved: A Young Child's Transformation of His Favorite Story." In *Memory and Affect in Development: Minnesota Symposium on Child Psychology*, edited by C. A. Nelson, 26: 87–114. Hillsdale, N.J.: Erlbaum.

MILLER, P., AND MEHLER, R. 1994. "The Power of Personal Storytelling in Families and Kindergartens. In *The Need for Story: Cultural Diversity in Classroom and Community*, edited by A. H. Dyson and C. Genishi, 38–56. Urbana, Ill.: National Council of Teachers of English.

NELSON, K. 1996. *Language in Cognitive Development: The Emergence of the Mediated Mind*. Cambridge: Cambridge University Press.

THE NEW LONDON GROUP. 1996. "A Pedagogy of Multiliteracies: Designing Social Futures." *Harvard Educational Review* 61: 60–92.

OPIE, I. 1993. *The People in the Playground*. Oxford: Oxford University Press.

RAMSEY, P. 1998. *Teaching and Learning in a Diverse World: Multicultural Education for Young children*. 2d ed. New York: Teachers College Press.

SHEPARD, L. 1991. "Negative Policies for Dealing with Diversity: When Does Assessment and Diagnosis Turn into Sorting and Segregation?" In *Literacy for a Diverse Society: Perspectives, Practices, and Policies*, edited by E. Hiebert, 279–298. New York: Teachers College Press.

STREET, B. 1995. *Social Literacies: Critical Approaches to Literacy in Development, Ethnography, and Education*. London: Longman.

SUTTON-SMITH, B., MECHLING, J., JOHNSON, T. W., AND MCMAHON, F. R., ED.1995. *Children's Folklore: A Source Book*. New York: Garland Publishing.

VYGOTSKY, L. S. 1962. *Thought and Language*. Cambridge: MIT Press.

———. 1978. *Mind in Society*. Cambridge: Harvard University Press.

———. 1987. *L. S. Vygotsky, Collected Works: Volume 1, Problems of General Psychology*. New York: Plenum Books.

WILLIAMS, R. 1965. *The Long Revolution*. Harmondsworth, England: Penguin.

WILLIS, P. 1990. *Common Culture: Symbolic Work at Play in the Everyday Culture of the Young*. Boulder, Col.: Westview Press.

Nine

The Young Reader as a Self-Extending System: Motivational and Cognitive Underpinnings

JOHN T. GUTHRIE

Early in her writing, Marie Clay envisioned the young reader as a self-improving system. In 1979 she wrote, "The end point of early instruction is reached when the children have a self-improving system. This consists of a history of successful reading of books, a set of operations just adequate for reading a more difficult text for the precise words and meanings of the author. In Smith's terms (1978) they have a 'theory of the world' which works and they are testing that theory and changing it successively as they read more books" (Clay 1979a, 8). These capacities for self-improvement depend on self-monitoring. Clay suggested that independent readers are distinguished by their monitoring of their own reading. They discover things for themselves when they cross-check new words or information. Independent readers self-correct frequently as they recognize words and construct new ideas from texts. In her later writing, Marie Clay (1991, 1998) evolved her thinking by adopting the phrase, "self-extending system." Within this change, Marie introduced the notion that children are not merely gaining cognitive competence implied by the term "improvement," although skills do increase. She was pointing to the development of self, including the acquisition of cognitive self-monitoring, the growth of conceptual knowledge, the refinements of reading interests, the development of and appetites for literary experience. This chapter explores how the child's intrinsic motivation contributes to reading development.

Clay was emphatic about self-improvement as an aim of teaching. She claimed that a teacher's goal is to develop independent readers. To build independence, Clay (1979a) suggested that teachers should give students ways to detect errors and encourage their attempts to correct errors in word recognition and meaning-making. She suggested that effective teachers "give clues to aid self-correction . . . and when he works out a word or text for himself help him to know how he did it. Ask him 'How did you know?'" (43).

For four months in 1980, I had a rare opportunity to visit Marie Clay at Auckland University. During that visit, we discussed her vision of children becoming self-improving readers. The idea is simple. It is akin to the adage that if you give a man a fish, he enjoys a meal; but if you teach a man to fish, he can eat for a lifetime. If you teach a child to self-improve, the child becomes her own agent of growth. The child becomes independent in *doing,* but also in *learning.* However, there is a chasm between the vision and the reality. Actually teaching self-improvement is more daunting than it initially appears.

Clay's vision of the self-improving reader was rooted in cognition and language. The child detects errors and corrects them. Sensing unclear meaning, the child attempts to clarify it. As operations of language and cognition, these functions of the self-improving reader have received extensive research and attention from teachers. However, equally important to success in self-improvement is a set of affective, motivational, dispositional characteristics of the young child. At the simplest level, a young reader must want to improve and believe that she can learn.

It seems self-evident that self-improvement is associated with the desire to be competent and the belief in one's capacity for increasing competence. Yet these motivational aspects of self-improvement in reading are central; they are not peripheral, nor are they possible luxuries that may follow successful reading. Self-improvement in reading rests equally on cognitive and motivational underpinnings, and these relationships are complex.

This chapter explores how young children become engaged and motivated as readers. It also looks at how a series of barriers may obstruct this process. This contribution explores how intrinsic motivation for reading develops, and how motivation contributes to self-improvement in young children's reading.

What Is Intrinsically Motivated Reading?

By the time children have reached age ten, some have become avid, competent, motivated readers. These children read different kinds of books because they enjoy them. They may have favorite authors, pursue topics of personal interest, or read socially in a book club. The reading activity is performed for its own sake. They are excited by the book, intrigued by the characters, or charmed by the information. These attributes describe intrinsically motivated behavior (Deci 1992; Gottfried 1990; Ryan, Connell, and Grolnick 1992), and they apply to reading as aptly as other activities, such as having a conversation, playing a sport, doing a science experiment, or writing a letter. Children who read because they want to read are *intrinsically motivated.* When a child's reason for reading is an incentive offered and controlled by another person, the reading activity is *extrinsically motivated.* A competent ten-year-old may read for extrinsic reasons, such as rewards and prizes, as well as intrinsic reasons, such as enjoyment of the plot or the topic.

To explore the myriad reasons children read, we have interviewed them, held focus groups with them, and conducted questionnaire studies. The outcome was a variety of reasons for reading that broadened our understanding of motivation. Based on multiple methods of inquiry, we have identified at least eleven dimensions of motivation that can energize reading and serve as the basis for self-improvement (Guthrie and Anderson 1999). Several of these reading motivations are intrinsic, including curiosity (the desire to learn about the world around us through reading), involvement (the desire to be immersed or engrossed in a book), and preference for challenge (the desire to figure out a complex plot or a difficult idea by reading). Students who enjoy reading for its own sake usually give one or more of these reasons for their choices of books. Extrinsic motivations for reading include recognition (desire to be acknowledged publicly for one's achievements), grades (a teacher evaluation of reading achievement), competitiveness (the desire to be better than one's peers in reading), and tangible rewards (prizes or money for accomplishing a goal). Two other aspects of motivation are *self-efficacy*, children's belief in their capacities to read successfully, and *social interaction*, children's enjoyment in sharing reading and maintaining social relationships through literacy. It seems that the act of picking up a book and reading it may appear simple, but the interests, affects, and motivations that underlie the choice and the pursuit are not simple.

Who Are the Intrinsically Motivated Readers?

Children who are intrinsically motivated to read display different characteristics than do children who read for extrinsic incentives. Intrinsically motivated readers are engaged in reading as a meaningful, enjoyable, self-enhancing pursuit. By the age of ten, intrinsically motivated readers have gained a repertoire of cognitive strategies for finding books of interest, getting the main idea, self-monitoring, understanding, and remembering what they have read that is personally significant. In contrast, extrinsically motivated readers at age ten use superficial strategies for accomplishing tasks. Their goal is rarely to gain deep understanding. It is more frequently to complete the text, finish the book, or answer the question. With these extrinsic goals, children reduce their cognitive effort and do minimal work to win the prize. When the external goal is attained, their reading usually ceases.

The engaged reader who is highly motivated and strategic is likely to read widely and frequently. Wigfield and Guthrie (1997) found that fourth graders who were in the top third in motivation read more than three times as much as children who were in the bottom third for motivation. Whereas highly intrinsically motivated readers spent more than thirty minutes per day reading for their own enjoyment, less intrinsically motivated students read for pleasure less than ten minutes per day.

It is intrinsic motivation that energizes avid reading; thus it is significant to the notion of the self-improving reader. Further, the amount of reading and print exposure have a dramatic impact on children's competence in reading (Cunningham and Stanovich 1997); frequent reading in and out of school is the single strongest predictor that a child will be a competent reader. Self-improving readers, then, are active, motivated readers who seek books on their own interests and read to satisfy their curiosity. These motivations empower students to use their cognitive strategies to more fully enjoy stories or exposition. The extent to which a child is a self-improving reader has been established by age ten. By late elementary grades, the self-improving system rests on a foundation of intrinsic motivations for reading, such as curiosity, involvement, and preference for challenge.

What Happens to Intrinsically Motivated Reading over Time?

We have been discussing children aged nine and ten and comparing those who are intrinsically and extrinsically motivated in reading. Unfortunately, by this age, relatively few children are intrinsically motivated readers. Several studies using diaries and questionnaires have shown that the typical ten-year-old reads ten minutes per day or less for his own enjoyment (Anderson, Wilson, and Fielding 1988; Wigfield and Guthrie 1997). A large-scale national questionnaire conducted by the National Assessment of Educational Progress (NAEP) (Campbell, Voekl, and Donahue 1997), reported that 26 percent of nine-year-olds read five pages or fewer daily for school and homework (low), about 15 percent read eleven to fifteen pages per day (moderate), and 17 percent read twenty or more pages per day (high). Differences in achievement between the low and moderate readers on the NAEP test were extremely large and statistically significant. Although wide and frequent reading is the single highest contributor to reading competence at age nine and ten, less than 20 percent of the population can be considered to be reasonably active, engaged readers.

The story of intrinsic motivation in reading is one of decline. If children are asked, "Do you enjoy reading?" or "Are you interested in reading books?" they are much more likely to reply negatively as they progress through the elementary school years. From grades three to eight, children decline in intrinsic motivation for reading (Harter, Whitesell, and Kowalski 1992; Wigfield, Eccles, and Rodriguez 1998). Whereas 80 percent of third graders are likely to say, "I am interested in reading," only 20 percent are likely to make that same affirmation by grade eight. According to McKenna, Kear, and Ellsworth (1995), attitude toward reading (liking to read) declines in the elementary school years. A student with a positive attitude says, "I like reading." This attribute of liking is not the same as motivation. A student may like reading but not be intrinsically motivated to read frequently. We are familiar with the sentiment, "I like to read, but I do not do it often." Across the elementary years, students with high achievement, from grades one to six, maintain positive attitudes toward reading, whereas students with low achievement show a steady decline in their reading attitudes. Even low achievers hold positive attitudes in grade one, but their attitudes decline consistently each year unless their reading competency is radically increased.

The dilemma is obvious. To be self-improving as a reader in grades four and five, children need intrinsic motivation for reading, but such motivation is relatively rare at grades four and five. Moreover, the proportion of students who are intrinsically motivated decreases from grades three to eight. If the self-improving system and reading engagement are not well established by grades four or five, the chances of sustaining or increasing them are threatened thereafter. To understand and, potentially, to reverse this decline, we need to explore the development of intrinsic motivation for reading in young children. What is its course of development, and what are the qualities of home and school that influence intrinsic motivation?

How Does Intrinsically Motivated Reading Develop?

Shared Book Reading

A substantial number of young children from birth to age three enjoy the world of books. Many young children have been read to by parents, grandparents, and siblings. This experience of joint storybook interaction is the first encounter with reading for most children and is essential to laying the foundations of intrinsic motivation for reading.

The nature of the young child's interaction with significant others in storybook reading varies dramatically. For some children, the experience is frequent, rich in conversational interchange, and affectively positive. For other children, however, joint storybook reading is relatively rare and strange, conducted with a more rigid view of the correct rendering of the text. It is viewed as skill building rather than as an enjoyable form of entertainment (Baker, Scher, and Mackler 1997).

Children who are fortunate enough to have extended-family members dedicated to their enjoyment and learning through early literacy activities will experience all the prerequisites for the development of intrinsic motivation, including frequent participation in the activity of reading. Such children say "Let's read a book" as though they are an equal member of the team. As they participate, these children recognize a cognitive challenge in the activity. They perceive that they can follow a character in the story and will anticipate hearing the end. They recognize and enjoy the challenge of learning the names of the characters or objects in the books.

In this context, children acquire a disposition for continued participation—that is, they ask to read frequently, they want to read more books, and they seek people to share book reading. This positive disposition, or *intention to read,* is a cornerstone of the intrinsic motivation for literacy. It has been documented, albeit loosely, that children who experience frequent participation in early literacy activities perceive the cognitive challenge involved, enjoy the doing and learning, display a positive disposition for literacy interactions, and are likely to develop intrinsic motivation for reading. However, this is only the first phase. The attainment of reading expertise is not yet complete, and therefore the attainment of intrinsic motivation for reading is not fully accomplished.

Learning the Written Code

The second phase of intrinsically motivated reading development occurs when children discover the nature of written language. At various ages from three to six, children perceive the written code and acquire concepts of print. Marie Clay's (1979b) phrase *con-*

cepts of print is apt. Children learn that books have fronts and backs, letters have shapes, words have sequences of letters, and their own names can be spelled. As children learn to associate their spoken language with the written code, the notion of reading takes on added meaning and significance. In this phase, children may enjoy participating in the joint activities of naming letters or reading a limited set of familiar words. They may be fortunate to experience the first two ingredients of intrinsically motivated behavior: active participation and enjoyment in the activity of learning the written code.

When the written code predominates children's consciousness of what it means to read and be a reader, a serious obstacle to intrinsically motivated reading arises. As children confront the written code, effective learners recognize that there is a cognitive challenge facing them. Acknowledging that the code is complex, these children are sober, or at least modest, about their abilities. If they see concretely how difficult it is to read new words and learn new aspects of the alphabetic principle, children appraise their own capacity for learning realistically. They will set lower estimates of their own ability and lower goals for their own reading. Gaa (1973) worked with first graders in setting goals for their acquisition of the written code. Children who set goals for the letters, letter sounds, and words they would learn to read and received teacher responses to their learning showed lower self-efficacy for reading than children who were not provided with this intensive interaction with code learning. Children without the interactive opportunity were more likely to be unrealistic, saying, "I can read anything" and "I can learn any words." The tutored students were more realistic and more reserved. In addition, Foorman et al. (1998) showed that first graders with explicit instruction in the code had lower attitudes toward reading than children with literature-based teaching and little explicit code instruction. However, the explicit instruction group gained more competence in word recognition. If young children recognize the challenge of learning concepts about print and gaining competence in the written code, their self-appraisal of their ability and their attitude toward reading temporarily declines, reflecting a realism about the cognitive challenges in literacy development. If children succeed at this early coding stage and if their experiences with code learning are enjoyable, the chances for continued development of intrinsically motivated reading are good.

From the phase in which reading emphasizes joint storybook interaction, to the phase in which reading also includes learning the written code, the nature of the cognitive challenge shifts. Because the definition of a reader has transferred from book sharing to interactions with the written code, intrinsic motivation for reading also shifts. To be an intrinsically motivated reader in the written-code phase, children need the opportunity to be successful participants, to enjoy learning, to embrace the cognitive challenge, and to acquire a disposition for continued understanding and participation in interactions with the written language. In this phase, the meaning of the information that the code is expressing is not irrelevant, but it is secondary. Biemiller (1970) documented that as children learn the alphabetic principle, they focus more attention on the code and less on the meaning of the text. This shows in the children's oral reading errors. For a temporary period, their errors are less sensitive to meaningful context and more sensitive to the letter sounds and letter sequences at this stage of development. As children gain competence in reading and writing letters and words, intrinsically motivated reading is redirected to competence in these aspects of language.

Although competency in learning the written code is valuable, it is not sufficient for the development of intrinsic motivation. Code-learning activity must be enjoyable for its own sake, endowing a sense of pride and engendering a desire for new opportunities for written code learning. In this phase, the engaged reader finds literacy interactions that foster code learning, and creates opportunities to extend the knowledge base of phonology and orthography that underlies word reading and, ultimately, mature literacy.

These early phases of intrinsically motivated reading are cumulative. The dispositions for shared book reading are retained and expanded as children undertake the processes of coding print to language. As intrinsic motivations for word reading are acquired, they supplement and extend intrinsic motivations for the previous phase of joint book sharing. The child's concept of reading is expanding and touching the extremes from broad narrative meaning to letter- and word-coding processes.

Comprehending Print

The third phase of development in the intrinsically motivated reader is initiated when the child becomes a comprehender of printed meanings beyond the word. Having gained enough command of the code to recognize a range of letters, words, and spelling patterns, the child increases rapidly in the ability to comprehend written texts. At this phase, "being a reader" means reading the story to its conclusion yourself. Comprehending print implies being self-sufficient in understanding the author's message. The ingredients for developing intrinsic motivation, in this phase, consist of successful participation in reading for the enjoyment of understanding. Complexity, the child's need for competence and relatedness, the need to know, ascends to prominence. Inquisitive children who want to read the next book by an author or a new book on a favorite topic, such as airplanes or elephants, will fulfill needs for knowing about the world around them. They use their new-found competencies in coding to meet their need for understanding texts.

Intrinsically motivated reading, at this phase, is motivation for understanding and enjoying the internal and external world. Children who fail to develop intrinsic motivations may well have acquired simple word reading or comprehension competencies. However, a lack of frequent participation, enjoyment, recognition, challenge, or the shared satisfaction in new understanding will preclude the growth of disposition for more reading.

In this phase, many students do not acquire intrinsic motivation for reading. Although they are able to read words and understand texts at an adequate level, their experience does not fulfill the necessary prerequisites for intrinsically motivated reading. Consequently, they become those who *can* read but *don't*. They become functional aliterates who are capable of comprehending books and articles but choose not to read for enjoyment, information, or self-improvement.

Reading as Inquiry

Reading is a form of inquiry when it serves personal goals, enabling young readers to expand their knowledge and experience according to their own tastes. Self-directed learning is essential for inquiry literacy and depends on a new wave of intrinsic motivation for reading. As children move beyond ages nine and ten into discipline-based learning in science, history, geography, and literature, effective literacy depends on self-direction and self-regulated use of strategies. At this stage, being a reader includes setting goals, locating print resources, judging relevance and importance, extracting critical details, combining information with prior knowledge, and synthesizing what is learned. This phase demands constructing goals, critically evaluating texts, and managing time for literacy activities at a new level. Previous phases of intrinsic reading motivation development will not suffice to ensure the necessary motivations for reading as inquiry.

In this phase, students enjoy extending their autonomy. They construct personally significant topics to read about, find resources that appeal to them, and construct creative and unique interpretations. Motivation for reading inquiry is based on the enjoyment of autonomy and the desire to be an agent of one's own growth. In this phase, self-improvement refers not to developing skill in coding the written language or comprehending an author's message, but to enhancing the self as a knowledgeable, sentient being. In this phase, children are motivated to grow as persons through reading.

None of the preceding phases of motivational development ensures that this one will occur successfully. Although some students are motivated to follow an author's message in a story or book, they are not inquirers. Research by Wigfield and Guthrie (1997) showed that the reading motivation of involvement—the enjoyment of getting lost in a book—is independent of the motivation of curiosity. Some individuals have one of these aspects of intrinsic motivation, some have both, and still others have neither. Participating in inquiry, enjoying the process of learning through problem solving, acknowledging and embracing the challenge of investigation, and possessing a disposition for new learning through self-direction are highly important and relatively unique to this phase. There is a significant research base that describes the contexts and environments needed for motivational development in this phase (McCombs and Whistler 1997).

How Does Intrinsic Motivation Develop?

First, it is valuable to clarify the meaning of intrinsically motivated activity. Ed Deci and his colleagues at the University of Rochester have examined the topic extensively. Several of his colleagues (Ryan, Connell, and Grolnick 1992) stated:

> We define intrinsic motivation as an innate, rather than derivative propensity to explore and master one's internal and external worlds. It is manifested as curiosity and interest, which motivate task engagement even in the absence of outside reinforcement or support. Intrinsic motivation represents an organismic tendency that plays an

important role in the development of energizing the exercise and elaboration of one's capacities, . . . Intrinsically motivated behavior is . . . done for its own sake or for the satisfaction inherent in the process of the activity . . . Extrinsic motivation, on the other hand, pertains to activity that is more directly instrumental or adaptational, based upon people's needs to respond to socially prescribed demands, limits, and patterns of behavior. When extrinsically motivated, individuals behave in order to attain some external reward, avoid some threat, gain some recognition by another, or conform to some extant value. (169–170)

For young children, many activities are intrinsically motivated. Such activities include eating, sitting in mother's lap, and playing with favorite toys. Children do these naturally and without external rewards. These activities will be pursued for their own sake and enjoyment. However, a number of activities are not easily learned independently and immediately enjoyed for their own sake. For example, riding a bicycle, swimming, playing a musical instrument, writing a story, and reading a book are activities that are performed most frequently with support and interaction from significant others. As children perform these activities, they acquire motivations surrounding the nature of the social interaction that is occurring. If children's basic psychological needs are met in the course of these interactions, their motivations will become intrinsic. If, however, the interactions are less need fulfilling and more externally controlled and determined, the child's motivations for performing them will become relatively more extrinsic than intrinsic.

The basic psychological needs that young children bring to most interactions and activities include the needs for competence, relatedness, and autonomy, according to Deci and Ryan (1985). As indicated in the previous definition, these needs are innate, as fundamental as the physiological needs for food, comfort, and safety. The competence need refers to children's desire to be capable of doing valued things, such as walking, talking, and solving problems creatively. In reading acquisition, the need for competence is fulfilled as children are able to comprehend stories that are read to them, gain expertise in recognizing letters and words, and understand independently an author's meaning. Competence here refers to a successful completion of cognitive and language processes and to the understanding that results from them.

Children's need for relatedness refers to their desire for security in an interpersonal milieu. If early reading experiences in book sharing or recognizing environmental print are shared with significant others, children gain intrinsic motivation for these early literacy activities. In older students, needs for relatedness may be met by sharing books with friends, learning about topics in common with peers, and reading literature expressive of the human experience. As literacy activities fulfill needs of relatedness, the act of reading becomes intrinsically motivated.

Young children's need for autonomy is related to the desire to control their environment. A youngster may be insistent about wearing a particular piece of clothing on a given day. Such insistence reflects the desire to exercise control over the world rather than be controlled by it. As children exercise control over which books they read, how long they spend in the activity, and the nature of their book interactions, they acquire intrinsic motivations for reading. In contrast, if children are controlled by parents or teachers in their literacy interactions, they may become extrinsically motivated to read. Without the opportunity to make choices and exercise their autonomy in reading, children's reasons for engaging in literacy will be externalized (Connell and Wellborn 1991). They will read to meet expectations and obtain rewards offered by others, but not to pursue their interests and extend their sense of self.

A fourth need is children's desire to know and understand. As Berlyne (1960) has shown, the need to explore is as basic as the need for food. In fact, mammals that are hungry and placed in a new environment will devote time to exploring the environment before they satisfy their hunger by eating. Young children explore constantly, and the frequent question "Why?" symbolizes their insatiable craving to know. In this context, the need to know has an experiential aspect. Children who want to hear a story repeatedly are seeking to relive an experience. With each rereading, the child knows the character and understands the adventure in new ways, as well as enjoying them in old ways. Children who follow favorite authors, pursue intriguing topics, or enjoy satisfying their curiosity through reading are fulfilling their need for knowing and experiencing. Simply understanding something we have been puzzled by is inherently gratifying, and this gratification may occur at any age.

The psychological need to know, which has also been called the need for cognition, supports competence, but is not the same as competence (Cacioppo et al. 1996). Although the need for cognition requires some competence in listening or reading, the need to know is a need to understand the surrounding world through reading. Although competence is important to an individual's self-efficacy as a reader, the sense of being capable of reading is not the same as feeling and being knowledgeable. A fulfilled need for competence in literacy enables the person to say "I can read" or "I can enjoy books." However, the need to know is fulfilled when the person is able to say "I do enjoy what I have learned through literature" or "I do find it satisfying to understand this topic more fully." Competence refers to the process of being a reader (procedural), whereas the need for knowledge refers to the substantitive content of literature or information (declarative) that the exercise of reading processes generates.

Intrinsically motivated reading is based on these basic psychological needs. For example, when a child's need for competence is met, the child believes in her capacity to read effectively. She can say, "I read pretty well." Feeling competent enables the child to read easily and for enjoyment. The need for relatedness is associated with a social aspect of reading motivation. Fulfillment of the need for relatedness enables the student to participate in reading as an interpersonal activity. Likewise, when the individual's need for autonomy is met, the person is able to responsibly exercise choice to extend his reading interests. If the individual believes he has genuine options and control over which options to pursue, he is likely to become intrinsically motivated in the selection and activity associated with the chosen option.

Finally, the need for knowing is related to two aspects of intrinsic motivation, curiosity and involvement. Curiosity refers to individuals' enjoyment in learning about the world around them through reading; it emphasizes nonfiction reading and scientifically oriented ways of knowing. The motivational aspect of involvement often refers to pleasure in a literary work. This form of knowing through literacy consists of entering the fictional world of the author. The distinction between curiosity and involvement illustrates that there are multiple avenues for knowing that have developed differently for different individuals. These different motivational aspects are relatively independent of each other. Individuals may be high on one or another, high on all, or low on all. They are not bound to one another, perhaps because individuals vary in the nature of the need-fulfilling literacy interactions that they experience before the age of nine or ten.

Intrinsically motivated readers have been fortunate to enjoy literacy interactions in which these basic psychological needs are fulfilled. The needs for competence, relatedness, autonomy, and knowing may be connected to all aspects of literacy: shared book reading, learning the written code, independent comprehension, and inquiry through reading as a lifestyle. Unfortunately, the different phases of literacy development through which most people progress also hold threats to the acquisition of intrinsic motivation for reading. Each phase requires a new set of cognitive challenges and a new type of motivational development. If these challenges are met, the individual may continue developing intrinsic motivation. However, if a child is thwarted by cognitive failure or interpersonal limitations, reading motivations may not develop at all or the individual may become extrinsically oriented. In the next section, we discuss these contextual influences more fully.

Contextual Influences on the Development of Intrinsically Motivated Reading

How do contexts provided by parents, teachers, or schools influence the kinds of motivations children develop? First, we reiterate the distinction between intrinsic and extrinsic motivational orientations. A child who is intrinsically motivated to read will read for its own sake, will seek and meet the challenges of reading new books, will enjoy the stimulation of novelty, and will exert effort to understand fully or complete the experience of a book-reading activity. By comparison, the extrinsically motivated child views reading as a means to an end. Reading is a way of obtaining a reward or incentive provided by a significant other, such as a parent or teacher.

A context that is extrinsically motivating sets in place a structure consisting of reading tasks to be accomplished. Rewards for successful completion, such as prizes, are stipulated and awarded. Children in this environment exhibit a strong tendency to choose easy tasks in order to obtain the reward, and to avoid challenges in order to increase their chances of success. With extended experience under extrinsic incentives, children acquire an extrinsic orientation that includes preference for easy assignments, reliance on the teacher for help, dependence on the teacher's opinion, and submission to external sources of evaluation (e.g., grades) rather than self-appraisal (Flink et al. 1992).

Children who experience extrinsic incentives and controlling parents or teachers acquire a typical set of perceptions. These children believe that the teachers are in control of their reading and that external recognition for success is the highest premium. Because they are not in control of their outcomes, children's efforts are linked to rewards but not to their comprehension or enjoyment of reading. If these conditions are sustained, children become dependent upon external structures, evaluations, and tangible rewards for reading. In this situation, achievement, in terms of comprehension abilities reflected on tests, declines (Barrett and Boggiano, 1988; Boggiano and Barrett 1985). In contrast, intrinsically motivated reading develops when students' literacy interactions are successful in meeting their needs for competence, relatedness, autonomy, and knowing. In other words, reading activity that is enjoyed for its own sake develops when parents and teachers enable students to understand the level of their own competence. If children can see what they can and cannot read effectively, they gain a realistic self-concept that enables them to make good choices about which books to read and when to persist in the face of difficulties. When the context for reading is supportive of children's competence, relatedness, autonomy, and knowing, these same qualities are infused into their motivations for reading. Thus, children possess a sense of self-efficacy for reading, integrate literacy interactions into their social lives, exercise freedom of choice in their reading activities, and continually extend their experience and world knowledge through reading.

Conclusion

At the outset, we alluded to Clay's emphasis on the reader as a self-improving system. She revised the phrase to refer to a self-extending system in later publications (Clay 1991). Although the term *improvement* may be viewed narrowly in terms of achievement by some individuals, the term *extension* refers to the broad scope of self-development that is characteristic of mature readers. Although Clay underscored the cognitive foundations of this self-extending system, this chapter proposes the motivational conditions that naturally accompany that cognitive foundation. At the youngest age, children who are intrinsically motivated to read will expand their literary experience, their knowledge base, and their belief in themselves as they participate in reading. In contrast, children who are more extrinsically motivated will gain more rewards and reinforcement. However, they are less likely to experience understanding and a sense of themselves as self-extending readers than are intrinsically motivated readers. As Clay and others have explained and documented, cognitive supports for reading competencies are needed to attain the goal of helping children become self-extending readers. In addition, we have seen in this chapter that explicitly designed supports for intrinsically motivated reading are equally vital to the attainment of self-extension. The potential barriers to intrinsic motivation for reading are encountered throughout the course of reading development because the cognitive challenges of reading shift. From shared book reading, to learning the written code, to independent comprehension, to reading inquiry, new motivational acquisitions are needed. Contextual supports for intrinsic motivation need to recur in new forms as children develop literacy, just as the cognitive supports recur in new forms throughout elementary schooling. When the conjunction of cognitive and motivational processes occurs, children's chances of becoming sustained in their self-extensions are enhanced.

References

ANDERSON, R. C., WILSON, P. T., AND FIELDING, L. G. 1988. "Growth in Reading and How Children Spend Their Time Outside of School." *Reading Research Quarterly* 23: 285–303.

BAKER, L., SCHER, D., AND MACKLER, K. 1997. "Home and Family Influences on Motivations for Literacy." *Educational Psychologist* 32: 69–82.

BARRETT, M., AND BOGGIANO, A. K. 1988. "Fostering Extrinsic Orientations: Use of Reward Strategies to Motivate Children." *Journal of Social and Clinical Psychology* 6: 293–309.

BERLYNE, D. E. 1960. *Conflict, Arousal, and Curiosity.* New York: McGraw-Hill.

BIEMILLER, A. 1970. "The Development of the Use of Graphic and Contextual Information as Children Learn to Read." *Reading Research Quarterly* 6 (1): 75–96.

BOGGIANO, A. K., AND BARRETT, M. 1985. "Performance and Motivational Deficits of Helplessness: The Role of Motivational Orientations." *Journal of Personality and Social Psychology* 49: 1753–1761.

CACIOPPO, J., PETTY, R., FEINSTEIN, J., AND JARVIS, B. 1996. "Dispositional Differences in Cognitive Motivation: The Life and Times of Individuals Varying in Need for Cognition." *Psychological Bulletin* 119: 197–253.

CAMPBELL, J. R., VOEKL, K. E., AND DONAHUE, P. L. 1997. *NAEP 1996 Trends in Academic Progress* (NCES Publication No. 97–985). Washington, D.C.: U.S. Department of Education.

CLAY, M. M. 1979a. *The Early Detection of Reading Difficulties: A Diagnostic Survey with Recovery Procedures.* 2d ed. Auckland: Heinemann.

———. 1979b. *Reading: The Patterning of Complex Behaviour* 2d ed. Auckland: Heinemann.

———. 1991. *Becoming Literate: The Construction of Inner Control.* Portsmouth, N.H.: Heinemann.

———. 1998. *By Different Paths to Common Outcomes.* York, Maine: Stenhouse.

CONNELL, J. P., AND WELLBORN, J. G. 1991. "Competence, Autonomy, and Relatedness: A Motivational Analysis of Self-System Pocesses." In *Self Processes and Development. The Minnesota Symposia on Child Development*, Vol. 23, edited by M. R. Gunnar and L. A. Sroufe, 43–77. Hillsdale, N.J.: Erlbaum.

CUNNINGHAM, A. E., AND STANOVICH, K. E. 1997. "Early Reading Acquisition and Its Relation to Reading Experience and Ability 10 Years Later." *Developmental Psychology* 33 (6): 934–945.

DECI, E. L. 1992. "The Relation of Interest to the Motivation of Behavior: A Self-Determination Theory Perspective." In *The Role of Interest in Learning and Development*, edited by A. Renninger, S. Hidi, and A. Krapp, 43–70. Hillsdale, N.J.: Erlbaum.

DECI, E. L., AND RYAN, R. M. 1985. *Intrinsic Motivation and Self-Determination in Human Behavior.* New York: Plenum Press.

FLINK, C., BOGGIANO, A. K., MAIN, D. S., BARRETT, M., AND KATZ, P. A. 1992. "Children's Achievement-Related Behaviors: The Role of Extrinsic and Intrinsic Motivational Orientations." In *Achievement and Motivation: A Social-Developmental Perspective*, edited by A. K. Boggiano and T. S. Pittman, 189–214. New York: Cambridge University Press.

FOORMAN, B. R., FRANCIS, D. J., FLETCHER, J. M., SCHATSCHNEIDER, C., AND MEHTA, P. 1998. "The Role of Instruction in Learning to Read: Preventing Reading Failure in At-Risk Children." *Journal of Educational Psychology* 90: 37–55.

GAA, J. P. 1973. "Effects of Individual Goal Setting Conferences on Achievement, Attitudes, and Goal-Setting Behavior." *Journal of Experimental Education* 42: 22–28.

GOTTFRIED, A. E. 1990. "Academic Intrinsic Motivation in Young Elementary School Children." *Journal of Educational Psychology* 82 (3): 525–538.

GUTHRIE, J. T., AND ANDERSON, E. 1999. "Engagement in Reading: Processes of Motivated, Strategic, Knowledgeable, and Social Readers." In *Engaged Reading: Processes, Practices, and Policy Implications*, edited by J. T. Guthrie and D. E. Alvermann, 17–45. New York: Teachers College Press.

HARTER, S., WHITESELL, N. R., AND KOWALSKI, P. 1992. "Individual Differences in the Effects of Educational Transitions on Young Adolescents' Perceptions of Competence and Motivational Orientation." *American Educational Research Journal* 29: 777–807.

McCOMBS, B. L., AND WHISTLER, J. S. 1997. "The Learner-Centered Classroom and School: Strategies for Increasing Student Motivation and Achievement." In *The Learner-Centered Classroom*, edited by B. L. McCombs and J. S. Whistler, 63–101. San Francisco: Jossey-Bass.

McKENNA, M. C., KEAR, D. J., AND ELLSWORTH, R. A. 1995. "Children's Attitudes Toward Reading: A National Survey." *Reading Research Quarterly* 3: 715–726.

RYAN, R. M., CONNELL, J. P., AND GROLNICK, W. 1992. "When Achievement Is Not Intrinsically Motivated: A Theory of Internalization and Self-Regulation in School." In *Achievement and Motivation: A Social-Developmental Perspective*, edited by A. K. Boggiano and T. S. Pittman, 167–188. New York: Cambridge University Press.

SKINNER, E. A., WELLBORN, J. G., AND CONNELL, J. P. 1990. "What It Takes to Do Well in School and Whether I've Got It: A Process Model of Perceived Control and Children's Engagement and Achievement in School." *Journal of Educational Psychology* 82: 22–32.

SMITH, F. 1978. *Understanding Reading.* 2d ed. New York: Holt, Rhinehart and Winston.

WIGFIELD, A., ECCLES, J. S., AND RODRIGUEZ, D. 1998. "The Development of Children's Motivation in School Contexts." In *Review of Research in Education* Vol. 23, edited by P. D. Pearson and A. Iran-Nejad, 73–118. Washington, D.C.: American Educational Researchers Association.

WIGFIELD, A., AND GUTHRIE, J. T. 1997. "Relations of Children's Motivation for Reading to the Amount and Breadth of Their Reading." *Journal of Educational Psychology* 89: 420–432.

Ten

What Does Good First Teaching Mean?

IRENE C. FOUNTAS AND GAY SU PINNELL

The first few years of school are a child's introduction to the kind of learning that will be required for success in school and later in life. Patterns of learning are established, and a body of knowledge that will be foundational to all of the rest of learning must be acquired—that is, the child becomes literate. In the first years of school we expect that children will progress from only a few vague ideas about reading and writing to capable, fluent use of reading and writing as tools for learning. Achieving this goal depends on the first teaching that children experience in school, especially for children who depend on school for most of their literacy learning.

In this chapter, we examine ten characteristics of what we call *good first teaching*. Although we recognize the great importance of preschool experiences and the need to support literacy opportunities in children's homes, our focus here is limited to what we can provide in school settings and how we can teach reading and writing, which as literacy educators, is our concern, our experience, and our expertise.

1. Good first teaching begins with a belief that all children can learn to read and write.

"The learners are ready but the school is not ready to demand learning from them and to deliver the opportunities they need" (Clay 1998, 206).

Historically, a body of research has suggested that one factor in students' success is whether or not their teacher believes that they can learn (Baker and Crist 1971; Silberman 1970). Apparently that belief system leads the teacher to make unconscious decisions about which opportunities to provide for the learner. Unfortunately, remedying the situation is not so simple as just helping teachers suddenly decide that all children can learn. Beliefs are deeply rooted, often at a subconscious level, and result from the life and professional experiences that all of us have had.

Whether or not there is a clear research base to support teacher belief as a major factor in learning, the concept makes sense to us, given our experiences. When children appear to be tired, for example, sympathetic teachers may encourage naps rather than engage them in instruction. With the best of intentions, a teacher may deprive a child of an opportunity to learn (and at the same time provide rest during the day so that the child will, naturally, be able to stay up later at night). So, achieving good first teaching for all children requires that as teachers we engage in self-examination and hold an open view of what is possible.

What makes a difference in teachers' beliefs about students' ability? It might be the previous performance of that child or the teacher's own experiences with children who exhibit characteristics such as a high or low levels of distractibility. Stereotypes about siblings and family members can interfere with our ability to perceive children's strengths and use those strengths as a basis for learning.

Reading Recovery has helped many teachers expand and renew their belief that all children can learn to read and write. Reading Recovery teachers serve the lowest achievers in literacy, one by one. They accept all children as potential learners and challenge themselves to reach each learner's starting point. The fact that so many children who receive intensive individual tutoring in Reading Recovery make accelerated progress is confirmation that if we can find the way to adjust the school program to children (rather than the other way around), we can find a way to teach all children.

Seeing children's strengths and building on them is key to strengthening one's own belief in children. In Reading Recovery, teachers are able to see the tangible results of their work. So, Reading Recovery teaching represents not only an opportunity for the child to learn, but for the teacher to learn from the experience. Classroom teachers and Reading Recovery teachers who observe evidence of accelerated learning on the part of a child who was thought not to be able to learn are changed by the experience. The experience "ups the ante," so that the search is on for ways to teach every child.

For a teacher working in a classroom with twenty-five or thirty children, Reading Recovery as a one-to-one intervention is not the teaching model, although it may confirm the possibility of every child's learning. The classroom involves a different challenge. Children learn as individuals and we see evidence of the progress in individuals; but we often organize children into groups for efficient and effective teaching, as well as for the benefits of social learning. Classroom experiences are widely varied and include many opportunities to use reading and writing for a variety of purposes. The classroom program must be organized so that many routes to learning are possible and there are multiple levels, so that all children in the class are met at their starting points. If we believe that all children can learn, then we must make the opportunities possible; this means adjusting the school program—sometimes through providing individual help, sometimes through providing smaller groups with a more intensive focus, and sometimes through engaging in different kinds of literate activity.

2. Good first teaching is based on a teacher's understanding of the reading and writing processes.

Good first teachers understand that teaching is not a simple series of prescribed steps to be undertaken in rote manner. No matter how sound a guide or set of materials may be, instructional effectiveness absolutely depends on their informed use. All reading programs are successful with most students; none is successful with all students. Every program has some gaps and some weaknesses. It may be impossible for one approach or one program to provide for the needs of all the diverse learners in our schools. The effective teacher knows that she will be observing her own students carefully as they learn within an instructional approach or program, and she will be filling in the gaps in learning that may occur. Teaching decisions are based on knowledge of:

- The processes of reading and writing
- The children you teach
- How to make a match between the two
- How to use materials in ways to support the learning process

Teaching has been called an art, a craft, and a science. Whatever name applies (and we suspect that all three are appropriate), it is obvious that teaching is complex. Moment-to-moment decisions arise from the body of understandings developed over time. According to Clay (1998), good teaching "arises out of the understandings teachers have of their craft and never out of prescriptive programs" (130).

Teacher's understandings are rooted in their own observations of what children actually do. You can learn how to help children read and write by observing what experienced and inexperienced readers and writers do, and thus you can continually document the development of the critical processes. Observations of the children you teach then makes sense as you build understanding of the individual routes they are taking to those common outcomes (Clay 1998).

The prescriptive curriculum is often resorted to when administrators do not trust teachers (or themselves) to create a curriculum that effectively and efficiently makes the most of learning for all children. It is thought that if the curriculum is systematically applied, even if some children are going over concepts and skills they already know and others are finding learning quite difficult, everyone has the best chance of acquiring the knowledge they need. We would describe such an approach as a "hit or miss" curriculum. Indeed, without systematic assessment and good knowledge of what children know, it is quite difficult to create lessons that work and to make them into a curriculum that supports high achievement. But systematic observation can free teachers from the prescriptive curriculum because they have a knowledge of outcomes and can see evidence of learning along the way.

Looking at Reading

Examining children's reading behaviors on a regular basis not only assists teachers in making the complex decisions related to planning reading lessons, but guides their moment-to-moment interactions with children in a way that makes the interactions more powerful. The excerpt in Figure 10–1 is from a running record[1] of Lauren's reading of *Ginger* (Fear 1995). The √ marks indicate accurate reading.

167

Text	Child's Reading
Ginger, p. 1	
Oh, no! Ginger needed to find a new	√ √ √ √ √ √ √ √
	house
	———
home.	home
She walked all around town.	√ √ √ │a- r-√ two │SC
	——— ———
	│around town│
She looked up one street and	√ √ √ √ √ √
she looked down another.	√ √ √ √
Ginger, p. 9	
Ginger went to the next door.	√ √ √ √ √ √
A woman let her in.	√ √ √ √ √
Ginger looked all around and sniffed the air.	√ √ √ √ √ smelled│R √ √R
	———
	sniffed │
She smelled broccoli. Ginger was hungry,	√ √R √ √ √ √
but she didn't like broccoli!	√ √ √ √ √
This was not the place for Ginger.	√ √ √ √ √ √ √

FIGURE 10–1 *Lauren's reading of* Ginger

Lauren read *Ginger* with high accuracy (97 percent of words were read correctly). She knew or could solve almost all of the words that she needed to read this text, which is at a level that average first graders can read toward the end of the year. Accurate reading provided evidence that she was checking on her own reading and was reading for meaning. Most of what she read made sense, sounded right, and looked right. Further, her reading was phrased and mostly smooth sounding. Lauren observed punctuation marks with appropriate pauses and stops. Her substitutions also indicated that she was working for meaning throughout this text. On page three, she substituted *house* for *home* and did not self-correct. That miscue was close in meaning and also looked orthographically similar to the word in the text. On the next line, we see some evidence of word solving, as Lauren started to use the letter-sound information, the beginning two letters of *around*, at first saying them aloud. She sampled the visual information and, while checking the rest of the word, probably also thought about what would make sense and sound right. Thus, Lauren successfully used several different sources of information to figure out a word that was new to her. On the next word, *town*, she quickly said a known word, *two*, that was orthographically similar, but quickly self-corrected as she noticed different features of the word. Probably, though, she also was checking the meaning and knew that *two* simply would not make sense at the end of this sentence. These errors and self-corrections provide evidence of close monitoring, using several kinds of information in the text.

On page 9, we see further evidence of Lauren's checking behavior. She substituted the word *smelled* for *sniffed*, a miscue that made sense and began and ended like the word in the text. As indicated by this substitution, Lauren used three sources of information—meaning, language structure, and the visual features of the word. Yet she stopped and repeated the word again. At the end of the sentence, she hesitated again, going back to repeat the phrase. It sounded right to her, but we hypothesize that she knew something wasn't quite right. To render an absolutely accurate reading, Lauren would need to analyze the visual features of the word more precisely. What is important here is her monitoring behavior, the fact that she was detecting error and was working on information that did not quite fit. This behavior indicates active processing.

Looking at children's writing behavior as well as their products, and analyzing and interpreting them, can free you from the prescriptive curriculum. With an understanding of the desired outcomes, you can see evidence of learning and plan for group teaching and individual conferences that move writers forward.

Next, we look at a sample of writing behavior. In Selena's writing, presented in Figure 10–2, we see a very powerful message, full of personal meaning for this child. The piece of writing was prompted not only by Selena's own life circumstances but by her knowledge of a familiar text, *Who Will Be My Mother?* (Cowley 1983), which she had read in a guided reading group and reread several times. In fact, the picture on the front of Selena's book provides evidence of the connection between texts. She actually copied the title of the book for the front of her book. We believe that this text might have reminded her of her own experiences. The most important characteristic of this writing is that Selena is expressing in her own voice what is important to her.

As we look further at this piece of writing, we see a great deal of evidence that Selena is developing as a writer. The text contains many words spelled conventionally (for example, *my, mother, and, she, I, me, see, will, a, got, to, dad, not, big, love*). Her accurate spelling of the word *brother* (after attempting the spelling as *BUDR*) was the result of a conference with the teacher, who showed her that *brother* and *mother* were similar. We see how Selena was using letter-sound relationships as a strategy to spell words.

FIGURE 10–2   *Selena's writing sample*

BAK, NOO, HOO, HAV, UV, NEVR, KER (also written as *CER*), *COD*, and *TAK* all indicate the use of phonetic strategies. *NOO* (new) and *HOO* (who) indicate that Selena is beginning to understand the use of spelling patterns in words. We also notice that she is aware of words with silent letters (DIDE for died).

Her attempt at the word *little* is interesting. She wrote LIDLL, indicating her awareness of the sounds in words as well as the orthographic features, such as the double letter. As a writer, Selena understands how to stick with her topic and have a series of ideas about it. Her story was relevant to her title, and she had a series of events that are placed in order. She also had a conclusion that resolved a problem. This young writer is putting together many different kinds of knowledge. By looking carefully at children's writing, we develop our understandings of how individual writers build a writing process over time.

From observations of reading and writing behavior such as the ones presented here, we have evidence of how young children build a system for constructing meaning from written language and making it their own. As we observe and analyze many samples of behavior over the years, we add to our own base of knowledge about how children become literate.

3. Good first teaching is based on assessment that informs instruction and documents individual learning over time.

Observation of children's reading and writing behaviors is the key to good first teaching. Observing behaviors and analyzing them helps us to meet a child where he is as a reader and writer. According to Clay, "just as a listener tunes in to a speaker, so a teacher must observe, listen to, and tune in to a learner" (1998, 13). Good assessment

- uncovers specific behaviors that indicate children's strengths and knowledge base as a starting point for further learning
- is systematically applied so that reliable, valid information is collected
- provides information on how children use knowledge in a variety of contexts, most of which are close to the processes of reading and writing continuous text
- accurately inventories bodies of information (such as letter knowledge) but leaves openings to discover more about what children know
- includes procedures that are an ongoing, integral component of the classroom instruction
- includes more formalized procedures that provide good information for reporting, class assessment, end-of-year assessment, and placing children in texts

Assessment is a way of taking high-quality, sensitive observation, such as that described under the previous point, and placing it in ongoing, systematic processes that guide teaching. Even good observation needs to be systematized and documented over time if it is to fully support effective instruction.

A key assessment in early literacy instruction is the systematic record of reading behavior provided by running records. As a tool it has many uses, the most important of which is to document how children are building a reading process over time. It provides both qualitative and quantitative information to help us assess what children are able to do and to find the level and type of reading text that will support and challenge children so that they learn more about reading (Fountas and Pinnell 1996). Systematic collection and careful study of writing samples over time accomplishes the same detailed analysis, to include both content and mechanics. It is in the study of writing and reading samples that the curriculum for reading, writing, and word study can be developed to meet the needs of the children you teach.

4. Good first teaching engages children in a variety of authentic reading and writing experiences every day.

There is only one way to become a reader—by using strategies to read continuous text for a variety of purposes. And there is only one way to become a writer—by composing and constructing continuous text for many different purposes. Focused experiences, in which children give direct attention to aspects of composing or constructing text, are an essential part of the instructional plan, but the understandings that are developed must be closely related to children's daily use of knowledge and skills while writing and reading continuous text.

To ensure opportunities for children to write and read, we need to look carefully at classroom life and analyze the important literacy opportunities that are present there.

Extensive Amounts of Reading Daily

To learn how to process as a reader, children need opportunities to read a great deal of continuous text every day. We might ask ourselves a variety of questions to evaluate the opportunities. How much real reading do we actually see going on in the classrooms in our schools? Are children given opportunities to read fiction and nonfiction text? What would it mean to look at classroom after classroom and see some literacy activities but no children actually reading books? Encounters with text should range from easy reading to more challenging reading, but there is value simply in looking at the amount of text—the number of words organized into coherent text—that readers process daily.

Rereading of Familiar Material That Supports Phrased, Smooth Reading

Fluent processing of easy material is an important aspect of a reader's competence. Reading familiar material supports fluency. In a text that is very easy, readers have the opportunity to engage in rapid problem solving and can turn their attention to the meaning of the text and the sound of the language as they read. Younger children often reread their first books many times, enjoying the fluent act of reading. As they become able to read longer books, for example in second grade, rereading is not necessary. Only favorites might be taken up again, or parts of the book might be reread to get information or to perform for others. But, then, reading of easier texts or reading a whole series about the same character (for example, Arthur, Amelia Bedelia, or Cam Jansen) provides the opportunity for developing and supporting fluency on familiar materials.

Instructional Reading with Appropriate Supports and Challenges That Give Children Opportunities for Problem Solving

While easy reading builds fluency in processing, it is also necessary for children to extend reading competence by reading books that offer challenges. A book must be "just right" for instruction; that is, it must contain language structures, concepts, and words that the child either knows or can get to with his current reading strategies. A text that places slightly more demands on the reading process gives the reader the opportunity to engage in some "reading work," the in-the-head problem solving that extends the system. A self-extending system, as Clay (1991) describes it, as one that is expanded through use. Such a system means that readers have *learned how to learn* reading. This system is built through successful processing. Readers need problems to solve, so they must meet some challenges in each novel text, and they must use strategies to solve them.

In Figure 10–3, we look at a teacher's interaction with Jeremy while he reads *Baby Bear's Present* (Randell 1994). The left column presents the text and the middle column shows a representation of Jeremy's reading. The teacher was not taking a running record, but was simply observing, taking notes, and briefly interacting with the child as he read a text in a guided reading group. The reading behavior is coded here simply to present the actual reading information. The right column shows the teacher's (T) interactions with the child (C). Her comments are made very quickly so that the interaction will not disrupt the momentum of the reading; they provide light support that keeps the reader going and simultaneously brings to his attention ways to use information in the text.

For example, Jeremy substituted *had* for *has*, read to the end of the line, and then reread to self-correct, indicating that he was checking further, noticing the ending of the word. The teacher encouraged him with a comment. Then, in the next section, Jeremy read *said* for *is* without noticing the discrepancy between his reading and the text. The teacher decided that it would be appropriate to call Jeremy's attention to the discrepancy because he was learning how to check what makes sense with the print. She wanted him to use his knowledge of *known* words, such as *is*. In this case, Jeremy did know the word but was not using it as he processed the text.

The teacher's first move was to ask Jeremy to check on his reading, but Jeremy produced the sentence in the same way. She then read the sentence as he read it and asked him to find the word that didn't look right. Jeremy was not able to find the word that didn't fit. Finally, she drew his attention to the word and asked him what it was.

Text—*Baby Bear's Present*	Child's Reading	Teacher/Child Interaction
Mother Bear said,	√ <u>b-√</u> | R √ Bear |	
"Baby Bear has no toys."	√ √ <u>had</u> | SC √ √ has |	T-I like the way you fixed that.
Let's get a toy for Baby Bear.	√ √ √ √ √ √ √	
"Yes, let's," said Father Bear.	√ √ √ √ √	

"He is a good little bear."	√ <u>said</u> √ √ √ √
	  is
		T-Does that sound right? Try that again.
		C-Rereads the same.
		T-You said . . . . (points and reads as the child did).
		   Which one doesn't look right?
		C-Points to <u>bear.</u>
		T-This one doesn't look right (points to <u>is</u>). What's that word?
		C-Is.
		T- Try <u>is</u> and see if that would sound right.
		C-Rereads the sentence accurately.
		T-It sounds right and now it looks right too.

FIGURE 10–3 *Teacher-child interactions during Jeremy's reading of* Baby Bear's Present

This time, when Jeremy focused on the word, he was able to read it. The teacher then prompted him to read it in the sentence and to be sure that it made sense, sounded right, and looked right. He was being required to confirm for himself.

This interaction provides a good example of a teacher working to help a child monitor his own reading and use what he knows. When the first interactions did not result in the behavior he needed, the teacher shifted her prompting so that Jeremy was able to work it out. By engaging in this kind of reading work, supported by teacher interaction, children are learning how to solve problems as readers. This in-the-head reading work engages the child again and again in learning something about reading that he can use with other books.

Guided reading is an instructional context designed to help children learn to read by engaging in strategic reading work on novel texts (Fountas and Pinnell 1996). We describe guided reading as a setting in which children who are similar in their development of a reading process *at a particular point in time* can be brought together in a group for intentional teaching of reading. That setting enables the teacher to select an appropriate text for the group to read—one that is not too easy and not too hard. Thus, in guided reading, the goal is to help students edge up in their learning, with the skillful support of the teacher.

In guided reading the teacher selects a book that is "just right" for a group of children. Of course, even though these children are similar in their development of a reading process, they are individuals. The book is appropriate for each member of the group within a range of particular skills and interests. It provides a common experience through which the teacher can help each reader process better. Through an introduction to the book, the teacher fine-tunes the suitability of the book for children in the group (Clay 1998). The goal of the introduction is not to pre-teach a word or eliminate all problems that children might encounter while reading the text, but to provide a set for accessing the information in the text. In fact, we *want* children to encounter words that they do not know and work at figuring them out.

There should not be too many problems, because we want the reading to move along at a fast pace, with just a few challenges. The key is in the book selection and introduction. Then, the teacher guides children as they read the whole text (or a unified part of it) for themselves. Children will be doing "reading work" that is so essential with very little interruption by the teacher, who is guiding the processing at a few points of difficulty or sometimes reinforcing effective processing behaviors that are emerging. After the reading, the teacher and children revisit the text to learn more about the reading process. The teacher selects one or two powerful examples to bring to the children's brief attention following a discussion of the story.

Varied Writing Opportunities Daily

Writing is an increasingly important life skill, especially when we consider that written messages are functioning in broader ways (for example, electronic mail as communication). Through writing, people communicate ideas and give directions, so clear writing makes a difference. Writing is important for its own sake, as students learn to communicate clearly and set down their thoughts. It is also an important support for learning. Writers document their investigations. They record information to help them organize and remember it. They use writing to express their voices and understanding of the world. Moreover, there are important connections between learning in writing and learning in reading.

Learning to be a writer is accomplished through thousands of varied experiences in producing writing. There must be focused time for writing every day within which children can learn the craft and skills related to being a writer.

5. Good first teaching includes attention to letters and words and how they work.

It makes sense to design a curriculum in which children spend most of their time reading and writing for real purposes. While reading for meaning, every good reader uses a range of skills, including word solving, and the same is true for writing. Good readers and writers know about words. They have knowledge of

- an ever-increasing core of words that need little attention because they can be read or written automatically
- knowledge of the individual sounds and clusters of sounds in the language
- the variety of letter patterns that occur in words
- strategies for solving words that they only partially know or that are completely new

Competent word solvers know how to take words apart while reading for meaning and how to spell words while writing to communicate. Taking words apart while reading means that while the eye is moving along a line of print, the reader is very rapidly attending to visual aspects of words. The reader might bring to bear knowledge of letter-sound correspondence, recognize the word instantly as a known word, recognize clusters of letters within a word, recognize meaningful parts or endings. All of these actions take place in a smooth and coordinated way; readers check visual analysis with all other information in the text to be sure that it fits with the meaning and syntax of the sentence.

In writing, words are written letter by letter in a linear way. The writer might know some clusters of letters that represent sound sequences or might think of a cluster of letters as a meaningful unit (adding *ing* to a word, for example). The skillful writer will control a large body of words that are known and are written (or typed on the computer) rapidly, with ongoing monitoring but little conscious attention. Ultimately, each letter of a word must be recalled and written in sequence by the competent writer. Young children need to know how to make the directional movements necessary to construct individual letters, and how to put them in order onto the space of the page, with space between words. All of these understandings represent a complex set of interrelated strategies. How can we support children and get them on their way?

In their first experiences with print, children face a daunting task that is different from any previous kind of visual perception. They need to learn to discern the fine features that make a letter different from every other letter. Most of these differences are quite small (for example, distinguishing *h* from *n*) because our writing system is efficient to produce. So, distinguishing the word *oh* from *on* assumes that children have learned to look at print. Many children have not noticed such features of letters, although they will certainly have encountered print in the environment; many need assistance in where to look, what to look at, and what to look for (Clay 1998).

Good first teaching takes children from their first personal encounters with print to more generalized knowledge. For example, kindergarten and first-grade teachers use children's names very effectively to help children learn how to look at print. Name charts can be a wonderful resource; children are interested in their own names and the names of their friends. Some important understandings can be clustered around names. For example:

- My name is a word that is written the same way every time.
- There are letters in my name and some of the letters are in the names of other people.
- The letters in my name are in a particular sequence.
- I can connect the sounds I hear in my name with the letters.

Experiences such as putting together one's name as a puzzle (first with a model and then without a model) and linking one's name to words that are written on charts in group writing situations help to provide the beginning connections that children need.

It is true that arguments surrounding the word *phonics* batter the field of literacy education and that most (not all) of these arguments center not on *what* children need to know but how to teach it in classrooms. We believe that the key is good first teaching that is based on a teacher's understanding of how language systems are structured.

We propose that a major advantage to primary teachers is developing a way of thinking about the language/literacy curriculum. For too long we have put together eclectic approaches—a little of this and a little of that. Sometimes educators even talk about a literature-based or "whole language" approach with a little phonics sprinkled in or a phonics program with literature added in. Thinking in that eclectic way will lead us in a direction that we do not want to go, and instruction may become fragmented, ineffective, and inefficient.

Good first teaching provides many ways for children to learn and use reading and writing. Children will engage in varied activities through a language arts block—indeed throughout the day—and will take different understandings from them. It is important that all of the ways children use literacy be interconnected, just as language is interconnected as a learning system. It helps us to think about learning word solving in three different but interrelated settings. The instructional model shown in Figure 10–4 guides our thinking about the range of learning contexts that makes for both breadth and depth in learning (Pinnell and Fountas 1998).

Reading involves encountering continuous text and engaging in the processes necessary to gain meaning; that means solving the words within the process. Various kinds of reading contexts—reading aloud, shared reading, guided reading, and independent reading—all support word solving as part of the process. Teachers have an opportunity to draw children's attention to letters and words and how they work.

Likewise, writing contexts—language experience, shared writing, interactive writing, writing workshop, and independent writing—provide settings within which teachers can help children develop strategies for spelling the words they need in their

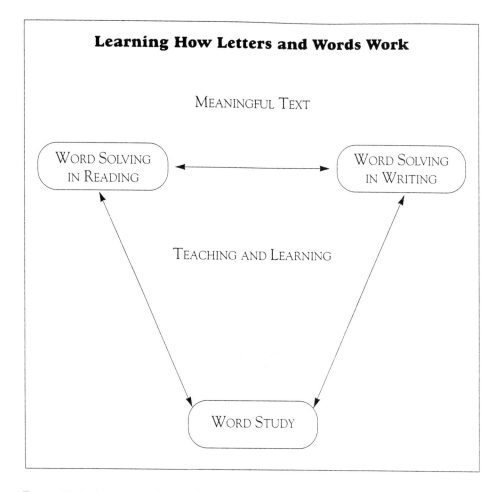

Learning How Letters and Words Work

MEANINGFUL TEXT

WORD SOLVING IN READING

WORD SOLVING IN WRITING

TEACHING AND LEARNING

WORD STUDY

FIGURE 10–4   *Learning how letters and words work*

writing. Interactive writing, in particular, provides opportunities for an explicit demonstration of how words work.

The third area we call *word study*. Here we recommend focused attention to words and word elements, with the goal of helping children use their knowledge within reading and writing contexts. Word study emerges from the teacher's observation of what children are demonstrating that they know about letters, sounds, and words. Knowledge of the language system and how it works within the reading and writing processes helps in determining what children need to know next.

Word study actively involves students in investigating and discovering things about words so that they learn the underlying principles that will help them to take words apart in reading and spell words in writing. Word solving takes place across many literacy contexts. Sometimes the teacher provides an explicit mini-lesson; sometimes children are engaged in independent investigations such as word sorting or building. The important thing about the three contexts represented in this model is that there are meaningful connections among them. Common examples that surface while children are reading or writing become the focus of a mini-lesson, and children might go on independently to find more words like the example or to sort words with that particular principle. A word that has been discovered and added to a chart of words in a certain category (for example, words with *er* endings) might be used in a group writing setting. We like to think about "echoes" across the curriculum, so that children are encountering and using understandings about letters, sounds, and words in many different ways to develop a breadth of knowledge they can use flexibly in many contexts.

6. Good first teaching takes place in a quality, organized environment that supports collaborative and independent learning.

In every environment human beings enter, they learn how to behave in that space— how to manage their learning and interact with each other. That is certainly true of the classroom. What would a classroom look like if every aspect of the physical space and the way people used it were organized to promote self-managed independent learning? An important part of learning is learning *how* to learn; for example, learning how to

- interact with others in positive and constructive ways
- check on oneself, monitoring one's own behavior and learning
- use and care for materials
- complete tasks, alone or in cooperation with others
- make choices and respect the choices of others
- work independently in a self-disciplined way
- use reading and writing as tools for learning and, in the process, learn more about reading and writing

All of these skills are important for adults. We can see the roots of their development as young children work independently and in groups in quality learning environments. An environment in which supplies are carefully organized and labeled signals to children that there are routines and procedures for selecting, using, and caring for materials.

Part of good first teaching is organizing and caring for the environment in a way that provides structure and predictability for the children. When children know where supplies are and how to find and use them, they can give more attention to the learning tasks in which they are involved. Also, when all members of the class are using the classroom materials and equipment in an orderly way, learning is better supported and teachers have time to teach.

Creating order is not just a matter of organizing a beautiful environment, although that is certainly basic to the process. We also need to think about explicit ways to teach the necessary routines of the classroom. Teaching routines does not mean spending hours on rules or being unnecessarily rigid and dictatorial. It simply means that when twenty or thirty people work together all day in one small room, they can accomplish more if everyone knows what is expected as they work together.

Often, teachers explain or tell children what to do. For young children we believe that it is more effective to collaboratively construct guidelines for working together, to demonstrate the behaviors that are important, and to enable them to practice, as much as needed, the desirable behaviors. For example, using a "browsing box" for independent reading seems like a simple process. It might involve going to a particular box, selecting some books, reading each of the books in entirety, reading a book to a partner, returning the books to the box, and going to the next activity in the child's schedule of independent work. For most young children, that series of actions is not familiar. It will help to have them practice the routine a few times with the support of the teacher and to reflect on how well they completed the task.

Every routine that children are expected to carry out in the classroom, from using the stapler to putting books back on the bookshelf to selecting writing materials, must be explicitly demonstrated and taught. Routines are freeing to the teacher and children because everyone can engage in important learning conversations rather than the teacher's constantly "directing traffic."

7. Good first teaching requires appropriate materials and resources to enable children with diverse strengths and needs to engage in reading, writing, and word study.

A range of language and literacy activities is needed to support children's learning across a broad spectrum of understandings. The quality of those activities will suffer if appropriate materials are not there to support the process. We have said that good first teaching is not a "program" and it is not materials. That's true. We think of materials as a necessary-but-not-sufficient factor. The classroom must be alive with materials that attract students' attention and support their learning. Here, we discuss materials to support literacy learning, but we recognize that there must also be a wide range of hands-on materials to support learning in content areas such as science and mathematics, as well as a rich provision of art materials.

For literacy and language learning, the range includes

- information books
- poetry, nursery and other rhymes, songs, chants, and word play
- "big" books to support shared reading
- books that support beginning reading
- books of folktales, fairy tales, poetry, and legends

- concept books, such as counting books, photography on a topic, or ABC books
- books by recognized authors and illustrators

The classroom collection will include books to read aloud to children, books that children can explore on their own even if they cannot read all of the words, books that children can read in their entirety for independent reading, and books that are arranged in a gradient of text for guided reading and other purposes. The whole collection must reflect our multicultural society so that children not only see people like themselves in the books they encounter, but they see and learn to respect other groups in society.

Materials to support writing will also be needed. A well-provisioned and well-organized writing center will not only make it possible for children to select and use materials with less help from the teacher, it will suggest to students how to make their work more interesting and of a higher quality. For example, having different sizes and kinds of paper, markers, a stapler, colored pencils, book covers, and other materials available in trays suggests to students ways to vary the presentation of their ideas.

When students engage in word study, there must be active inquiry into the way words work. Materials such as magnetic letters, word tiles, and word cards for sorting can be used by students independently. As they work with manipulative materials, children can apply understandings that they have discussed with the teacher, but they are likely to go on to discover more about words.

Visually, the classroom for young children must invite literacy learning from the very walls. Teachers successfully use interactive writing, with children's art, to provide reading materials that children can visit independently. Interactive word walls and word charts provide a visual summary of completed and ongoing analyses (Pinnell and Fountas 1998; Hall and Cunningham 1999). Easels, pocket charts, an overhead projector, and other equipment are helpful.

8. Good first teaching requires a large block of daily instructional time for literacy.

Without sustained time for high-quality teaching, children will be shortchanged. At no time in a child's life is it more important to have uninterrupted time for learning with skilled teaching. If we are serious about all children's achievement in literacy, then we must commit at least two and a half hours of uninterrupted time daily for the language arts. That means looking critically at school schedules to eliminate wasted time (such as inefficient ways of moving children to special area studies and long programs on the intercom). It also may mean integrating some important content areas such as science and social studies. After all, children need to write and read about something interesting, and content area learning can provide a meaningful focus. This does not mean eliminating some hands-on investigation time; it does mean using those productive morning hours for language and literacy in ways that will often include reading and writing about content area topics.

181

9. Good first teaching is paired with safety nets for children who need something extra.

If our responsibility as educators is to adjust the school program to educate every child, then good first teaching will not be quite enough. The level of support and the kind of support will obviously need to be adjusted for some children. We need dynamic and rich literacy programs in preschools and kindergartens; yet despite participating in such programs, some children enter the first grade with limited knowledge of and experience with print. There are a variety of reasons, including moving often, poor attendance, and confusion about how the print system works.

Whatever the reason, safety nets are needed to ensure an adequate level of support. Good first teaching will provide what most children need in order to engage with the processes of reading and writing and develop independent systems. A small number of children who will need the extra help must have it during that critical period. The most effective time for intervention in literacy is after the child has had an opportunity to learn in a rich classroom for about a year. Then, if he has not engaged with the reading process, one-on-one help will be needed.

Reading Recovery provides an ideal safety net because the individual tutoring setting allows the teacher to analyze the child's behavior in detail, construct interactions and a series of encounters with text that support this particular child's strengths and needs, and superbly sequence a program that will support accelerate learning. Why do we provide this kind of intensive, high-quality help so early? Why not wait? We argue that within the context of our literate society, first grade is not too early. As children learn more about using reading and writing, the complexity increases geometrically. A child who does not yet understand what the system is about cannot profit from classroom experiences the way most of the other children can, even if good first teaching is going on.

> You can see the doors to effective literacy learning beginning to close during that first year of school. That is why early intervention programs are suggested—in an attempt to stop doors from closing before it is too late. Or, more accurately, as insurance against those doors closing. (Clay 1998, 209)

It simply makes sense to catch most of the children who are having difficulty by providing this early intensive support. Reading Recovery will move almost all children into a position of independent reading and writing so that they can participate fully in classroom instruction. For a very few, ongoing special help of various kinds will be needed.

Safety nets and good first teaching go hand-in-hand. Sometimes we have erroneously assumed that improving classrooms will mean that we do not need safety nets such as Reading Recovery, and it is true that the numbers who appear to need extra help can be greatly reduced by good preschool, kindergarten, and first-grade programs (provided that children have the opportunity to experience all three). But we cannot eliminate all safety nets, even though the classrooms are doing an excellent job. In fact, as classroom teaching improves, the need for safety nets for a few will be even more noticeable.

> My guess is that if we increase literacy achievement with a good preschool, preparatory, and Grade 1 program we will produce a greater need for an early intervention program for the lowest achievers; and we will have created a bigger gap to bridge. (Clay 1998, 218)

10. Good first teaching is not a program you can buy, but is the result of an investment in professional development.

We began this chapter with two factors that are critical in children's learning—the teacher's belief that a child can learn and the teacher's understanding of learning processes. All the other factors we have described here also depend on teacher expertise. The task of teaching all children is daunting for new teachers and remains a challenge even for experienced teachers. The key to good first teaching is good professional development for teachers, and that means teacher education that is more than a one-shot deal or even a two-week summer workshop. Currently, of all educational ventures in the United States, teacher education is the most fragmented and piecemeal.

We have learned from Reading Recovery some powerful ways to support teachers' learning. While the focus is certainly different, we propose that some of the characteristics of teacher development present in Reading Recovery can give direction to professional development for classroom teachers. For example:

- Teachers engage in collaborative inquiry, in which they observe and analyze children's behavior, talking with each other to support the process.
- Teachers examine student work to gather evidence of children they know or almost know, to hypothesize what children need to know, and to decide what will be the most effective teaching.
- Teachers support each other through talk that helps them ground their observations, clarify their analyses and conclusions, and build theoretical understandings.
- Understandings to be developed are close to the act of teaching and have immediate reality for those involved.
- Teachers learn over an extended period of time while they are monitoring the learning of young students.
- Observation of live teaching sessions is an integral part of almost every professional development session so that teachers can learn how to observe student behavior and make moment-by-moment teaching decisions.
- On-site assistance and coaching help individual teachers in their work in schools.
- Teachers are involved in planning for their own learning.

All parties interested in improving education must be interested in helping *teachers* achieve their goals. Teacher education at colleges and universities, as it is currently delivered, is not the entire answer. A concerted effort is needed to find and deliver excellent models of preservice and inservice teacher development that build the kinds of understandings that help teachers continue to learn from their own teaching and to form supportive learning groups.

What is possible?

The ten principles numbered in this article are not placed in order of priority. We have to face the fact that all are necessary. Is it possible to ensure good first teaching for all children? Given that provision, is it possible for all to learn? Our work in Reading Recovery and in primary classrooms has changed our own view of what is possible. We know that it is possible to ensure joyful, competent literacy for virtually all children. We also have had a glimpse of what it's going to take. Turning around expectations that a group of children will fail to achieve independent literacy will take decisive policy and professional will. Standards, policies, and requirements are useless unless there is commitment on the part of educators at the school building level to create a quality program for the children who enter their doors. To meet the challenge of literacy for all requires teamwork and mutual support, as well as commitment to the long-term rather than to quick fixes (Allington and Cunningham 1996).

Children, especially those who are vulnerable for economic or other reasons, need more than one good year of instruction, so it will not be enough to improve teaching in one classroom. Good first teaching is not what happens in one classroom, and it is certainly not what happens when you adopt a particular reading program, no matter how good it is. Good first teaching means several years of high-quality instruction, intervention, and extra support for those who need it, and a range of supports (for example, quality materials and professional development) that will help teachers do their jobs better. Ultimately, children's early literacy achievement will depend on the quality of good first teachers.

Note

1. The running record (Clay 1993a) is a tool for recording the details of reading behavior. The teacher sits beside the child, both looking at the text that the child is reading. A coding system is used to record reading behavior, including significant behaviors such as repetition, substitution, and successive attempts at words. For more information about how to take and use running records, see Clay 1993a; Fountas and Pinnell 1996; and Johnston 1997.

References

ALLINGTON, R. L., AND P. M. CUNNINGHAM. 1996. *Schools That Work: Where All Children Read and Write*. New York: HarperCollins.

BAKER, J. P., AND CRIST, J. L. 1971. "Teachers Expectancies: A Review of the Literature." In *Pygmalion Reconsidered,* edited by J. Elashoff and R. E. Show, 48–64. Worthington, Ohio: Charles A. Jones.

CLAY, M. M. 1991. *Becoming Literate: The Construction of Inner Control.* Portsmouth, N.H.: Heinemann.

———.1993a. *An Observation Survey of Early Literacy Achievement.* Portsmouth, N.H.: Heinemann.

———.1993b. *Reading Recovery: A Guidebook for Teachers in Training.* Portsmouth, N.H.: Heinemann.

———.1998. *By Different Paths to Common Outcomes.* York, Maine: Stenhouse.

COWLEY, J., 1983. *Who Will Be My Mother?* Bothell, Wash.: Wright Company.

FEAR, S. 1995. *Ginger.* Illus. N. Carpenter. Boston: Houghton-Mifflin.

FOUNTAS, I. C., AND PINNELL, G. S. 1996. *Guided Reading: Good First Teaching for All Children.* Portsmouth, N.H.: Heinemann.

HALL, D. P., AND CUNNINGHAM, P. M. 1999. "Multilevel Word Study: Word Charts, Word Walls, and Word Sorts." In *Voices on Word Matters: Learning About Phonics and Spelling in the Literacy Classroom,* edited by I. C. Fountas and G. S. Pinnell, 114–130. Portsmouth, N.H.: Heinemann.

JOHNSTON, P. H. 1997. *Knowing Literacy.* York, Maine: Stenhouse.

PINNELL, G. S., AND FOUNTAS, I. C. 1998. *Word Matters: Teaching Phonics and Spelling in the Reading/Writing Classroom.* Portsmouth, N.H.: Heinemann.

RANDELL, B. 1994. *Baby Bear's Present.* Illus. I. Lowe. Crystal Lake, Ill.: Rigby.

SILBERMAN, M. L. 1970. "Teachers' Attitudes and Actions Toward Their Students." In *The Experience of Schooling,* edited by M. Silberman, 86–96. New York: Holt, Rinehart and Winston.

Eleven

Revealing and Telling: The Socialisation of Attention in Learning to Read and Write

COURTNEY B. CAZDEN

Becoming literate requires learning to attend to new features of the world. More obvious are the features of written language itself: in the beginning, the alphabet and the spatial patterns of letters and lines; later, larger aspects of text structures and the connecting words that mark them. Less obvious and harder to learn, but just as critical in the beginning, are features of already automatised actions, such as the sounds being produced in one's own speech.

These learnings can be called the "socialisation of attention." In using the term "socialisation," I want to emphasise the nonnatural, linguistically and culturally variable, aspects both of these language features themselves and of the kinds of human help given in learning them.

A large binary contrast in the forms of such help—termed acquisition versus learning—was first conceptualised within theories of second language learning and teaching. Subsequently, this contrast has been widely invoked in discussions of all kinds of language learning—oral and written, second language and second discourse, etc. Here, for instance, are Gee's (1990) definitions of the terms:

> *Acquisition* is a process of acquiring something subconsciously by exposure to models, a process of trial and error, and practice within social groups, without formal teaching. It happens in natural settings, which are meaningful and functional in the sense that the acquirers know that they need to acquire the thing they are exposed to in order to function and they in fact want to so function. This is how most people come to control their first language.
>
> *Learning* is a process that involves conscious knowledge gained through teaching (though not necessarily from someone officially designated as a teacher) or through certain life experiences that trigger conscious reflection. This teaching or reflection involves explanation and analysis, that is, breaking down the thing to be learned into its analytic parts. It inherently involves attaining, along with the matter being taught, some degree of meta-knowledge about the matter. (146)

Paper presented at a symposium at the New Zealand Council for Educational Research in honor of Marie Clay, December 1991.

Having defined these two processes by contrast with each other, Gee then qualifies their separateness:

> Much of what we come by in life, after our initial enculturation, involves a mixture of acquisition and learning. However, the balance between the two can be quite different in different cases, and different at different stages in the developmental process. (146)

In writings on literacy education in the United States, this contrast—unmitigated by such qualifications—has been particularly strong and particularly unfortunate. Advocates of "whole language" argue for a pedagogy designed on the model of first language acquisition that can too easily be understood or misunderstood as requiring no formal teaching. Advocates of "phonics" argue for the necessity of just such formal teaching, which can, in turn, too easily be understood or misunderstood as substituting workbook exercises for reading and writing real texts.

There are welcome signs of an erosion of this dangerously oversimplified binary opposition in literacy education (and in second language teaching), and even in corrections of too selective interpretations of what happens so successfully with first languages in the home (Cazden 1992). For example, Holdaway (1990) quotes Gee's definitions given above and then adopts the hybrid term "acquisition learning," because "early speech, emergent literacy, developmental play, and emergent thought can be seen to involve a far greater use of both 'metacognitive awareness' and what might be called 'natural instruction' to a far greater extent than was implied by the initial distinction between acquisition and direct instruction" (2).

To summarise a less polarised view: Human minds seem to learn best from a rich presentation of concrete cases, preferably good prototypical ones; but the mind cannot record for later generalising every feature of every case. And so the role of assistance —given less consciously by parent to child, more deliberately by teacher to student or class—is to focus attention on the most significant features, or those features that particular learners seem to be ignoring. The teacher both selects examples and focuses attention at the moment of encounter.

Marie Clay's work (1985; 1991) has helped me to conceptualise a more complex continuum of experiences with print that are mediated for the learner by different kinds of social assistance. Two points on that continuum of assistance, both intentional and carefully planned, I call "revealing" and "telling."

Consider one teaching strategy from the very successful New Zealand Reading Recovery Programme for six-year-old children who have not caught on to reading (already imported into Australia and the United States and just beginning in Britain at the end of 1991). One component of the programme is helping children attend to the sounds in their own speech. During each individual tutorial session, the child composes a message—at first just one sentence—on a topic of the child's choice, and writes it with the tutor's help that Clay and Cazden (1990) have analysed as kinds of scaffolds.

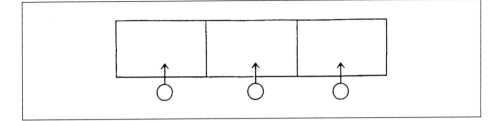

FIGURE 11–1

One kind of help involves a technique adapted from Soviet psychologist Elkonin (1973). The tutor draws a set of boxes that match the number of sounds (not letters) in the word. So, for example, there would be a set of three boxes, not four, for the word *made*, as shown in Figure 11–1.

The tutor demonstrates how to slide counters up into the boxes, left to right, as she says the word with exaggerated slowness. The child imitates her actions, identifies any letters heard in the process, and finds the boxes they belong in.

For learners, the activity of having to slow pronunciation in order to match the finger action makes possible a new kind of attention to the sounds of their own speech. The teacher's language is directed to involving the child in the activity, in which the child will come to attend in a new way. Thus, a teaching technique has been developed that successfully teaches phonemic awareness by revealing the sound structure to the child without explicitly telling the child linguistic labels or orthographic rules.

Each Reading Recovery lesson provides many instances of this kind of assistance. And "shared book experience"—the typical New Zealand junior class activity of reading to children from an enlarged "big book" resting on an easel-like stand—provides analogous assistance by means of masking cards. As Holdaway (1979), one of the originators of shared book experience as a classroom activity, says:

> It is vital that when we choose to talk about some detail of print, every eye is observing that detail at the same time as the accompanying sounds are uttered. Only then are we teaching the crucial eye-voice-ear link which makes print intelligible in the earliest stages of reading. (76)

Figure 11–2 shows a masking device calling attention to the word *groan*. Note the device's flexibility as to the size of the focal print unit—from a single letter to an entire line.

The terms "reveal" and "tell" come from Donaldson's 1978 book, *Children's Minds*. This still-excellent book was given special prominence in the British government's *Report of the Committee of Inquiry into the Teaching of English Language* (DES

FIGURE 11–2   *A masking card in shared reading (Holdaway, 1979, p. 76)*

1988) as the only child development reference. Here are two quotes, both referring to the importance of teaching the complexities of English spelling:

> The nature of the correspondence system [between sounds and letters] should be *revealed* as soon as possible. (73)

> If the system they are dealing with does involve options [i.e., many: many correspondences rather than 1: 1], we should *tell* them so. (105; emphasis added in both quotes)

These two sentences could have been synonomous for Donaldson's purposes. But in the context of recommendations concerning knowledge about language for students of different ages, they are not. "Telling" is not the only way of ensuring that important information is "revealed." Donaldson's choice of words differentiates well, even if more than she consciously intended, between alternative ways of communicating about language to children: focusing their attention so that features of language will be revealed and tacit knowledge about them implicitly acquired, versus explicit telling in some kind of metalinguistic terms. As instructional strategies, each has its value.

Why Revealing Is Sometimes the Best Strategy

There are at least two reasons why revealing can be more helpful than telling, especially for young learners. First, information learned from telling often seems to be indigestable for later use. Readers have trouble applying phonics rules in "sounding out" unfamiliar words in reading, and there is little evidence that writers can use grammar lessons about parts of speech and the components of complete sentences to improve their texts.

Second, attempts to tell some general statement about the way written language works risk oversimplifying complex reality. In the Reading Recovery case, Clay and Watson's 1982 longitudinal research shows, for example, that the most common words that six-year-old children learn to write without help during the Reading Recovery Programme reveal to the child that many letters represent different sounds, not just one: for example, that the letter *a* represents the five different sounds in the words *a*, *at*, *play*, *father*, and *said*. Conversely, the seeming security of being told a "rule" may make it less likely that the learner will independently pay attention to variations in the pattern as they are encountered.

However, as Gee suggested in his qualification, forms of assistance do not usually come (outside the laboratory, that is) in pure form. Even though the goal of both Clay and Holdaway is to help beginning readers and writers construct complex action systems, not to teach testable knowledge, both suggest the value to learners of some special literacy vocabulary. For example, in a teacher's manual for an early set of shared book materials, Handy and Holdaway (1975) "suggest that from the very beginning teachers use the standard technical vocabulary in teaching new skills, such as *root word* or *simile*" (unpaged). Whereas features of print can be revealed, labels for them have to be told.

Why Telling Is Necessary Sometimes, Too

For all students, labels like "left" or "root word" may aid generalisation and should also facilitate teacher-student communication. For students older than those in Clay's research, there is another reason why telling about some feature, and metalinguistic discussion of it, is sometimes essential. This reason follows from the difference between primary and secondary socialisation.

Socialisation refers to the general process of internalisation through which human beings become members of particular cultures. It is more often applied to the primary socialisation that takes place during childhood within the family; but it should also be applied to secondary socialisations throughout life to specialised forms and uses of language in school, community, and work settings.

As an example that may make the larger point clear, consider again the Elkonin boxes, but now from the perspective of teachers learning to be Reading Recovery tutors. Clay has found that during the year-long Reading Recovery training, one of the most difficult concepts for teachers to learn is the distinction between the number of speech sounds in a word and the number of letters, presumably because adults' mental representation of words has been so deeply influenced by experience with print (Clay and Cazden 1990, 221).

The important point is that, in this case of secondary socialisation as a teacher, the new learning contradicts the old. The old conception of words as being composed of letters is not wrong, but in a new situation, for a new purpose, a new conception of words as being composed of sounds is necessary. Talking about this contrast metalinguistically—whether using the colloquial word *sounds* or the technical term *phonemes*—is essential.

More often than we may realise, literacy behaviours expected in school and university do contradict students' previous experience. Five-year-olds may have been taught to print their names in capital letters at home, but the teacher expects lower-case manuscript writing. Primary grade children may have held an appreciative audience with episodic stories in the kitchen, but the teacher expects more topic-centred narratives during sharing time (Cazden 1988). And, to shift to adult learners, Chinese students may be well-practiced in embedding the point of a paragraph near the end (perhaps as an implicit expression of politeness), but teachers of English as a second language want the topic sentence right at the beginning (Ron Scollon, personal communication, October 1991).

Where such differences between primary and secondary socialisations exist between home and school—or first culture and second culture—the teacher's goal should not be to eradicate prior learning but to supplement it. We seek additive, not subtractive, bilingualism in the broadest sense. In such situations, revealing—even where it would be possible—runs the risk of "naturalising" the new ways and implying that the learner's previous actions—whatever they may be—are stupid, illogical, deficient, or just plain wrong. Instead, we need to talk about both the old and the new ways of using language and the differences of situational appropriateness, and often of power, that differentiate them. That requires some form of telling—or better, of explicitly talking about.

As a case in point, an old problem has taken on a new urgency in New Zealand tertiary education. December 1991 (when I was in New Zealand to participate in the symposium honouring Marie Clay) was the end of the first year of a partial integration of the Auckland College of Education with the University of Auckland. Teachers in training for primary schools and early childhood centres, formerly trained only at the college, now have to take some of their courses at the university. In those courses, they were facing new writing standards, especially in the essay questions in year-end examinations. Grades were just becoming public and there was concern about the results among faculty at both institutions, especially about the early childhood students, many of whom were Maori and Pacific Island women highly regarded in their communities for their work with children but educationally not prepared for these new demands.

As we talked about the problem, it seemed essential that the faculty members of the two institutions come together to articulate what kinds of writing are important for students to do and then to figure out how best to help the college students become bicultural in their writing competencies. (Because New Zealand universities do not have a tradition of expository writing courses for first-year students, it seems possible that some regular university students could benefit from such help as well.)

New Zealand historian W. H. Oliver (1991) has recounted what he learned when he came to terms with such cultural differences in language use for the first time (albeit from the opposite direction) during a temporary professional job. He was helping "to do biculturalism by helping to produce *The Dictionary of New Zealand Biography* in Maori as well as English. It was a trying experience, in the end richly rewarding" (100).

> Much that I had taken for granted about the uses of language had to be forgotten. Certain kinds of English are suitable for different purposes; in particular, spoken English and written English work to different sets of rules. In English we were looking for a plain, economical, expository kind of writing. Spoken out loud, it is still a piece of writing. It is different, I was given to understand, in Maori. There was much dispute as to what the norms of spoken Maori are, but it was unquestioned that they must prevail, not only in terms of the expressions used but also in terms of the structure of the piece of writing. Translation was a matter of taking the English essay to pieces and building it up again into a new Maori text. Probably I should not have had to wait until my sixties to learn that. (100)

Many writers imply that language and literacy socialisation is always successful as long as the learning environment is at least minimally adequate. But resistance does occur. Familiar examples are immigrant children resisting speaking the language of their primary socialisation at home if the language of the school is also the language of the wider society, or speakers of nondominant dialects resisting speaking a standard dialect despite its availability at school and on television.

Writing about the general field of socialisation of cognition, Goodnow states: "I seek an account of socialization that goes beyond saying that the individual must be regarded as agent or actor, or that influences are bidirectional. . . . Even if much of one's life is spent in puppet fashion, there remain at least the occasional times when one notices the strings and decides to cut them" (1990, 280).

One vivid example of cutting such strings is African American law professor Patricia Williams' book *The Alchemy of Race and Rights* (1991), which is subtitled (but only on the paper jacket) *The Diary of a Law Professor*. The book begins:

> Since subject position is everything in my analysis of the law, you deserve to know that it's a bad morning. (3)

The book continues with a complex mixture of personal experience, slave narratives, technical explanations of contract law (which is the author's speciality) and metalinguistic discussions (derived from feminist literary criticism) of the impossibility of analysing law from a "subject position" within the conventions of traditional legal writing.

Williams' book is a highly sophisticated work, though it suggests the power, even when its used in simpler ways, of sometimes resisting and deliberately violating prevailing language conventions—a power that requires critical understanding of those conventions and the meanings that they make it easier or harder to express.

Gilbert (1991), speaking of "place, parameter and play" in the Australian controversy over the teaching of specific genre forms (Reid 1986), also argues that "breaking the rules of protocol—breaking generic conventions—can be politically very powerful" (7). Citing Gee's distinction between acquisition and learning, Gilbert agrees with him that the critical reflection on discourse practices that such rule breaking requires, a process he calls "liberating literacy," "almost always involves learning, and not just acquisition" (Gee 1990, 154).

The concept of critical literacy is more commonly applied to reading, but it applies to writing as well. In the words of literary theorist Robert Scholes (1982), "Instruction . . . must both socialize and desocialize. That is, students need to acquire the interpretive [and expressive] codes of their culture, but they need to see them as codes" (14, emphasis in the original).

Socialisation, especially initial socialisation into ways of using oral and written language, can be accomplished by revealing. But secondary socialisation (as for historian Oliver) and desocialisation (as by law professor Williams) requires telling, or talking about, as well.

Conclusions

While many teachers would no doubt agree on the need for both revealing and telling—or, in other words, for some mix of apprenticeship and more explicit discussion—two big questions remain for future research.

First, what is the optimal mix for particular learners—at different ages, with different previous literacy experiences, and facing different demands?

Second, when we do engage in some kind of telling, what is the most useful metalanguage for teachers, and then for students? Linguists of various persuasions will advocate their wares. In the United States, a version of Chomsky's transformational grammar came and went through the schools. The British Kingman report (DES 1988) stayed with traditional descriptive grammar. In Australia, systemic grammar after Michael Halliday is being advocated by a strong group of genre educators led by linguist James Martin.

However, Ronald Carter (1990), Director of the Language in the National Curriculum (LINC) project for teacher development in Britain, puts it right:

An analytical model is not a pedagogical model. . . . The payoff for any applied theory of language is not its power as a theory; what counts is its relevance to classroom practice. (6, 14)

Acknowledgments

This chapter originated as a talk at an earlier tribute to Marie Clay: a symposium on the occasion of her retirement at the annual meeting of the New Zealand Association for Research in Education in Dunedin, 2 December 1991. It was subsequently published with other symposium papers in *Educational Psychology* (1992).

Some colleagues hearing or reading about "revealing" have wondered why I didn't use a more familiar term like "inquiring" or "discovering." The important difference is that both inquiring and discovering refer to mental activities of learners, whereas revealing, parallel to immersing and telling, refers to the pedagogical actions of teachers.

Marie Clay, I was happy to learn, understood that difference and liked the term. In a recent book, she contrasts kinds of teacher assistance with a personal example:

> Cazden has written about three ways of teaching—by teacher telling, by teacher revealing, or by the learners working it out for themselves. For example, an expert can "tell" me how to solve my computer problem and talk me through it; or my colleague can "reveal" what needs to be done to get me into a new procedure, which I only come to understand as I try it under scaffolded support and use it effectively; or I can try to "discover" the solution on my own. Which is the "right" procedure? That depends on my expertise: the more I know, the more I can solve myself or work out from the expert's instruction; but the less I know, the more I need a helping hand from someone who sees where I am and *what my learning problem is.* [As an alternative to teacher telling or learner discovering] a third position close to Cazden's "revealing" is for literacy teachers *to actively support the early formative stages of perceptual processing so that children make successful responses, and through doing so come to know how to make them without external support.* (1998, 68–69, emphasis in the original)

My examples and Clay's are from first language literacy learning. But, as I realized in adapting these ideas for an audience of second language teachers in Hong Kong, the continuum of kinds of assistance, and their probable relationship to learner age and expertise, may be useful for thinking about assistance to second language learning as well.

References

CARTER, R. 1990. *Knowledge About Language and the Curriculum: The LINC Reader.* London: Hodder and Stoughton.

CAZDEN, C.B. 1988. *Classroom Discourse.* Portsmouth, N.H.: Heinemann.

———. 1992. *Whole Language Plus: Essays on Literacy in the United States and New Zealand.* New York: Teachers College Press.

CLAY, M. M. 1985. *The Early Detection of Reading Difficulties.* 3d ed. Auckland and Portsmouth, N.H.: Heinemann.

———. 1991. *Becoming Literate: The Construction of Inner Control.* Portsmouth, N.H.: Heinemann.

———. 1998. *By Different Pathways to Common Outcomes.* York, Maine: Stenhouse.

CLAY, M. M., AND CAZDEN, C. B. 1990. "A Vygotskian Perspective on Reading Recovery." In *Vygotsky and Education,* edited by L. Moll, 206–222. Cambridge: Cambridge University Press.

CLAY, M. M., AND WATSON, B. 1982. *The Success of Maori Children in the Reading Recovery Programme.* Report prepared on research contract for the Director General of Education, Department of Education, Wellington, New Zealand.

DEPARTMENT OF EDUCATION AND SCIENCE. 1988. *Report of the Committee of Inquiry into the Teaching of English Language* (The Kingman Report). London: Her Majesty's Stationery Office.

DONALDSON, M. 1978. *Children's Minds.* London: Fontana.

ELKONIN, D. B. 1973. "USSR." In *Comparative Reading: Cross-National Studies of Behavior and Processes in Reading and Writing,* edited by J. Downing, 551–579. New York: Macmillan.

GEE, J. 1990. *Social Linguistics and Literacies: Ideology in Discourses.* London and New York: Falmer.

GILBERT, P. 1991. "On Place, Parameter and Play: Exploring the Cultural Possibilities of Genre Work." Plenary address at the Literacy Education Research Network Conference, Sydney University of Technology, November 1991.

GOODNOW, J. L. 1990. "The Socialization of Cognition." In *Cultural Psychology: Essays in Comparative Human Development,* edited by J. W. Stigler, R. A. Shweder, and G. Herdt, 159–286. Cambridge: Cambridge University Press.

HANDY, L., AND HOLDAWAY, D. 1975. *What Do You Do? Teacher's Manual.* Auckland and Sydney: Ashton Scholastic.

HOLDAWAY, D. 1979. *The Foundations of Literacy.* Sydney: Ashton Scholastic.

———. 1990. "The Social Dynamics of Acquisition Learning." Paper prepared for the Australian Reading Association, Canberra, July 1990.

OLIVER, W. H. 1991. "Belonging to the Land." In *Pakeha: The Quest for Identity in New Zealand,* edited by M. King, 92–104. Auckland: Penguin.

REID, I. 1986. *The Place of Genre in Learning: Current Debates.* Deakin University, Australia, Centre for Studies in Literary Education.

SCHOLES, R. 1982. *Semiotics and Interpretation.* New Haven: Yale University Press.

WILLIAMS, P. 1991. *The Alchemy of Race and Rights.* Cambridge: Harvard University Press.

Twelve

Teacher Development:
The Best Investment in Literacy Education

CAROL A. LYONS AND GAY SU PINNELL

Children come to school bearing the sum total of their home and community experiences. Their learning depends on the teaching they experience in those first years of school. The process of teaching is complex and requires a broad base of knowledge. In addition to their knowledge of subject matter, elementary teachers need a range of other understandings and skills, not only for their work with young children, but in order to contribute to the community of learners in any educational setting.

Our particular interest is in the literacy achievement and well-being of children who must depend on school for the teaching that they require. Literacy is not a privilege; it is a right. Without highly competent literacy, individuals find themselves in marginal roles in our society; conversely, the good of society depends on a highly literate citizenry.

Although we now know a great deal about how to help children become literate, we have not constructed the delivery systems that will make all of our schools and classrooms places where that can happen. To do so, we must go beyond particular teaching methods or materials and think about the process of learning and development at every level of the education system. Our experience has given us some idea about the extent of the effort that will be required. A key factor is the development of teachers' knowledge and skills. What do teachers need to know? How do they acquire the necessary skills and learn to use their knowledge effectively?

This chapter is divided into four sections. In the first section, Teacher Learning, we discuss what teachers need to know over and above their subject matter, and how they acquire this knowledge. Section two focuses on how to support the development of teachers from the point of view of teacher educators. Our discussion centers on developing teachers' potential for working with children and colleagues to build effective schools. In section three we offer five principles to guide teacher development that have emerged from our studies of effective classroom and Reading Recovery teachers. In the last section, we discuss how to build a community of learners in the process of change. Within each section, we draw from research and practice in the Literacy Collaborative at the Ohio State University and the Reading Recovery program.

Through our work with teachers and children in both of these educational ventures, we have expanded our understanding of what can make a difference in the literacy education of primary-age children.

Teacher Learning

What do teachers need to know?

First and foremost, teachers need to learn how to be effective teachers of children. Being an effective teacher means coordinating a complex set of analyses and actions. It is a decision-making process. For example, in the course of any one instructional moment, we might be considering the following:

- Based on the sum of my experience with him, what does this child know?
- What can he do without any help?
- What does he need to know *next*?
- Why is this new learning important at this point in time?
- Under what conditions can he engage in the process without help?
- What kind of help would be most beneficial to him and move him forward in learning?
- What will help him learn a *process* rather than simply getting the right answer? That is, how can my teaching help him learn generative processes that will carry over into other situations?
- Does he know the nature of the task I am asking him to perform, or do I need to teach the task before I teach the process?

Answering such questions captures only a little of the complex problem solving in which the teacher engages, and it is all happening on the run, while the teacher is interacting with a child or a group of children. Here are some more questions of a reflective nature:

- What was the child learning about the processes involved?
- What supported his learning of this process? For example, how did the text, read or written, his own oral language, and his background of prior knowledge support learning?
- How did the teaching interactions and examples support learning?
- What opportunities did I create to engage the child actively in the process?

In asking these questions, we are assuming that our goal in teaching is to help children learn generative processes that they can apply in many ways. They are "learning how to learn" at the same time that they are acquiring specific pieces of information, such as vocabulary words. We may be teaching behaviors or information directly (for example, we may demonstrate a process for the child or direct his attention to a powerful example), but we cannot directly teach the "in-the-head" strategies that we want the learner to develop. That is, the learner must learn something about how to learn. We call this process teaching *for* strategies.

Teaching *for* strategies means that teachers' interactions with children are designed to support this kind of generative learning (Clay 1991). By drawing a child's attention to the visual features of a word, we do not have a specific goal of simply learning that word. We may want the child to learn how to conduct a left-to-right visual analysis of the letters in the word, a process that the child can use on any word, and although it may take many experiences to become skillful and flexible in conducting the analysis, once the skill is learned it can be applied again and again (Clay 1993). Thus the child has learned much more than the particular word in focus.

Here's another example. A child is reading the text slowly, haltingly, word by word. The teacher coaches the child to put his words together so that they sound like talking. The goal here is not to make that single reading "expressive," but to encourage the reader to become more sensitive to the syntax and meaning of the text he is reading and to process more fluently. The process to be learned is how to access the language systems that help to maintain fluency, and to coordinate those systems with visual analysis of print at the same as comprehension.

We are talking here about a way of thinking through our teaching. So, what teachers know includes not only a repertoire of specific techniques and knowledge of materials, but also a kind of problem-solving process. For more than a decade, we have been involved daily in listening to teachers talk about their teaching. The educational processes in which we have been engaged require talking while observing, as well as reflective discussion. We have learned much from hearing teachers think out loud about their teaching decisions, and from hearing them discuss how their theories have changed over time. The teacher's theory is always incomplete, in that teaching each new student helps to expand the understandings related to this complex activity. Encountering students who have difficulty may require us to revise our theories, so we are constantly in the process of learning about teaching while we are doing it.

How do teachers acquire complex understandings about the learning and teaching processes and learn to use their knowledge effectively?

First, we will discuss aspects of the thinking process that effective teachers develop while teaching children, and then we will draw examples from several years of our observation of and conversations with classroom and Reading Recovery teachers to describe the reasoning and thinking processes of effective teachers.

We start with the assumption that every system is connected. As the learner acquires new knowledge, he builds a network of understandings to support the new knowledge. This network is made up of relevant prior knowledge as well as new understandings constantly being acquired. The learner himself has constructed this network of meanings, and he constantly uses it to make sense of and acquire new knowledge. For example, a young child who is just learning to write may compose a text from his oral language, a system that he has learned first at home and expanded at school. The particular word he wants to write is probably one that he has heard and knows, but to write it, he has to connect what he knows about sounds in the word and how those sounds are connected to letters or letter clusters. When he writes the word, he has to connect it to the directional movements he has learned to make in connection with a letter. These processes are so interconnected that we do not think about them separately. In becoming literate, however, there is overt evidence that these connections are being made. When a young child learns, he has constructed a mental map built on prior knowledge and use of language and text to make sense and to communicate his thoughts and needs. Learning means adding to, deleting from, or rearranging that map.

Teachers have to construct an idea of the child's developing mental map if they are to help the child take on new learning in an efficient and effective way. The only way we can derive an understanding of the child's mental map is by carefully observing behavior, analyzing the behavior as evidence, and engaging in an investigative process. An individual teacher might describe the process like this:

1. *Listen and watch.* The first step is to listen and watch. Observation is quite systematic in that there might be a series of initial assessments that provide a rich foundation of information. But observation does not stop there. It is an ongoing part of the teaching process. It is through observation that I build my theory of how this learner is processing information and add to my theories of how people, in general, learn.

2. *Probe.* Out of the observation come ways of interacting with the learner that provide even more information about the processing at this point in time and under these conditions. The questions and interactions arise from my general knowledge. I am always thinking about the series of alternative explanations for specific behaviors. This series is built through case examples of work with individuals or groups, and is strengthened by reflection and discussion with my colleagues.

3. *Select hypotheses.* From my repertoire of explanation, I narrow the focus to probable interpretations of behavior and then probe again.

4. *Test.* Then, I begin to test hypotheses by interacting with children, based on my theory. All the time, I am observing and interpreting behavior for evidence of change that would support or reject the hypothesis. The more experience I have with different children, the greater my repertoire and the more accurate my hypotheses.

5. *Reassess.* If the evidence indicates that the hypothesis is correct, I continue to use that understanding in my teaching interventions with children, starting the observation and assessment cycle again. If the evidence suggests that the hypothesis is inaccurate, the teaching is not helping the child. A critical skill of teaching is detecting when the child is not engaging in learning the process. In that case, the cycle starts again but I may call in a colleague or specialist, or I may apply some specialized knowledge, going back to the original assessments and reconsidering the process.

This thinking process is not, by any means, purely sequential. It is recursive in nature, with constant recycling of the processes and renegotiation of current thinking. We are constantly observing and evaluating during our teaching interactions. Further, it is not usually a conscious process; that is, teachers are focusing on and thinking about the child, acting instructionally, and revising as they go.

This process is not a lesson plan to be followed like a script, although there will be some planned structures that make the interactional context possible. For example, a teacher may have selected a text for reading with a child or group of children in mind. For a particular group, she will have thought through some possible challenges and supports, and she has some ideas about how she might activate prior knowledge as children begin to read the text. She also has a general idea of what these children need to learn at this point in time. But the power of teaching is in the moment-to-moment interactions that take place during the lesson. It is in the ways the teacher can call children's attention to powerful examples that help them develop an understanding of the process. Becoming proficient at teaching interactions requires the kind of self-regulation described above. Our study of effective teachers indicates that they

- enjoy the challenge of analyzing students' behaviors and creating powerful and varied opportunities to help each student learn how to read and write
- have learned how to demonstrate and help children use what they know to resolve unknown words encountered while reading and writing
- continuously monitor the effects of their instruction on student behavior and develop alternative plans and teaching procedures if a child is not making adequate progress
- expect the child to make accelerated progress and do not give up on the child or themselves until their goals are met
- have learned how to plan, organize, guide, and monitor their own behavior and change when the child's behavior suggests that he or she has not learned a particular lesson

As the following example illustrates, effective teachers have the capacity to infer from a student's verbal and nonverbal behaviors what the child may be thinking and why he is responding in specific ways.

An example from a Reading Recovery teacher.

When Michael entered Reading Recovery he recognized thirty-six letters by sight and could write his first and last names. He could not read or write one word, nor hear and write sounds in a dictated sentence. The *Concepts About Print* assessment indicated that he knew one concept—the front of the book—but had few other notions of how print works. He did not attend to print, nor had he acquired left-to-right directional behaviors. During the first six weeks of lessons, the teacher used a variety of texts in reading and writing activities to enable Michael to acquire more letter knowledge and to learn how to use this knowledge to construct meaning. These experiences enabled him to learn how to attend to and visually scan letters within words, and words within sentences, while reading; and to hear and record sounds and letters in sequence while writing. By demonstrating how to use information to link known words and word parts to analyze unknown words, Michael developed critical behaviors that generated new learning and facilitated accelerated progress. After eight weeks of instruction, he was becoming an independent strategic problem solver, and the Reading Recovery teacher was able to examine his reasoning processes and infer from them the basis of his subsequent behavior. She was able to provide a hypothetical rationale to accompany each move Michael made because she had provided him with many opportunities to accomplish each aspect of his problem solving during the eight weeks they had been working as partners.

Text: *Lazy Mary* (level 6) Michael

A sip "I don't hear a <u>p</u> at the end."

———

splash
of cold water.

Teacher comment: Michael looked at the first letter and thought of a word that would make sense that began with an s and he probably thought sip would make sense. But when he said "sip," he heard a p at the end of the word. Then he looked at the last letter of the word sip to see if there was a p at the end. When he didn't see a p, he said aloud "I don't hear a p at the end."

A sprinkle

———

splash [hesitation] "no <u>k</u>."
of cold water.

Teacher comment: Michael did not see a p at the end of the word but he noticed that there was a p in the word right after the first letter. He needed to think of a word that made sense and began with sp. He decided to try sprinkle. The word sprinkle fit structurally and it made sense. However, after saying the word aloud, he heard a k and noticed that the unknown word did not have a k in it. The word in the text did not look like sprinkle. He had to think of a word that looked right.

A splash "Yea, splash, that word looks right."

———

splash

A splash
of cold water
if you don't!

Teacher comment: Through a process of elimination, Michael thought of a word that would look right and make sense. He noticed and analyzed the relevant features in the unknown word and regulated his behavior to search for and determine the best-fit solution. It is important to note that each word tried was meaningful; meaning drove his problem solving.

Michael thought of and followed his own plan, monitored his own behavior, and devised several idiosyncratic methods for resolving the conflict he was facing. He was becoming self-regulated. But without explicit teaching, it is doubtful that he would have developed the ability to learn effectively how to engage in this complex reasoning.

An example from a classroom teacher.

A teacher is introducing the book *Keep the Lights Burning, Abbie* to a group of second graders. In guided reading lessons, teachers select a text that will be within the control of a group of children who are similar in their reading development. The text will offer support in that children will be able to use their prior knowledge to understand the text and predict what might happen in it. They will know most of the words or be able to get to them by using the strategies they currently have. The text will offer some challenge and opportunity for problem solving so that children can learn more about the reading process. In this example, a teacher has selected a chapter book with a historical setting.

> *Teacher comment: The children in this group had shown evidence that they could sustain their reading and their interest in a longer book, but they hadn't yet read something that was distant in time. I wanted to stretch their thinking to understand problems not related to their own world. While the children know most of the words in the book, some place names will offer a challenge. I knew I needed to draw their attention to long words and how to take them apart. I also needed to help them understand the plot—the importance of keeping the light burning.*

Before reading, the teacher and children had a conversation about the book, then the children would read a section of the book for later discussion. The story introduction seems like a conversation among friends, but the teaching is intentional. It helps the children to bring more understanding to the story and perhaps unlocks some difficult words in advance. First, the teacher introduces the title, setting, theme, and characters. Here we give only two segments of this introductory conversation.

TEACHER: Let's look at the cover of the book while I tell you a bit about our new story. This is a true story about a young girl named Abbie. Abbie lived a long time ago on an island with her parents and three younger sisters. Her father got stuck in town during a terrible storm and Abbie had to keep the lighthouse lit for all the sailors. She had to be very brave and work very hard while her father was away.

BECKY: This is real? She really did this? Where was it?

TEACHER: Yes, Abbie Burgess really did this. The island is called Matinicus Island and it is off the coast of Maine.

> *Teacher comment: I started by giving the children an overall description of the story—who the characters were and what the important events would be. I wanted them to be interested in the main character, Abbie, and in the importance of the job she had*

to do. I also have noticed that the children tend to hesitate at long, multisyllable words and sometimes find unfamiliar names like Matinicus difficult. I wanted to help them find ways to approach multisyllable words.

TEACHER: See if you can find *Matinicus* on the page. What do you notice about it?
SHEILA: It has a capital letter. It's like a name.
TEACHER: Uh-huh. Anything else?
BECKY: It's a really long word.
TIFFANY: It has "mat" and "in."
SHEILA: And "us" too at the end! Cool! It's all parts.
TEACHER: Those parts can help you if you have trouble with the name.

Teacher comment: I said "Matinicus" so that they could hear me pronounce it, but I wanted them to notice things about the word that would help them. They could look for parts that they could recognize and pronounce and make an attempt at taking the word apart. As with any place name, pronunciation might have to be looked up later, but a good reader can learn to approach a multisyllable word. I wasn't concerned that they learn the precise word for later use; I wanted them to develop strategies for taking words apart.

TEACHER: What do you think it would be like to live over a hundred years ago on a small island?
TIFFANY: There was no TV or electricity and all the kids had lots of chores to do.
SHEILA: Yeah, they might not even have any schools.
BECKY: I bet they had boats instead of cars to get places.
SHEILA: It looks really cold and windy there. Everything's blowing.
TEACHER: You're right. That's how it was for Abbie and her family. Let's take a look through the book and see what happened.

Teacher comment: This group of children has not had much experience reading historical fiction. I want them to understand that the story takes place a long time ago, and there are many differences between those times and these. I wanted them to be able to put themselves in the place of the characters in the story and imagine what it is like. In all stories, it's important that they think about what they already know and try to connect that knowledge to the book they're reading. That's part of the strategy for understanding, and I'll help them continue to access that knowledge as we talk more about the plot.

Learning to Support the Development of Teachers

The examples above provide a brief glimpse into how effective teachers think while teaching. Although it's hard to capture, and still harder to teach, this foundation of knowledge underlies all efforts to educate children. We have to ask the question: Does teacher education, as it is currently delivered, have the capacity to provide all of the necessary support that teachers need? And the answer would have to be "no." If we are serious about creating the kind of dynamic teacher development programs necessary to serve today's students, much more will be needed than our current systems provide. For example, universities and colleges are the vehicle for initial preparation of teachers, and the largest inservice course is the master's degree. Although much valuable learning occurs, the education is often distant from the day-to-day problems of teaching and does not promote the kind of intensive reflection needed to build the system. Inservice courses are generally run just about the same way. Although they provide some practical ideas, they do not provide sustained support for developing the thinking processes.

Achieving literacy for all requires that we examine how effective teachers have acquired these complex abilities and skills. Undoubtedly it will mean evaluating and, if necessary, revising current approaches and expanding our educational support for teachers to accommodate new designs for learning. In this section, we look at two teacher development programs that provide some direction in this process.

A teacher developer is one who engages in a process of thinking about how teachers learn to teach. Let's revisit the investigative process that a teacher uses in her work with children. Could it apply to the development of teachers? We think so. As we teach children, we want to be learning more and more about the processes involved in teaching. It helps to have a person with experience and expertise guiding and supporting what we do. In a collaborative way, teachers can help each other analyze and reflect on their work. Sometimes the process is guided by a teacher educator, at other times by a peer with more experience in a particular instructional approach. In a sense, each of us who engages in the process is a teacher educator; here we will call this role the *developer*. The developer has a multifaceted role. For example, he or she conducts inservice sessions or classes that involve teachers in examining new techniques and approaches. Part of the discussion will be to look at cases to illustrate processes. The more the group participates in analyzing examples of teaching, the more active their learning, but the most powerful process is what we would call *in-class assistance*, sometimes called *coaching*. In this setting the developer has the opportunity to help a teacher learn from her teaching. The goal here is to help the teacher become conscious of the examples offered daily in her own classroom. In a sense, through this reflective process, she is learning how to teach more effectively while teaching. Through experience, case examples inform the teacher's theory, and subsequent instruction is more powerful (Pinnell 1994).

A teacher developer might talk about assisting teachers in their learning in the following manner:

1. *Watch and listen.* My task is to observe teaching in the classroom context. This process might involve observing a teacher working with an individual child, a small group of children, or a whole class. I listen to the learning conversations that

are going on, look for evidence of learning on the part of children, and analyze the situation to connect teaching moves to the evidence of learning. This analytic knowledge is connected to the road map of teaching and learning in my own head. Based on my understanding, I decide what to bring to the teacher's attention about the quality of the teacher/learning situation.

2. *Probe.* My discussion with the teacher provides support for her to talk about her teaching. Describing behavior, raising awareness of interaction patterns, and articulating problems help to identify the variables that make this particular lesson effective.

3. *Select hypotheses.* The teacher and I draw inferences about what supports learning for this child or group of children. We explore what actions or decisions can make learning more effective. For example, perhaps the selection of different texts or the use of more-precise language may support the child's learning. At the same time, engaging in the selection of hypotheses helps both of us to get better at the process, and we are working to better understand how these interactional plans help the child build internal systems of strategies for reading and writing. Learning takes place, and the hypothesis is held in reserve for another teaching opportunity.

4. *Test.* Alerted by our learning interactions, the teacher is more aware of behavioral evidence of learning and the new hypothesis of teaching in further interactions with the child or children. She watches for the opportunity to use the new thinking to confirm or support the hypothesis. I help her in the process by building further observation on the work that we have done together. In this way, I can provide ongoing feedback and support for the teacher's *own* analysis. Typically, observations are sequenced over time so that we can construct together an ongoing working hypothesis about these children and their learning. At the same time, we are learning more about how to think about teaching and learning.

5. *Reassess.* Reassessment is cyclic over time. The whole investigative process is a search for what works and why it works. I help the teacher participate in the investigative process, realizing that solutions are tentative until they are tested for an extended period of time. What she is learning, though, is what to watch for. As a developer, my role is to ask the probing questions that prompt the teacher to consider new possibilities. The teacher's behavior shifts as new learning is taken on; but over time, the repertoire of behaviors and responses to children are internalized so that they are instantly available as needed.

Next, we present two examples from our experience. In the first, two Reading Recovery teacher developers, Rose Mary and Mary, share understandings and lessons they have learned after fourteen years of experience in training Reading Recovery teachers and teacher-leaders. In the second example, a teacher developer for the Literacy Collaborative at the Ohio State University shares her insights about the teaching and learning processes gained from working with classroom teachers.

Comments from an Interview with Two Reading Recovery Teacher Educators.

Thinking about how adults learn.

Like all human beings, teachers have an innate desire to learn. If the instructor attempts to understand what the adult knows and the adult is a reflective practitioner, learning will occur. Our experience has shown that teachers who are forced to take Reading Recovery training do not have the level of commitment needed to succeed. Learning requires commitment, tenacity, and desire.

You can tell when teachers have learned a concept or skill by observing shifts in four areas: (1) conversations and teaching of children; (2) goals they set for themselves; (3) discussions about theory and practice with colleagues; and (d) how they reflect and analyze their learning. Like children, adults learn when the content is purposeful, and teaching involves explicit demonstrations, clear explanations, goal setting, positive reinforcement, coaching, and ongoing support.

Suggestions for helping teachers learn.

It is important to develop a safe and trusting context for learners so that they are willing to take risks, knowing that they will be supported. From the first class forward, it is important to be accepting of all responses and to praise efforts of risk-taking, partially right responding, and articulation of current understandings. However, this does not mean an anything-goes atmosphere. Acceptance of "having a go" and gentle explanation, reference, and specific possible examples will facilitate the learning without discouraging participation.

Our suggestions for staff developers include the following:

1. Provide varied and many different kinds of opportunities for individuals to construct their own understandings through shared experiences. Demonstration behind a one-way glass, conversation with others while observing teachers and students, specific feedback, and analysis of student-teacher interactions that have occurred during the demonstration lesson are powerful ways to learn.
2. Never stop teaching children. It is through your work with children that you continue to build and refine your own theories of learning, which in turn inform your teaching. Teaching children enables you to become more observant and analytical. The more teaching experiences you have, the more opportunities you have to observe the idiosyncratic nature of the learning process. Without varied teaching experiences, you are less likely to be efficient and effective. Finally, you earn respect and gain credibility when examples used during the professional development class are from your own teaching.
3. Provide an overview of the scope of learning that the class will be working on together throughout the year. Establish roles, responsibilities, and expectations for the group early on, and continue to revisit and reevaluate these goals throughout the year. Foster a trusting environment by preventing surprises. Working in pairs or small group develops trust. Humor helps, too.

4. Listen carefully to what the teachers are saying and try to understand their perspectives. Ask for and provide feedback. Respond to questions and needs promptly, not one or two weeks later.
5. Talk about the learning process. Help individuals understand that learning is complex and takes place over time. Foster common goals and a shared agenda by listening to concerns from individuals or the group. What are they finding difficult? What do they want more information about? What concepts need to be revisited? Provide time for the group to share concerns, then be responsive to their concerns by involving the group in a problem-solving process that results in a plan of action.
6. Be positive, supportive, encouraging, empathetic, straightforward, and honest. Have high expectations, but offer help beyond the typical instructional settings. Relax and enjoy the process.

Comments from an Interview with Melissa, a teacher developer for the Literacy Collaborative at the Ohio State University.

Thinking about how adults learn.

I believe that all teachers want to learn how to do their jobs better. I base my work on that assumption, and my job is to help them. It's all about change; we are all changing all the time. It is much easier to learn when we focus on one child at a time. If we can analyze and interpret the behavior of one child, thinking from his perspective, figuring out what he knows and needs to know, we also learn something about learning. When that understanding is internalized repeatedly, I can help the teacher lift that knowledge to generalizable levels. Observation is a key to learning.

I can tell when a teacher has acquired a new concept or skill by observing practice and listening to talk about practice. Often, I observe a teacher working with a class or group of children, and I see a shift in behavior that makes learning more powerful. But I also watch for a shift in the teacher's own language as she reflects on her teaching. She might say "I think I did that better this time" and tell why. That is more important than my telling the teacher what to do because it indicates that she has a process for reflecting on her teaching and evaluating it herself.

Suggestions for helping teachers learn.

I believe that the key is close observation of children's behavior. You also have to prove some explicit suggestions for teaching. It is a balancing act between explicit instruction, independent practice, and individual inquiry. As a developer, I provide the context for teachers to think on their own. Some suggestions for teacher developers are:

1. Avoid one-shot inservice sessions. The learning must be connected.
2. Provide some concrete descriptions of specific techniques; be practical enough that teachers can try these techniques out on their own. But don't let the teacher development stop there.

3. Help teachers analyze their teaching by looking at the interactions with their students. This can be done during inservice class experiences and on-site coaching. A dynamic staff development program includes a variety of learning settings—a class or study group that meets regularly over time, individual conferences, classroom observation, and coaching.

4. Teacher development is best when it includes demonstration and conversation. My own teaching is a powerful tool. The teachers in my building know that I teach children in classrooms every day and draw from that experience. I can demonstrate techniques with their children, but teaching is not a display of techniques. It is observing and working with a group of children over time, making decisions about their learning, and acting on those decisions. Shared conversations about that learning process are powerful in helping all of us learn more.

5. Provide shared experiences such as observation behind the one-way glass, as in Reading Recovery, group observation in a classroom, or group observation of videotapes.

6. Engage the group in conversation surrounding the act of teaching, and help them apply principles across settings.

7. From the first minute you step into a classroom, see yourself as a helper. You are helping the teacher to do anything that needs to be done.

8. Teachers need different kinds of help at different times. For example, a new teacher (or one moved to a new grade) may need to focus on management or classroom environment. More-advanced teachers need to look deeply into their observations of children.

9. Be open to listening in general—not just coaching in a formal situation.

10. When working in a teacher's classroom and helping her to evaluate instruction, make it clear that anything said is confidential, so that teachers will be encouraged to take risks in self-evaluation.

11. Use observation as a basis for planning staff development sessions and for coaching on an individual level. Watching a teacher's interactions with students will help you determine what information they are gaining from their own observations and what needs to be clarified or analyzed further.

In these examples, we have described the thinking processes of three extraordinary teacher developers. From Reading Recovery, Rose Mary and Mary's reflections have provided insights into what they have learned about teaching children and teachers. We looked at Melissa's analysis of her own classroom teaching and her work as a literacy coordinator or teacher developer, supporting the learning of other teachers in her school. It is important to emphasize that the same processes flow across their work; each facet informs the other. For these three educators, the work with teachers in particular is grounded in the work with children. It is probably true that constant reflection on and analysis of the teaching of others informs their own teaching of children.

Principles to Guide Effective Teacher Development

Several principles have emerged from our study of teachers over the years. These principles are illustrated by the work of Rose Mary, Mary, and Melissa, but they are related to the hundreds of teachers and teacher developers we have observed and listened to over time.

1. *Teacher development is effective when there is a balance between demonstration of specific teaching approaches and the reflection and analysis needed to build the process of thinking about teaching.* Of course, teacher development does not take place in a vacuum. Teachers want to learn specific techniques that they can use with children, and they want help in selecting materials and engaging the actions related to the approach. So, teacher developers engage groups in viewing or learning about some particular instructional techniques so that they can apply them and analyze them. Once teachers are engaged in trying the new techniques or refining approaches that they have previously used, powerful learning conversations can take place. (Specific instructional approaches are embedded in both Reading Recovery and the Literacy Collaborative. Participants who enter the training programs for these teacher development efforts are shown these procedures and techniques in a clear, explicit way over several years of training. By participating, they agree to engage in the instructional processes.) In our view, the real learning is related to developing the processes of reflection, analysis, and hypothesis formation that teachers learn in the process of trying and testing any new techniques. Teacher development really begins after a demonstration or exploration of a technique has taken place and the developer can engage teachers in self-reflection.

2. *Teacher development is effective when complex ideas are experienced, analyzed, and discussed across a variety of learning contexts.* The effectiveness of the in-class coaching described here is related to the fact that the teacher developer has engaged the participants in a variety of learning experiences. Teacher education would be inefficient if we had to depend on teaching and assisting one teacher at a time with all of her learning, but when we combine group sessions with extension into classroom settings, powerful learning can occur. What are some of these group situations? Figure 12–1 outlines aspects of a dynamic teacher development program that provides extended support to teachers over time. The program depends on providing a number of learning contexts, within each of which interaction among the teacher developer and teachers takes place. Learning is embedded in these interactions; the context makes the conversation possible. For each context, we provide a brief rationale, a description of expected outcomes, and a description of the interactional nature of learning.

3. *Teacher development is effective when it is grounded in the practice of teaching children.* As teacher developers work with children and with teachers, work in one area informs the other. Daily practice with children constantly builds the conceptual map that the teacher developer draws for powerful interactions with teachers.

Experiences to Support the Development of Teachers

Context	Definition	Rationale	Interactional Learning
Case investigations	Collect and analyze data on individual students over time, including observations of behavior and assessment results. Capture changes over time in daily increments. Case studies and case examples inform teaching.	Investigation provides a basis for common, shared experience in analyzing children's behavior. Teachers learn how to: • look for evidence of learning over time; • relate learning to ongoing instruction; • use evidence as a basis for instructional decisions; • share case examples and learn from others.	The developer guides teachers to talk about what they have noticed in their examination of children's behavior. In the process, the teachers • develop a common language for talking about complex ideas; • achieve a conceptual level by grounding their talk in behaviors; • develop and express conceptual understandings of the learning process and what it looks like.

FIGURE 12–1   *Experiences to support the development of teachers*

Experiences to Support the Development of Teachers

Context	Definition	Rationale	Interactional Learning
Demonstration and group analysis	As a group, teachers observe a demonstration of teaching. This demonstration might involve a teacher working with one child or someone teaching a small group or class. Live demonstrations and videotapes provide the context.	Demonstrations provide an effective way to get inside instructional processes. Teachers use the knowledge they are building from their case investigations to observe "on the run" a teacher working with children. In this way, they • access the teaching and observations of others in the group; • practice analyzing teaching and learning while it is taking place; • develop an investigative stance to teaching.	The developer guides the group to talk about what they are seeing and to describe it at a conceptual level, asking participants to support their claims with evidence. Freed from teaching, participants can articulate their observations and understandings of the learning process.

FIGURE 12–1 *Experiences to support the development of teachers*

212

Experiences to Support the Development of Teachers

Context	Definition	Rationale	Interactional Learning
Coaching	The teacher developer observes and talks with individual teachers during and after working with children. The process includes brief demonstrations by the coach but largely focuses on helping the teacher analyze teacher and student interactions.	The developer works with an individual teacher who is teaching children in her own classroom. The goal is to help the teacher apply learning; uncover problems; and develop a plan for working with children that will be operationalized, tested, and revised. Observation and coaching take place close to the act of authentic teaching and build over time to help teachers • put knowledge developed though case investigations together with their understanding of the context for learning. • learn how to carry on these analytic operations without the support of the teacher developer.	Learning conversations take place throughout the coaching process. The teacher has an idea of her goals and some of the problems she is experiencing in reaching those goals. She has knowledge of children, but may not know how to use that knowledge efficiently and effectively in instructional decision making. Through discussion, the coach addresses the teacher's goals and problems, as perceived, and assists her to use those ideas to expand her knowledge base.

FIGURE 12–1 *Experiences to support the development of teachers*

Experiences to Support the Development of Teachers

Context	Definition	Rationale	Interactional Learning
Monitoring student progress	Gathering evidence of student learning is an integral part of an effective teacher education program. Teachers systematically assess and record student scores and other evidence of achievement (such as work samples) on an ongoing basis and discuss evidence with the teacher developer.	Collection and evaluation of formal and informal student achievement data: • keeps the teaching grounded in reality; • informs the overall design of the instructional program for children and the teacher development program; • helps teachers see the outcomes of their work with children. Data reveal how children can generalize prior knowledge to new contexts. They also help in looking at the systems and how they are connected.	The teacher developer engages teachers in looking at data in several ways, promoting a rich discussion of practice: • individual teachers may look at scores, ongoing records of behaviors, and collections of work from the children they teach. • group of teachers may periodically look at evidence of learning of the children in the whole school.

FIGURE 12–1   *Experiences to support the development of teachers*

When we began our work in Reading Recovery, we believed that daily work with children helps teacher leaders win credibility among the teachers in their training classes. We no longer hold this view. Work with children is far more important than a simple issue of winning your stripes; it facilitates the growth of case knowledge and helps the teacher developer understand all the possible ways to detect learning.

There are different paths of progress, and the teacher developer's map must be complex indeed if she or he is to help other teachers discover evidence of learning. This discovery of evidence of learning through close observation and analysis informs the teacher developer's own theories of learning and effective practice. It builds the flexibility needed to teach the same process in multiple ways. In order to assist teachers in this thinking and learning process, the developer must have wide and current experience in it. Teachers in the development group are working daily with children either individually or in groups; their understandings are being tested not only in the inservice class or context, but in their daily work. Contexts like case investigations focus on the children that the teachers have daily responsibility for.

4. *Teacher development is effective when it involves learning conversations surrounding the act of teaching.* We can plan instructional activities for teachers. Every session in every context needs a well-designed structure so that there are expectations and efficient and effective use of time. But the plan must call for time to talk. The teacher developer skillfully elicits, connects, and guides talk so that conceptual understandings are built into the process. Each of our four contexts involve interactional learning. Talk enables teachers to act, state interpretations and conclusions, support their statements with evidence, and inform and support each other in the process. Thus, they learn to state their conceptual understandings at the current level. As with any human being involved in any kind of learning, talking during the process helps teachers to use language to learn. Successful teacher developers intentionally plan for problem-centered interaction.

5. *Teacher development is effective when it is supported by a learning community that shares a language that can be used to communicate about complex ideas.* In the process of talking about children and teaching, the participants in a group develop a set of shared meanings and a language to talk with each other. It takes time to build this shared language, but as the communication expertise of the group expands, so too does the individual teacher's map of learning. The teacher educator selects the case, the problems for the group to consider, and the demonstration of teaching. The developer allows time for teachers to make and articulate hypotheses about the specific case or example under observation. Everyone views the examples from a different perspective, one that has emerged from work with children. Because of the richness of the examples and discussion, they begin to see how learning manifests itself in different ways. As group, they learn to analyze behavior and make hypotheses about the plan for further learning. The process helps them become more flexible in the ways they address a problem. Rather than fol-

lowing a set prescription, they are encouraged to think about the multiple approaches available to them. They learn to adjust their teaching so that if one approach does not work, they can detect the problem and adjust to an individual learner or to the learners within a group. With only one person's view present, the chances for remedying a situation is limited. A community of learners who share insights is highly supportive. Teachers help each other become more skillful and reflective, and every member of the team has credibility because every member works with children.

Building a Community of Learners in the Process of Change

It is obvious that effective teacher development depends in large part on building a community of learners. Education is a process of change, but change will not be lasting unless a community of people becomes committed to the new learning and to helping each other learn (Darling-Hammond and McLaughlin 1996). How do we build a community of learners? Once we know how to do it, how can that process be replicated in school after school? The typical way that educational reform is disseminated involves transferring information so that one group of educators simply imitates what another is doing. In doing so, they may be missing the key ingredient—how a community of learners is built to work together. The variety of experiences, the chance to talk and listen and to examine teaching, build community among the teachers who share an experience (Lambert et al. 1995; Lieberman 1996).

Teacher developers must create an environment within which differences are seen as strengths. There may be differences related to beliefs about learning and teaching, in patterns of social interactions, in skills and knowledge. All of these differences must be a recognized part of the strengths of the group, and every individual must take a learning stance. That is, everyone must be engaged in ongoing learning. There is no such thing as perfect teaching. The teacher educator has a plan for what the teachers need to know, but also has a model for how to help them get there. Within that plan, flexibility is required to adjust to changing circumstances. Flexibility has to do with moment-to-moment adjustments when the context or materials change. The teacher is observing and adjusting to the learner in order to support further learning. We don't stick to our plan rigidly if we see that learning is not taking place.

All members of the group must have high expectations for the outcomes. There is a mutual goal. The goal and agenda belong to the group, and the group's common vision guides the process. In pursuit of this vision, every member of the group agrees to examine his or her own views and to listen to others.

There are expectations of the members of the community, and those expectations are high. Members of the group know what the expectations are and work to meet them. Observation data on children's learning help the group measure their own progress.

Group dynamics are an important consideration. Good group interaction—conversation that supports learning—depends on every individual's willingness to risk voicing opinions and to listen to others. At any given time, we need listeners and talkers, but everyone in the group needs a chance to do both.

Finally, a community of learners has at its heart mutual respect. Every individual is comfortable in questioning and willing to express views. When there are problems, those problems are shared. Team problem solving, once learned, continues to build skills even while problems are addressed and solved.

If we are to build the capacity we need to fully support teacher development, there must be many teacher educators in every school and school district. So, we need to think about models that encourage experienced teachers to take on the new learning that they will need to support other teachers in the process (Darling-Hammond and McLaughlin 1996).

Teacher development will not succeed if it is handed down from a state or university level as a set of instructions or demonstrations of process. As Bradley (1998) has said so clearly, "Legislating and mandating prescriptive practices will never be as effective or as essential as a skillful teacher in the classroom" (18). Even though good descriptions, always available in the literature, are helpful, teacher development takes place at the school level. We need to find ways to build capacity at the district and school-building levels so that teachers have the support networks they need to keep on learning. We have observed two dissemination plans that accomplish this capacity building: Reading Recovery and the Literacy Collaborative at the Ohio State University. We briefly describe these here as a way of illustrating the kinds of designs that will be necessary if we are to help every teacher teach effectively and powerfully.

Reading Recovery.
In this early intervention program, teachers work individually with a special group of children who are having difficulty in learning to read and write (Pinnell 1989; Pinnell, Fried, and Estice 1991). According to Wilson and Daviss (1994), "Reading Recovery offers U.S. education its first real demonstration of the power of a process combining research, development (including ongoing teacher education), marketing, and technical support in an orchestrated system of change" (76). Staff development is a key process, as described above. Staff developers make use of a one-way glass screen to provide shared experience in observation and decision making. They also provide individual coaching and assistance to teachers in schools. Teacher-leaders are provided a year of training in residence at a university site; in the process they learn to teach children effectively, to analyze their own teaching, and to teach teachers. These key staff developers are located at the district level and sometimes at regional levels. They provide graduate-level classes to teachers that incorporate all elements (with credit offered by a local university or college).

Staff development in Reading Recovery is ongoing in that there is an intensive initial year of training and regular continuing teacher development as long as teachers are involved in the program. As they become more experienced, Reading Recovery teachers visit each other to assist in learning. Always they are encouraged to work together and to work with classroom teachers in school teams to discuss individual children and support their progress (see Clay and Watson 1982; Gaffney and Anderson 1991; Lyons 1993; and Lyons, Pinnell, and DeFord 1993 for further information).

The Literacy Collaborative at the Ohio State University.
The Literacy Collaborative project, begun at Ohio State University and extending to approximately two hundred schools and five universities, offers a supportive learning network for classroom teachers. Taking a comprehensive view of literacy development in the early years, the Literacy Collaborative project works to build capacity at the school level. This comprehensive plan includes safety nets, outreach to parents, and a range of staff development support for teachers (Fountas and Pinnell 1996; Pinnell and McCarrier 1994). The major delivery system includes year-long nonresident preparation of a literacy coordinator who then works as a staff development person within the school building. The literacy coordinator continues to teach children in classrooms and provides ongoing teacher development through an initial class, ongoing study groups, and in-class demonstration and coaching.

Learning about teacher development.
These two literacy projects provide examples of connected, ongoing teacher development. Both Reading Recovery and the Literacy Collaborative emphasize

- ongoing teacher development of a high quality and intensive nature
- direct demonstration of skills and procedures
- systematic, ongoing observation of children and the forming of hypotheses about learning
- reflection on teaching with the assistance of a more expert other
- conversation and mutual support among members of a learning group
- a dissemination plan that develops capacity at the local level
- a local staff developer who continues the practice of teaching children and who draws on experience
- an ongoing supportive national network that collects data on children's achievement and organizes continuing education for the teacher developers

Although Reading Recovery and the Literacy Collaborative do not provide a complete picture of what needs to be accomplished in the education of teachers, they offer insight into what it's going to take. Too many piecemeal solutions have been tried and failed. If we are serious about providing literacy as every child's right, then teachers must be skilled beyond materials or programs. As Bradley said in an article in *Reading Today*, "We teach people, not third grade or college or special education or Reading Recovery or Success for All. Learning is about change, and change is about increasing and deepening our understandings so we can accept, reject, or question our knowledge" (1984, 18). Through this reflecting and questioning process, knowledge is shared across the teaching profession. What is needed is a design to support the process so that learning builds upon learning, rather than dissipating teaching techniques in short-term projects.

References

BRADLEY, D. H. 1998. "Addressing School Reform: What's Essential and What's Not." Forum in *Reading Today.* Aug./Sept., 18.

CLAY, M. M. 1991. *Becoming Literate: The Construction of Inner Control.* Auckland: Heinemann.

———. 1993. *Reading Recovery: A Guidebook for Teachers in Training.* Portsmouth, N.H.: Heinemann.

CLAY, M. M., AND WATSON, B. 1982. "An Inservice Program for Reading Recovery Teachers." In *Observing Young Readers,* edited by M. M. Clay, 192–200. Portsmouth, N.H.: Heinemann.

DARLING-HAMMOND, L., AND MCLAUGHLIN, M. 1996. "Policies That Support Professional Development in an Era of Reform." In *Teacher Learning: New Policies, New Practices,* edited by M. W. McLaughlin and I. Oberman, 202–218. New York: Teachers College Press.

FOUNTAS, I. C., AND PINNELL, G. S. 1996. "Good First Teaching with a Second Chance to Learn." Chapter 15 in *Guided Reading: Good First Teaching for All Children,* 189–199. Portsmouth, N.H.: Heinemann.

GAFFNEY, J. S., AND ANDERSON, R. C. 1991. "Two-Tiered Scaffolding: Congruent Processes of Teaching and Learning." In *Literacy for a Diverse Society,* edited by E. H. Hiebert, 184–198. New York: Teachers College Press.

LAMBERT, L., WALKER, D., ZIMMERMAN, D. P., COOPER, J. E., LAMBERT, M. D., GARDNER, M. E., AND SLACK, P. J. F. 1995. *The Constructivist Leader.* New York: Teachers College Press.

LIEBERMAN, A. 1996. "Practices That Support Teacher Development: Transforming Conceptions of Professional Learning." In *Teacher Learning: New Policies, New Practices,* edited by M. W. McLaughlin and I. Oberman, 185–201. New York: Teachers College Press.

LYONS, C. A. 1993. "The Use of Questions in the Teaching of High-Risk Beginning Readers: A Profile of a Developing Reading Recovery Teacher." *Reading & Writing Quarterly: Overcoming Learning Difficulties,* 9: 317–328.

LYONS, C. A., PINNELL, G. S., AND DEFORD, D. E. 1993. *Partners in Learning: Teachers and Children in Reading Recovery.* New York: Teachers College Press.

PINNELL, G. S. 1989. "Reading Recovery: Helping At-Risk Children Learn to Read." *The Elementary School Journal*, 90 (2): 159–181.

————. 1994. "An Inquiry-Based Model for Educating Teachers of Literacy." *Literacy, Teaching and Learning: An International Journal of Early Literacy* 1: 29–42.

PINNELL, G. S., FRIED, M. D., AND ESTICE, R. M. 1991. "Reading Recovery: Learning How to Make a Difference." In *Bridges to Literacy: Learning from Reading Recovery,* edited by D. E. DeFord, C. A. Lyons, and G. S. Pinnell, 11–36. Portsmouth, N.H.: Heinemann.

PINNELL, G. S., AND MCCARRIER, A. M. 1994. "Interactive Writing: Easing the Transition to Literacy." In *Getting Reading Right from the Start: Effective Early Interventions,* edited by E. Hiebert and B. Taylor, 149–170. Needham Heights, Mass.: Allyn and Bacon.

WILSON, K., AND DAVISS, B. 1994. *Redesigning Education.* New York: Henry Holt and Co.

Thirteen

The Political and the Professional in Education:
An Unnecessary Conflict?

PETER MORTIMORE AND JO MORTIMORE

Introduction

In England education is high on the political agenda. The government's public pronouncements, however, have done little to lift teachers' morale at a time when
requests for early retirement are rising and recruitment to the profession is falling.

In this chapter, we explore why so many modern politicians and officials appear to
dislike teachers so much. Of course teachers are not above criticism. In a number of
countries their organizations are reactionary, elitist, or resistant to change. In our
experience, however, teachers appear to be less greedy and more socially conscious
than many other occupational groups, and are more likely to feel a duty to work for
what they see as a worthwhile cause.

We maintain that the current malaise has two main causes: ministers' failure to
understand the psychology of teachers, and the unwillingness of the numerous teacher
associations to rise above their historical differences and unite in a single structure.
The consequence of the first is that, by failing to understand the importance that
teachers place on teamwork, ministers and officials misinterpret teachers' reactions to
their policies of selective rewards as an unwillingness to recognize individual differences in competence. The consequence of the second is that the profession is unable
to speak with one voice and is subject to the government's ability to divide and rule.

If the goal of raising standards—held by government and teachers alike—is to be
achieved, there is an urgent need to improve relations between those charged by the
electorate to provide political leadership in education and those whose role it is to
implement policies—and without whose support the most inspiring leadership will
come to nought.

We consider that politicians and officials could learn much from the work of
Marie Clay. She built her work around a sound understanding of, and sympathy for,

This chapter was previously published in the *Journal of Education for Teaching* 24: (3), 1998, by Carfax Publishing
Ltd., UK.

teachers. She recognized them as partners and accorded them respect. That is part of the reason why her brainchild, Reading Recovery, is highly valued in so many parts of the world.

Background

The eighteen years of Conservative Party rule in Britain from 1979 to 1997 introduced a number of radical changes to the organisation of education, which were accompanied by a sharp deterioration in relations between central government and teachers, particularly in England.[1] The changes—some of them welcome but others bitterly opposed—and the ensuing tensions within the education system have been fully recorded, so will not be repeated here. Suffice it to say that the approach of the 1997 British general election, which the Labour Party was expected to win—and won handsomely—was seen by many in the education service as heralding a new era of recognition and partnership between the politicians who decree the policies and the professionals who have to implement them. This chapter argues that the new era has yet to begin.

On the first of May 1997—election day—we were in the west of England working with heads and teachers. The atmosphere was electric—tense anticipation and cautious excitement, tinged with a collective holding of breath. The following morning, in an even larger group, the mood was unlike anything we had experienced in twenty years of professional gatherings. If any of the assembled heads and teachers were not overjoyed with the election results, they did not show it. The delight and goodwill were almost tangible.

The new Labour government, at that moment, could have had the teaching profession eating out of its hand. With publicly expressed, positive expectations of what teachers could contribute to the raising of standards, it could have capitalised on the groundswell of support and created a partnership capable of developing, in England, an education system for the twenty-first century. Instead, the education ministers have exhibited many of their predecessor's negative attitudes towards, and low expectations of, teachers. The power of positive expectations has long been recognised in social science research and many government reports have urged teachers to raise their expectations of pupils. Yet ministers seem unable to apply the same psychology to the nation's teachers.

In England, low expectations of teachers are, in part, a consequence of the profession's inability to stand up for itself. We suggest that the history of the teaching profession in England, with its different interest groups, has prevented the emergence of a unified profession that is able to speak with authority on behalf of its members. A divided profession—too conscious of individual rivalries—when faced with a reforming government reacts defensively. Such a reaction—just a short step away from expressions of victimisation—further spurs the government into ignoring legitimate concerns. Our comments apply specifically to England, although similar concerns have been raised in the United States (Chrispeels 1997) and Australia (Smyth, Shacklock, and Hattam 1997).

The Government and the Teaching Profession

The new government, to its credit, wasted no time in demonstrating that it is a "can do" administration. It has thrown itself into action with commendable energy and reforming zeal. And it has, of course, taken some very positive steps. The planned reduction in the size of infant classes, guaranteed education for all four-year-olds, extra money for books and for improvements to buildings, a concerted drive to raise standards of literacy and numeracy, the decision to create a General Teaching Council—and, more recently, the allocation in the spending review of nineteen billion pounds over three years—all indicate an impressive start to the government's first term of office.

Such changes have generally been welcomed by the teaching profession and extend the common ground that exists between it and the government. Both parties want standards to continue to rise and both agree that there is still scope for improvement at all levels (even though the results in the national General Certificate of Education [GCSE] have increased slightly each year for the last ten or so years[2]). We suspect that few teachers would argue with the ghovernment's view that demonstrably incompetent colleagues should be removed from schools or that teachers need to be well trained in all aspects of their work. Why, therefore, have the government's relations with so many members of the teaching profession—after such a short time—reached the point where "an air of disappointment—even betrayal—is still palpable in many of the nation's staff rooms" (*Times Educational Supplement*, 1 May 1998)? We believe that it is not the government's educational *ends* with which the profession takes issue—but with many of its *means*.

Writing on the first anniversary of Labour's election victory, the secretary of state commented that teachers "had expected soft words and what I have given them is hard action" (Blunkett 1998). We sense that many heads and teachers wanted both. They probably felt that they deserved some words of appreciation and encouragement after the cutbacks and opprobrium at the hands of previous Conservative Party ministers. Instead, teachers experienced a year of negative comments which focused on the failing minority at the expense of the competent and committed majority. Teachers certainly wanted some hard action to improve the conditions which so many of them, and their pupils, had endured over the years of Conservative rule, and many wanted a measure of equity to be returned to a system damaged by excessive marketisation policies. Instead, just as with the former government, the teaching profession appears to be seen as the problem rather than as part of the solution. Is it surprising, therefore, that teachers are reported as being in a state of "gloom" (Hackett 1998)?

The government's criticisms of teachers cannot all be dismissed out of hand. But they seem to us to be based on grains of truth, unfairly exaggerated. Whilst—as in any occupational group—there are some "whingers" who resist change and some shirkers who need to be weeded out, many teachers are expressing legitimate concerns. We will give eight examples of policies or actions which, despite the government's undoubted good intentions, are seen by many teachers as counterproductive to the task of raising national levels of achievement. Part of the problem is that these "top-down" policies have not had the benefit of sustained critical discussion with the profession. Indeed, they appear to have been generated by an antiteacher culture inherited from the previous government.

1. "Naming and Shaming"

One of the first actions of the new government was publicly to draw attention to the problems of eighteen "failing" schools. Teachers' reactions to this "naming and shaming" were seen as protecting the interests of a profession deemed unwilling to acknowledge—and deal with—incompetent teachers and failing schools. No one can justify the damage to children's education of protracted and halfhearted attempts to improve a failing school. But the government's desire to be seen publicly to be taking a hard line obscured the fact that some schools had been thrust into their unenviable position by the previous government's policies on "opting out"[3] and parental choice and by being pressurized by their respective local education authorities (LEAs) to accept "hard to teach" pupils whom neighbouring schools (some of them grant maintained) had refused or excluded. The adverse publicity from the "naming and shaming" damaged the already fragile confidence of staff and students and made it even harder to recruit the "new blood" needed to energize improvement efforts.

2. League Tables

The continuation of the previous government's policy of publishing crude league tables of pupils' achievement in national attainment tests[4] and of GCSE results maintains the pretense that schools' results are wholly independent of the background and prior attainment of the pupils entering them. It also sets school against school in ways which go against the collegial grain of many teachers and heads. Teachers who have voiced concerns over league tables have much evidence on their side. As the school effectiveness literature demonstrates, it is seldom possible to designate an entire school as "effective" and "attempts to describe schools uniformly as 'good or bad' are genuinely unhelpful" (Sammons, Thomas, and Mortimore 1997). Schools vary in their effectiveness between subjects, over time, and in relation to different groups of pupils. All serious analyses of school performance have shown that only the top and bottom of the range are significantly different. The rest are often clustered closely together and appear different only because of the rankings which lend the tables a spurious validity (Goldstein and Spiegelhalter 1996). Most importantly, research has shown that the performance of pupils is affected by both the efforts of the school *and* pupils' home background. Attempts to single out improving schools are confounded by the inability of all but well-informed data analysts to distinguish between those schools which have improved because the teachers have changed their patterns of teaching, or the organization has been modified, or the schools' funding has improved, or because the schools' control over admissions now allows them to recruit "easier to teach" pupils from more advantaged homes (Mortimore and Whitty 1997).

3. Socioeconomic Disadvantage

Ministers have repeatedly criticized teachers for arguing that, as a group, economically disadvantaged pupils cannot be expected to perform at the same level as others. They are on record as saying that "poverty must not be seen as an excuse for failure" (Byers 1998). In the past, some teachers may well have used pupils' disadvantage unjustifiably—to excuse low expectations and poor performance. Regrettably, some may still do so. But the reality is that, throughout the developed world, poverty and disadvantage are associated with lower academic performance—even in the United States, which has had numerous programmes to redress the educational consequences of economic inequality (U.S. Department of Education 1992). Children from disadvantaged families suffer physically—through poorer health and less energy; emotionally—through greater family tensions; psychologically—through the risk of lower self-esteem; and educationally—through reduced opportunities for help at home. A review of the evidence demonstrated that disadvantage is a cause of, rather than an excuse for, failure (Mortimore and Whitty 1997).

If families are coping with low income, inadequate diet, poor health, bad housing, and the stigma of poverty, is it surprising that their children are likely to do less well in competitive, norm-influenced public examinations than children who come from families with every material advantage? In England, the key measure of achievement is the competitive GCSE examination taken by sixteen-year-olds. Currently, approximately 40 percent of boys and 50 percent of girls reach the accepted benchmark of success (five A*–C grades). Each time these percentages increase slightly there is a media-led public outcry that standards must be slipping. Given this constraint on rising grades in a competitive system, the reality is that pupils from disadvantaged backgrounds are less likely to succeed than their advantaged peers, and that schools with predominantly disadvantaged intakes are less likely to do as well as others. Individual pupils and schools which "buck the trend" do so as a result of extraordinary efforts. But it is inevitable that in a system in which success is, in a sense, rationed, their success can only be achieved at the expense of others.

4. Current System of School Inspections

The abolition, by the last government, of Her Majesty's Inspectorate (HMI) and the creation of the Office for Standards in Education (Ofsted) radically changed the nature and the culture of national inspection.

Prior to the change, inspection of schools was carried out by HMIs recruited from senior teachers in schools and colleges, with a chief inspector drawn from their ranks. Ofsted was set up in 1992, subsuming HMI, as a nonministerial governmental department independent of the Department for Education and Employment. Its role is to undertake regular inspections and produce public reports on all state-funded schools, local education authorities, and teacher training in England. Inspections are undertaken by teams of accredited independent inspectors which have entered into competitive tendering for contracts. The teams recruit specialists who have both appropriate qualifications in the subject they are required to inspect, and general experience of pedagogy.

Whilst, in some ways, the new arrangements are an improvement on those of the former HMIs and local authority inspection services (for example, in the much more systematic approach to "failing" schools), our view is that the current system is unsatisfactory in a number of important respects.

First, the commercial arrangements, involving competition between contractors for inspection contracts and a system of unstable and constantly changing inspection teams, have led to an overall inconsistency of judgement (*Times Educational Supplement*, 22 May 1998). Moreover, the inability of teams to provide advice on improvement has reduced the value of the exercise to schools (Ofstin 1996).

Second, the endeavours by Ofsted to judge and to quantify the achievement and progress of pupils, regardless of the context of the school and without systematic use of value-added analyses, has led to the proliferation of unreliable—and, consequently, unfair—judgements (Gray 1998).

Third, the integrity of Ofsted has been seriously damaged through the use of flawed research studies which, ironically, have been used to support the claim for Ofsted to have even greater powers over other parts of the education system (Mortimore and Goldstein 1997).

Fourth, the scale of the inspection programme and the overheads of the office mean that the costs of Ofsted are high (in the region of 140 million pounds per year) and contrast starkly with the limited budget available to most schools for books and equipment. If the costs (including the opportunity costs) of the host school are also taken into account, questions about the cost-effectiveness of the enterprise become extremely pertinent—and surely, as has been suggested, warrant an inquiry from the National Audit Office (Bright 1998).

Fifth, the culture of inspection—as promoted more by the comments of the Chief Inspector than by the inspection of individual schools—has become strident and punitive instead of, as in the days of HMI, rigorous yet supportive. It is not surprising that aspects of the work of Ofsted have been criticized so roundly by both an earlier Senior Chief HMI (Bolton 1998) and the founding head of Ofsted (National Committee of Inquiry into Higher Education 1997).

The government, so far, has publicly rejected all criticisms of Ofsted. If it wishes to improve its relations with the teaching profession, it needs to reconsider whether this is a wise and productive stance.

5. Beacon Schools

The government's beacon schools initiative will make available 1.8 million pounds to up to one hundred schools considered by Ofsted to be outstanding. Schools will each receive between twenty thousand and fifty thousand pounds to help them disseminate their success via publications, seminars, and computer links. The initiative is another example of ministers' positive ideas which, lacking the critical input of practitioners, are in danger of missing the mark. In theory, it seems entirely reasonable to expect schools which are doing particularly well to act as models for those labouring under difficulties (although what works in one school may not translate to other schools in different settings). But teachers who visit—or are visited by staff from—beacon schools, which are privileged in terms of extra funding or in the type of pupils they attract, may grow resentful of the inequity rather than be impressed by the pedagogy. Whilst the beacon logo may look good on school notepaper, it may prove a hostage to fortune in the long term. Some of the innovative City Technology Colleges, created by a previous Conservative administration, grew to regard their "beacon" label less as a badge of excellence and more as an albatross.

6. Advanced Skills Teachers

The government intends to create a small cadre of "super teachers" with enhanced status and salary in order to demonstrate that professional careers in the classroom are worthwhile and that high levels of pedagogical skills will be rewarded. Teachers' opposition to the plan has been interpreted by the government as the reactions of an egalitarian group in the profession which is unwilling to recognize exceptional achievement. No serious consideration seems to have been given to the possibility that the opposition is on purely pragmatic grounds. Ministers have surely underestimated the importance of teamwork in schools and neglected the difficulty such posts may create for their holders—and their colleagues. Can it be justifiable—or wise—to single out such a small number and say to them, in Moriarty's words, "There's so little money that even a small pay award has to be staggered in April and December, but you can have a prize for excellence instead" (Moriarty 1998). (Imagine you are one such post holder, receiving an enhanced salary and expected to influence other teachers, and you encounter difficulties with a particular class. How would you retain credibility amongst your less well-paid peers?) Furthermore, the idea that particularly talented teachers can be persuaded by higher salaries to stay in the classroom for the whole of their careers may be unrealistic. Teaching is extremely demanding; talented teachers may well "burn out." The transition from classroom teacher to head or inspector, far from being a problem, may be in the best interests of both individuals and the schools.

7. Summer Literacy Schemes

Summer holiday literacy schemes are, in principle, an excellent idea. If the pioneering schemes achieved no more than the provision of three weeks of supervised, enjoyable, and worthwhile literacy-related activities for children (particularly those with working mothers), they were money well spent. However, amassing evidence of whether they had achieved their prime purpose—to raise the reading standards of slow readers before they reached secondary school—called for careful monitoring of reading levels before and after participation. The immediate and overenthusiastic official comments on the efficacy of the schemes not only implied that ordinary teachers in primary schools were failing to achieve comparable progress, but turned out to be premature. Independent monitoring by the National Foundation for Educational Research revealed that the testing carried out on the scheme had been flawed and that the reading levels of participants, in common with those of pupils who had not attended the schemes, had, in fact, declined over the summer (Sainsbury 1997).

8. Teachers' Hours and Holidays

Ministers have drawn attention to the limited working hours of schools and the length of teachers' holidays. Whilst teachers' contractual hours may be shorter and their holidays undeniably longer than in many other occupations, most teachers work much longer hours than their pupils (and than those in many other professional groups), as surveys carried out by the government's Office of Manpower Studies and the School Teachers' Review Body (STRB) illustrate (STRB 1994). It is also the case that many teachers are under considerable stress—witness the increasing size of the annual exodus of those seeking early retirement on health grounds (3,053 in 1997–1998) (*Education Journal*, June/July 1998). We believe that a radical review of the hours of schooling, the length of teachers' holidays, and, most importantly, the number of terms in the school year, needs be undertaken in order to formulate a new contract. But we also believe that such a review has to be carried out by the profession *in partnership* with parents, rather than being performed by the government and then imposed upon teachers.

Why Are Ministers Misjudging Their Relations with Teachers?

Our view is that ministers and their officials are misjudging their relations with teachers because they are failing to understand the psychology of teachers. As a consequence, they are misinterpreting many of the statements and reactions of the profession. Teachers are seen as over-defensive in relation to other occupational groups. There is probably some truth in this, but, we would argue, it is for two good reasons.

The first reason stems from the nature of the teaching task. Teachers spend much of their time isolated from their colleagues and surrounded by young learners. As a result, although few would probably admit it openly, they can feel isolated and exposed. This vulnerability helps generate a strong need for teamwork and peer support. Moreover, the skills of teamwork and cooperation are what teachers try to instil in pupils—and what they are constantly being told that society (and, in particular, industry) needs.

The second reason is that teachers have been criticized and blamed for the last fifteen or so years. They have been held to account for the failures of the system. Yet the most rudimentary analysis of educational policies over this period shows that it is the *system* which has been appallingly mismanaged by the previous government. The confusion surrounding the introduction of, and subsequent alterations to, the national curriculum, the wholesale changes to the methods of testing, and the reduction in the proportion of the gross domestic product being devoted to education (from 6.8 percent in 1975 to 5.1 percent in 1993) speak for themselves (Centre for Educational

Research and Innovation 1996). Small wonder, therefore, that the teaching profession appears beleaguered.

Ministers and officials seem to consider anything less than wholehearted endorsement of their policies as hostile opposition. They interpret teachers' "defensive" attitudes as an unwillingness to accept criticism or to recognize individual differences in competence. In such circumstances the government, like its predecessor, is using shame, fear, and top-down *diktats* as the motivators for change. This is the rationale underlying naming and shaming, league tables, and punitive inspection practices. Yet there is sound research evidence from the school effectiveness literature that praise and rewards are far greater motivators (for pupils and for teachers) than are derision and punishment (Rutter et al. 1979; Mortimore et al. 1988). Surely such positive characteristics should govern the education system as a whole.

What Could the Government Do?

We believe the government should cultivate a better understanding of the psychology of the profession, which would lead to a more accurate perception of teachers' attitudes and behaviours. Strategies should be based on the principles of social psychology and motivation theory. We suggest three specific strategies. First, ministers, in their public pronouncements, need to focus more directly on teachers' achievements and contributions to society (rather than adding these as a minor counterpoint to criticisms and then protesting when the media report the main negative substance of their remarks). Ministerial expressions of appreciation of, and trust in, teachers as a professional group (not just accolades for a chosen few at an Oscars-like ceremony[5]) could begin to reverse the decline in relations.

Second, ministers need to find better ways of consulting with the profession and of involving it in developmental policies which allow the experienced practitioner some flexibility. Neither inundating schools with formal documents nor discussing ideas with a minority of handpicked supporters is right. There is an urgent need for a more constructive dialogue—in which concerns can be aired and alternatives considered—between politicians elected to provide policy leadership and teachers charged with policy implementation, whose support is critical. Indeed, the prime minister himself—when leader of the opposition—is quoted as acknowledging that "no worthwhile reform can take place without the positive engagement of teachers" (*Times*, 10 January 1997). If ministers fail to promote an appropriate role for the profession, they will not only waste a valuable opportunity—as, arguably, has happened in Australia (Smyth, Shacklock, and Hattam 1997)—but will risk teachers engaging in unprofessional activities. Strikes or working to rule could again become the norm, rather than the last resort.

A crucial third step is to trust teachers as full professionals—which means encouraging them to formulate their own initiatives. The profession is a repository for vast amounts of good practice which have been tempered in recent years by the constraints of successive waves of government-enforced reforms. Moreover, some of the beguiling but basically shallow ideas currently holding sway are likely to founder and will need to be replaced by more thoughtful, *practice-tested*, strategies.

Is this a dewy-eyed, idealistic vision? We believe not. Rather, it is based on research findings about the "ownership" of ideas and initiatives and on current thinking in the international business world which places a premium on initiative, creativity, and trust (Handy 1997; World Bank 1995).

The Art and Science of Teaching

Nobody knows for certain what attracts people to teaching. It might be the sense of a vocation to promote knowledge and see children learn and develop, or the relative freedom that teachers have traditionally enjoyed to plan and organize their work and to exert control over others. Some may be attracted by the opportunities to spend the long holidays pursuing their interests, whilst others may simply be drawn to a job that—having spent so long in their own schools—they think they already know. It is probable that most teachers are drawn to the profession, as we were in our day, by a mixture of altruism and self-interest.

We are certainly not arguing that all teachers are beyond reproach. As in any large group in society, some members will be much better than others. Some will seek to blame everyone else for poor outcomes. A few will be motivated by revolutionary politics and will seek to exploit any peer dissatisfaction for their own political ends. In our experience, however, teachers as a whole are more idealistic and more public-spirited than many other occupational groups.

For anyone who has attended school—and that means most of us—teaching seems to be the most transparent of occupations, with less mystique than many other walks of life. Most people, if asked, would probably claim to understand what teachers do. But, whilst most are familiar with the daily pattern of teachers' work, far fewer understand the complexity of the pedagogy[6] and, as a result, underestimate the skills required. Teachers, in deploying the art and science of their profession, are expected to have an expert knowledge of their subject plus a range of skills:

- organisational skills to sort out materials and sources of information, to create the right atmosphere, and to organize suitable opportunities for pupils to learn and to be challenged
- analytical skills to enable them to break down complex bodies of knowledge into coherent components
- synthesizing skills so that ideas can be built into arguments, propositions, and theories
- presentational skills for providing information to pupils of varying ages and abilities and, increasingly, for explaining their work to parents and guardians
- management skills so that the dynamics of individual learners, groups, and classes can be effectively coordinated

- assessment skills so that pupils' work can be judged and appropriate feedback given informally—through question and answer techniques—and formally—through tests and examinations
- self-evaluative skills so that their teaching performance can be continually monitored and improved
- social skills so that they are able to relate to the needs and talents of a range of pupils and communicate with them, with parents, and with external agencies

Effective teachers weave together knowledge and pedagogy, managerial and social skills, imagination and sensitivity, in order to stimulate and support learning. Their complex role is actually extremely daunting, but is largely taken for granted by the media and the general public. Teachers, moreover, do not operate in a vacuum. They work within a context of values stemming from the nature of the society in which they operate, the ethos of their school, and their own particular beliefs. They also have a curriculum—in England, a national curriculum—and an assessment framework with national testing of pupils at ages seven, eleven, fourteen, sixteen, and eighteen. The techniques employed in instruction were a matter for personal choice until developments such as the "literacy hour" started to specify even these. Amidst a welter of statutory specifications, dedicated material, and official guidelines, teachers are expected to evoke motivation and to ensure that learning takes place. Teaching, in a nutshell, is the means to an end: pupils' learning.

It is sometimes argued that teaching should only be deemed effective if it is clear that it has led directly to learning. The argument runs that teaching is an interactive process, and if no learning has taken place, there cannot have been adequate teaching. However, in reality no one can guarantee learning. Determined pupils can, and do, resist it. Somewhat frustratingly, we also know that effective learning can take place in the absence of effective teaching, and even despite poor teaching—which can sometimes heighten motivation in learners. Learning can also be a cumulative process in which the groundwork laid in one school year does not appear to bear fruit until the next, or something may "click" and be understood some time after it was first introduced to the pupil, perhaps by a different teacher in an earlier school year. Furthermore, pupils can learn as a result of many factors which have little to do with school teaching: through conversation with parents or other adults, playing with friends, reading books, watching television, "surfing" the Internet, or thinking through issues for themselves. It is therefore difficult to judge with any precision the effectiveness of particular teachers on pupils' learning.

An Insecure Profession

In comparison with that of law or medicine, the status of the teaching profession is low and its claims to be a profession at all are still contested (Ozga and Lawn 1981). The origins of the profession—and of its representative associations—lie in the development over the past 150 or so years of different kinds of schools, serving pupils from different social groups and requiring differently qualified teachers (Ironside and Seifert 1995). The constituent parts of today's public education service are rooted in Joseph Lancaster's monitorial system, in endowed grammar schools, and in trade schools (Aldrich 1998).

There are currently six major professional associations representing teachers. Their separate geneses and ideologies reflect historical differences in the range of schools and members' qualifications and the different roles, career expectations, and even pay, between the sexes. These different histories mean that the teaching profession, rather than speaking with one voice, suffers from "endemic divisiveness" (Gardner 1998). The profession has never formed one large powerful body. Paradoxically, as one of the most highly unionized groups in the workforce, teachers might have been expected to present a united front. But history (thus far) has triumphed, and loyalties to individual associations, with their idiosyncratic backgrounds, have prevented the emergence of a united profession.

Successive governments have been able to capitalize on this disunity in order to achieve changes in practice or in conditions of service. For example, the previous administration began to reduce its predecessors' commitments to the steady improvement of teacher education (such as the extension of training from two to three years and the introduction of a bachelor of education degree). It also fostered a variety of schemes to bring untrained people into the classroom (of which a so-called "mums' army" of untrained staff was the most blatant); abolished the probationary year for newly qualified teachers; failed to introduce a General Teaching Council; and encouraged the erroneous view that teacher training was open to the whims of "trendy" academics.[7]

Since no single body can speak for the profession, teachers, thus far, have been unable to resist successive governments' imposition of policies which they believed to be inherently damaging to the education system. Unlike the members of the medical and legal professions, teachers have no collective voice. Instead, the profession is represented by a number of different associations which combine trade union functions and professional roles. In our view, the coexistence of such bodies has prevented the emergence of a strong and united profession, able to represent teachers' interests to the government of the day and to secure from it the trust and respect it deserves. Thus, the profession has not been in a position to be proactive, with its own agenda for improvement. Nor has it the stature to challenge "teacher-bashing" or to moderate the numerous initiatives being foisted on schools.

What Should the Teacher Associations Do?

The long-awaited General Teaching Council (GTC) may help. But such a body will always remain a creation of government. We hope the GTC will become an independent arbiter of standards and not join what Humes (1994) scathingly calls "the laundering agents of public policy" (56). But even if the GTC works well and government allows it independence, its function will be mainly regulative so that there will still be a need for a complementary unified body dealing with professional and trade union matters.

We acknowledge that earlier moves by the associations towards mergers have come to nought. The three largest associations—the National Union of Teachers (NUT), the National Association of Schoolmasters and Union of Women Teachers (NASUWT), and the Association of Teachers and Lecturers (ATL)—have, in the past, passed conference resolutions calling for professional unity, and the ATL and the Professional Association of Teachers (PAT) have held formal talks about merging but failed to reach agreement. However, the associations have submitted common claims to the School Teachers' Review Body, many local branches work harmoniously at LEA level, and the current GTC movement owes much to cooperation between the different organisations.

The divided associations are products of the old system. Once they had some rationale, rooted in their histories. Now the conditions that produced divisions have disappeared—and so, we argue, should the separate and competing associations. Surely now is the moment to put aside rivalries and historical differences and work towards compromise for the sake of a greater good: the creation of a unified professional force. Now is the time to "think the unthinkable" and to create one association which can stand up for teachers as fully fledged professionals and resist thinking of them as "hard-done-by" victims.

We recognize that the changes we propose will not be popular with *all* teachers. Members who feel strong emotional links with their own particular associations will not warm to the notion of a bigger, less personal body. Those for whom the annual conferences are the high spot of the year—when they can give vent to their feelings of injustice and have them beamed via television news into millions of homes—will no doubt resist pressure for change. So will the small number of teachers who are politically motivated and who strive for revolutionary changes in society as a whole. There is evidence to suggest, however, that such a move would prove popular amongst some teachers (Rafferty 1998). In the United States it is likely that the two biggest teacher unions will merge and by so doing produce the largest single professional employees union in the country.

Why should the current leaders support a proposal to relinquish their roles and make their several associations redundant? Because the creation of a single body would unify and strengthen the profession. If individual leaders were to take a truly dispassionate look at the bigger picture, the potential benefits of teacher unity—not just for the profession but for the education system as a whole—might inspire in them the courage to take such a decisive step.

Implications for Teacher Education

We have argued that, over recent years, the approaches of both political parties to the teaching profession in England have been characterized by an unwillingness to trust practitioners. This lack of trust has extended to those in higher education who have responsibility for the training of new teachers. In fact, teacher trainers have often been seen as the "real problem." It is for such reasons that a new Teacher Training Agency (TTA), working directly for government and overseeing all training courses, was established. The agency has imposed a national curriculum for initial teacher training and has approved a programme of regular inspection undertaken by Ofsted. It has also fostered the idea of school-based teacher training, thus adding to the already heavy burden of school teachers' duties and creating small, non-cost-effective training courses in competition with higher education.

The teacher associations and those responsible for teacher education in higher education have not, traditionally, enjoyed close relations. The two groups have seldom been in open conflict, but, because they have not worked towards common goals, they have established neither a rapport nor a realisation of how much they both depend on the quality of new trainees. The establishment of the GTC and of one unified teacher association would provide an opportunity to end this anomaly. These bodies, rather than the TTA, should assume responsibility for the profession and for its initial and continuing training. Working with higher education would enable the profession to promote the highest standards and to benefit from developments in learning and teaching.

Conclusions

It is clear from our visits to schools abroad that many English schools have great strengths and that their teachers have the capacity to lead the world with their skills, commitment, and professionalism. We were disappointed by the lack of publicity given to the excellent performance by English pupils in the science component of the Third International Mathematics and Science Tests. In the special tests of problem solving—a skill so sought after by employers—undertaken outside of the mathematics and the science tests, English pupils scored highly. Yet because there has been such an emphasis on failure, these achievements have been largely overlooked. In contrast, the mathematics results—in which English pupils did much less well—are frequently used as an example of how poorly our pupils are performing. The punitive atmosphere engendered by a selective emphasis on poor results, league tables, negative inspection techniques, and naming and shaming has encouraged many who do not know much about publicly funded, local-authority schools to fear the worst. There is a danger that such negativism will create a self-fulfilling spiral of lowered confidence, feelings of inadequacy, and, for many, a desire to leave the profession. As the United Nations Educational, Scientific, and Cultural Organization (UNESCO) states: "When teaching as a profession is ill-regarded in a society, that ill-regard reflects itself on the entire system of organized education" (1988, para. 17).

Currently in England there is low morale in the profession, record numbers of vacancies, and declining numbers of high-quality applicants for teacher training—the opposite of what is needed if our nation is to prosper and if we are to succeed in becoming the "learning society" of the twenty-first century. No government likes to admit that any of its approaches have been misguided. We hope, however, that this government will have the courage to acknowledge the need for a change of emphasis and that ministers, rather than seeking to justify their stance (or simply attacking this critique) will reflect on our analysis and grasp the challenge it proffers. Similarly, we hope that the teacher associations will resist the temptation to see us as outsiders meddling in their affairs.

We have heard much about the potential of the British government's "third way" and of the "mutualism" underpinning it. We think that restoring the confidence of the teaching profession provides a perfect opportunity for the government to demonstrate what these concepts can mean for education. But the profession must play an active part in that process. We believe that, if the English teacher associations were to break their historical ties, bury their differences, and join forces in a united association, they would become a powerful advocate for the professionals they represent and, indirectly, for the children their members teach.

The work of Marie Clay provides an encouraging model for both parties. This can produce an outcome which is greater than the sum of the two separate contributions. The key ingredients, as in so many aspects of our educational enterprises, are trust and mutual respect. For the sake of future generations of learners and teachers, we hope that British government and the English teacher associations will have the courage and the generosity of spirit to learn from Marie Clay's model.

Notes

1. This chapter refers specifically to England. Scotland and Northern Ireland each have different education systems and Wales has a separate inspection system.

2. The GCSE is an examination taken by most sixteen-year-olds at the end of their statutory schooling. Results are compiled annually by the Department for Education and Employment (DfEE). See, for example, DfEE 1997.

3. Under the Conservative administration, schools were encouraged to "opt out" of local education authority (LEA) control and, instead, to adopt "grant maintained" (GM) status. This means that they receive their funding directly from central government, rather than the funding being allocated "second hand" via the LEA. Since the LEA takes a percentage of the money to cover the costs of central services (such as advisory services, building and site maintenance services, special needs, school meals, and transport), GM schools, by choosing the different status, receive a greater amount of money and have control over how it is spent.

4. All pupils are assessed in national tests on their attainment at the end of "key stages" of the national curriculum. These tests are taken at ages seven, eleven, and fourteen. At age sixteen most pupils take their GCSE examinations.

5. The government intends to hold regional awards ceremonies, leading to one national televised ceremony, for up to six-hundred teachers and classroom assistants nominated in categories. Schools will be invited to nominate candidates and a panel, chaired by a well-known industrialist, will select the winners.

6. The Greek word *pedagogy* literally means "the care of boys," but is more commonly taken to mean "the art and the science of teaching."

7. Since 1984, successive governments have maintained tight control of teacher education, initially through the Council for the Accreditation of Teacher Education and latterly through the work of the Teacher Training Agency. All training is subject to rigorous inspection. A cluster of government circulars have specified the precise allocation of time to be spent on the various courses and in schools.

References

ALDRICH, R. 1998. "Teacher Training in London." In *London Higher: The Establishment of Higher Education in London,* edited by R. Floud and S. Glynn, 223–246. London: Athlone Press.

BLUNKETT, D. 1998. Cited in an interview with G. Hackett, *Times Educational Supplement,* 1 May.

BOLTON, E. 1998. "HMI—The Thatcher Years." *Oxford Review of Education* 24 (1): 45–55.

BRIGHT, M. 1998. *Observer,* 3 May.

BYERS, S. 1998. Address to the International Congress on School Effectiveness and Improvement, Manchester, January.

CENTRE FOR EDUCATIONAL RESEARCH AND INNOVATION. 1996. *Education at a Glance: OECD Indicators.* Paris: Organization for Economic Co-operation and Development.

CHRISPEELS, J. 1997. "Educational Policy Implementation in a Shifting Political Climate: the California Experience." *American Educational Research Journal* 34 (Fall): 453–481.

DEPARTMENT FOR EDUCATION AND EMPLOYMENT. 1997. "Top Performers Highlighted in New Performance Tables." Press Release 367/97. London: DfEE.

Education Journal. 1998. "Reply to a Parliamentary Question on 4 June 1998." (June/July): 31.

GARDNER, P. 1998. "Classroom Teachers and Educational Change 1876–1996." *Journal of Education for Teaching* 24 (1): 33–49.

GOLDSTEIN, H., AND SPIEGELHALTER, D. 1996. "League Tables and Their Limitations: Statistical Issues in Comparisons of Institutional Performance." *Journal of the Royal Statistical Society* A 159: 385–443.

GRAY, J. 1998. "The Contribution of Educational Research to the Cause of School Improvement." Professorial lecture, Institute of Education, April.

HACKETT, G. 1998. "Blunkett Regrets Teachers' Gloom." *Times Educational Supplement*, 1 May.

HANDY, C. 1997. "Schools for Life and Work." In *Living Education: Essays in Honour of John Tomlinson*, edited by P. Mortimore and V. Little, 117–127. London: Paul Chapman Publishing.

HUMES, W. 1994. "Teacher Education in British Columbia and Scotland: A Response." *Journal of Education for Teaching* 20 (1): 47–58.

IRONSIDE, M., AND SEIFERT, R. 1995. *Industrial Relations in Schools.* London: Routledge.

JUDD, J. 1998. *Independent*, 6 May.

MORIARTY, H. 1998. *Guardian Education*, 14 July.

MORTIMORE, P., AND GOLDSTEIN, H. 1997. *The Teaching of Reading in 45 Inner London Primary Schools: A Critical Examination of OFSTED Research.* London: Institute of Education.

MORTIMORE, P., AND WHITTY, G. 1997. *Can School Effectiveness Overcome the Effects of Disadvantage?* London: Institute of Education.

MORTIMORE, P., SAMMONS, P., STOLL, L., AND ECOB, R. 1988. *School Matters: The Junior Years.* London: Paul Chapman Publishing.

NATIONAL COMMITTEE OF INQUIRY INTO HIGHER EDUCATION. 1997. *Higher Education in the Learning Society* (The Dearing Report), Report 10, Teacher Education and Training: A Study. London: Her Majesty's Stationery Office.

OFSTIN. 1996. *Improving School Inspection: An Account of the Ofstin Conference.* Hexham, Northumberland: Ofstin Working Group.

OZGA, J., AND LAWN, M. 1981. *Teachers' Professionalism and Class.* London: Falmer.

RAFFERTY, F. 1998. "Hankering After Unity." Conversation with Hank Roberts. *Times Educational Supplement*, 24 April.

RUTTER, M., MAUGHAN, B., MORTIMORE, P., AND OUSTON, J. 1979. *Fifteen Thousand Hours: Secondary Schools and Their Effects on Children.* London: Paul Chapman Publishing.

SAINSBURY, M. 1997. *Summer Literacy Schemes.* Report to the Department for Education and Employment by the National Foundation for Educational Research. London: DfEE.

SAMMONS, P., THOMAS, S., AND MORTIMORE, P. 1997. *Forging Links.* London: Paul Chapman Publishing.

SCHOOL TEACHERS' REVIEW BODY. 1994. *First Report on 1994 Teachers' Workload Survey.* London: STRB.

SMYTH, J., SHACKLOCK, G., AND HATTAM, R. 1997. "Teacher Development in Difficult Times: Lessons from a Policy Initiative in Australia." *Teacher Development* 1: 11–19.

Times. 1977. Editorial, 10 January.

Times Educational Supplement. 1998. Leader, 1 May.

Times Educational Supplement. 1998. 22 May.

UNESCO. 1988. *Report of the Joint ILO–UNESCO Committee of Experts on the Application of the Recommendation Concerning the Status of Teachers.* Geneva and Paris: ILO/UNESCO.

U.S. DEPARTMENT OF EDUCATION. 1992. *National Assessment of the Chapter 1 Program: The Interim Report.* Washington, D.C.: U.S. DOE.

WORLD BANK. 1995. *Priorities and Strategies for Education: A World Bank Review.* Washington D.C.: World Bank.

Fourteen

Theoretical Privilege and Researchers' Contribution to Educational Change

VIVIANE M. J. ROBINSON AND JAMES C. WALKER

When Reading Recovery is evaluated using the criteria of dissemination, utilization, and early impact, one concludes that it has been one of the most successful educational interventions of its time. There must surely be lessons to be learned, therefore, from an examination of the theories of change that inform this multilevel intervention. In contrast to most current approaches to educational change, Reading Recovery has not set out to reform, let alone restructure, existing school and classroom provision for the teaching of early literacy. It has kept its focus firmly on the individual learner, and on the creation of conditions outside regular classrooms that will enable students in the program to progress fast enough to catch up with their classmates. At the systemic level, Reading Recovery was designed to create an infrastructure that can work in parallel with students' regular programs, rather than to change the original provision under which these students had difficulty learning. That infrastructure includes separate national or regional systems for training teachers and tutors in Reading Recovery, and a distinctive curriculum and pedagogy delivered in out-of-class individual instruction.

One lesson to be learned from the success of Reading Recovery, therefore, is that it may be easier to remediate the problems of learners by bypassing the systems in which those problems arose, rather than by directly engaging with those systems. Certainly the highly individual focus of Reading Recovery, and the belief that failure is inevitable for a certain percentage of young learners in junior classrooms, make this approach seem logical. Ten years ago, however, the first author discussed the possibility that, although the bypass strategy might increase the possibility that Reading Recovery would be adopted by national and state systems, it might jeopardize the continued progress of learners as they shift from individual tuition back to regular class programs that lack many of the features thought necessary to sustain their gains (Robinson 1989). In raising this possibility, however, the author was careful to acknowledge that the intervention challenges raised by the attempt to reform some aspects of mainstream provision are even greater than the challenge of creating space within that system to install the Reading Recovery infrastructure.

239

This chapter explains the risks involved in engaging rather than bypassing existing practice and provision, and outlines an approach to intervention and intervention research that may convert those risks into learning opportunities for both the putative reformers and the practitioners and policymakers they seek to influence. In summary, we argue that researchers with a reform agenda are frequently caught in a dilemma between the acceptance of that agenda and the effectiveness of their proposals. The probability of acceptance increases to the extent that a reform agenda is broadly compatible with the thinking and values that inform current policy and practice, yet such compatibility may threaten the effectiveness of those reforms when current thinking is implicated in the problems that motivate the attempt to change. On the other hand, even though reform proposals that challenge current values are more likely to be effective if they are acted upon, they are less likely to be implemented (Cousins and Leithwood 1986; Nisbet 1994).

It seems, then, that the dilemma between effectiveness and acceptance will force the reform-minded researcher to choose between co-optation and a principled but ineffectual critique of the status quo. We argue that there is a third alternative, in which the views of reformers and practitioners are treated as competing theories whose efficacy is investigated in a manner that treats both perspectives fairly (Robinson 1993). Pursuit of this alternative is difficult, because it requires researchers to reject epistemological and methodological principles that privilege either their own or practitioners' theories. It requires instead that differences between researchers and practitioners be resolved through mutually educative inquiry rather than through interpersonal or political persuasion. This is not to say that inquiry that is designed to reveal and resolve such differences will succeed in doing so; there are many instances when the conditions for such inquiry cannot be established, and others in which competing interests overwhelm any common ground. However, we reiterate that the dilemma of effectiveness and acceptance is far more likely to be resolved if interventionists and researchers treat objections to reform agendas as theory competition that requires further inquiry, rather than as opportunities for political or personal persuasion.

We proceed by explaining how differences between researchers and practitioners can be conceptualized as theory competition, and how such theories can be identified and evaluated. After giving the broad outline of such inquiry, we argue, through examination of reform-oriented research, that much of it fails to resolve the acceptance-effectiveness dilemma because it either privileges the theory of the researcher (*R-theory*) or, as seen in more recent forms of inquiry, privileges the theory of the relevant practitioners (*P-theory*). Although we refer to the contending theories as R-theory and P-theory, we recognise that theoretical disputes may occur within as well as among these groups. Our argument is applicable to the investigation and resolution of any disagreements about the desirability of particular practices, including those practices in regular classrooms that may not be conducive to the continued progress of Reading Recovery graduates.

Differences Between Researchers and Practitioners as Theory Competition

We have suggested that differences between researchers and practitioners should be construed as a process of theory competition and resolved through evaluation of the relative adequacy of each theory. Although the word *theory* is usually associated with researchers and not practitioners, we use the term to mean a set of understandings about how to achieve desired consequences in given sets of circumstances. In this sense, theories are held, whether implicitly or explicitly, by both researchers and practitioners. A particular teacher of reading has a theory that leads her to employ a phonics approach, whether or not she can articulate that theory. A researcher has a different theory, which leads her to advocate a whole language approach. The two theories are in competition, not in the sense of a conflict of interest between persons, but in the epistemological sense that they represent two different solutions to the problem of how to teach reading (Walker and Evers 1982).

Faced with theory competition, protagonists frequently assume the validity of their own views (*privilege* their theory) in their attempts to overcome the resistance of the opposition. The alternative we advocate is one of critical dialogue, in which the theories of the protagonists are clarified, then evaluated in terms of their relative strengths and weaknesses as accounts of the practical problem and sources of potential solutions (Robinson 1993, 53–58). The dialogue may or may not occur as a face-to-face encounter—the point is that proponents of a theory are fair-minded in their treatment of its competitors.

The argument for a methodology of theory competition through critical dialogue is both epistemological and practical. Our knowledge is likely to be expanded when we consider more possible sources of knowledge rather than fewer (i.e., serious consideration of the competitor may improve our knowledge of the reading process), and the stronger the set of available solutions from which we may choose, the more likely our problems are to be solved. Critical dialogue also strengthens a collegial approach to professional practice; we not only surface and share our views, but we respect and seek to learn from those whose views are different.

Theory competition through critical dialogue means that a researcher who is critical of an educational policy or practice should first identify the theory of practice (we consider policy to be a form of social practice) that leads practitioners to employ it, then evaluate the adequacy of that theory in comparison to the theory of practice that is suggested by his or her critique.

It may not be obvious why we are advocating inquiry into the relevant *theory of practice*, rather than comparative evaluation of the *practices* that are advocated by researcher and practitioner. After all, much research has been done into the relative merits of such practices as the phonics and whole language approaches to the teaching of reading, without locating each practice in the practical theories of the actors that employ it. Our reason for focusing on theories of practice is that they generate the practices that researchers wish to alter, and unless practitioners alter their relevant theories, they will not willingly (indeed, they cannot) alter the targeted practices. In addition, those same theories are the source of practitioners' objections to the advice of researchers, and they are likely to persist unless the reasoning that generates them is directly engaged. By engaging rather than bypassing theories of practice, researchers gain a better understanding of what causes the practices that they contest, and what is involved in seeking to alter them. Such inquiry may also help practitioners to surface the tacit knowledge that informs their practice, and thus to join with researchers in the evaluation of its adequacy.

Inquiry into practice requires an understanding of the nature of practice and of theories of practice. We take a practice to be a *solution* to a practical problem, and as we make clear later, to call it a solution is to say simply that it is in place, not that it is adequate. A teacher's practice of leaving school promptly after class is his solution to the problem of how to manage his stress and his child-care responsibilities; a state's mandated phonics reading curriculum is its solution to the problem of how to overcome the recent history of poor performance on national tests of early literacy. Given that practices are solutions, we understand these practices by understanding the problem-solving processes that gave rise to them, evaluate them by judging their adequacy as solutions, and contribute to their improvement by showing how an alternative practice may better solve the problem.

A theory of practice proposes (a) the practices that serve as solutions to practical problems; (b) the assumptions, values, and causal reasoning, implicit or explicit, that gave rise to those practices, and (c) the intended and unintended consequences of those practices. Although the methods for describing practices and investigating consequences are well established, more needs to be said about how one investigates the reasoning that led practitioners to settle on the practices or policies that are the target of reform. Sorting this out requires a theory of problems and of problem solving.

Problems and How They Are Solved

The philosopher of science Thomas Nickles defines a problem as "all the conditions or constraints on the solution (variously weighted) plus the demand that the solution (an object satisfying the constraints) be found" (Nickles 1988, 54). Nickles calls these conditions *constraints* because they rule out or make problematic some possible solutions that might otherwise be admissible. They do not define the set of permissible solution alternatives, but determine or constrain to a greater or lesser degree *what counts as* an admissible solution. Given the everyday understanding of a constraint as a barrier that prevents people from doing what they want to do, it is important to remember that by ruling out options that would otherwise be admissible, constraints, in Nickles' sense, also help to identify which options can be ruled in.

Constraints include both the conditions set by the problem solvers themselves, which reflect their own ethics, values, and assumptions, and those set by others, which they believe must be included within the constraint set, such as regulations and resource limits. A problem is solved by examining how various strategies would satisfy a developing constraint set and then adjusting the constraints, their relative emphases, and the solution strategies, until problem solvers are satisfied with the degree to which they have been integrated. Using Nickles' definition of a problem, we can understand, for example, the implementation of Reading Recovery by identifying the constraints that dictated how it was introduced. The two key constraints to be satisfied, which were themselves in considerable tension, were protection of the integrity of the instructional practices that constitute the technology of the program, and adoption of the innovation by host systems whose approaches to literacy instruction were often quite different from that of the innovation.

The constraint-inclusion account of problems makes clear that problems are solved by integrating the constraints taken as a set, rather than by maximizing a favored one or two, or by reaching a compromise among them all. Solving the problem of how to implement Reading Recovery was not a matter of maximizing the integrity of the innovation, nor of maximizing the number of adopting systems, but of designing practices that integrated both these constraints. The solution is evident in three key implementation practices. First, Reading Recovery is delivered through its own separate infrastructure rather than through regular classroom instruction, which simultaneously protects the integrity of Reading Recovery technology and prevents high levels of threat to the host system. Second, Reading Recovery tutors act as a "redirecting system" that monitors whether variations that are observed in or requested by potential host systems are compatible with the principles underlying the innovation (Robinson 1989, 36). Third, the assessment and instructional practices of Reading Recovery supplement rather than challenge the practices of the junior school classrooms from which Reading Recovery students are drawn. Although this is a conservative strategy, it has enhanced the likelihood of adoption by very diverse host systems.

Developing new practices (new solutions) or maintaining existing practices (old solutions) requires a theory of practice that will include an account, implicit or explicit, of the problem's constraints and the practice or practices that may integrate them. Understanding this process requires us to distinguish between a theory of practice that is *implicit* in the practice (a theory-in-use) and one that is *explicit* in the mind of the practitioner (an espoused theory).

Espoused Theory and Theory-in-Use

A theory of practice may be an espoused theory, a theory-in-use, or both (Argyris and Schön 1974, 1996). A practitioner will advance an espoused theory to explain or justify a practice. Espoused theory is determined by asking a practitioner (and obtaining an honest answer) about what the practitioner knows, believes, and values. A practitioner's theory-in-use is implicit in the practice itself and must be derived from observations of the practice in question or from corroborated reports of the performance of the practice. A practitioner's espoused theory and theory-in-use may or may not be congruent or equivalent, and a practitioner may or may not be aware of the theory-in-use that is implicit in any particular practice.

The Evaluation of Solution Adequacy

To say that a practice is the solution to a problem is to say only that it is in place, not that it is desirable. If researchers are to engage practitioners in a fair-minded evaluation of the efficacy of current and alternative practices, they must employ criteria that both parties accept as appropriate to the complexities of the problem situation.

The criteria that are acceptable to practitioners, at least as a starting point, are revealed by the prior constraint analysis, for those constraints are the criteria that have in fact determined solution adequacy. In terms of the above example, a fair-minded evaluation would involve consideration of how well the balance has been struck, in the implementation of Reading Recovery, between flexible adaptations to diverse host systems and protection of the integrity of the innovation. To restrict the evaluation to these criteria, however, is to privilege the practitioner's perspective in a way that precludes questioning his or her formulation of the problem. A researcher might argue that the quality of regular classroom instruction should be an additional constraint, so that more reading failures are prevented and the gains of Reading Recovery graduates are more likely to be sustained once they return to the regular classroom. However, researchers who introduce such additional evaluative criteria run the risk of privileging their own theory if they assume the superiority of their constraint set over that employed by the practitioners they seek to influence.

The dilemma between acceptance of the original constraint set or risking rejection of the alternative can be resolved by the use of a second, coherence criterion of solution adequacy (Walker 1987, 1991). Whereas the first, the effectiveness criterion, asks whether the solution satisfies the constraints set on the resolution of one particular problem, the second, the coherence criterion, recognizes the interconnectedness of problems by evaluating whether or not the solution is compatible with what we know about how to resolve all the problems in a problem set. For example, the coherence criterion would prompt a dialogue about whether better literacy instruction in regular classrooms would increase the adoption of Reading Recovery by overcoming objections to the program that are based on concerns about how gains made during individualized instruction can be sustained in regular classrooms with inadequate literacy practices. Thus, if Reading Recovery practitioners accept the idea that, in addition to solving the implementation problem, they must address the problem of creating classrooms that will sustain gains, they will enlarge their espoused constraint set to include improvement of the quality of regular classroom instruction. In short, even though the coherence criterion moves beyond the P-theory of a given problem, it still refers to practitioners' interests by showing how implications of that particular P-theory may not be compatible with the P-theory they might wish to adopt in solving a related problem.

The Search for an Alternative Practice

People institute change when they are dissatisfied with current practices and when they have confidence in an achievable alternative (Prochaska, DiClemente, and

Norcross 1992). Even though practitioners understand that their current practice is inadequate, they will *not change* it until they learn that it is possible to design and enact a practice that meets their new constraint set. If reform-minded researchers are to assist in this process, they must move beyond the theory that generated their critique of practice to the formulation of a new theory of practice that meets the constraints that practitioners and researchers have agreed are appropriate. Researchers who do not privilege their own theory will become involved in this attempt without presuming that theories of practice that give greater weight to the new constraint will be any more adequate than those they seek to replace. For example, it may prove impossible to make an impact on regular classroom practice without engendering such a high level of threat in the host system that adoption of the innovation is jeopardized. On the other hand, it may be possible to design ways of reducing the tension while preserving the principles and values that each constraint represents. Researchers and practitioners who are open-minded about the relative efficacy of the old and new implementation practices will continue to evaluate the results of any new practices to see whether they turn out to be more effective and more coherent than the practices they replace.

In summary, researchers critique practice when they believe that inappropriate weighting has been given to one or more constraints selected by their preferred theory. Their critique implies that it is possible to employ an alternative practice that weights the constraints in the desired pattern. Researchers privilege their theory when they fail to inquire into the accuracy of these assumptions. Such inquiry involves uncovering the theory of practice that sustains the practices they criticize, and evaluating that theory against a constraint set that is acceptable to both parties. In addition, it involves inquiring whether the alternative practices meet these constraints more effectively than those already in place.

In the remainder of this chapter, we illustrate our thesis about theoretical privilege and its implications for educational change by discussing two research programs: one that privileges R-theory and one that privileges P-theory. For the former, we have chosen a recent study by Wells and Serna (1996), which is part of a long-standing research program on tracking and detracking in United States high schools (Oakes 1985, 1992). We chose to study this program because, although the research program of which it is a part has been influential among academics, it has, in the words of its leader, had far less impact than desired on those practitioners and policymakers who make decisions about whether or not to track (Oakes 1992). We argue that R-theory is privileged in the Wells and Serna study, and, because the approach to theory that these authors exemplify is also found in other studies belonging to this same program (Oakes and Guiton 1995), we suggest that its limited impact may be attributable to the adversarial reaction that such a methodological stance engenders (Robinson 1998).

We discuss the privileging of P-theory through the work of the Israeli researcher Freema Elbaz, who has been critical of how some researchers have belittled and bypassed what she calls "teachers' knowledge" (Elbaz 1983). We argue that in attempting to give due recognition to such knowledge, Elbaz unwittingly privileges practitioners' theories in a way that limits her intended contribution to their development.

Research on Tracking and the Privileging of R-Theory

Tracking, or *streaming* as it is known outside the United States, is a highly controversial strategy for allocating students to different curriculum subjects or to differing levels within those subjects. It is controversial because even though it is intended to be a meritocratic allocation process, it usually results in a form of within-school segregation, with students from differing social and racial groups allocated to different levels or curriculum tracks. Low achieving students perform less well in tracked than in untracked classes, probably because of the relative quality of teaching and curriculum resources available to students in the two kinds of provision (Oakes and Guiton 1995).

The more recent research on tracking has analyzed the efforts of some high schools in the United States to detrack all or part of their curriculum. In one such study, Wells and Serna (1996) set out to explain the resistance of what they call *local elites* to the attempts of ten racially and socioeconomically mixed schools to implement detracking reforms. The six high schools and four middle schools involved were spread across the United States and varied greatly in size. Each school was visited three times over a two-year period to collect data through field observations, document analysis, and interviews with teachers, parents, community leaders, and administrators.

Our earlier account of the nature of practice suggests that the resistance of elite parents should be viewed as a practice and therefore as their solution to a problem, the nature of which can be determined in principle at least by discovering the constraints to which it is responsive. At first glance, it seems as if Wells and Serna are committed to this interpretive task, for they describe one of their purposes as helping educators and policy makers understand the various manifestations of local political resistance to detracking. However, their explanation of parental resistance turns out to be very different from the parents' explanation. Rather than treat these competing explanations as an opportunity for theory testing, they privilege their own framework (R-theory) by assuming that it is both more accurate and morally superior to that held by those who resist detracking (P-theory). We defend our conclusion that R-theory is privileged by first outlining the authors' explanation of resistance and comparing it with that claimed by those doing the resisting. Second, we describe and illustrate precisely how we see privilege occurring and how it could have been avoided. We conclude our discussion by examining the implications of theoretical privilege for the achievement of the authors' reform goals.

Competing Explanations of Resistance

Wells and Serna understand parental resistance to detracking through the lens of Bourdieu's theory of cultural capital. They assert that the education system rewards the consumption patterns of the dominant classes, and that such rewards promote the educational achievement of those who display them. Cultural elites conceal the arbitrary link between social and cultural capital and achievement by appealing to "intelligence" and "merit" to defend their privileged status. The resistance of elite parents to detracking can thus be explained by their efforts to maintain their children's access to the most prestigious classes and programs—resources that will in turn contribute to the reproduction of the cultural and symbolic capital that they inherited from their families.

Not surprisingly, Wells and Serna's theoretical framework produces an explanation of parental resistance that is very different from that offered by the parents themselves. Whereas Wells and Serna explain parental resistance in terms of parents' desire to maintain the status and privilege that they associate with their children's educational provision, parents themselves argue their case in terms of the relative educational quality of tracked and untracked programs. Although both theories affirm the value of cultural diversity in quality schooling, the researchers assert that even those who see advantages in having their children mix with those from diverse cultures seek to limit that integration to the hallways, rather than extend it to the classrooms.

We have no objections to Wells and Serna's use of R-theory to suggest alternatives to the explanations put forward by parents themselves. Indeed, we have already discussed the fact that the motives that actors report for their own actions (espoused theory) may not match their actual motives and beliefs, especially when actors anticipate that admission of certain motives will bring social disapproval. Rather, our criticism of Wells and Serna is that while they use Bourdieu as a resource to challenge parents' accounts, they do not see parents' accounts as a resource for challenging the validity of their own views. It is the one-sidedness of the challenge that leads us to judge them as privileging R-theory.

The Evidence That R-theory Is Privileged

A methodology that tests rather than assumes the validity of R-theory requires that (a) the competing theories be understood in their own terms, (b) the points of competition between them be identified precisely, and (c) data collection and analysis processes be designed to produce fair tests of those differences.

To identify P-theory in its own terms is to identify the constraints parents are concerned about, and the logic that leads them to believe they are better satisfied by tracked rather than untracked arrangements. Instead of doing this, Wells and Serna conflate their description of parental views with Bourdieu-inspired critique. The authors' analysis of the following quotation, taken from an interview with a white woman whose son is in an honors program, illustrates our point.

> I think a lot of those Latinos come and they're still Mexicans at heart. They're not American. I don't care what color you are we're in America here and we're going for this country. And I think their heart is in Mexico and they're with that culture still. It's one thing to come over and bring your culture and to use it, but it's another thing

to get into that . . . and I'm calling it the American ethic. They're not into it and that's why they end up so far behind. They get in school and they are behind. (1996, 101)

Wells and Serna describe this statement as "explain[ing] her opposition to detracking," "exposing her sense of entitlement," illustrating the idea of the "deserving minority," showing the woman to be denying the value of nonwhite students' and parents' own culture, and illustrating "cultural racism." Although the complete interview transcript might justify such conclusions, the authors have considerably more work to do to provide a convincing case. First, the woman is describing why she believes Latinos are behind in school, not why she is opposed to detracking, and the links between the two are unclear. Perhaps she believes that those who have not embraced the American ethic will reduce the academic focus of her son's classes. Second, the accuracy of the attribution of entitlement and the reasonableness of the authors' critical stance toward the alleged disposition must be established. Is the alleged sense of entitlement based on racial and cultural stereotypes, or is it based on personal and cognitive attributes that this woman believes are required by students in different types of educational programs? If the latter, are these beliefs arbitrary, or are they grounded in this woman's actual experience of different types of educational programs? If stereotypical reasoning explained this woman's attitudes, P-theory could be legitimately redescribed through the work of Bourdieu; if not, then its early intrusion will prevent discovery of its logic. Wells and Serna do not pursue these distinctions, because for them and for Bourdieu, the reasons for opposition to such reforms have been prejudged: "Bourdieu identifies 'practices'—actions that maintain or change social structures—within strategically oriented forms of conflict. These strategic actions must be rooted back into the logic or sense of entitlement that underlies these practices" (107); that is, detailed empirical investigation of P-theory is unnecessary because the logic of parental opposition is already demonstrated by R-theory as one of entitlement.

In the above example, R-theory is privileged by reading motives from the functions that specified practices perform within R-theory; the opposition of elite parents is a strategic practice in Bourdieu's terms, and therefore it is motivated by a sense of entitlement. The following examples show a second way in which the authors' explanations are privileged by reading actors' motives directly from the consequences of their practices.

. . . [elite parents'] practices were aimed at maintaining the track structure, with separate and unequal educational opportunities for "deserving" and "undeserving" students. (2–3)

. . . [elite parents employ practices] to prevent structural change that will challenge their status and privilege. (3)

In the data from our ten schools, we have identified at least four political practices, shrouded in a discourse of the arbitrary, that the local elites employ to undermine and co-opt meaningful detracking efforts in such a way that their children continue to benefit disproportionately from educational policies. (18)

In each of these statements, the authors link their description of parental practices (maintain track structure, prevent a structural change, undermine detracking) with their consequences in a way that implies that those consequences were intended. From the fact that parents did resist, that their resistance helped maintain tracking, and that tracking is highly inequitable, one cannot infer that parents were motivated by a desire to maintain that inequity. To infer the psychology of actors directly from consequences in this way is to make the logical mistake of assuming that all consequences are intended (Flew 1985, 21). Motives cannot be read directly from consequences, but must be established independently by arguing that it is reasonable to infer certain mental states given how the relevant actors behave under different circumstances.

For example, the claim of parents that their opposition is motivated by concerns about academic and disciplinary standards in untracked programs, and not by a desire to defend status and privilege, could be tested by detailed and sensitive probing of their reactions to a hypothetical detracked program that had high academic and disciplinary standards. In fact, Wells and Serna seem to anticipate such a test when they write:

> . . . the real stakes [for elite parents] we argue, are generally not academics at all, but rather status and power. For example, if a school does away with separate classes for students labelled "gifted" but teachers continue to challenge these students with the same curriculum in a detracked setting, the only "losses" the student will incur are their label and their separate and unequal status. Yet in a highly stratified society, such labels and privileged status confer power. (1996, 96)

The hypothetical example shows precisely the kind of test required to tease out whether it is the desire for status and power or concern over educational quality that is driving parental opposition. If parents had been interviewed in detail about their reaction to untracked high-quality provision and had demonstrated attitudes that were closed to actual or possible examples of such programs, the reader could have a great deal more confidence in the authors' conclusions that these parents were motivated by status and power. If, on the other hand, respectful probing of parental views showed that they were open to the possibility of quality untracked provision for their children, and that they preferred such provision to a quality program that was tracked, the balance of evidence swings, at least on this dimension, in favor of P-theory. It should be noted that the respect that is accorded P-theory in such informal testing processes is not incompatible with stringent critique of that theory. However, the process does require that P-theory be understood in its own terms before it is critiqued, that the points of competition between P-theory and R-theory be identified precisely, and that the data collection and analysis process be designed to produce fair tests of those differences.

In arguing that Wells and Serna privilege their own theory, we are not claiming that they intended to do so. It is their theory-in-use and not their espoused theory of research practice that is problematic. As they wrote, "Our intention is not to criticize these powerful parents in an unsympathetic manner. Yet we believe that too often the cultural forces that shape such parents' agency as they try to do what is best for their children remain hidden from view and thus unquestioned" (96).

Paradoxically, these authors' research practice may be counterproductive to their own reform goals. It is methodologically counterproductive because respect for theoretical diversity is essential to strengthening the validity of both our explanations of tracking and our knowledge of how to design alternative practices that meet warranted objections to both tracking and detracking. It is politically counterproductive because Wells and Serna's privileging of their own theories will likely lead those practitioners whom they seek to understand to deny that the researchers have done so, and to be less rather than more likely to join any inquiry into how to resolve the problems that tracking has brought. In short, although their research is motivated by a desire to reduce inequity and social fragmentation, Wells and Serna perpetuate such fragmentation by treating those with differing views as opponents to be defeated rather than as potential participants in the search for a solution to a reformulated problem (Hostetler 1995). Elite parents may agree that tracking has inequitable features and still resist detracking because the problem their resistance is solving is how to protect the education of their own children, and they have taken little responsibility for the problem of how to provide equitable opportunities for all children. Given the intersection of these two problems, more progress is likely to be made by acknowledging the importance of both problems and exploring together how one can be solved without the other being sacrificed.

The Attack on R-Theoretical Approaches

Having illustrated and argued against R-theoretical privilege, we now show how, conversely, privileging practitioners' theories is equally unlikely to improve educational policy and practice. The first point to note is that we are not alone in recognizing the error of ignoring practitioners' points of view, values, and situational understandings. Indeed, one way of reading certain major trends and new developments in educational research over the past two or three decades is to see them as assertions of the importance of understanding the world of practice in terms that are comprehensible to practitioners, if not in practitioners' own terms.

This shift in focus is part of a wider epistemological trend, often described as *postpositivism*, in which traditional models of educational knowledge that present generalizations based on putatively theory-free data were rejected in favor of contextualised understandings that capture the subjective consciousness and social and cultural positions of researched individuals and groups. We locate our proposed methodology of theory competition through critical dialogue within the postpositivist tradition. Positivist approaches have done justice neither to the complexities of the world of practice nor to the experience, knowledge, and skill of practitioners (Walker and Evers 1994).

We share, for example, with the action research tradition (e.g., Carr and Kemmis 1983, 152–155) a regard for Lewin's (1946, 1948) initiation of a tradition of scholar-practitioners. Like Lewin and unlike some action researchers, we also stress the importance of integrating science and practice (Argyris, Putnam, and McLain-Smith 1985, 7). This is a key point if we hold that theory competition through critical dialogue is the way forward in developing knowledge for the improvement of educational practice; many who have rejected positivism have rejected science along with it, because they mistakenly identify positivism with science. Typically, those who take this position will view science, as do Carter and Doyle (1996, 122) in their review of research on narrative and the life history of teachers, as characterized by "technical rationality." They interpret "the forceful emphasis on teachers' personal knowledge" as reflecting "in part . . . a general reaction against the technical rationality that has characterized much of teacher education policy and practice, a rationality that stressed the acquisition and testing of research-validated [(i.e., R-theoretical—VMJ and JCW)] teaching skills."

It is ironic that such writers as Carter and Doyle, who rail against science, should invoke Schön's (1983) notion of epistemology of practice, when Schön, along with his colleague Argyris, advocates *integrating* science and practice. Having equated science and positivism, writers like Carter and Doyle then reason that because science has nothing to offer educational practice, to the extent that R-theory is "scientific" (and this may be presumed to be a large extent), R-theory should be rejected. On this account, if R-theory has any role at all in educational research, it is a subservient one in support of P-theory. Because R-theory has no substantive role as a source of possible solutions to educational problems, it cannot be in competition with P-theory. R-theory becomes methodological only, a source of methods for helping practitioners get the best out of P-theory. It is unquestioned that educational change will necessarily involve practitioners' own knowledge, beliefs, and values. The core of the question is whether P-theory is sufficient; that is, whether the present content of practitioners' understandings is sufficient to improve educational practice.

We believe that the confusion of necessity and sufficiency has led to the intended or unintended privileging of P-theory. An example is the either/or approach to the relation between R-theory and P-theory, often sustained by explicit or implicit assumptions about the incommensurability of the two (Kuhn 1970). It may be suggested that one cannot adopt R-theory (because, for example, it is positivist) and at the same time adopt P-theory (because it is antipositivist). Even if one wanted both, or some accommodation between the two, this would not be possible because, being incommensurable, they cannot be rationally compared and critically evaluated. Given that the trend in this line of thinking is against "science," this amounts to a systematic attack on R-theory, at least at the substantive level, as a potential source of guidance on educational practice or, in our language, as a source of solutions to the problems of practitioners.

Research on Teachers' Knowledge and the Privileging of P-Theory

We commence our consideration of P-theory privileging with an example from what we might call *practicalist* research on teachers' knowledge. Freema Elbaz's widely noted study of the development of teacher knowledge in curriculum development is part of a contemporary reassertion of the craft tradition of teachers' knowledge, a reassertion whose characteristic methods involve uncovering teachers' thinking and telling their personal stories. Elbaz (1991) has extended the thinking in her 1983 study by using influential work on narrative and story telling (Carter 1995; Connelly and Clandinin 1987) and on biography and autobiography (Butt and Raymond 1987; Butt, Raymond, and Yamagishi 1988). According to Connelly and Clandinin (1990, 2), "education is the construction of personal and social stories," and so teachers' professional knowledge must, crucially, be knowledge of those stories, including how to hear them, tell them, and participate in their construction.

Along with Tom and Valli (1990), we note that this view of professional knowledge has been criticised as antiscientific (Gage 1985) and risking restriction to the conservatism inherent in reliance on the wisdom of practice (Zeichner 1983). We believe that these criticisms, valid though they might be, do not get to the heart of the matter, at least insofar as our concern is to produce research that contributes to the improvement of practice. From our point of view, rejection of science and practitioner conservatism count against a research method or tradition if these characteristics are related to a failure to have a practical effect. Both of these characteristics limit the impact of Elbaz's intendedly practical research. In criticizing Elbaz's study, we stress that our criticisms are directed at her methodological assumptions about the relation between educational research and educational change. The merits of the substantive content of her study have already been clearly stated by Westbury and Reid (1983):

> By reporting in vivid detail an analysis of the insights and ideas of one teacher, Sarah, as they emerged in a series of long interviews, [Elbaz] brings into full view the hopes, the concerns and the style of thought of many teachers who want not advancement but the opportunity to "open windows" for their students. Sarah is clearly where the action is, her problems are clearly the problems of the schools, and her excitement is the real excitement of education. We have an account here of a woman who is moving her world and, as she does so, is growing and changing (viii).

The celebration of the practitioner, however, does not in itself address the question of how to improve education when current practice is inadequate to address current problems, unless we assume that self-discovery (aided perhaps by researchers) of implicit practitioner knowledge is sufficient to solve practical problems.

Having found "expert" knowledge wanting, Elbaz turns to the notion of practitioners' knowledge. She notes (1983, 6) that traditional models of curriculum development (e.g., Tyler 1949) give a central role to experts and largely exclude teachers; that is, they privilege R-theory. Elbaz (1983, 7) rightly points out the paradoxical nature of the ensuing situation: "Teachers' active role in the creation of new instructional arrangements is denied, but they are credited with a generous share of the responsibility for failure."

Declaring the orientation of her research to educational change, Elbaz then cites approvingly the work of Schwab (1969), "who has argued that the theoretically [i.e., R-theoretically—VR and JW] derived conceptions of curriculum with which we have been operating lack both the power to generate serious discussion in the field and the power to order and regulate practice or bring about change" (8). We agree, and as we did in the example of research on tracking, we explain this practical impotence of R-theory by pointing to its failure to capture the constraint sets of practice. We also agree with the spirit of Elbaz's enlistment of other critics of the domination of R-theory in relation to curriculum development, and with her observation that research on teaching before the 1980s had generally viewed teachers in a negative and fragmented way. Similarly, we applaud her condemnation of the view that teachers are lacking in knowledge of their own (Elbaz 1983, 9–11). Where we part company with Elbaz, and likely with many researchers on teacher thinking and teacher knowledge, is on her solution to this problem: "The single factor which seems to have the greatest power to carry forward our understanding of the teacher's role is the idea of teachers' knowledge" (1983, 11). In other words—and this appears to be the assumption of much research on teacher thinking—the way to order practice and promote change, for example through curriculum development, is the articulation and application of teachers' practical knowledge. This is what we mean by *practicalism*.

We part company with Elbaz here because of the relation that she asserts holds between teachers' knowledge (P-theory) and the researcher's perspective and conceptual framework (R-theory). In her research on the knowledge of one particular teacher, Sarah, the treatment of that knowledge as the single most powerful factor amounts in practice (Elbaz's practice as a researcher), and so in R-theory-in-use, to privileging Sarah's P-theory. Moreover, many of Elbaz's espoused theoretical statements are congruent (Argyris and Schön 1974, 23) with her theory-in-use as we reconstruct it here. According to Elbaz, the role of the researcher is to assist the practitioner to articulate her practical knowledge: "The most important lesson to be learned from this study is that it is possible for teachers to become aware of and articulate their own practical knowledge, and that this process can lead to greater self-understanding and personal growth" (1983, 170).

Indeed, there is, finally, no necessary role for a professional researcher at all, so long as "some measure of formality" is maintained, because "the process is one of giving form to one's knowledge," and "the second party might be another teacher, a non-teaching but curious friend, or a notebook." When it comes to a practitioner and his or her notebook, the situation is essentially the same as totally self-managed action research, the limiting case where researcher and practitioner are one and the same person.

From our point of view there is a problem with this limiting case, for unless there is some form of critical dialogue with others, there will be no theory competition, and therefore solutions to the problems of practice will be limited to whatever critical review and innovative thought can be generated from within the practitioner's own P-theoretical resources. Of the various likely outcomes of such P-theoretical introspection, one of the most serious is a breakdown in problem solving and a consequent frustration and loss of confidence on the part of the practitioner.

Of course, such frustration is a common enough feature of teachers' professional experience, and Sarah's is no exception. Moreover, in one important instance Elbaz is quite clear about the reason—P-theoretical failure:

> Interestingly, it is in the area of evaluation that Sarah's practical knowledge faltered. Here again she relied on commonsense methods, such as talking to students about their work in other classes, but this rightly did not satisfy Sarah. She bemoaned the lack of "precisely calibrated instruments" for evaluating the course. Finally her inability to evaluate the course was an important factor in Sarah's disillusionment with it. (1983, 81)

It is ironic that Elbaz dismisses Sarah's inclination to look to R-theoretical knowledge ("precisely calibrated instruments") to solve her problem; "It is surprising that she did not apply her ingenuity about classroom techniques in this area to develop classroom methods of assessing effects of the Learning Course" (81–82). The next step, of course, is to condemn Sarah for privileging R-theory.

> This gap in Sarah's practical knowledge of curriculum suggests a form of theoretical bias: Sarah regarded evaluation as an area of expertise, amenable to the use of precisely calibrated instruments. Awareness of her ignorance . . . made her reluctant to rely on the rough-and-ready evaluation methods she might herself develop, and seemed to paralyze Sarah's resourcefulness in this area. (82)

But this either/or thinking is unnecessary and arises only because of *a priori* privileging of P-theory. If neither P-theory nor R-theory is privileged, it is possible to look at both for potential solutions to the evaluation problem and to avoid Sarah's ultimate disillusionment with a basically sound educational program. Elbaz's hypothesis that the solution to the problem lay in the rough-and-ready techniques that would be generated from Sarah's practical knowledge remains untested, as does her assumption that such a solution would be better than one derived from "expert" knowledge. Elbaz's research methodology does not allow such testing because it is restricted to the development and articulation of the practitioner's knowledge.

What then is the teachers' knowledge to which form needs to be given, and how does this knowledge grow? To answer the second question first: This knowledge increases as the practitioner gains experience. This does not mean, however, that this experience does not include "theoretical knowledge of subject matter, and of areas such as child development, learning and social theory." Rather, it means that these "are integrated by the individual teacher in terms of personal values and beliefs and as oriented to her practical situation." To this is added firsthand experience of students, a repertoire of instructional techniques and classroom management skills, and a knowledge of the social structure of the school and the community (Elbaz 1983, 5).

It is critical here to notice the bind into which such practicalist teacher-knowledge research can lead. On one hand, Elbaz insists that knowledge that does not come in the form of "practical knowledge," as she understands it, is of no use for the improvement of educational practice. On the other hand, she acknowledges that practical knowledge contains "theoretical knowledge of subject matter, and of areas such as child development, learning and social theory . . . integrated by the individual teacher in terms of personal values and beliefs and . . . oriented to her practical situation." The critical question is, "How is such knowledge integrated into the teacher's practical stock?" One point is clear—it cannot be through the methodology of research on teacher thinking employed by Elbaz. Presumably it can be through the kind of learning that occurs in initial or preservice teacher education, and there have been many recent studies that explore teachers' knowledge development in order to understand how better to plan teacher education programs (e.g., Grossman 1990; Richardson 1996; Shulman 1987). Maybe, also, theoretical knowledge can be integrated into the practical stock through the teacher's own reading or continuing formal professional education, although it is not clear how this would be consistent with the restrictions placed on the role of "experts."

The point we are making is that Elbaz's account of practical knowledge is internally inconsistent and also inconsistent with her theory of educational research methodology. P-theory in her sense of "practical knowledge" cannot be entirely experiential in nature and growth if it is to include the (R-theoretical) content that Elbaz acknowledges may be present. For a teacher to develop Elbaz's practical knowledge, there must be a critical dialogue with educational research, and where there is a conflict, an intellectual competition of views; that is, an interaction between P-theory and R-theory.

How has this no doubt unintended inconsistency arisen? One possible explanation is that epistemology has become mixed up with politics. A recurring theme in this kind of literature is that R-theory, and the professional theorists whose theory it is, are in a more powerful position than practitioners whom they may oppress, albeit unintentionally. If so, steps need to be taken to restore the balance of power and eliminate oppression of practitioners by researchers. This line of reasoning is buttressed by portrayals of positivism as the theory of a power elite in government and industry in the political economy of advanced capitalist societies. This approach can lead to a feeling of guilt amongst researchers who, rightly enough, do not wish to oppress practitioners but to support them in the improvement of educational practice.

What evidence is there for this explanation? In the case of Elbaz's study, there is some evidence. For instance, R-theory is self-consciously suppressed by the researcher as "bias," and the researcher corrects herself, in interviewing Sarah, for any notion of "objectivity" that might be clinging to "the fringes of my awareness, as a strong situational constraint that subtly influenced me to favour a more detached style of interviewing." Elbaz has confused the essential requirement that as a researcher she understand clearly what her interviewee is saying, in her own terms, with a disavowal of any substantive R-theory of her own that she might usefully share with the practitioner (1983, 25–26).

The same confusion exists in Elbaz's more recent writing, in which she draws on poststructuralist approaches to privilege the language and conceptual categories of practitioners, thereby preventing domination by experts. She thus sets apart the language of teacher thinking (and research thereon) and preemptively dismisses the possibility of engagement with expert discourse (Elbaz 1991; Elbaz and Elbaz 1988). There is a critical methodological distinction to be made between research in which the objective is to support and record the articulation of P-theory, and research that assumes that once this has been achieved, there is a need for P-theory to engage R-theory. Undoubtedly educational researchers have, intentionally or unintentionally, stifled or ignored the voices of practitioners, and studies such as Elbaz's are valuable in showing the kinds of approaches and sensitivities necessary to support practitioners in making their voices heard. This will mean, at certain stages of the research, that the researcher refrains from putting forward other views because there are questions of power and respect to be addressed. Ultimately, however, it shows teachers no respect to withhold critical comment and the challenge of alternative views. To do so is to privilege P-theory and to patronize practitioners.

Summary and Conclusion

We have sought to show that theoretical privilege in educational research inhibits the production of findings that are likely to contribute to the improvement of educational practice. Theoretical privilege is a methodological posture through which, by attention to and use of one theoretical framework to the exclusion of another, competition among theories, and critical dialogue between their proponents, is curtailed. We have suggested that in educational research two sorts of privilege have occurred: privileging of the theories of researchers, or R-theory, and privileging of the theories of practitioners, or P-theory. We have attempted to show through close examination of two quite different examples that methodologies that privilege either researchers' or practitioners' theories jeopardize collaborative research relationships, the improvement of educational practice, and the advancement of knowledge.

Because Reading Recovery has been implemented without directly challenging the theories of practice that inform the mainstream teaching of the students it serves, the problem of theoretical privilege has not loomed as large for Reading Recovery staff as it might have otherwise. There may come a time, however, when, in the interests of prevention or improved follow-up results, a more direct engagement with mainstream provision is preferred. If this happens, Reading Recovery staff will face the challenge of advocating change in others while being open to reciprocal influence. When such conversations are grounded in evidence and argument and conducted with mutual respect, they offer the potential for learning more about the theory and practice of literacy learning.

Although we have spent most of this chapter being critical, our intention has been to elucidate some conditions under which educational research is more likely to lead to improvement in educational practice. We have not provided examples of research that seeks to observe such conditions, although we have done so elsewhere (Robinson 1993). Further profitable inquiry along these lines will involve both useful critical examination of past research and the development and implementation of research designs that privilege neither R-theory nor P-theory, but promote a healthy critical dialogue between them.

References

ARGYRIS, C., PUTNAM, R., AND MCLAIN-SMITH, D. 1985. *Action Science*. San Francisco: Jossey-Bass.

ARGYRIS, C., AND SCHÖN, D. A. 1974. *Theory in Practice: Increasing Professional Effectiveness*. San Francisco: Jossey-Bass.

———. 1996. *Organizational Learning II: Theory, Method and Practice*. Reading, Mass.: Addison Wesley.

BUTT, R. L., AND RAYMOND, D. 1987. "Arguments for Using Qualitative Approaches in Understanding Teacher Thinking: The Case for Biography." *Journal of Curriculum Theorizing* 7 (1): 62–93.

BUTT, R., RAYMOND, D., AND YAMAGISHI, L. 1988. "Autobiographic Praxis: Studying the Formation of Teachers' Knowledge." *Journal of Curriculum Theorizing* 7 (4): 87–164.

CARR, W., AND KEMMIS, S. 1983. *Becoming Critical: Education, Knowledge and Action Research*. London: Falmer Press.

CARTER, K. 1995. "The New Narrative Research in Education." In *Review of Research in Education*, 21 edited by M. W. Apple, 211–254.

CARTER, K., AND DOYLE, W. 1996. "Personal Narrative and Life History in Learning to Teach." In *Handbook of Research on Teacher Education*. 2d ed., edited by J. Sikula, T. J. Buttery, and E. Guyton. New York: Simon and Schuster/Macmillan.

CONNELLY, F. M., AND CLANDININ, D. J. 1987. "On Narrative Method, Biography, and Narrative Unities in the Study of Teaching." *Journal of Educational Thought* 21 (3): 130–139.

———. 1990. "Stories of Experience and Narrative Inquiry." *Educational Researcher* 19 (5): 2–14.

COUSINS, J. B., AND LEITHWOOD, K. A. 1986. "Current Empirical Research on Evaluation Utilization." *Review of Educational Research* 56 (3): 331–364.

ELBAZ, F. 1983. *Teacher Thinking: A Study of Practical Knowledge*. London: Croom Helm.

———. 1991. "Research on Teachers' Knowledge: The Evolution of a Discourse." *Journal of Curriculum Studies* 23 (1): 1–19.

ELBAZ, F., AND ELBAZ, R. 1988. "Curriculum and Textuality." *Journal of Curriculum Theorizing* 8 (2): 107–131.

FLEW, A. G. N. 1985. *Thinking About Social Thinking.* Oxford: Blackwell.

GAGE, N. 1985. *Hard Gains in the Soft Sciences: The Case of Pedagogy.* Bloomington, Ind.: Phi Delta Kappan.

GROSSMAN, P. L. 1990. *The Making of a Teacher: Teacher Knowledge and Teacher Education.* New York: Teachers College Press.

HOSTETLER, K. 1995. "Getting Serious About the Questions of Democracy." *Educational Theory* 45 (1): 101–117.

KUHN, T. S. 1970. *The Structure of Scientific Revolutions.* 2d. ed. Chicago: University of Chicago Press.

LEWIN, K. 1946. "Action Research and Minority Poblems." *Journal of Social Issues* 2: 32–46.

———. 1948. ED. *Resolving Social Conflicts.* New York: Harper and Row.

NICKLES, T. 1988. "Questioning and Problems in Philosophy of Science: Problem-Solving Versus Directly Truth-Seeking Epistemologies." In *Questions and Questioning,* edited by M. Meyer. Berlin: Walter de Gruyter.

NISBET, J. 1994. "Policy-Oriented Research." In Vol. 8 of *The International Encyclopedia of Education.* 2d ed., edited by T. Husèn and T. N. Postlethwaite, 4556–4562). Oxford: Pergamon.

OAKES, J. 1985. *Keeping Track: How Schools Structure Inequality.* New Haven: Yale University Press.

———. 1992. "Can Tracking Research Inform Practice?" *Educational Researcher* 21 (4): 12–21.

OAKES, J., AND GUITON, G. 1995. "Matchmaking: The Dynamics of High School Tracking Decisions." *American Educational Research Journal* 32 (1): 3–33.

PROCHASKA, J. L., DICLEMENTE, C. C., AND NORCROSS, J. C. 1992. "In Search of How People Change: Applications to Addictive Behaviors." *American Psychologist* 47 (9): 1102–1114.

RICHARDSON, V. 1996. "The Role of Attitudes and Values in Learning to Teach." In *Handbook of Research on Teacher Education.* 2d ed., edited by J. Sikula, T. J. Buttery, and E. Guyton. New York: Simon and Schuster/Macmillan.

ROBINSON, V. M. J. 1989. "Some Limitations of Systemic Adaptation: The Implementation of Reading Recovery." *New Zealand Journal of Educational Studies* 24 (1): 35–45.

———. 1993. *Problem-Based Methodology: Research for the Improvement of Practice.* Oxford: Pergamon.

———. 1998. "Methodology and the Research Practice Gap." *Educational Researcher* 27 (1): 17–26.

SCHÖN, D. S. 1983. *The Reflective Practitioner.* New York: Basic Books.

SCHWAB, J. J. 1969. "The Practical: A Language for Curriculum." *School Review* 78: 1–23.

SHULMAN, L. S. 1987. "Knowledge and Teaching: Foundations of the New Reform." *Harvard Educational Review* 57 (1): 1–22.

TOM, A. R., AND VALLI, L. 1990. "Professional Knowledge for Teachers." In *Handbook of Research on Teacher Education*, edited by W. R. Houston. New York: Macmillan.

TYLER, R. W. 1949. *Basic Principles of Curriculum and Instruction*. Chicago: University of Chicago Press.

WALKER, J. C. 1987. "Democracy and Pragmatism in Curriculum Development." *Educational Philosophy and Theory* 19 (2): 3–10.

————. 1991. "Coherence and Reduction: Implications for Educational Inquiry. *International Journal of Educational Research* 15 (5): 505–520.

WALKER, J. C., AND EVERS, C. W. 1982. "Epistemology and Justifying the Curriculum of Educational Studies. *British Journal of Educational Studies* 30 (2): 312–29.

————. 1994. "Research in Education: Epistemological Issues." In *The International Encyclopedia of Education*. 2d ed., edited by T. Husèn and T. N. Postlethwaite. Oxford: Pergamon Press.

WELLS, A. S., AND SERNA, I. 1996. "The Politics of Culture: Understanding Local Political Resistance to Detracking in Racially Mixed Schools." *Harvard Educational Review* 66 (1): 93–118.

WESTBURY, I., AND REID, W. A. 1983. Foreword *Teacher Thinking: A Study of Practical Knowledge*, by F. Elbaz. London: Croom Helm.

ZEICHNER, K. M. 1983. "Alternative Paradigms of Teacher Education." *Journal of Teacher Education* 34 (3): 3–9.

Fifteen

Forging an Interactive Relationship Among Research, Theory, and Practice: Clay's Research Design and Methodology

NOEL K. JONES AND M. TRIKA SMITH-BURKE

Clay's research in early literacy acquisition has been broad in scope—both in terms of the range of variables she has investigated and in the variety and flexibility of her research design and methodology. Over her career Clay's work has achieved a level of synthesis and generalization that includes, in addition to her own research, the theory and research findings of others and the wisdom and expertise of educational practitioners. Another characteristic of Clay's work is the manner in which she revises and reestablishes relationships between seemingly opposing fields, such as research and practice, quantitative and qualitative research, theory and instruction, case study and group research, and regular and special education. Clay has integrated information from these fields in the development of a general theory of literacy acquisition and in the design of a highly successful early literacy intervention program, Reading Recovery. However, as Clay (1997, 2) stated:

> It becomes more and more difficult to bring such concepts together as people research their separateness. Polarities run for cover into their respective enclaves when challenged. If you try to bring them together in some middle position the attack or counter arguments will come from both sides, and I can vouch for that. I like to be able to reconceptualize the polarities and complete the circles of interactive effects.

This chapter is organized into five parts: Clay's Values and Beliefs, Clay's Early Research, Design of Measurement Procedures for Beginning Literacy, The Development of Reading Recovery, and Reading Recovery as Part of a Comprehensive Approach to Literacy Instruction. We conclude with a summary of Clay's contributions to research and evaluation design and methodology against the broader spectrum of expectations of the academic world and of the political world of educational governance and administration.

Clay's Values and Beliefs

Both the scope and the quality of Clay's work firmly establish her reputation as a major contributor to the field of education. Throughout her work, there is a remarkable coherence and an interconnectedness not only of ideas, but also of values.

Three strong value commitments are apparent in all of Clay's work: (1) a commitment to rationality and scientific methodology in addressing issues both of knowledge construction and of practical action; (2) a developmental perspective from which she views educational issues in terms of learning, growth, and change over time, and which is grounded in a belief that all children have the potential and the right to become successful learners; and (3) a belief in the necessity of a reciprocal relationship between theory and educational practice and genuine respect for the contributions of educational practitioners and researchers.

Scientific Methodology

Clay's dedication to rationality and scientific methodology is apparent in her writings and in her research studies, where she is always careful to limit her conclusions to those supported by evidence and to maintain objectivity and avoid bias. Clay understands that bias can be built into a researcher's inquiry, choice of hypotheses, research design, and data-collection methods, as well as into interpretations of evidence. She also understands that the methodology must fit the research questions and issues being addressed. Her understanding and her training as a developmental psychologist influenced her design choices, as she began her investigations into the beginnings of literacy, approaching the question of how children learn to read in the same way that a biologist might approach a new ecological system (Clay 1982), by taking an atheoretical stance and observing and recording as much as she could, using reliable, systematic sampling and observation techniques.

Developmental Psychology

Clay's interest in the acquisition of reading and writing grew out of her work as a developmental psychologist and lecturer in school psychology at the University of Auckland in the 1960s and her year of study at the Institute of Child Development at the University of Minnesota. She wondered if the numbers of children who were referred to school psychologists as failures in classroom learning could be reduced, and noted that the majority of children referred had serious difficulties in learning to read and write. Clay's developmental orientation and value commitment to children and their learning potentials has both motivated and guided her research career and the development of theory. For example, her theory of literacy acquisition was constructed to account for the varied learning paths of all children, not only for successful literacy acquisition, but also for a wide range of difficulties in learning to read and write, and how children experiencing difficulty can, with appropriate interventions, become successful learners. Clay's work has powerfully influenced an emerging policy that almost universal learning is an important criterion for judging educational systems.

Reciprocity Between Theory and Practice

A third value is Clay's commitment to a reciprocal relationship between research and practice. Extensive, long-term involvement in educational applications of a particular set of theories is uncharacteristic of most researchers and theorists. Clay's involvement with program development and implementation is unusual in both its depth and duration. It is, perhaps, even more significant that she has created a productive interplay among theory, research, and applications—extending and revising theory on the basis of activity in the field, and refining and developing programmatic applications on the basis of theoretical constructs and research findings.

Throughout her engagements with teachers and administrators, Clay has consistently shown respect for their expertise. Although Clay is committed to the canons of evidence and reasoning of academic communities, she recognizes that educators must act immediately when they teach children and run schools, and that a different kind of knowledge forms the basis of practice. Clay understands that teachers must make pragmatic decisions; however, her research and evaluation design for Reading Recovery deliberately provides for the systematic collection and interpretation of data in order to revisit the consequences of those pragmatic decisions and assess their soundness.

Clay's linkage of research and educational applications resulted in a comprehensive research career that has focused on the goal of successful early literacy learning for all children. It has led her to use a wide range of theories applicable to learning and teaching, information processing, perception, educational systems, educational change, teacher development, curriculum implementation, and evaluation, as well as all aspects of cognitive and language research relevant to literacy development. Her engagement with applications has enabled her, in turn, to further refine and elaborate theory.

Clay's Early Research

As an academic in developmental and school psychology, Clay understood that a great deal of school maladjustment is due to unsuccessful literacy learning. Research into early literacy learning fit well with Clay's goal of knowledge development through scientific methodology and her wish to contribute to the work of educators. The problem Clay faced was how to investigate early literacy acquisition so as to understand the nature of the reading and writing processes during the acquisition stages and to determine what children must learn, how they learn, the degree of variability in learning, and the factors that account for individual differences in learning.

Clay chose to conduct an intensive longitudinal study of children in their first year of schooling in New Zealand, where literacy instruction begins shortly after children enter school at age five (Clay 1982). She studied all the children who entered school during one year in five schools that were representative of the socioeconomic makeup of urban New Zealand. She made weekly observations of each child, eliciting samples of their drawing (at first), writing, reading, and language over the period of a year. She also administered a battery of seventeen tests within two weeks of each child's reaching the ages of five, five-and-a-half, and six.

From a developmental perspective, Clay was dissatisfied with the level of understanding of literacy acquisition current in the 1960s. There were no studies of literacy acquisition similar to longitudinal research in language development, and therefore no credible theories of literacy development grounded in close observation over time. Clay was particularly interested in the developmental paths of children who have difficulty in learning to read, but she felt their difficulties would have to be understood in relation to the development of more successful children of the same age. Was it possible to detect when the process began to fail? Noting the limitations of extant theory, she began her investigations from an atheoretical, no-hypothesis stance to data collection (Clay 1982).

In contrast to the individual case studies of language development research, Clay observed the progress of one hundred children through the course of each child's first year in school. Her investigation centered on the range of differences in learning and on possible explanations of why some children fail to realize their learning potential. Sensitive to the effects of instruction on learning, she used a large sample that enabled her to generalize across several classrooms, teachers, and schools; however, she was careful to limit her findings to observations of similar populations receiving similar instructional treatments.

Clay has commented several times about the advantages of a longitudinal research design as a basis for understanding the course of literacy development. In discussing the work of Biemiller (1970), she notes that

> He used a probe test approach at different ages and the averaged findings look like a stage-wise description of progress . . . Failure to explore the longitudinal approach using frequent observation seems to have produced a description of reading acquisition in terms of global averages which do not help us to teach individuals. They also mask the effects that different types of instruction might have on individual progress. (Clay 1991, 12).

Clay's initial study combines quantitative and qualitative methodologies. Her quantitative research used appropriate techniques for sampling, data collection, and analysis. She used established psychometric measures for much of the test battery, and the measures she developed were subjected to appropriate statistical analysis to ensure their reliability and validity. Clay's design and methods were also consistent with the conditions of qualitative research. She collected rich data systematically at frequent intervals; used reliable and standardized methods of observing and recording; developed new concepts on the basis of observed patterns in the data (e.g., self-corrections in reading); and then used those concepts to enrich data collection. She allowed observation to guide her development of theory; but she schooled herself to remain open to new discoveries, new concepts, and new theoretical constructs arising from her extensive observations.

The comprehensive design of Clay's original study included both closed tasks and open tasks. As closed tasks, she used established, reliable measures to collect psychometric and language data on each child at six-month intervals. As open tasks, she elicited samples of children's drawing, writing, and reading at weekly intervals. This enabled her to investigate the means and correlations among literacy and language performance, psychological traits, and sociocultural factors across high, high-average, low-average, and low progress groups of children derived from her data. However, a more apt characterization of her research, and perhaps the greatest impact of her findings, concerns the concept of a grounded theory.

> A grounded theory is one that is inductively derived from the study of the phenomenon it represents. . . It is discovered, developed, and provisionally verified through systematic data collection and analysis of data pertaining to that phenomenon. Therefore, data collection, analysis, and theory stand in reciprocal relationship with each other. One does not begin with a theory, then prove it. Rather one begins with an area of study and what is relevant to that area is allowed to emerge. (Strauss and Corbin 1990)

The term *grounded theory* did not come into use in academic and research literature until 1967, when it was introduced by Glaser and Strauss (1967), but Clay was undoubtedly aware of its roots in the biological, social, and cognitive sciences and shared the concerns of Glaser and Strauss concerning theory development.

The vast majority of experimental studies in early literacy followed the paradigm of group comparison, testing one or more hypotheses by comparing groups and manipulating and controlling variables so that any observed effects can be attributed to specified independent variables. One limitation of such research is that its value depends upon the justification of the hypotheses being tested. If the hypotheses are derived from weak theory, the experiments are of little value. Clay saw little evidence to support a theory of early reading acquisition, and, therefore, little reason to use an experimental design.

Another limitation of group comparison designs is that individual data are aggregated and reported only as group means. Clay comments: "Research studies hide the complexity of child learning by reporting group averages, but a pooled average may not describe any individual" (Clay 1998, 226). A third serious limitation of group comparison designs using closed tasks is that the data collected represent the outcomes of children's learning, "Those error-free end results, which are the outcome of many false starts, half-correct processes, and much self-correction en route to a recognizable product or achievement" (Clay 1998, 257).

In contrast, the design Clay used allowed observation of this emerging, tentative behavior that progressed gradually to become controlled, secure knowledge. The use of open tasks and frequent observations made it possible to detect the variability of individual paths to literacy achievement. In short, Clay's design was productive for theory development because it was thoroughly grounded in the data from children who were closely observed during what was, for most of then, the formative period of literacy acquisition.

Clay and her colleagues (see Clay 1982) used a variety of research designs. They applied methods similar to those in her original study with children in their third year of schooling to investigate the progression of literacy development beyond initial stages and to confirm categories of behavior observed in younger children. Clay also used experimental designs to test hypotheses flowing from theory. In one such study, e.g., she showed that young, naive readers are much less bothered by disorientation of print (inversion, reversal, scrambled sequence) than more experienced readers are. When she had the opportunity to observe the literacy acquisition process in a set of quadruplets, Clay chose a case study, longitudinal approach. All of these studies are discussed in *Observing Young Readers* (1982). Studies designed to extend or verify elements of her theory followed rigorous standards without concern for direct application. However, as is discussed below, her research agenda was also influenced by a desire to be helpful to educational practitioners at all levels.

Clay's Theory of Literacy Acquisition

Clay's theory of literacy acquisition in continuous text (Clay 1991, 1982, 1975, 1966) has become a foundation for subsequent research and evaluation designs, including Reading Recovery. Five key ideas within Clay's theory are particularly relevant to her assessment tools and to her evaluation design for practical applications.

1. Clay's theory of literacy acquisition is about learning to read and write continuous texts more than it is about methods for teaching literacy. According to Clay,

   > A theory of reading continuous texts cannot arise from a theory of word reading because it involves the integration of many behaviors not studied in a theory of reading words. (It must, of course, explain the role of word reading and letter recognition within the theory of reading continuous text.) (1993b, 7)

   Children learn to construct meaning through the use of language while using a complex semiotic coding system as input and impetus to their thinking. They must learn to divide their attention to maintain a focus on story or text meaning, while also attending to sentence meaning, language structures, and print. When children encounter difficulty in text, they must be able to shift attention to the level of processing that will enable them to solve a problem, quickly reestablishing meaning if it has been interrupted.

2. Clay's theory emphasizes change over time, as learning and development move forward. Clay and many others have shown how a number of concepts, conventions, and operations must be learned and come under the child's control as the child develops from nonreader to reader and from nonwriter to writer. Significant changes over time result from: (a) the gradual establishment and revision of concepts, (b) an increasing store of items of knowledge, (c) the development of strat-

egies for working on print, such as monitoring one's own performance in both reading and writing, (d) greater facility in attending to different and more complex sources of information simultaneously and in shifting attention when needed, and (e) continuous new learning about oral and written language forms and structures through literacy experiences (Olson 1995). Clay "assumes that the child begins to read . . . with limited knowledge and primitive response patterns which change in two ways: (1) learning about each of these areas expands; and (2) ways of working on the interrelationships of these areas develop" (1993b, 7).

The concept of change over time also refers to the gradual establishment of particular knowledge or skills and how to use them flexibly. Clay explains that anything a child can write has to take three journeys:

> The *first journey* is from unknown to partially known to just known, to easily produced, to never wrong in any context and in many variant forms.
> The *second journey* is from very slow to labored production to fast execution . . .
> The *third journey* is finding and continually adjusting its placement in the orchestration of the whole system of written language as understood by the learner at any particular time. (1998, 156)

The notion of change over time helps to explain growth and changes in the quality of abilities, as well as inconsistent learning performance, and reading and writing behaviors that are often regarded as inappropriate and ineffective, such as making an error on the basis of context and first letter only (such as reading *truck* for *tank*). Such behavior may represent an important phase of growth for a specific child at a particular point in time, mirroring the approximations and partially right responses documented in oral language research (Clay 1991). The persistence of such behavior, however, despite appropriate opportunities to learn may become problematic. Clay's notions about the gradual development of control, fluency, flexibility, and integration of knowledge are useful in understanding how children learn to read and write (Clay 1993b). However, recognizing the gradual emergence of knowledge and strategies that change over time complicates efforts to measure literacy learning at very early levels.

3. A third element in Clay's theory is her understanding that reading and writing are reciprocal. Clay points out that, given the opportunity, children in the emergent and early learning stages acquire overlapping but different pools of knowledge about written language from experiences in reading and in writing. For example, writing fosters a slow analysis of language, highlighting letter forms, sequences, and combinations and their relationships to sound, and brings attention to the detailed features of written language in ways that reading often does not (Clay 1998; Goswami and Bryant 1990). Writing knowledge provides information that can help the child in reading. "However, the reciprocity does not occur spontaneously. The teacher must remember to direct the child to use what he knows in reading when he is writing and vice versa" (Clay 1993b, 11).

4. Clay's theory recognizes that children come to literacy knowledge in very different ways, and the explanations for difficulties in acquiring literacy are also diverse, arising from differences in language development, experiences with books and print, motivation, memory, ability to divide attention, understanding the need to maintain a focus on meaning, attention to and isolation of speech sounds, identification of letter and word forms, directional conventions, concepts about print, inappropriate habituated behaviors, and the ability to link sound and letter sequences. Other research programs have too frequently assumed that all children acquire literacy in much the same way. Clay also points out that "Theorists and researchers have proceeded with too little attention to the role of instruction, and the distinction between usual sequences and necessary sequences for learning." (Clay 1991, 17; Vellutino et al. 1996).

5. Finally, Clay points out that successful learners acquire a learning system that continually extends control over reading and writing processes as they engage in activities involving continuous texts. This "self-extending system" for literacy learning (Clay 1991) is similar to, but not identical to, those systems of strategies that children have developed from infancy to learn language and to learn about the world. Clay innovation, Reading Recovery, is an intervention strategy based on skilled teaching that provides struggling young learners a second chance to develop a self-extending literacy-learning system.

Design of Measurement Procedures for Beginning Literacy

Clay's early research studies were motivated partly by her desire to help teachers and school administrators (Clay 1982). As her research evolved, she faced the task of developing assessment tools that would be consistent with her theory of literacy acquisition: They had to be highly sensitive to change over time; to allow insights into partial learning; to span all areas that contribute to successful literacy learning; to highlight individual differences; to reflect a literacy–learning system in formation; and, at the same time, to be easily administered and interpreted by classroom teachers.

The result, Clay's *An Observation Survey of Early Literacy Achievement* (1993a), was the first large-scale application of her research on literacy acquisition to the field of education. Based upon her theory, Clay's survey tasks capture observations of children's reading and writing performance on continuous texts, but they also include tasks to assess knowledge in areas that contribute to reading and writing abilities, such as letter identification, concepts about print, knowledge of phonemic awareness, word knowledge, the ability to hear phonemes and record them in writing, and oral reading of progressively more difficult texts, as well as emerging strategies for learning in each of those areas. Clay considers that interpreting the data according to her theory is as important as deriving a score on each measure.

Because this assessment occurs when literacy learning is just beginning, a broad range of observations is necessary to establish assessment procedures that reflect the diversity in children's learning—differences in opportunity, pace, concepts, awareness, understandings, knowledge of items, interests, motivations, and strategies. This approach also enables educators to assess children's knowledge as it changes over time.

> I value highly an approach to research which attempts to capture the ways in which children change over time in a reading program, an approach too rarely taken in reading research. It is not enough to administer achievement tests before and after a program or to probe deeply into the reading process. An important additional source of research information lies in accounts of what changes occur in what children in what sequences as they learn in their classroom programs. As a researcher this has interested me; it is, of course, what concerns the teacher. (Clay 1982, xiv)

For optimal validity and reliability, Clay's observation survey tasks are administered individually, with standardized conditions, directions, and probes to elicit evidence of partial knowledge or strategic operation. Clay knew that an important condition of standardization in performance assessment is that each child must comprehend what is being asked of him or her. The teacher or observer uses specified language to restate directions and to urge the child to respond in some way. Clay views language as a source of measurement error for young children—not only language directed to a child, but also the child's challenging task of constructing a language response (Wood 1988). Thus she developed several tasks that invite children to demonstrate their knowledge through their actions, such as Concepts About Print, an interaction between the child and a simulated text guided by an observer, rather than through verbal response (Clay 1993a, 1998).

Clay's observation survey measures have high construct and face validity because they are directly and obviously relevant to the reading and writing of continuous texts. Further, they have high reliability—measurement error is greatly reduced because the tests are administered individually with standardized procedures by teachers trained to use these measures. Several of the observation tasks would perhaps qualify as criterion measures because they assess children's developing knowledge in limited domains, such as letter identification, concepts about print conventions, and ability to hear and record sounds in words. As criterion measures they are useful as a basis for informing instruction for children from ages five to seven or eight. Although these measures yield reliable rankings of children during this period, the learning ceilings of several of these tasks limit their usefulness for assessing longitudinal development beyond the early stages of literacy acquisition.

It is interesting to consider why Clay abandoned traditional norm-referenced group achievement tests, and the psychometric principles for constructing such tests, for the study of the early acquisition of literacy. Standardized tests yield valid comparisons of mean scores derived from groups of students who are already reading, but they are not sensitive to variability in emerging knowledge. Therefore, these tests are not useful as baseline measures for assessing the longitudinal development of beginning literacy. Test responses that are either right or wrong obscure the processes by which children arrive at their responses, as well as children's developing knowledge or partially correct responding, important information for beginning instruction. Different children can receive similar scores for very different response profiles, making the results difficult for practitioners and parents to interpret. The amount of measurement error does not allow for reliable comparisons of growth over a short period of time. Clay points out that

> It is easy to arrive at false assumptions about a process as complex as learning to read. Firstly, we are likely to average a vast amount of evidence in order to arrive at a program decision. Secondly, we may do this on the basis of superficial or highly selected observations. Thirdly, our assumption may be the result of an oversimplified, logical analysis of the task which bears little relationship to the ways in which individual children learn. (1982, xi)

Standardized tests lend themselves to all three types of errors.

The stability of Clay's observation survey tasks also make them valuable to researchers studying the development of reading and writing abilities over time. Clay comments that "Powerful statistical analyses have shown that these procedures which permit more detailed recording of individual responses than a normative test nevertheless have proved to be sound measurement devices" (Clay 1982, 6). They are also extremely valuable to classroom teachers: they help teachers see how children go about the tasks of reading and writing, and they enable teachers—through repeated observations—to perceive their children's progress and to adjust instruction accordingly. These same measures are useful to administrators who wish to evaluate schools, teachers, and programs because they provide baseline information as well as ongoing records of progress over time.

Clay's observation survey tasks appear to be relatively simple, but they represent a significant innovation in educational practice, both for instruction and for program evaluation. As such, they are often misunderstood and therefore misused. Their purpose is to assess individual children's literacy knowledge and ability at a particular point in time, not to predict future school performance.

Some practitioners would like to use one or more of these measures in isolation, but Clay specifies that the entire set of tasks is needed to depict a young child's emerging literacy abilities. Because the tasks differ in terms of quantity, quality, and types of items, scores from separate tasks cannot be combined or compared; however, used as benchmarks several times during the year, such scores may be more valuable for group comparisons of early literacy achievement than scores from standardized tests, a serious consideration in program evaluation. Clay has also shown that these measures are reliable for identifying children experiencing difficulty learning to read and write and for ranking children within a group at a particular point in time.

Clay's belief that these observation survey measures can be used effectively by teachers stands in contrast to the American tradition of testing and test interpretation being performed by specialists. She believes that these measures belong in the hands of teachers because close observation should serve as the basis for instruction.

Clay has treated the measurement of early literacy as a complex issue. Given (1) the range and diversity of knowledge among beginning readers and writers, (2) the emerging nature of knowledge in young children on the road to literacy, and (3) the changing nature of a child's literacy knowledge over time (even sometimes from day to day), a child's knowledge or level of performance cannot be reduced to a single score on a single task, or to a ranking on a single measure. Clay's view has significance for the design of research into early literacy learning, as well as for intervention efforts and programs.

The Development of Reading Recovery

Clay's Observation Survey was welcomed by educators who understood the reliability of these measures for identifying the children who were at greatest risk of failure in literacy learning. Practitioners' insistence that she also provide help in devising ways to teach these children struck a responsive chord in Clay's value orientation, leading to a redirection of her career. The problem was how to develop instruction that would succeed in changing the learning paths of children who were encountering the greatest difficulty. Clay's theory of emergent literacy and early literacy learning was a starting point, but she had to decide two key things: what her overall strategy for instruction would be, and how she would work to develop instructional theory and methods. The instructional strategy she chose was to coach low-progress children to use the strategies and processing systems that she had documented for high-progress beginners, an approach that follows rather naturally from her conviction that reading and writing are learned behaviors. High-progress learners are able to develop a self-extending system for learning to read and write through a combination of modeling, incidental teaching, formal tuition, and personal discovery and confirmation (at home and at school). Clay was convinced that low-progress children could develop a similar system, but that they would probably need much more explicit teaching and support, tailored to the individual's learning patterns and addressing any confusions.

Clay's approach was to collaborate with and to document the practice of excellent teachers working over time with several children. As methods were tried, in-depth discussions probed an understanding of the child's thinking in relation to his performance and the teacher's thinking in relation to her perceptions of the child and her own prior notions about learning and teaching. In short, Clay used a grounded theory approach: She used observations of children and teachers to develop theory, she used theory to guide selection of methods, she applied the methods to practice in a systematic way, and she used detailed observations and records to confirm or revise theory and procedures.

Clay's research program consisted of a series of eight studies, extending from 1976 to 1991. The first six of these studies were done during the development phase of Reading Recovery Clay (1993b).

In the Development Project, Clay worked with one teacher during the first year to develop an initial set of procedures. In the second year she worked with five additional teachers to determine whether experienced teachers without specialist training could use the procedures effectively, and how the program might need to vary from school to school (Clay 1993b, 62). During the second year, only a set of procedures and a lesson format were trialed. The lesson format was a series of high-scope tasks (tasks that allow each learner to participate at his or her own level, pace, and purpose), beginning with

- rereading familiar books
- taking a running record of a child's independent reading of yesterday's new book
- working with magnetic letters to strengthen letter and word knowledge
- writing a story
- reassembling a cut-up strip on which the story was written
- introducing a new book
- reading the new book with instructional support and teaching

A great deal of flexibility was allowed during the second year to see what worked best under what conditions. Again, Clay used a grounded theory approach to determine parameters for the instructional program within schools. The teacher/pupil ratio, duration of the lessons, and teacher use of time were all decisions of the teacher with school staff, and these variables were investigated through extensive discussion with special teachers and school personnel and through examination of patterns of data.

Clay's research during this instructional development phase might be summarized as follows:

- The research program consisted of a series of studies and teaching-learning initiatives that methodically addressed a progressive set of questions about teaching procedures, teacher-training possibilities and procedures, program operations, decisions about when to end a child's program, and sustained effects over one year and over three years.
- The work of practitioners and the effects of their instruction on children's learning formed the content of the investigation for every research question. Children's learning progress was the data source for judging effectiveness.
- Research methods depended upon the questions addressed and whether Clay was judging the effectiveness of a particular approach or exploring a new one.
- The initial study for each research question was replicated in an independent study.

Clay's respect for and trust in practitioners, as well as her values, are evident in her research design for developing Reading Recovery. It is interesting that Clay's research methodology became the basis of the teacher training program for Reading Recovery. As one teacher taught a child behind the one-way, soundproof viewing screen, Clay and the other teachers discussed what they thought was going on in the lesson. Afterwards the demonstration teacher was asked to describe what she had observed and to explain the student's actions and her teaching decisions.

This model illustrates the complexity of teaching decisions about individual children. Both the teacher and the child act, and both have reasons for their actions, which may or may not be available to conscious reflection (Clay 1991). The role of the teacher is to precisely observe the child's responses in order to make inferences about the child's thinking. In parallel fashion, teachers' actions reflect their understandings about literacy learning and their assumptions about a particular child. Teachers use the child's behaviors as feedback for their teaching and their evolving development of theory. The continuous interplay between what teachers and children are *doing* and *thinking* facilitates teachers' construction of personal theories about each child that are grounded in observational data. When a group of teachers observe a tutoring session and talk about what they are noticing, all group members have the opportunity to consider multiple explanations in light of the actions of the child-teacher dyad before them. Gaffney (1994) depicted this model as a 2 × 2 matrix: *child, teacher × doing, thinking*. Analysis of the interactions among these variables will create tension between existing assumptions and observed responses. The teacher group, all observing a common lesson, may engage in questioning and discussion in which all participants improve the fit between their observations and their assumptions.

This line of questioning builds consensus about what was observed and inferred and makes public the reasoning behind teaching decisions. However, it also requires teachers to verbalize their theories about how children process information and why a certain procedure might be used in response to a hypothesis about a student's behavior and thinking. It also stimulates a reexamination of each teacher's current understandings of reading and writing processes and how they are acquired. This methodology is appropriate when knowledge production is the goal, as well as in a training program when knowledge acquisition and use are goals. Clay's Replication Study of 1979 showed that this approach to teacher training produced effective student learning for a much larger group of teachers, even when instructional time for children was considerably reduced.

Another issue concerned deciding when to stop a child's intervention program. Clay established three criteria for a successful intervention: A child had to perform within the average of his class, but he also had to demonstrate that he had established a self-extending learning system. However, Clay had to demonstrate that these criteria were valid in terms of continued learning progress at an appropriate rate over time, her third criterion for a successful intervention. For this reason, Clay launched a three-year study that showed that the children for whom the intervention had been discontinued successfully continued to achieve within the average of the age cohort. The children who had not been discontinued successfully and had not developed a self-extending learning system fell significantly below this average at the end of their third year in school. In other words, the criteria for discontinuing children had successfully differentiated those who had established an effective self-extending system for learning in school classrooms from those who had not.

Clay's research design to show the effectiveness of Reading Recovery is frequently criticized because she did not use an experimental group comparison design (Program A versus Program B, or Program A versus Control Group). However, no other intervention treatment was available for comparison. Clay rejected the alternative of comparing Reading Recovery children to children who were not given the program on the grounds that it would be unethical to withhold service from any child who needed it. The only alternative was to compare their progress with other children of the same age who were receiving the same classroom program but who did not qualify for Reading Recovery (Clay 1993b, 60). In essence, then, Clay has reversed the direction of comparisons: The typical group-comparison research design is intended to show that two groups of children who are equal at the start are made unequal through an intervention. Clay's design compares two groups who are unequal at the start, demonstrating that after the intervention they become relatively equal.

Critics have also criticized the Reading Recovery research design because the process of discontinuing a student from the program appears to be judged relatively; that is, in comparison to the average of a particular class or school group. However, there is a second requirement for discontinuing—that the child demonstrate a self-extending learning system. Determining the presence of a self-extending system is not a simple matter; however, the decisions of experienced Reading Recovery personnel appear to yield reliable judgments, and the validity of these judgments is demonstrated repeatedly as children continue to progress after the intervention is stopped and continue to achieve within the average range for their age group. This conclusion from Clay's three-year study (1993b) has been replicated longitudinally (Pinnell, DeFord, and Lyons, 1988; Askew et al. in progress) and cross-sectionally (Jaggar and Smith-Burke 1994, Jaggar and Simic, 1996; see also Askew et al. 1998) in a number of school systems in North America.

Clay's work from 1976 through 1981 led to the creation of Reading Recovery, an early literacy intervention with great potential for dramatically reducing the number of children who have difficulty in learning to read and write. Without intervention, these children become a continual burden on educational systems. In addition, Clay and her colleagues demonstrated that the instructional procedures for this program could be successfully taught to teachers without specialist training and that the program could operate quite successfully in a variety of schools in New Zealand, and eventually in Australia and the United States (Clay 1994). We now turn to the challenges of (a) gaining acceptance for the idea of a highly skilled, targeted intervention, (b) creating a system that could not only be replicated in different settings, but that would continue to improve over time, and (c) successfully implementing this educational change in diverse cultures.

Reading Recovery as Part of a Comprehensive Approach to Literacy Instruction

Clay defines the problem of literacy failure largely in terms of schools' inability to accommodate to the diversity of skills and abilities among learners as they enter school. Schools tend to teach a single curriculum and expect a single developmental progression of all learners. Early literacy instruction must accommodate *to all types of diversity*. According to Clay:

> The mismatch between what schools require and the individual diversity of learners has been . . . institutionalized in school systems. The delivery system for education is group or whole class instruction, not individual instruction which societies believe they cannot afford. *Classes are instructed but classes do not learn; only individuals learn.* (1998, 223, emphasis added)

Additionally, within any society educational norms of performance, developmental sequences of behaviors for specific age groups, and requirements in terms of curriculum and teaching all tend to be based on the concept of average performance. Clay goes on to say:

> Diversity of any kind does not fit well within such expectations. Can educational practice escape from expectations of "average for age" and that children must take common paths to common outcomes? . . . Modern societies claiming to value diversity, and wishing to mainstream learners who were previously kept apart, need ways of escaping from the tyranny of the average. (223–224)

Industrial nations today are not willing to tolerate the amount and degree of literacy failure that schools are producing (Allington and Walmsley 1995). Educational researchers have long argued that all children can learn, but that schools and educational practices must change in order for this to occur. Crevola and Hill (1998) argue convincingly for zero tolerance of literacy failure.

Prevention is often suggested as a response to diversity and to the problem of school failure. Pianta (1990) describes three types of prevention strategies: a primary prevention strategy that addresses a single variable known to be a major cause of literacy failure; a secondary prevention targeted to just those individuals who demonstrate profiles most highly correlated with failure outcomes (see also Vellutino et al. 1996); and a tertiary prevention strategy for the small percentage that are not helped by the first two programs. Schools and many researchers of the issues of early literacy failure tend to stake their resources on a primary intervention strategy, such as all parents reading aloud to their children or strong phonemic awareness programs in all preschools and kindergartens (Griffin, Snow, and Burns, 1998).

However, Clay points out that primary intervention strategies alone will not work because they do not address the differences found among young learners. As part of a comprehensive educational effort including good classroom teaching (a kind of primary prevention in Pianta's terms), Reading Recovery instruction provides the lowest achieving first-grade children with a second chance to learn literacy, what Pianta refers to as a "secondary prevention" strategy. Through her research Clay demonstrated the two positive outcomes of Reading Recovery instruction: (a) it reduces the number of children who pose problems for a school system by their failure to learn according to grade-level expectations, and (b) it identifies the small percentage of children who will be referred for further assessment and longer-term service (i.e., tertiary prevention). Drawing on systems theory, Clay realized the limitations of developing only an instructional framework and a teacher-training model (Clay 1987). More was needed.

Thus, the challenge for Clay was to create a design that could disseminate Reading Recovery to different cultures and different governmental structures while ensuring the integrity and quality of the program. The program must

- ensure the depth and quality of professional training for Reading Recovery teachers in any new implementation
- convince the educational system that early intervention worked by demonstrating that it satisfied the three criteria for success
- provide continuous feedback to teachers that their efforts with individual children were successful or, if not, provide the information to make them so
- be flexible enough to enable Reading Recovery professionals to work with diverse populations, the varied organizations of schools and school systems, the varied organization of higher education, and different political and governmental structures
- collect ongoing research data that would be useful for questions and challenges that could not be anticipated
- allow for continual growth in understanding by the professionals working in the program and educators and administrators working alongside the program
- respond to new theoretical and research developments that offer promise of improvement and greater understanding

In short, the challenge Clay faced was how to disseminate the program, how to maintain its integrity while working within new educational systems, and how to allow for change and improvement without losing the program's essential quality or effectiveness.

To meet this challenge, Clay created Reading Recovery with four interacting components (shown in Figure 15–1):

- Individual instruction for first graders at risk of literacy failure.
- A three-tiered staffing model.
- An implementation design to introduce, maintain, and institutionalize Reading Recovery in large systems such as those at district, region, or state levels.
- A monitoring and evaluation component to evaluate student success and provide information that would improve the implementation of all aspects of the program.

These components are discussed below.

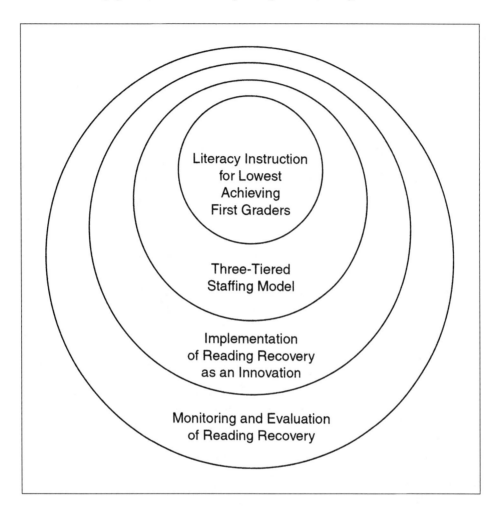

FIGURE 15–1   *The four components of the reading recovery program*

Instructional Component

Short-term, supplemental, daily, individual instruction is provided by highly trained teachers for the lowest achieving first-grade children. The keys that will promote accelerated learning and establish a self-extending learning system that can continue beyond the intervention are the lesson framework described in the "Development of Reading Recovery" section: close observation, the menu of possible procedures within each part of the lesson, the careful matching of texts and instruction to individual children, and the development of a system of cognitive strategies.

Three-Tiered Staffing Model: Differential Roles and Expertise with Common Practice

Three different roles were created—the Reading Recovery teacher, the teacher-leader, and the trainer of teacher-leaders—all grounded in the common practice of teaching the "hardest-to-teach children," but each requiring differentiated expertise. For each role, ongoing professional development is also required in order to maintain and improve the implementation of Reading Recovery and introduce piloted changes from research and practice. Teacher-leaders and trainers of teacher-leaders enter with different qualifications in order to function according to the demands of their respective roles. Developed to parallel the training of Reading Recovery teachers, the training of teacher-leaders and trainers has evolved from excellent practice, using a grounded theory methodology. The responsibilities associated with each role are described below.

Trainers of Teacher-Leaders

Trainers of teacher-leaders work in university training centers and hold faculty appointments. They are required to hold doctorates in education (including expertise in early literacy) or closely related fields and to attend an additional year of intensive training in Reading Recovery. Their responsibilities include teaching Reading Recovery children; conducting initial training and ongoing professional development for teacher-leaders; providing technical assistance to training sites (problem solving to improve the implementation of the program); overseeing the collection, analysis, and reporting of data and information about the program to training sites and local, state, and national audiences; keeping abreast of the latest research related to Reading Recovery in order to answer questions that arise from practice and new research; conducting research in related areas; attending professional development of trainers; and contributing to both the national Reading Recovery program—through the National Reading Recovery Trainers Group—and to their home university.

Teacher-Leaders

Teacher-leaders (called tutors in some countries) work in sites that may include one or more school systems. (A training site may be one large district or a "provider site" consisting of multiple small districts. Both employ one or more teacher-leaders and designate a site coordinator to assist with administrative matters.) Teacher-leaders are required to hold a master's degree in education; have experience as teachers of early literacy; have human relations, organizational, and communication skills; and be capable of providing new learning within their system. They attend a year of training at a university training center. Clay (1987) sees them as the key implementers of Reading Recovery in a training site. Goodlad (1977) states:

> The systems of which the school is a part exercise enormous constraints which are essentially conservative and which serve to discourage change and innovation. These systems are not only the formal political ones of the state and local organization for education, they are also the informal ones, exerting subtle pressure by way of implicit and explicit expectations of schooling. . . . If change is to occur at anything like a more

rapid rate than is characteristic of the whole, the existence or creation of a *redirecting system of considerable salience* (emphasis added) may be critical. (cited in Clay 1987, 42)

Realizing the nature of change and the natural resistance to innovation, Clay considers teacher-leaders to be the "redirecting system . . . which must be insistent, persistent and consistent over continued crises" (1987, 42).

Teacher-leader responsibilities include teaching children in Reading Recovery; providing initial training and ongoing professional development for Reading Recovery teachers; assisting the development of school Reading Recovery teams, consulting with Reading Recovery teachers about the hardest-to-teach children; overseeing the collection, analysis, and reporting of data to the school superintendent, school board, schools, and the general public. Teacher-leaders use data to resolve instructional and implementation issues at the school and district levels. They are encouraged to function with the site coordinator as a member of a district Reading Recovery team for planning and coordinating program implementation with other district literacy initiatives; to attend professional development sessions organized by the university training center; to present at regional and national conferences; and to disseminate information about the program to different audiences in their area.

Reading Recovery Teachers

Reading Recovery teachers are selected for their records as excellent teachers of early literacy, three years of teaching experience, good human relations skills, and the capacity to take on new learning. Most teach four children in Reading Recovery for half of the school day, and in the other half of the day are assigned another job based on the staffing model selected by the school's Reading Recovery team to meet school needs. These models range widely, from entering primary classrooms to support good classroom literacy instruction, to teaching English as a second language or resource room teaching, to sharing a primary class with another teacher. The Reading Recovery teacher, the principal, and other primary teachers make up the school's Reading Recovery team, which implements the program according to its purpose, design, and *Standards and Guidelines of the Reading Recovery Council of North America* (1998). The Reading Recovery teacher also communicates information about the program within the school, coordinates services for Reading Recovery children, and helps the school team complete an annual report on the program. Given both sets of responsibilities and depending on the selected staffing model, the Reading Recovery teacher may work with as many as fifteen to thirty children each day.

The differentiated roles within Reading Recovery allow for flexibility in the system for problem solving and provide a way for information to flow from "practice" to the trainer level in order to inform possible modifications for instruction, administrative procedures, or aspects of implementation. This design also allows for piloting potential changes based on new insights from theory or research before the changes are disseminated to the total system. For example, when Clay produced *Reading Recovery: A Guidebook for Teachers in Training* (1993b), she refined and added procedures and integrated new insights into the rationales for instructional procedures based on her research and that of others. The three-tiered system not only provides a communication network among Reading Recovery professionals, but also provides professional development sessions concerning when, why, and how these changes might be used; it also includes follow-up during school and colleague visits to ensure quality implementation of the changes.

Implementation of Reading Recovery as a System Innovation

The third component, the implementation of Reading Recovery, involves managing the change process as Reading Recovery is adopted, implemented, and eventually institutionalized by each school within a district. One key to successful implementation is maintaining internal coherence within Reading Recovery to ensure quality, while relating to the host system (Gaffney and Paynter 1994). This relationship involves cooperation, communication across levels of hierarchical systems, initial and ongoing training across systems, organizing and collaborating for the benefit of children, ongoing data collection, and sustaining or modifying the different aspects of implementation to maintain quality. Reading Recovery is not exempt from everyday issues such as student or teacher absences, district testing policies, competing priorities for student and teacher time, or transiency of student populations. And, as Fullan and Miles (1992) observe, resistance should be viewed as normal when implementing curricular change, and it should be treated with understanding, not demonstrations of impatience. The teacher-leader functions as the redirecting system and steers the course for successful implementation at the district level. Reading Recovery teachers do the same at the school level. In discussing the patterns of change, Fullan (1993) stresses the need to be internally cohesive, but externally oriented. To this end, trainers from university centers offer technical assistance and problem solving to training sites.

Clay has identified five stages of implementing Reading Recovery as an innovation in an educational system. The first stage involves getting started—developing an informed group of administrators and teachers at both school and district levels, building a training facility, training one or more teacher-leaders, and then training the first group of Reading Recovery teachers.

The second stage involves sustaining the beginning program within each participating school, moving toward *full coverage,* i.e., having enough trained Reading Recovery teachers to serve the lowest achieving first-grade children in the school, (approximately 15% to 20% depending upon need), and broadening ownership through dissemination of information about the program at both school and district levels. The teacher-leader must support teachers' refinement of their teaching, identify and resolve problems by using data, and document the stories of successful children and teachers.

The third stage involves reaching full coverage in participating schools. With full coverage and quality teaching there should be a significant reduction in the number of those who need long-term special services. Important concerns at this stage are expanding the program to other schools throughout the district; sustaining and refining the quality of the program; ensuring communication, collaboration, and cooperation among classroom and Reading Recovery teachers; networking across education systems; and writing up and disseminating results.

The fourth stage concerns questions of size and scale as the program expands to regional and state levels. There are two national networks in the United States that help address problems of expansion: the North American Reading Recovery Trainers' Group and the Reading Recovery Council of North America. Within these groups there is the potential to conduct research, as well as a wealth of experience across systems from which training sites may benefit.

The fifth stage focuses on the paradox of success in mature and vintage sites. Owing to the success of the program, the apparent need for it becomes invisible and, consequently, support for the program may decrease. At this stage it is important to keep the program viable in the changing climate of schools. Other potential problems come from routinization of teaching, drifting away from Reading Recovery procedures, and inefficient implementation, all of which may affect program results negatively; these issues must be addressed quickly by school and district teams. To increase teaching capacity within schools, it is also important to rotate new teachers into Reading Recovery, thus providing schools with more trained teacher capacity and flexibility in achieving full coverage. Changing demographics and state policies also provide challenges. Critical to the success of the implementation is national Reading Recovery data collection, which provides answers to evaluation questions and enables all Reading Recovery professionals to monitor the success of the program both locally and nationally.

Monitoring and Evaluating the Reading Recovery Program

The fourth component of Clay's model is the ongoing data collection of student outcomes. In the United States, data are collected on all of the observation survey tasks at the beginning of the year, on three tasks at end of the year, and on all measures when children enter and exit the program. Clay's alternative evaluation design for Reading Recovery provides a sound way to track individual as well as group progress. This design is a simultaneous replication design at an individual and site level (Frymier et al. 1989). Each child is required to achieve certain benchmarks before leaving the program (i.e., scoring within or above average band[1] achievement of the cohort *and* demonstrating a self-extending system of strategies to solve problems with materials appropriate for at least the end of first grade) and to continue to learn over time. The design is also replicated systematically across training sites diverse contexts and with diverse populations, by trained and in-training teachers, at sites at different stages of implementation, and across multiple years.

In addition, from year to year, each district should identify at the end of kindergarten the cohort of children in each school who need Reading Recovery services in order to determine the number of Reading Recovery teaching slots that will be needed. In this way the training site can clearly assess changes in the number of children retained or needing special services as the program expands toward full coverage in each school and in each district. Additional functions of data collection include quality assurance and program improvement.

Each district may also extend data collection to measure whether a significant portion of students have maintained their gains from their success in Reading Recovery either cross-sectionally or longitudinally. Rowe (1995) demonstrates an interesting way of plotting data in box and whisker plots, showing the average achievement and range compared to a random sample from the same cohort over time. He has demonstrated the remarkable post-program achievement of Australian Reading Recovery program children over time. Askew (in progress) has just completed two longitudinal studies that demonstrate that Reading Recovery students maintain their gains over several years on standardized tests, slightly below the mean but within the average band where one would expect them to be. Cross-sectional follow-up studies from Texas and Boston (cited in Askew et al. 1998) and in New York (Jaggar and Smith-Burke 1994; Jaggar and Simic 1996) also provide evidence of Reading Recovery's success in different contexts over time.

Summary and Conclusions

In 1993, Carl Kaestle published an article in the *Educational Researcher* titled "The Awful Reputation of Education Research." This was the first in a series of articles that address the ineffectiveness of educational research to make a positive difference in schools. For the most part, the enormous gap between theory and practice still exists.

However, Clay's work offers one notable exception. Clay has avoided participating in nonproductive, contentious debates between polar positions such as whole language versus phonics, descriptive versus experimental designs, or individual versus group data (for a discussion of these issues and an example of these debates, see Pressley and Allington, in preparation; and Vellutino and Scanlon, in press). Instead, Clay has focused steadfastly on her evolving interests, the purposes of her research, and her belief in children's ability to learn.

Her perspective as a developmental psychologist, her commitment to scientific methodology, and her firm belief in the reciprocity between theory and practice have led her to develop a comprehensive theory of literacy learning and an instructional intervention as she has pursued what is possible to maximize human potential and the opportunity to become literate. The focus and purpose of her work have shifted over time, from the development of her grounded theory of how children learn to read and write continuous text, to observation measures reflecting her theory that are to be used by nonspecialist teachers, to Reading Recovery instruction and teacher training, and then to the design of an implementation system for dissemination of Reading Recovery as an innovative, not-for-profit, early intervention component of a comprehensive design to teach early literacy. Throughout her work, Clay found the appropriate design and methodology to fit her particular purpose. As an example, her unique evaluation design holds those using it accountable for the learning of each and every child taught in Reading Recovery.

Implementation of Reading Recovery began in New Zealand in 1978; it became a national program in 1984. Implementation in the United States began in 1984 (Pinnell et al. 1988). Since then, Reading Recovery has become one of the most effective and widely disseminated early intervention programs available in the world. The development of Reading Recovery has shifted thinking away from remediation after failure has occurred to prevention through early intervention based upon skilled teaching. Reading Recovery is built on Clay's broad repertoire of theories and research designs and methodologies; her respect for the different traditions of research; her respect for the expertise of teachers and staff developers; and her realistic understanding of daily life in schools.

The enduring contribution of Clay's theory of how children read and write continuous text has changed the way both researchers and practitioners think about early literacy development. A second significant contribution has been her demonstration that productive school reform may be achieved by forging an interactive relationship among research, theory, and practice.

Note

1. Average band is defined as one-half a standard deviation both below and above the mean.

References

ALLINGTON, R., AND WALMSLEY, S., EDS. 1995. *No Quick Fix: Rethinking Literacy Programs in America's Elementary Schools*. Newark, Del.: International Reading Association.

ASKEW, B. J., FOUNTAS, I. C., LYONS, C. A., PINNELL, G. S., AND SCHMITT, M. C. 1998. *Reading Recovery Review: Understandings, Outcomes, and Implications*. Columbus, Ohio: Reading Recovery Council of North America.

ASKEW, B. J., KAYE, B., WICKSTROM, C., AND FRASIER, D. In progress. *Subsequent Progress of Former Reading Recovery Children: Two Longitudinal Studies*.

BIEMILLER, A. 1970. "The Development of Use of Graphic and Contextual Information as Children Learn to Read." *Reading Research Quarterly* 6: 75–96.

CLAY, M. M. 1966. "Emergent Reading Behaviour." Ph.D. diss., University of Auckland.

———. 1975. *What Did I Write?* Portsmouth, N.H.: Heinemann.

———. 1982. *Observing Young Readers: Selected Papers*. Portsmouth, N.H.: Heinemann.

———. 1987. "Systemic Adaptations to an Educational Innovation." *New Zealand Journal of Educational Studies* 22 (1): 35–58.

———. 1991. *Becoming Literate: The Construction of Inner Control.* Portsmouth, N.H.: Heinemann.

———. 1993a. *An Observation Survey of Early Literacy Achievement.* Portsmouth, N.H.: Heinemann.

———. 1993b. *Reading Recovery: A Guidebook for Teachers in Training.* Portsmouth, N.H.: Heinemann.

———. 1994. "Reading Recovery: The Wider Implications of an Educational Innovation." *Literacy, Teaching, and Learning* 1 (1): 121–194. Reprinted from A. Watson and A. Badenhop, eds., 1992. *Prevention of Reading Failure.* London: Ashton Scholastic, and with permission of author.

———. 1997. "The Future Research in Reading Recovery." Presentation at the First North American Leadership Academy, Strengthening the Operation of Reading Recovery. San Diego, Calif., July 1997.

———. 1998. *By Different Paths to Common Outcomes.* York, Maine: Stenhouse.

CREVOLA, C. A., AND HILL, P. W. 1998. "Evaluation of a Whole-School Approach to Prevention and Intervention in Early Literacy." *Journal of Education for Students Placed at Risk* 3 (2): 133–157.

FRYMIER, J., BARBER, L., GANSNEDER, B., AND ROBERTSON, N. 1989. "Simultaneous Replication: A Technique for Large-Scale Research." *Phi Delta Kappan* 71 (3): 228–231.

FULLAN, M. 1993. *Change Forces.* Philadelphia: Falmer Press.

FULLAN, M., AND MILES, M. 1992. "Getting Reform Right: What Works and What Doesn't?" *Phi Delta Kappan* 73: 744–752.

GAFFNEY, J. S. 1994. "Adding Power and Richness to Reading Recovery Teacher Training." Presented at the Second International Reading Recovery Conference, July 1994, Palm Springs, Calif.

GAFFNEY, J. S., AND PAYNTER, S. Y. 1994. "The Role of Early Literacy Interventions in the Transformation of Educational Systems." *Literacy, Teaching, and Learning* 1 (1): 29–42.

GLASER, B., AND STRAUSS, A. 1967. *The Discovery of Grounded Theory: Strategies of Qualitative Research.* Chicago: Aldine.

GOODLAD, J. 1997. *Networking and Educational Improvement Reflections on a Strategy.* Washington, D.C.: National Institute of Education.

GOSWAMI, U., AND BRYANT, P. 1990. *Phonological Skills and Learning to Read.* Philadelphia: Farmer Press.

GRIFFIN, P., SNOW, C. E., AND BURNS, M. S. 1998. *Preventing of Reading Difficulties in Young Children.* Washington, D.C.: National Academy Press.

JAGGAR, A. M., AND SIMIC, O. 1996. *A Four-Year Study of Reading Recovery Children in New York State: Preliminary Report.* New York: New York University Reading Recovery Project, School of Education.

JAGGAR, A. M., AND SMITH-BURKE, M. T. 1994. *Follow-up Study of Reading Recovery Children in Community School District # 2, New York City.* New York: New York University Reading Recovery Project, School of Education.

KAESTLE, C. F. 1993. "The Awful Reputation of Education Research." *Educational Researcher* 22 (1): 23–31.

LYONS, C. A., PINNELL, G. S., AND DeFORD, D. E. 1993. *Partners in Learning: Teachers and Children in Reading Recovery.* New York: Teachers College Press.

OLSON, D. 1995. "Writing and the Mind." In *Sociocultural Studies of Mind*, edited by J. Wertsch, P. del Rio, and A. Alvarez. Cambridge, Mass.: Cambridge University Press.

PIANTA, R. C. 1990. "Widening the Debate on Educational Reform: Prevention as a Viable Alternative." *Exceptional Children* 56: 306–313.

PINNELL, G. S., DeFORD, D. E., AND LYONS, C.A. 1988. *Reading Recovery: Early Intervention for At-Risk First Graders.* Arlington, Va.: Educational Research Service.

PRESSLEY, M., AND ALLINGTON, R. in preparation. *What Should Reading Instructional Research Be the Research Of?* Albany: State University of New York.

ROWE, K. J. 1995. "Factors Affecting Student Progress in Reading Recovery: Key Findings from a Longitudinal Study." *Literacy, Teaching and Learning* 1 (2): 57–110.

READING RECOVERY COUNCIL OF NORTH AMERICA. 1998. *Standards and Guidelines of the Reading Recovery Council of North America.* Columbus, Ohio: Reading Recovery Council of North America.

STRAUSS, A., AND CORBIN, J. 1990. *Basics of Qualitative Research: Grounded Theory Procedures and Techniques.* Newbury Park, Calif.: Sage Publications.

VELLUTINO, F. D., AND SCANLON, D. M. In press. "Focus, Funding, Phonics—What's the Point? A reply to Pressley and Allington." *Issues in Education*.

VELLUTINO, F., SCANLON, D., SIPAY, E., SMALL, S., PRATT, A., CHEN, R., AND DENCKLA, M. 1996. "Cognitive Profiles of Difficult-to-Remediate and Readily Remediated Poor Readers: Early Intervention as a Vehicle for Distinguishing Between Cognitive and Experiential Deficits as Basic Causes of Specific Reading Disability." *Journal of Educational Psychology* 88 (4): 601–638.

WOOD, D. 1988. *How Children Think and Learn.* Cambridge, Mass.: Basil Blackwell.

Contributors and Their Connections with Marie Clay

Billie J. Askew, Professor, Department of Reading and Bilingual Education, College of Education and Human Ecology, Texas Woman's University, Denton

I was introduced to Marie's work in the 1970s when professors Margaret Griffin and Rose Spicola brought her to Texas Woman's University. Her ideas were revolutionary—challenging my assumptions and expectations about literacy teaching and learning. Her influence continues, providing new and unexpected ways of thinking about what is possible. Marie Clay continues to gently prod, thoughtfully challenge, and generously support explorations of possibilities in my work and in the work of so many others. Thank you, Marie, for "stirring the waters" for all of us!

Courtney Cazden, Charles William Eliot Professor of Education Emerita, Harvard Graduate School of Education, Cambridge, MA

I first met Marie Clay at a reading research conference in the United States, and then went to New Zealand in 1983 for the first of many visits at her invitation. I was there most recently in December 1999 and was honored to be able to attend the launching of the "reconstruction" of Clay's *Observation Survey of Early Literacy Achievement* for children learning to read in the Maori language.

Anne Haas Dyson, Professor, Education: Language, Literacy, and Culture, University of California, Berkeley

I first met "Marie Clay" quite by happenstance while browsing in an Austin, Texas bookstore in the mid-seventies. I was a young teacher, completely disillusioned with the "approach" approach to childhood literacy (e.g., "language experience," "literature," "basal"). Each approach seemed written for imaginary children, never as lively, or as confusing, as my own. The book *What Did I Write?*, and the child writing adorning its cover, gripped my attention. It promised intellectual interest in and respect for children's actions—not didactic prescriptions for teachers. My own research path began there, that day, in the bookstore aisle.

Irene Fountas, Professor, School of Education, Lesley College, Cambridge, MA

Early in my teaching career I was drawn to the meticulous, insightful work of Clay as it helped me understand the nature of learning and reflect on my teaching of young readers and writers. As life happens, I had the good fortune of studying her work in early intervention and then developing a collegial relationship that has made the earlier conversations with text take on new meaning in my work with children and teachers.

Janet S. Gaffney, Associate Professor, Department of Special Education and Center for the Study of Reading, University of Illinois at Urbana-Champaign

Marie appreciates a good question. I save mine for her. I keep a list—just in case. Periodically, I delete, revise, and add questions. Each time we meet, she lets me ask *all* of them. Marie is a master of responding to questions in ways that reveal some kernel of truth so clearly that I cannot imagine ever thinking how I thought before. Whether the question is about learning, teaching, schooling, or conducting research, almost always her answers snap me back to seeing things from a child's point of view. Marie will have more time when I finally get this.

John T. Guthrie, Professor of Educational Psychology, Human Development, University of Maryland, College Park

I was fortunate to visit Marie extensively in 1979 in Auckland. She was writing her first findings surrounding Reading Recovery, which led to exciting discussions. She also introduced me to the print-rich cultures that are New Zealand schools and communities. My interest in literacy as a motivated cultural practice originated in that experience.

Charlotte S. Huck, Professor Emeritus, The Ohio State University, Columbus

Marie Clay is one of the most professional persons I have ever known. I have long admired the care and precision of her research on Reading Recovery, children's early writing, and teacher education. In her quiet yet determined way, she has earned the respect and admiration of all who have been privileged to work with her. She has enriched my personal and professional life, and I'm proud to call her my friend.

Peter Johnston, Professor, Reading Department and National Center on English Learning and Achievement, State University of New York at Albany

Marie's insightful writings have stimulated and informed my thinking since my teacher education classes in New Zealand. As a model, Marie is always disciplined and principled in her work, circumspect in her claims, and respectful of teachers and children. Her concept of the self-extending system is one of a handful of powerful ideas that can be applied to all levels of education.

Noel K. Jones, Associate Professor, Language and Literacy Education, and Reading Recovery Trainer, Department of Curricular Studies, Watson School of Education, University of North Carolina, Wilmington

Working within the Reading Recovery network, my association with Marie Clay has expanded and revised my understanding of literacy acquisition and raised many new questions about language and literacy development. Clay's writings and dialogue continually challenge thinking to probe more deeply or to move in unanticipated directions. Her ability to help others see puzzling issues in a broader, more informed perspective is a teaching model to which I aspire.

Carol A. Lyons, Professor, School of Teaching and Learning, The Ohio State University, Columbus

I first realized the interdisciplinary extent of Marie Clay's work in the late 1970s when my neuropsychology professor commented that in order to understand how theoretically driven research is designed to address practical questions we should read *Reading: The Patterning of Complex Behavior* by Marie Clay. Marie has taught me, through example, that every child and teacher can teach you something about the teaching and learning process IF you listen carefully, observe closely, and ask pertinent questions. Marie Clay's research, writing, and actions speak volumes.

Stuart McNaughton, Director, Woolf Fisher Research Centre, School of Education, University of Auckland, New Zealand

I took undergraduate and graduate developmental papers that Marie taught at The University of Auckland, and she cosupervised my doctoral thesis. After returning to Auckland I cotaught developmental and reading papers with her and worked directly and indirectly with her on a number of research projects.

Peter Mortimore, Professor & Director; Educational Researcher, Institute of Education, University of London
Jo Mortimore, Freelance, Institute of Education, University of London

We first met Marie Clay when she spent a year at the Institute establishing the British Reading Recovery Programme. We soon learned that Marie was a most unusual person who combined a hard-nosed, no-nonsense approach to problem solving with a warmth and sympathy for people. These attributes served her well as she laid the foundations for our work with schools. Our English Reading Recovery teachers and tutors have been greatly inspired by her knowledge and skill as well as by her remarkable vision.

David Olson, Professor, Centre for Applied Cognitive Science, Ontario Institute for Studies in Education, Toronto

I am attracted to the work of Marie Clay both because of her knowledge of and commitment to cognitive theories of literacy and because I see her as overcoming a weakness I see in my own work, namely, the notorious gap between theory and practice. My own work, *The World on Paper* (Cambridge University Press, 1994), focused on just what readers and writers are doing and more specifically what they think they are doing. Clay not only contributes to this theory, she has provided an informed, implemented pedagogy.

Gay Su Pinnell, Professor, School of Teaching and Learning, The Ohio State University, Columbus

Marie Clay's visionary theories and system designs have had worldwide influence on educators' views of children, learning, teaching, and schooling. Her work has made a profound difference in the learning of many thousands. I have been privileged to be one of those learners for the past two decades. I continue to learn daily from her writing, her research, her teaching, and her leadership.

Bridie Raban, Mooroolbeek Professor of Early Childhood Education, Director of the Early Education Research Unit, Department of Learning and Educational Development, Faculty of Education, The University of Melbourne, Australia

Marie always gives others the impression that she has time for them. Throughout the last twenty-five years of knowing Marie, she has always listened to our concerns as we struggle to incorporate her ideas into our work. She never forces her view, she relies on evidence and inquiry—her persistence, patience, humility, and fortitude act as lodestars for us all. Thank you, Marie, for being such a powerful and gentle teacher.

Viviane Robinson, School of Education, University of Auckland, New Zealand

When I went to Marie as a graduate student asking for a course to be offered on intervention, she obliged, because she herself was committed to the idea of doing research that made a difference and served children. The course brought together practitioners and full-time students in the study of what was to become my career theme—the relationship between social science research and practice.

M. Trika Smith-Burke, Professor, New York University, New York

I have often been called an educational amphibian. Clay has given new meaning to this phrase. Her ability to hold the tension of opposites, such as individual and group research, learning and teaching, norm-reference and criterion evaluation, and the stance of practitioner and researcher shows us that it is not a matter of "either/or" thinking, but "both/and" thinking, combined with a clear goal which has made her work so highly theoretical *and* practical, providing a way for *all* children to become literate.

Jim Walker, Professor of Education, School of Teaching and Educational Studies, University of Western Sydney, Nepean, Australia

I became intrigued by Marie Clay's work when I was Dean of Education at the University of Canberra, Australia (1990–94), where there was a strong Reading Recovery program. Since my work has always concentrated on the relation between research/theory and practice, I became interested in how Marie Clay's approach contributed to improvements in the quality of educational experience and outcomes.

Barbara Watson, National Director Reading Recovery, Auckland College of Education, New Zealand

I have had the privilege of working with an exceptional educator who provided me with opportunities to learn, and encouraged, challenged, shared, supported, and enriched my professional life for more than thirty years. There have been almost parallel paths—one from my late start in undertaking a first degree continuing through to gaining a Doctorate; the other as a teacher assisting in the early development of Reading Recovery and continuing as a participant in an ever-expanding international enterprise. Exciting years, during which I was inspired by Marie Clay always to ask questions and to strive to seek to understand more about children's learning and teachers' teaching.